"Being situated on a harbor, which attracted the first Dutch settlers, made New York's fortune. Its exceptional vitality was also a contributory factor. Wealth, poverty, liberty, violence, a melting pot of races and cultures . . ."
Hélène Trocmé

*Photograph: "Theoline", Pier II, East River, 1936*

ENTRANCE

"The subway often generates prolific ideas, due to the movement, the busy throng, the traveler's alert state of mind, as he clatters under streets and rivers, under the foundations of enormous buildings . . ."

Saul Bellow

*Photograph: Interior of the El station at Columbus Ave/72nd St, 1936*

PUSH   PUSH

DROP
NICKEL
HERE

**"**My memory of Manhattan is that of a simpler, friendlier city. . . . There was no underground subway but, on the other hand, outings on the elevated railway represented, for a young boy, the height of enjoyment.**"**

Mirwin Edman

*Photograph: The Bowery, beneath the 3rd Ave El, c. 1940*

EVERYMAN GUIDES
PUBLISHED BY DAVID CAMPBELL PUBLISHERS LTD, LONDON

NEW YORK ISBN 1-85715-806-7

© 1994 David Campbell Publishers Ltd
© 1994 Editions Nouveaux-Loisirs, a subsidiary of Gallimard, Paris.

All rights reserved. No part of this publication may be reproduced, stored in a retrieval system or transmitted, in any form or by any means, electronic, mechanical, photocopying, recording or otherwise, without the prior written permission of the copyright owners.

First published September 1994
Second edition September 1996

NUMEROUS SPECIALISTS AND ACADEMICS HAVE CONTRIBUTED TO THIS GUIDE:
SPECIAL THANKS TO:
IN NEW YORK: Luis R. Cancel (Commissioner, City of New York Department of Cultural-Affairs), Carole Sorelle (Assistant Commissioner for Public Affairs), Seymour Durst, Gordon McCollum
IN PARIS: Henri Peretz, Barry Bergdoll, Alain Dister

EDITORS: Élisabeth de Farcy, Catherine Fouré, Sophie Lenormand, Anne Magniant, Frédéric Morvan, Cassie Springer, Béatrice Viterbo, Delphine Babelon, Paule du Bouchet, Cécile Dutheil
CO-ORDINATION IN NEW YORK:
Laurence de Bélizal (text) and Alexandra Rose (picture research)
LAYOUT: Alain Gouessant, Yann Le Duc, Laurent Gourdon
PICTURE RESEARCH IN FRANCE: Tanguy Cuzon du Rest
NATURE: Sarah Elliott, Philippe J. Dubois, M. Goutsh, Sidney Hornstein, M. Waldman
HISTORY: Hélène Trocmé, Janette Sadik-Khan, Ed Stancik, Nancy Green, Kim Hopper, Ken Sheppard
LIFESTYLES: David Abrahamson, Walter A. Friedman, Nina Gray, Benoît Heimermann, Doris Hering, Louise Kerz, Michael Kerker, Brooks McNamara, Cassie Springer, Peter Watrous
ARCHITECTURE: Ed Dolkart, Isabelle Gournay
NEW YORK AS SEEN BY PAINTERS: Jonathan Weinberg
NEW YORK AS SEEN BY WRITERS: Lucinda Gane
PRACTICAL INFORMATION: Béatrice Coron, Leah Dickerman, Walter A. Friedman, Peter D. Meltzer
ITINERARIES: Norman Brouwer, Ed Dolkart, Isabelle Gournay, Serge Gavronski, Nancy Green, Catherine Hodder, Seth Kamil, Rod Knox, Anka Mulhstein, Ed O'Donnell, Hélène Trocmé, Elisa Urbanelli

ILLUSTRATIONS:
NATURE: Philippe Biard, Jean Chevallier, François Desbordes, Bernard Duhem, Gilbert Houbre, Patrick Merienne, Jean Torton, Jean Wilkinson
ARTS & TRADITIONS: Pierre-Marie Valat
ARCHITECTURE: Bruno Lenormand, Jean-Marie Guillou, Valérie Malpart, Claude Quiec
ITINERARIES: Bruno Lenormand, Philippe Biard, Hubert Gauger, Donald Grant, Marc Lacaze, Pierre-Marie Vallat
MAPS: Bruno Lenormand and Christine Adam, Claire Cormier, Stéphanie Devaus, Jean-Claude Senec, Catherine Totems, Olivier Verdy, (colorists)
COMPUTER GRAPHICS: Paul Coulbois

PHOTOGRAPHERS: Laurence de Bélizal, Ted Hardin, John C. Fletcher

WE WOULD ALSO LIKE TO THANK:
MUSEUM OF MODERN ART: Richard Oldenburg (Former Director), Jeanne Collins (Former DIrector, Public Information), Lucy O'Brien (Writer/Editor, Periodicals and Special Projects)
FRICK COLLECTION: Edgar Munhall (Director), Jack Kennedy (Public Relations)
WHITNEY MUSEUM: David Ross (Director), Jack Kennedy (Public Relations)
METROPOLITAN MUSEUM: Philippe de Montebello (Director), Barbara Burn (Executive Editor), Kent Lydecker (Deputy Director for Education), Mary Doherty (Photo and Slide Library), Lina Komaroff (Assistant Museum Educator)
THE CLOISTERS: Mary Shepard
SOLOMON R. GUGGENHEIM: Thomas Krens (Director), Lisa Denison (Collections Curator), Samar Qandîl (Rights and Reproductions), Joan Young (Administrative Curatorial Assistant)

TRANSLATED BY SUE ROSE.
EDITED AND TYPESET BY BOOK CREATION SERVICES, LONDON.
PRINTED IN ITALY BY EDITORIALE LIBRARIA.

EVERYMAN GUIDES
79 BERWICK STREET
LONDON W1V 3PF

# NEW YORK

EVERYMAN GUIDES

# CONTENTS

# ▲ NEW YORK

**1** GEORGE WASHINGTON BRIDGE **2** LINCOLN TUNNEL **3** HOLLAND TUNNEL **4** HUDSON RIVER **5** NEWARK BAY **6** BAYONNE BRIDGE **7** GOETHALS BRIDGE **8** STATUE OF LIBERTY **9** GOVERNORS ISLAND **10** ELLIS ISLAND **11** VERRAZANO NARROWS BRIDGE

**26** BROOKLYN BRIDGE **27** LONG ISLAND SOUND **28** TRIBOROUGH BRIDGE **29** QUEENSBORO BRIDGE

HACKENSACK

WEEHAWKEN

NEWARK

NEWARK INTERNATIONAL AIRPORT

HOBOKEN

JERSEY CITY

BAYONNE

Upper Bay

STATEN ISLAND

Lower Bay

CONEY ISLAND

Atlantic Ocean

New York State

Yonkers

Teterboro Airport

22

1

Bronx Park

Edgewater

Bronx

New Jersey

21

17

20

18

28

2

4

19

27

Manhattan

25

15

24

La Guardia Airport

29

12

16

23

Flushing Meadow

Queens

Forest Hills

Long Island

Brooklyn

John F. Kennedy International Airport

Jamaica Bay

Floyd Bennett Field

Rockaway Point

# HOW TO USE THIS GUIDE
*(Sample page shown from the guide to Venice)*

The symbols at the top of each page refer to the different parts of the guide.

■ NATURAL ENVIRONMENT

● KEYS TO UNDERSTANDING

▲ ITINERARIES

◆ PRACTICAL INFORMATION

The itinerary map shows the main points of interest along the way and is intended to help you find your bearings.

The mini-map locates the particular itinerary within the wider area covered by the guide.

●▲■◆

The symbols alongside a title or within the text itself provide cross-references to a theme or place dealt with elsewhere in the guide.

★ The star symbol signifies that a particular site has been singled out by the publishers for its special beauty, atmosphere or cultural interest.

At the beginning of each itinerary, the suggested means of transport to be used and the time it will take to cover the area are indicated:

🚢 By boat
🚶 On foot
🚲 By bicycle
🕐 Duration

---

## THE GATEWAY TO VENICE ★

**PONTE DELLA LIBERTA.** Built by the Austrians 50 years after the Treaty of Campo Formio in 1797 ● *34,* to link Venice with Milan. The bridge ended the thousand-year separation from the mainland and shook the city's economy to its roots as Venice, already in the throes of the industrial revolution, saw

🚶 Half a day

**BRIDGES TO VENICE**

# NATURE

# ■ CLIMATE

New York City's
climate resembles the
weather conditions that prevail along the
northeast coast of Asia. Frontal systems and the close proximity
of the ocean combine to accentuate great fluctuations in
temperature. This means that although New York is in a
temperate latitude, hurricanes, heat waves, blizzards and
spectacular weather changes can occur almost overnight. During
some years the temperature can vary considerably from -13°F in
winter to 106°F in summer, in other words by as much as 119°F.

**POSITION OF THE JET STREAM IN WINTER AND SUMMER**
Jet stream: strong winds traveling from west to east at very high altitudes and generated by the interplay between hot and cold air masses and the coriolis force.

WINTER

SUMMER

**ARCTIC AIR**
Arctic air from Siberia crosses central Canada and sweeps into the city, bringing bitterly cold weather in its wake.

Breezes from the west become less humid as they come into contact with the Appalachian Mountains.

Great masses of hot, humid air traveling northward and eastward from the Gulf of Mexico bring hot, humid and clammy weather as well as occasional showers.

*Lake Huron*

**DETROIT**

*Lake Erie*

**TORONTO**

**CLEVELAND**

**APPALACHIAN MOUNTAINS**

**WASHINGTON**

**PHILADELPHIA**

*Delaware Bay*

*Chesapeake Bay*

*Gulf Stream*

**THE "CANYON" EFFECT**
In Manhattan, high-rise buildings have unpredictable effects on the wind. The "canyon" effect – typically found in Downtown and Midtown – is produced when the wind bounces off the ground and the sides of the skyscrapers to form columns of rising air.

16

During extremely cold snaps, the Hudson River can become partially blocked with ice.

The ocean is responsible for violent storms in this area. At times the east coast of North America has some of the world's most changeable weather.

Temperatures can hit, and occasionally soar above 100°F in the summer. Hoses, fountains, even fire hydrants – in certain neighborhoods – are urban solutions to cooling off at such times.

When the city is beset by thick fog, the tops of Manhattan's highest skyscrapers disappear – as the Woolworth Building has done here – transforming the skyline.

In March 1993, a blizzard swept the east coast, from the Gulf of Mexico to Canada. A mass of cold air (-20°F) collided with a mass of hot air (85°F) and the difference in temperature caused snowstorms and tornados.

LAKE ONTARIO

NEW YORK

BOSTON

ATLANTIC OCEAN

Coastal regions enjoy milder weather in the winter and cooler weather in summer than areas farther inland.

**THE CAUSE OF A DEPRESSION**
When hot, humid air coming in from the Gulf of Mexico and cold air coming down from Canada collide, they generate a coastal storm.

**THE FORDHAM GNEISS**
Formed a billion years ago, gneiss is
Manhattan's oldest subsoil rock. It
outcrops in various places in New York,
as here on the northern tip of the island.

The islands at the top of New York Bay, which form one of the
main indentations along the eastern coast of the United States,
were created by geological conditions in the region's distant
past. Because the coastline's navigable waterways are wide, deep
and fairly long, ships can be easily piloted down them and
moored. New York's location, at the mouth of the Hudson
River, on a sheltered bay that opens into several other navigable
waterways, has played a crucial role in stimulating the city's port
growth, contributing to its status as one of the major ports in the
United States. Of the five boroughs that make up Greater New
York, only the Bronx is
connected to the
mainland.

**17,000 YEARS
AGO.** During the
height of glaciation,
the site of New York was
covered with an ice sheet 1000
feet thick and the shoreline was 600
feet farther back to the east.

**10,000
YEARS AGO**
When the
glaciers melted, the
terminal moraine acted
as a dike and the valleys
hollowed out by glaciation (the
Hudson, East and Harlem rivers)
filled up.

**10,000
YEARS AGO
TO PRESENT**
The sea reached its
present level 4,000–
6,000 years ago, and the
shoreline's contours formed.

The bare face of a marble mass, 500 million years old, can be found in Isham Park, at the north end of Manhattan.

Since building work started in Manhattan, the landscape has altered and the shoreline has been modified. Certain sites in Manhattan are built on landfills – among them Battery Park, South Street Seaport, the World Trade and the World Financial centers.

| | |
|---|---|
| | Hudson River |
| | Landfills |
| | Mudbank |
| | Terminal moraine, composed of boulders deposited by the glaciers |
| | Rocky substratum or granite bed |

The fresh waters of the Hudson
River and the salt waters of New York Bay
converge along the western shore of Manhattan. Despite being
one of the busiest ports in the world, New York harbor remains
home to many species of wildlife. Here the resident marine
fauna mingles with seasonal fauna; certain migratory fish (bass,
sturgeon) spawn farther upstream in the Hudson. Paradoxically,
many species are abundant here; because of the pollution they
are in no danger of being caught for mass consumption. Crabs,
lobsters and shrimp live on the sea bed, while the peregrine
falcon dives from the dizzy height of the bridges.

Many of the piers of New York Harbor are in
varying stages of decay and form an
extraordinary micro-habitat in themselves.

Great black-backed gull

Herring gull

Ring-billed gull

**LAUGHING GULL**
This bird
migrates south
in winter
anywhere from the
Carolinas to South
America. It is a
familiar sight in the
harbor in spring and
summer.

**FOUREYE
BUTTERFLYFISH**
The Gulf Stream
provides the bay with
an annual influx of
tropical fish such as
groupers, snappers
and butterfly fish.

**BLUE CRAB**
Large numbers of this
crab can still be found
in New York Harbor.

**GULLS AND SEAGULLS**
Certain species, such as the great black-
backed gull and the herring gull, live here all
year round, as does the ring-billed gull.

**AMERICAN SHAD**
Every spring, shad navigate the harbor on
their way to their breeding grounds farther
inland.

**STRIPED BASS**
Fishing for this
predator takes
place around the
Statue of Liberty
in the fall.

**AMERICAN EEL**
New York's waters are a paradise for the
young eels spawned in the Sargasso Sea. They
swim up the Hudson River and its tributaries.

Aquatic fauna is plentiful around the harbor's piers, which are covered with starfish, while sea horses play hide and seek among the fronds of seaweed. Predatory fish (bass, eel) come here to hunt.

# ■ CENTRAL PARK

**MONARCH**
This butterfly spends every fall in the park on its way to Mexico.

For most migrating birds New York is between their winter quarters and their breeding ground.

Central Park was created in the mid-19th century, so that New Yorkers without access to the countryside could enjoy some of its benefits on a small scale. The park, which extends over 840 acres, not only provides New Yorkers with somewhere to go for a breath of fresh air but also is of considerable importance to many species of wildlife, including birds, butterflies and dragonflies. This lush haven in a forest of concrete is a stopover, for several hours or several days, for various migrating birds.

**AMERICAN REDSTART**
With its outspread tail, this bird resembles a huge butterfly. It is one of the most common passerines in North America.

**SCARLET TANAGER**
This bird, which prefers to feed on caterpillars, leaves South America in the spring and nests in May in the oak trees of Central Park.

The cardinal has extended its range northward but can be found here year round.

**CARDINAL**
The male has bright red plumage, whereas the coloring of the female is drab brown.

**BLUE JAY**
The blue jay lives in the park all year round and can easily be distinguished by its call, from which it derives its name: "dchay-dchay-dchay". The jay is fairly tame and extremely fond of corn or peanuts in the winter.

**BALTIMORE ORIOLE.** This bird builds its nest in the shape of a ball suspended from a branch, occasionally using such materials as fishing wine.

**CAPE MAY WARBLER**
Regarded as one of the most beautiful species of its family, the striped warbler is always found near spruce trees. Its migratory path takes it through Central Park.

**YELLOW-RUMPED WARBLER**
This is the only representative of the warbler family to spend winter in the region of New York.

**MOURNING DOVE**
This dove derives its name from its rather melancholy call, which is similar to that of the owl.

**COMMON GRACKLE**
These birds breed alone but feed in flocks in the winter.

# ■ CITY FLORA AND FAUNA

**GERMAN COCKROACH**
This insect is perfectly suited to city life. In 18 months, a pair can produce 130,000 offspring.

Although it consists mainly of concrete, steel and glass, Manhattan provides a home for various animals and plants which, over time, have grown accustomed to their man-made environment. Not surprisingly, this unpromising habitat has attracted mainly adaptable species, especially those that were introduced by man, such as sparrows, starlings and pigeons. These animals and birds, some of which were brought over from the Old World, quickly multiplied in the absence of direct competition, creating fresh problems for the city's inhabitants.

**STARLING**
This bird, which was brought over from Great Britain in 1890 and released in Central Park, is now a common sight throughout the city.

**NORWAY RAT**
This European "immigrant" lives in Central Park, in tunnels, and in some tenements.

**TREE OF HEAVEN**
This tree is easily propagated and can be seen growing here and there in cracks in the sidewalk and the façades of houses.

**PEREGRINE FALCON**
Until very recently threatened with extinction, this falcon has adapted to large American cities, where it helps to control the population of pigeons, sparrows and starlings. Pairs nest in New York on the piers of bridges or on skyscrapers.

**ROCK DOVE**
Some old monuments have been ruined by this bird's droppings.

# HISTORY AND LANGUAGE

A scene depicting the
Algonquin way of life (below),
painted by Théodore de Bry
in the 16th century.

## FROM PREHISTORY TO THE 16TH CENTURY

**1000**
*Viking expedition to
North America led by
Leif Eriksson.*

**1492**
*First voyage of
Christopher
Columbus.*

**1521**
*Conquest of Mexico by
Cortes.*

Giovanni da
Verrazano, the
"discoverer" of New
York in 1524.

**THE INDIANS OF MANNAHATTA.**
As it is not known when the Asian
peoples who crossed the Bering
Strait arrived in the northeastern
part of what is now the United
States, it would be virtually
impossible to pinpoint when the site
of New York was first populated. In

the 16th century the area was occupied by Algonquin tribes
who lived by fishing, hunting and growing corn, squash and
beans. The only remaining trace of their existence in modern-
day New York is the name of the island of Manhattan ● 48
and a hotel, the Algonquin, on West 43rd Street.

**THE DISCOVERY OF NEW YORK BAY.** The French king
Francis I sent the Florentine navigator Verrazano to try to
find another route to Asia, north of the New World.
Verrazano, who sailed from Dieppe on board *La Dauphine*,
discovered and explored the bay in 1524. He immediately
appreciated its natural advantages ■ 20. However, this
discovery was not followed up, and it was not until 1609, over
eighty years later, that the Englishman Henry Hudson, then
employed by the Dutch East India Company, entered the bay
and sailed up the river which was to bear his name.

## 17TH AND 18TH CENTURIES

**1607**
*Jamestown, the first
permanent British
colony, is established
in Virginia.*

Peter Minuit buys
Manhattan from the
Indians for 60
guilders.

**1630**
*Boston is founded by
English Puritans.*

**1642**
*Montreal is founded by
the French.*

**A TRADING POST IS ESTABLISHED.** New Amsterdam, on
the island of Manhattan, was established in 1624 by the West
India Company. Peter Minuit, the settlement's first governor,
bought the island from the Canarsie Indians in 1626, and
brought Walloon settlers. New Amsterdam grew slowly. The
colony's prosperity was based on the sale of beaver skins,
otter skins and mink, as well as on tobacco farming, on the
site of the present Greenwich Village ▲ 210 and on the
Upper East Side ▲ 308. The first African slaves arrived in
New Amsterdam before 1630. Several Dutch farmers
established *boweries* ● 82
(farms) on the city's outskirts,
in such places as Brooklyn
▲ 366, Harlem ▲ 350, Yonkers
and the Bronx.

**THE CITY IS SEIZED BY THE
ENGLISH.** The struggle
between Holland and England
for supremacy at sea ended in
victory for the English. Charles
II, the king of England, presented his brother, the Duke of
York, with a vast territory including the Dutch colony of New
Netherland. New Amsterdam surrendered peacefully to the
English in 1664 and was immediately renamed New York. The
city expanded quickly; by 1700 it numbered nearly five
thousand inhabitants. Trade diversified; and flour became one
of the colony's main exports. This is why, to this day, the city's
coat of arms displays two barrels of flour against four
revolving sails of a windmill.

An Algonquin Indian and a Dutchman flanking the New York City seal, crowned with the American eagle.

**THE STAMP ACT.** In 1765, representatives from nine of the thirteen British colonies met in New York to protest against the imposition of a stamp duty on commodities; the act was repealed the following year. Tradesmen played a vital role in the initial phase of the struggle for independence by boycotting English produce. But the city was taken by the English in 1776 and became a stronghold of the Loyalists. After the end of the hostilities, in 1783, George Washington made a victorious entry into New York.

*1776*
*Declaration of Independence by the thirteen British colonies in America.*

Washington making a triumphal entry into New York in 1783.

**NEW YORK AS CAPITAL OF THE UNITED STATES.** This chapter in New York's history lasted from 1789 to 1790. The first president, George Washington, took his oath of office on the balcony of Federal Hall ● *85* ▲ *162*, which had been reconstructed after the revolution by the French architect Pierre Charles L'Enfant. The following year, the seat of the federal government was moved to Philadelphia. In 1797 Albany became the capital of the state of New York, and New York City's growth from that time onward depended purely on its economic role.

*1783*
*The War of Independence ends in 1783 with the Treaty of Paris, which recognizes the existence of the United States.*

## THE 19TH CENTURY

**BOOM TOWN.** By 1800 the city's population was more than 60,000. Over the next few decades, port activity escalated and New York's harbor became the busiest in the country ● *42*. In 1807 on the Hudson, Robert Fulton launched the first commercially successful steamboat. In 1818 the first regular shipping line between New York and Liverpool was established. Shipyards spread out along the East River, and the food and textile industries flourished. In 1820, the Stock Exchange replaced the open-air money market that had operated on Wall Street since 1792 ▲ *160.* In anticipation of further growth, a commission drew up a grid street plan for the city extending over the entire island of Manhattan ● *32.*

*1803*
*Napoleon sells Louisiana to the United States.*

*1860*
*Election of Lincoln.*

Warehouses and factories, such as this sugar refinery, were built along the East River.

**THE OPENING OF THE ERIE CANAL.** This canal connected the Great Lakes and the Atlantic, and it consolidated New York's supremacy as a port. By 1830 Manhattan had more than 200,000 inhabitants. The first horse-drawn buses appeared and a railroad running between New York and Harlem was built ● *36.*

**NEW YORK TAKES THE LEAD.** By 1860 the city was the largest in the U.S. The population increased with the arrival of numerous immigrants, especially Irish and German. Brooklyn's population had increased ten times in the space of thirty years, while that of Manhattan had quadrupled.

*1861*
*Outbreak of the Civil War, which ended in 1865 with victory for the North and the abolition of slavery.*

*1865*
*Lincoln is assassinated.*

*1876*
*Philadelphia Centennial Exposition.*

During the Civil War, New York remained in the Union and sent a great many men to fight for the North; the departure of troops leaving for the front was marked by rousing parades.

**1889**
*Construction of the Eiffel Tower in Paris.*

**1898**
*Spanish-American War in Cuba and the Philippines. The United States annexes Hawaii.*

$10,000 Reward

After years of impunity, Boss Tweed was brought to trial and convicted of theft; he died in a New York prison.

**1901**
*Death of Queen Victoria, who had reigned over the British Empire since 1837.*

**1914–18**
*World War One. The United States enters the war in 1917.*

**1917**
*The Communists seize power in Russia.*

Cast-iron structures ● *94* – office buildings with cast-iron façades – and "proto-skyscrapers" fitted with elevators, began to appear in the 1870's in downtown Manhattan, notably on Park Row. In 1856, 840 acres in the center of Manhattan were earmarked for a huge park ■ *22,* ▲ *314*. The Metropolitan Museum of Art was founded in 1870 ▲ *328*. During the Civil War, violent draft riots broke out in protest against conscription, claiming several hundred victims. In the post-war years the city government was controlled by the "Tweed Ring" under William "Boss" Tweed; he was convicted of corruption and removed from office in 1873 ● *40*.

**THE CONSTRUCTION OF THE BROOKLYN BRIDGE.**
Completed in 1883, the bridge joined the two most densely populated areas of the city ▲ *186*. Increasingly, New York was the gateway to the New World, and the Statue of Liberty ▲ *144*, given to the U.S. by France in 1886, welcomed immigrants as they entered the harbor. The city grew to such an extent that there was an urgent need for improved public transportation. Streetcars dating from the beginning of the century, and the elevated railway ● *36*, built in 1867, were electrified between 1890 and 1905, and a subway system was added in 1904 ▲ *236*.

**NEIGHBORING BOROUGHS ANNEXED.** By 1898 the city consisted of five districts: Manhattan, a commercial and residential area with over 1.5 million inhabitants; Brooklyn, a busy town with 900,000 inhabitants; and the less populous boroughs of the Bronx, to the north, Queens, adjacent to Brooklyn on Long Island, and Staten Island, to the south. Together, they created Greater New York, the most densely populated city in the United States, with 3.5 million inhabitants. The upper and middle classes had already started to move uptown in Manhattan, and in some cases to leave the city for the suburbs of New Jersey and Long Island.

## THE 20TH CENTURY

**THE SKYSCRAPER ERA.** The Flatiron Building ● *96,* ▲ *233*, dating from 1902 and 312 feet high, is one of the many skyscrapers built in the heart of Manhattan at the turn of the century.

They soon threatened to overshadow the streets and in 1916 the city government drew up a "Zoning Resolution", a set of regulations controlling the design of office buildings. This ordinance required architects to design towers with setbacks, establishing the characteristic shape of the skyscraper ● 96. By this time, Manhattan was connected to Long Island by bridges, and two new railroad stations had been built in the center: Pennsylvania Station ▲ 249, in 1910, and Grand Central Station ▲ 236.

**THE WALL STREET CRASH.** In the crash of October 24th, 1929, stock prices which had been overvalued by rash speculation plummeted. The Depression of the 1930's hit New York hard, but this period saw the completion of major projects such as the first bridge over the Hudson (the George Washington Bridge), the Empire State Building ▲ 242, and the Chrysler Building ▲ 266, as well as the start of work on Rockefeller Center ▲ 274. Fiorello La Guardia, the high-principled mayor elected in 1933, used federal aid as best he could to mitigate the devastating effects of the Depression.

**THE WORLD CAPITAL.** Many intellectuals and artists (including Albert Einstein, Marc Chagall, Piet Mondrian and Artur Rubinstein) took refuge in New York from a war-stricken Europe. After the victory of 1945 New York became the seat of the newly created United Nations. The organization's headquarters were opened in 1953 ▲ 264. Although by 1950 New York's population had reached almost 8 million, Manhattan had already begun to see a decline in the number of its own residents: some port activities were transferred to New Jersey and some manufacturing moved out of the city, which was handicapped by traffic congestion and inadequate maintenance. A new influx of poor immigrants increased the city government's financial burden ● 44.

**FINANCIAL CRISIS.** In 1975 New York teetered on the brink of bankruptcy, partly because of Mayor John Lindsay's lavish spending on social services. The banks refused to lend the city further funds and the state government offered a solution by establishing, in collaboration with the banks, the Municipal Assistance Corporation (Big MAC). This body imposed various austerity measures on the city, leading to deteriorating public services. However, New York remained unrivaled as a financial center and cultural capital and several new skyscrapers were added to Manhattan: the twin towers of the World Trade Center ● 103 in 1973, Battery Park City ▲ 141 and its development program for the banks of the Hudson ● 104, ▲ 138, in the 1980's. The bay, relatively deserted by shipping, has witnessed dazzling celebrations: the bicentennial of American Independence in 1976 and, in 1992, the gathering of large yachts in honor of Christopher Columbus, who, despite never having set foot on the North American continent, is considered its discoverer.

Panic on Wall Street (left). The Crash in October 1929 marks the start of the Great Depression.

*1933*
*Franklin Roosevelt launches the New Deal, intended to boost the flagging American economy in the grip of recession since 1929.*

*1941*
*The Japanese attack Pearl Harbor and the United States goes to war.*

*1949–53*
*Proclamation of the People's Republic of China and war in Korea. Also the beginning of the Cold War and McCarthyism.*

Fiorello La Guardia greets Albert Einstein in 1936.

*1963*
*John F. Kennedy is assassinated in Dallas.*

*1969*
*American astronauts Neil Armstrong and Edwin Aldrin walk on the moon.*

*1974*
*Nixon resigns following the Watergate scandal.*

*1989*
*Berlin Wall falls and the Communist bloc begins to crumble.*

*1993*
*Bill Clinton succeeds George Bush.*

# ● FROM NEW AMSTERDAM TO NEW YORK

New Amsterdam was a small, prosperous, peaceful town that slowly covered the southern tip of Manhattan, a site bought from the Indians in 1626. With its windmills and brick houses, it resembled Amsterdam, its parent city. In 1650, its population numbered barely one thousand people – mainly Dutch and English settlers. New Amsterdam was annexed by the English in 1664 and renamed New York.

**A TRADING POST**
The Dutch who settled on the island were employed by the new West India Company, founded in Amsterdam in 1621.

**FOR A HANDFUL OF GUILDERS**
Some historians maintain that Peter Minuit's purchase of Manhattan from the Canarsie Indians in exchange for some glass jewelry and trinkets worth 60 guilders (the equivalent of $24) was the first case in North America of Europeans' exploiting the Indians. However, it has never been determined whether Minuit intentionally took advantage of the natives' gullibility, or whether they felt at all cheated, since for several years they continued to visit the area to trade valuable skins with the Dutch.

**THE SKIN TRADE**
The prosperity of New Amsterdam was based on the sale of beaver skins, otter skins and mink. Between 1629 and 1635 the skin trade escalated: the number of beaver skins traded nearly doubled from 7,520 to 14,891 and the number of seal skins soared from 370 to 1,413.

**A CULTURAL CENTER IN THE MAKING**
In the 18th century intellectual life in New York was not as brilliant as in Boston or Philadelphia. However, King's College (below), the forebear of Columbia University, was founded in 1754, and a free-thinking press developed. By 1775 New York already numbered 25,000 inhabitants.

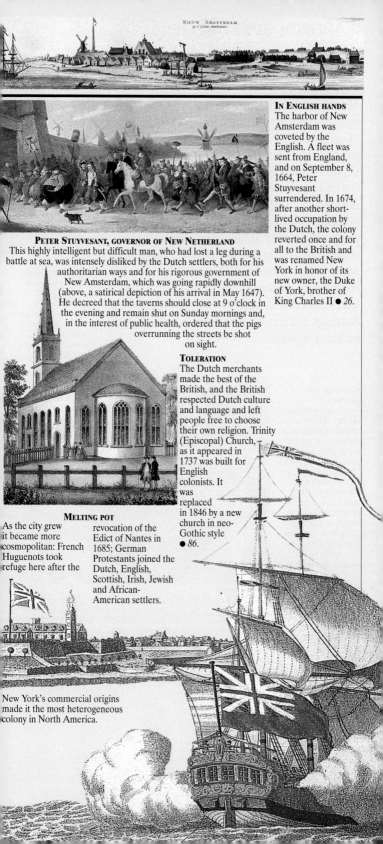

NIEUW AMSTERDAM
op 't Eylant Manhattans

## IN ENGLISH HANDS

The harbor of New Amsterdam was coveted by the English. A fleet was sent from England, and on September 8, 1664, Peter Stuyvesant surrendered. In 1674, after another short-lived occupation by the Dutch, the colony reverted once and for all to the British and was renamed New York in honor of its new owner, the Duke of York, brother of King Charles II ● 26.

### PETER STUYVESANT, GOVERNOR OF NEW NETHERLAND

This highly intelligent but difficult man, who had lost a leg during a battle at sea, was intensely disliked by the Dutch settlers, both for his authoritarian ways and for his rigorous government of New Amsterdam, which was going rapidly downhill (above, a satirical depiction of his arrival in May 1647). He decreed that the taverns should close at 9 o'clock in the evening and remain shut on Sunday mornings and, in the interest of public health, ordered that the pigs overrunning the streets be shot on sight.

### TOLERATION

The Dutch merchants made the best of the British, and the British respected Dutch culture and language and left people free to choose their own religion. Trinity (Episcopal) Church, as it appeared in 1737 was built for English colonists. It was replaced in 1846 by a new church in neo-Gothic style ● 86.

### MELTING POT

As the city grew it became more cosmopolitan: French Huguenots took refuge here after the revocation of the Edict of Nantes in 1685; German Protestants joined the Dutch, English, Scottish, Irish, Jewish and African-American settlers.

New York's commercial origins made it the most heterogeneous colony in North America.

New Amsterdam's first streets were laid out by the settlers along routes already used by people and livestock. At the beginning of the 19th century, as the city continued to spread northward, a coherent town planning program became an urgent priority and the state governor appointed a commission to design a "definitive" plan for Manhattan. Between 1807 and 1811, this commission perfected the existing grid system, which makes it simple for people to find their bearings and move easily from north to south and east to west.

**NEW AMSTERDAM**
The earliest plan parceling out Manhattan shows the allocation of plots of land to the Dutch settlers, the fort, several streets, the swamps and pasture land ● 74.

**A LOGICAL USE OF SPACE**
Post Independence the city spread out in an anarchic sprawl, at the mercy of projects initiated by private property developers. The members of the 1807 commission, who were wealthy merchants, took four years to make their recommendations. Since New York was primarily a business center, the grand designs that were a feature of older European cities and which the French engineer L'Enfant had followed in designing the federal capital of Washington were deemed pointless. New York needed a simple plan that would facilitate the sale of land as well as movement around the island and, most important, from one shore to another. The darker colored area on the *Commissioner's Map* of 1811 (opposite) indicates the size of the city at that time.

**CONTROVERSY**
Although the grid system was efficient and fairly easy to apply, town planners began in the mid-19th century to criticize its undue inflexibility which worked against Manhattan's topography. Their dream was to achieve a perfect symbiosis between city life, with all its advantages, and a more rural setting. Frederick Law Olmsted, the "father" of Central Park ■ 22 ▲ 314 (right), designed the park that William Cullen Bryant had campaigned for, feeling that the people of New York should enjoy open spaces similar to those in European cities.

At the beginning of
the 20th century the
major thoroughfares
devised by Olmsted
and his colleagues
were finally laid:
Riverside Drive and
the future Henry
Hudson Parkway,
▲ *356* (above, a view
at the turn of the
century) in
Manhattan, and also
Eastern Parkway and
Ocean Parkway in
Brooklyn. Various
means of locomotion
were accommodated
by an assortment of
slip roads and
footbridges. These
were later replaced by
highways, which were
better suited to motor
vehicles.

**A GEOMETRIC GRID**

There were to be 12
avenues running
north to south, 100
feet wide, with
numbering starting in
the east, bisected by
155 streets running
east to west, 60 feet
wide, with numbering
starting in the south.
These blocks were
then subdivided into
plots all roughly the
same size (25 by 100
feet). Not many
public squares and
open spaces were
provided because, in
the opinion of the
Commissioners, the
vast expanses of water
surrounding the city
made them
unnecessary. A
market, several
squares and a huge
parade ground for
military drills did,
however, appear on
the 1811 plan. But
these were soon
allocated and built
over, hence the
campaign led by the
press for a large park.

**THE EXODUS
NORTHWARD**
The new grid system
was to be applied
north of Houston St.
as far as 155th St. Not
a tree, stream, or hill
was spared (above, a
topographical map).
Around 1850 the grid
had reached 60th St.
Central Park
(opposite) ■ *22*,
▲ *314* was not
created until 1858.

The first public services appeared at the beginning of the 19th century, when the municipal government was faced with the inevitable problems caused by the expansion of a large city. However, the authorities were not completely free to act: they were often hampered by private companies unwilling to relinquish their share of some very lucrative markets. The authorities also had difficulty persuading the state of New York to allow them to create special departments to run their public services and undertake any necessary work.

### GAS AND ELECTRICITY

At the start of the 19th century, gas was the main source of power for lighting (below, a gas lamplighter in front of St. Thomas Church). In 1880 Broadway was equipped with an electric lighting system using the arc lamp. After inventing the incandescent bulb, Edison set up his own electricity company in New York in 1881. Buildings were first supplied

### SUPPLY OF WATER

Although water supply was one of the most pressing problems – being vital for sanitation and fire fighting – it was not until 1837 that work began on the Croton Reservoir (above), between 5th and 6th aves. and 40th and 42nd sts., on the site now occupied by the New York Public Library and Bryant Park. Completed in 1842, the reservoir was supplied by an aqueduct from Westchester County. Private homes had running water after the 1860's.

### POLICING

In 1844 a single police force of 200 men replaced the disparate units operating at the beginning of the century, which had consisted mainly of volunteers and part-time policemen. In 1853, the wearing of uniforms was made compulsory, which caused a great deal of dissatisfaction. But, from then on, the New York police force became a model for other American cities.

### TELEPHONE

The New York telephone system was inaugurated in 1878. Seven years later, the first long-distance trunk lines – New York–Boston, followed by New York–Chicago – were opened, the latter for the World's Columbian Exposition of 1893.

with electricity in 1882 and electric street lighting then became much more common. Below, men installing underground cabling around 1900.

The waterways of New York City.

1 : Cannonsville Reservoir
2 : Pepacton Reservoir
3 : Schoharie Reservoir
4 : Neversink Reservoir
5 : Ashokan Reservoir
6 : Rondout Reservoir
7 : West Branch Reservoir
8 : Croton Reservoir
9 : Kensico Reservoir

This underground section of New York at the corner of 6th Ave. and 50th St. was drawn in 1939. It shows the astonishing network of underground pipes that keeps the city alive. The orange cables supply power to the subway, the purple cables are for the telephone and telegraph system, the green pipes supply water, the red pipes supply steam for the district heating and the blue pipes carry gas. On the level below, the passageway to the subway can be seen, and to the left of that, the yellow sewage disposal pipe. Below that, the subway tunnels and, at the very bottom, 500–600 ft below the surface, the City Tunnel, supplying drinking water to the city.

## SANITATION AND PUBLIC HEALTH

In 1866 New York reorganized its Board of Health (opposite, inside a 19th-century ambulance), providing a team of health inspectors whose job was to enforce regulations. Some regulations were unrealistic, such as the one stipulating that every room in a building must have a window.

## STATE EDUCATION

Education was mostly private in 1842, when a department run by the Board of Education (composed of thirty-four elected members), was created to distribute the city's funds among its wards. The Board was also responsible for appointing teachers, choosing textbooks and syllabuses and building schools. Free public education was begun statewide in 1849 and, by 1860, 90 percent of all elementary school students attended public school. For many years, the main priority of state schools was to teach immigrants' children how to read and write and instill in them the values underlying democracy.

35

Ferries started running in the 18th century horse-drawn buses appeared in the 1830's, and, in 1870, the elevated railroad (the "elevated" or the "El") was built.

A solution to the problems caused by pollution and traffic congestion in the city was provided by the subway: the IRT (Interborough Rapid Transit) opened its first line in 1904. In 1955 the New York City Transit Authority, which had just been set up, became responsible for all the city's public transportation.

### FERRIES

These were the main method of transportation to and from Manhattan until the bridges were built at the end of the last century ▲ *188*. The first ferry started running in 1712, and many lines were opened during the steam era. In 1810 Cornelius Vanderbilt, the future railway magnate, laid the foundations of his fortune with the Richmond Turnpike Ferry, which ran between Staten Island and Manhattan. Since two of New York's five boroughs are islands, there is still a ferry service (notably the Staten Island ferry which operates a 24-hour service); 75,000 people use these ferries daily.

### TAXIS

It was not until 1907 that taxis were brought under regulation by the city authorities, who enforced meter inspection and set a minimum fare for each journey. The granting of licenses increased to such an extent that by 1937 the number of taxis had to be reduced from 21,000 to 14,000 (there are currently 11,787 taxis in New York) and a badge was designed for the hood (which is the origin of the name "medallion cab"). These official taxis have been painted yellow since 1970, and although there are a great many of them in Manhattan, they are not as easy to find in the other boroughs. Since there are still not enough of them, the number of unofficial taxis has increased to some 50,000.

The "El" traces sweeping curves high above 110th St.

### FROM THE "EL" TO THE SUBWAY SYSTEM

The elevated rail system had four routes which ran along 2nd, 3rd, 6th and 9th aves.,

making it possible to get from Harlem ▲ *350* to the Battery ▲ *142* in 40 minutes. The first pneumatic subway line, the City Hall Line, ran from City Hall ▲ *168* to

145th St., via the West Side ▲ *342*. Since then, the New York system, with 722 miles of track and 469 stations, has become the largest in the world. The City Hall station (above), which has been closed for the past fifty years, is still in its

original condition. On the other hand, nothing now remains of the elevated railway over the Bowery, which, with its two tracks, completely overshadowed the street (above). The last section of the 3rd Ave. line was not dismantled until 1955.

"The subway rolls and rumbles underground.
The bridges are shaken by railway lines.
The city trembles.
Shouts, fire and smoke,
Steam sirens sounding like raucous hoots."
Blaise Cendrars

### BAROUCHES AND HORSE-DRAWN BUSES

From 1831 privately owned vehicles had to share the streets with public transportation. The new horse-drawn buses created huge traffic jams, not to mention the problems caused by the horses

themselves (there were 80,000 in New York around 1880). This is why the El, despite its attendant noise and pollution, was seen as a great improvement.

# TRIAL BY FIRE

The numerous fire escapes that have disfigured the façades of many New York apartment buildings for over a century (to the amazement of foreign visitors) are a legacy of several catastrophic blazes in the early 20th century which made their construction obligatory. In the past, attracted by the bells and sirens of the fire engines, onlookers used to flock to the raging fires.

### FIRE AT THE TRIANGLE SHIRTWAIST COMPANY

On March 25, 1911, fire broke out in this factory near Washington Square, which employed 500 workers, mainly immigrant women. The garment workers' union had called, in vain, for additional fire escapes and for workshop doors to be left unbolted. Women, young girls and children died from suffocation or from jumping out of the windows (above, painting by Victor Joseph Gatto). The death toll was severe: 146 victims.

### CONSUMED BY FIRE

In 1776 and 1778, during the war of Independence, New York was devastated by arson attacks, attributed by turns to the Loyalists and to the Patriots. In December 1835, at the very time when the city was beginning to spread northward, a fire caused by a burst gas main broke out in Hanover Square ▲ 166 and in the narrow alleyways behind the docks. A strong wind carried the flames as far as South St., Broad St. and Wall St. For two days the flames raged Downtown, while the severe cold hindered the firemen; water froze in their hoses. In total, nearly seventeen blocks in the financial district were destroyed, including all the buildings from the Dutch period.

### FIRE AT CRYSTAL PALACE
Built for the Exposition of 1853, this huge building, thought to be fireproof, was totally destroyed by fire in 1858. Fortunately, there were no casualties.

### THE FIRE DEPARTMENT
Though impressive, with their gleaming red paint and clanging speed, fire engines could be rendered totally useless by adverse weather conditions. In March 1908, at a fire at the Equitable Building ● 97, ▲ 153 on Broadway, the water froze as it came out of the pumps.

### FIREMEN
It was not until 1865 that New York City created a professional, paid fire department. Before then, as was the case everywhere, fire fighting had been left to rival groups of volunteers (it was not unusual for them to come to blows at a fire), who were proud of their shiny equipment, their badges and their traditional parades. From the end of the 19th century, the meticulous organization, efficiency and the continually modernized equipment of the FDNY (Fire Department of New York City), were held up as a model for other cities. The department now employs more than 11,000 firefighters who deal with nearly 360,000 emergency calls per year, of which at least 100,000 are fires.

For lovers of "whodunits", New York is the metropolis where Ed McBain's cops use all means at their disposal to fight crime. Or there is the legendary Harlem of the 1960's policed by Ed Cercueil and Fossoyeur Johnson, the two cops created by Chester Himes. New York has always acted as a magnet for white-collar criminals highly skilled in the fields of administration and finance, and for the underworld, earning it the reputation of being a violent, dangerous city.

**CHARLES LUCIANO**
"Lucky" Luciano (above, the photos for his criminal record) became the godfather of all godfathers by arranging for the bosses of two rival gangs to be assassinated.

**THE SAINT SYLVESTER AT THE W. 47TH STREET POLICE STATION**
Drunkards, busy policemen and, in the foreground, a makeshift coffin containing the corpse of a woman who has just thrown herself out of the window of a nearby hotel. This 1939 illustration by Robert Riggs shows the police station for the area around Times Square, one of the most volatile parts of the city.

**PROHIBITION**
Adopted in 1920 (and repealed in 1933), this law was an unlooked-for bonus for New York's criminal elements. Instances of large quantities of contraband alcohol being destroyed by the police (below, on the docks of New York) did nothing to stop bootleggers from amassing huge illicit fortunes.

**"MEAN STREETS"**
In his film *Mean Streets*, Martin Scorsese evoked his experiences as an adolescent in one of New York's rough Italian neighborhoods where crime permeated the local community to such an extent that it became part of everyday life.

**BOSS TWEED**
In the mid-19th century, William Tweed, nicknamed "Boss" Tweed, made Tammany Hall (New York's Democratic machine) a byword for corruption. His consummate skill in electoral fraud and intimidation enabled him to control and systematically loot public funds.

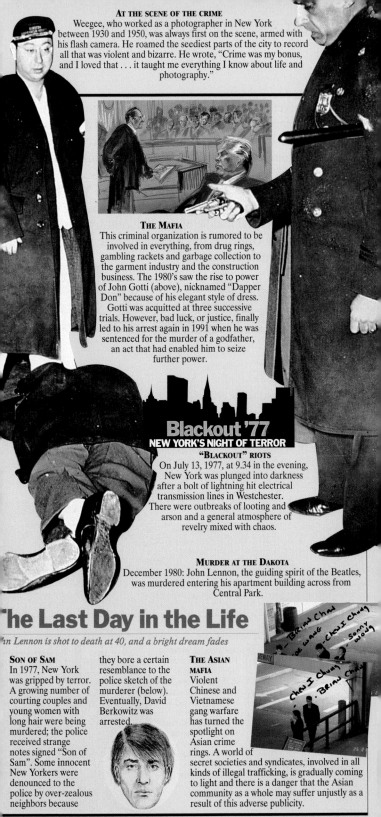

Weegee, who worked as a photographer in New York between 1930 and 1950, was always first on the scene, armed with his flash camera. He roamed the seediest parts of the city to record all that was violent and bizarre. He wrote, "Crime was my bonus, and I loved that . . . it taught me everything I know about life and photography."

### THE MAFIA

This criminal organization is rumored to be involved in everything, from drug rings, gambling rackets and garbage collection to the garment industry and the construction business. The 1980's saw the rise to power of John Gotti (above), nicknamed "Dapper Don" because of his elegant style of dress. Gotti was acquitted at three successive trials. However, bad luck, or justice, finally led to his arrest again in 1991 when he was sentenced for the murder of a godfather, an act that had enabled him to seize further power.

## Blackout '77
### NEW YORK'S NIGHT OF TERROR

### "BLACKOUT" RIOTS

On July 13, 1977, at 9.34 in the evening, New York was plunged into darkness after a bolt of lightning hit electrical transmission lines in Westchester. There were outbreaks of looting and arson and a general atmosphere of revelry mixed with chaos.

### MURDER AT THE DAKOTA

December 1980: John Lennon, the guiding spirit of the Beatles, was murdered entering his apartment building across from Central Park.

## The Last Day in the Life

*John Lennon is shot to death at 40, and a bright dream fades*

### SON OF SAM

In 1977, New York was gripped by terror. A growing number of courting couples and young women with long hair were being murdered; the police received strange notes signed "Son of Sam". Some innocent New Yorkers were denounced to the police by over-zealous neighbors because they bore a certain resemblance to the police sketch of the murderer (below). Eventually, David Berkowitz was arrested.

### THE ASIAN MAFIA

Violent Chinese and Vietnamese gang warfare has turned the spotlight on Asian crime rings. A world of secret societies and syndicates, involved in all kinds of illegal trafficking, is gradually coming to light and there is a danger that the Asian community as a whole may suffer unjustly as a result of this adverse publicity.

41

Giovanni da Verrazano, the first European to enter New York Bay, in 1524, immediately appreciated its natural advantages. The wide outer harbor (Lower Bay), itself sheltered from the ocean, opens out north of the Narrows into the magnificent Upper Bay, which also branches out into several secondary bays and channels washed by the tides. Although New York has not been the leading international port (Rotterdam having moved into the lead) since the middle of the 20th century, it is still the largest port in the United States with an average annual volume of forty million tons.

**DOCKERS AT WORK**
The completion of the Erie Canal in 1825 linked New York with the Great Lakes and the Midwest: a ton of wheat now took six days instead of twenty to reach New York from Buffalo and the cost of the journey plummeted from $100 to $10.

From 17th century to 1850

From 1945 onward

From 17th century to 1800

1880 to 1945

## A THRIVING HARBOR

The successive localization of port activities gives an idea of this site's enormous potential. In the 17th and 18th centuries everything was centered around the tip of Manhattan, especially its West Side. Gradually, during the 19th century, piers built perpendicular to the shoreline extended along the East River and the Hudson River (as far as 70th St.), on the New Jersey shoreline and in Brooklyn.

## SATELLITE VIEW

This shows every part of the coastline which has been developed to handle New York port traffic – that is Manhattan, Brooklyn ▲ *366*, Staten Island and New Jersey.

## THE LARGE TRANSATLANTIC LINERS

In 1818, some New York shipowners created the Black Ball Line, the first regular service between New York and Liverpool. Thirty years later the British Cunard Line set an example by replacing its large

sailing ships with steamers. Today after more than a century of heavy traffic, the New York City Passenger Ship Terminal welcomes fewer than 500,000 passengers per year.

## THE DEATH OF A GIANT

In February 1942, the *Normandie*, the most famous liner of its time, went up in flames while berthed on the Hudson River. It was capsized by the firemen, who deluged it with tons of water. In twelve hours, all that remained was wreckage.

## LEADING THE FIELD

At the end of the 19th century nearly half the United States' foreign trade passed through New York. The city exported timber, meat, cereals, flour and cotton from the South and imported tropical foodstuffs and manufactured products.

## THE PORT AUTHORITY

In 1921 the states of New York and New Jersey created the Port Authority of New York and New Jersey to centralize port activities and coordinate essential large-scale projects. At the end of World War Two, due to cramped conditions and restricted movement, most of the port activities were transferred from Manhattan to Brooklyn ▲ *366*, to Newark Bay and as far as Perth Amboy, on the coast of New Jersey.

In 1870, 83 percent of New Yorkers had on
relative born abroad. This was true in 199
for 40 percent of New Yorkers, of which 2
percent are African-American and 25
percent of Hispanic origin. Soviet Jews an
people from China, Korea, the Dominica
Republic, Cuba and other Latin-America
countries form the most recent wave of
immigrants. From Chinatown to Little Odessa,
the city is in a constant state of ethnic flux. New
immigrants arrive as others leave and the neighborhoods change
their identity: Harlem was Jewish before being Black, the Lower
East Side was Jewish and Italian before becoming Chinese.

### THE IRISH

By 1790 Irish settlers in
New York were as
numerous as those of
Dutch origin. More
arrived between 1820
and 1853, having been
forced to leave Ireland
for the New World by
famines, and by 1860
they constituted one-
quarter of the city's
population.
Predominantly
Catholic, they celebrate
St. Patrick's Day with
one of New York's
largest parades.

### THE JEWS

An initial immigration of Sephardic Jews in the 17th century was
followed by the influx of many German Jews in the mid-19th century
and Jews from Eastern Europe in the last three decades of that
century. The collapse of the Communist bloc has led to the arrival
of a new wave of Russian Jews.

### PUERTO RICANS AND OTHER HISPANICS

Before the Cubans,
who started to arrive
in the 1960's,
immigrants from
Puerto Rico began to
flock to East Harlem,
"El Barrio", between
1921 and 1924. In
1990 they numbered
900,000 (over 10
percent of the
population).

### THE CHINESE.

Recent
waves of Chinese
immigrants from
Shanghai, Taiwan and
Hong Kong, following
the Cantonese who
arrived in the 19th
century, have made

New York's Chinese
community the largest
in the U.S., surpassing
that of San Francisco.
Since quotas were
scrapped by the
Immigration and
Nationality Act of
1965, this Asian
immigration has
become less well
documented because i
is not so rigorously
controlled.

> " ... OF THIS MODERN ELDORADO, WHERE, LITTLE EUROPEAN CHILDREN WERE TOLD, THE STREETS WERE PAVED WITH GOLD, AND THE LAND SO VAST AND ABUNDANT THAT EVERYONE COULD FIND A PLACE IN IT. "
>
> FRANZ KAFKA

**THE GERMANS.** The first Germans arrived around 1710 and in 1790 accounted for 10 percent of the population. By 1860 they numbered 118,000, many of them shopkeepers. The major concentration of Germans was in a quarter called Deutschlandle, east of the Bowery, between Houston and 12th streets.

**THE BLACKS**
There were only 24,000 African Americans in New York in 1890 and 460,000 in 1940 – that is 6 percent of the population. Since then, a demographic shift has taken place, bringing many Blacks from the South to New York, and into mainstream business. In 1990, the Black community numbered more than two million.

**THE ITALIANS**
The Italians arrived later, primarily in the 20th century, and unlike earlier immigrants they came to the U.S. with the intention of returning to their homeland. The men generally emigrated alone, and once they had decided to stay, would bring over their families. By 1930 the Italians numbered 1,070,355; they shared the Lower East Side with the Jews working alongside them in the garment industry.

**THE OTHER COMMUNITIES**
Poles, most of them Catholic, are united by strong national traditions and celebrate this in the big Pulaski Day Parade on October 5th. In Astoria, Queens, there is an established Greek community, and The Bronx is home to many Armenians. Since 1964 many Haitians, Latin Americans and Asians (Japanese, Koreans and Indians) have also settled in New York.

BLACKWELLS ISLAND

# *STREET NEWS*

New York City, by turns repressive and hospitable, even occasionally aggressively charitable, has always been unpredictable in its aid to the homeless. During the 1980's their numbers rose at an alarming rate and their presence on the streets has never been so obvious as it is today. New laws have increased the capacity of adult shelters tenfold, resulting in more than twenty-four thousand available beds.

**BLACKWELL'S ISLAND**
This Welfare Island on the East River (above), now known as Roosevelt Island, seemed a suitable place for the detention of the infirm and the destitute. Some thirty charitable institutions, hospices, asylums, hospitals, prisons and shelters for single women were built here in 1935.

**THE FIRST SHELTER**
In 1734, on the site of what is now City Hall ▲ *168*, New York constructed a building intended to function simultaneously as a prison, a hospice and a workhouse. This provided care for the dying, a home for orphans and runaway slaves, and shelter for social misfits, the poor, and even criminals.

**EVANGELICAL MISSIONS**
After the Civil War, various Protestant missions sprang up in the city. Some, like the McAuley Mission (now situated at 90 Lafayette St.), still survive. Unlike the few existing night shelters, the missions are free of charge, but regular attendance at prayers is essential and strict discipline is still enforced in the dormitories.

**REHOUSING REPORT**
In July 1993, the Department of Homeless Services was created to respond to the problems of homelessness. The department currently houses about 5,500 families (a large majority young single mothers and their children) and 6,500 single people. It is estimated that one third of the latter are suffering from serious mental illness, aggravated by alcohol and drug abuse.

"... the tramps, the down-and-outs, the
shopping-bag ladies, the drifters and drunks.
They range from the merely destitute to the
wretchedly broken. Wherever you turn, they
are there, in good neighbourhoods and
bad."                                    Paul Auster

### JACOB RIIS
The Dane Jacob Riis
(1849–1914) arrived
in New York in 1870.
As a journalist on the
*New York Tribune* he
denounced the poverty
of immigrants, and
with his photographs
(left) campaigned
for social
reform.

### IN THE STREET
Thousands of
homeless New
Yorkers live in the
streets, in the parks,
in vacant lots and in
the subway. At times
these living quarters
acquire a
distinctive
identity and a
community

### PUBLIC SHELTERS
In December 1979 a
law was passed
requiring New York
City to provide public
shelters for all
"destitute and needy"
homeless men. It took
a second ordinance
for women to benefit
from the same law.
The refuge (below)
was set up in an
armory of the
National Guard
(W. 168th St.,
between Broadway
and Fort Washington
Ave.). Around 1985
the number of men
housed never
dropped below
1,200 per night.

### POTTER'S FIELD
Around 1869, the
poor were buried in
Potter's Field on
Hart Island, to the
northeast of the
city. The pine
coffins arrived by
ferry and the
gravediggers were
prisoners.

I AM HOMEL
AND HUNGRY,
ANYTHING
WILL HELP !!!

spirit. The
authorities will
turn a blind eye if
there are no
complaints from the
neighbors but a
"settlement" always
represents health and
fire hazards.

❝It was a magical refuge. New York had a lingo, a language all its own.❞

Jerome Charyn

**"THE BIG APPLE"**
New York is popularly called the "Big Apple", a custom dating from at least the 1930's, when jazz musicians took the name of a Harlem nightclub and extended it to the whole neighborhood and then to the city in general. In the mid 1970's, the New York Convention and Visitors Bureau used the phrase in an ad campaign to boost tourism.

English was increasingly spoken in the colony after the Duke of York succeeded the Dutch as its owner in 1664 ● *26*, although as late as 1760 a Manhattan lady could still write, "The English language is beginning to be more universally understood here." All kinds of languages and dialects gradually entered the city, due to trade and immigration, enriching the English spoken in New York.

## A POLYGLOT CITY

More than eighty languages are now spoken in New York. Spanish is the second most common language, after English, reflecting the high number of residents from Puerto Rico, the Caribbean, and Central and South America. Various other languages can be heard in daily business transactions: Yiddish in the diamond merchants' quarter (West 47th Street) ▲ *299*, Moroccan Arabic, Farsi and Bengali among newspaper vendors, Korean in fruit and vegetable stores, and Wolof between Senegalese street hawkers. Different languages can also be heard in all the ethnic enclaves scattered around the city: Cantonese in Chinatown ▲ *190*, Haitian Creole on the Upper West Side ▲ *342*, Ukrainian and Polish in the East Village, Hungarian in Yorkville, Armenian in Murray Hill and Spanish in East Harlem ▲ *350*. It is not unusual for children to learn English simultaneously with their mother tongue.

## STREET AND PLACE NAMES

Many street and place names still bear linguistic traces of New York's successive generations of settlers. Such is the case with the name "Manhattan" (formerly "Manhata"), which owes its name to the Delaware Indians. There are many theories about the original meaning of "Manhattan", but it probably meant something like "island" or "island with hills". The Dutch legacy can be seen in the names of Harlem and Gramercy (which came from the Dutch word *krummartsje*, meaning "crooked little swamp"). *Spuyten Duyvil* ("the Devil's waterspout") may possibly have been named after the treacherous waters at the confluence of the Hudson ● *20* and Harlem rivers, the Bowery (from *bouwerie*, "farm" ● *82*) and Brooklyn ▲ *366* (*breukelen*, reclaimed land). The English names of some Lower Manhattan streets ▲ *158* are derived from the Dutch: "*De Wall*" was translated into "Wall Street", and "*Maagde Paetje*" into "Maiden Lane".

A street in Chinatown (below).

# ART OF LIVING

**ELIZABETH SETON**
Elizabeth Seton (1774–1821), the first American-born saint, was canonized in 1975. She founded the order of the Sisters of Charity in New York.

In 1656 Peter Stuyvesant, the governor of New Amsterdam and a devout Protestant, tried to force the colony to embrace one religion. The West India Company was opposed to this move; it was afraid it might damage trade as New York was already a patchwork of different religions. Modern-day New York is home to more than one hundred religious denominations. Catholicism is the main religion, while the Jewish community is the largest outside Israel.

**JEHOVAH'S WITNESSES**
This is one of the largest evangelical movements in New York and is based in Brooklyn. Their two magazines *Awake!* and *The Watchtower* are published in at least 80 languages and boast a circulation of more than ten million copies. They are distributed door to door or in the street.

**ST. PATRICK'S CATHEDRAL.** This cathedral, the seat of the city's Roman Catholic archbishop, is on 5th Ave., between 50th and 51st sts., and was completed in 1906 ▲ *283*. It is consecrated to the patron saint of Ireland. The number of Catholics currently living in New York is estimated at 2.5 million.

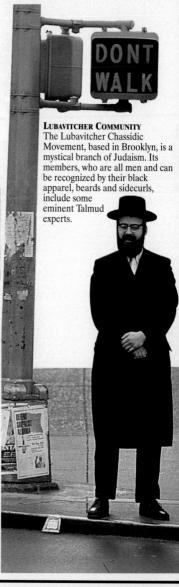

**LUBAVITCHER COMMUNITY**
The Lubavitcher Chassidic Movement, based in Brooklyn, is a mystical branch of Judaism. Its members, who are all men and can be recognized by their black apparel, beards and sidecurls, include some eminent Talmud experts.

**NATIVIST PROTESTANTS**
Protestantism was the main religion until the mid-19th century. But by 1864, following the immigration of Irish and German Catholics, half the population were Catholics. This cartoon by Thomas Nast, which depicts some parents protecting their children from the invading Catholic bishops, conveys Protestant distrust of Catholics, whom they criticized for their proposed changes to the educational system such as discontinuing Bible-readings and attempting to obtain state subsidies for their own schools.

> "IT WAS CLEAN, BUT NOT BRISK, NOTHING LIKE THE URGENCY
> OF NEW YORK, RUDE OFTEN, PREMISED ON A NOTION
> THAT TIME WAS FLYING."
>
> JANET HOBHOUSE

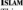

## ISLAM

This religion became widespread in New York only in the second half of this century. The Islamic Center of New York, opened in 1991, sits on the corner of 96th St. and 3rd Ave. Its axis forms an angle of 29 degrees with the street, so that the building is facing Mecca.

## JUDAISM

Over a million Orthodox Jews from Eastern Europe emigrated to America between 1880 and 1910. Many of them settled in New York. They started daily newspapers, theater companies, socialist political groups and unions. After World War Two, New York Jews gave their support to the creation of a Jewish state in Palestine and lobbied the government for economic and military aid to Israel.

## BUDDHISM

The impressive statue of Shinran-Shonin, who founded the Buddhist sect Jodo Shinshu, watches over the New York temple, built in 1938 on Riverside Drive. This statue, originally erected in Hiroshima, 1½ miles from the center of the explosion, was brought to New York in 1955 as a reminder of the horrors of

atomic warfare and a symbol of hope for lasting peace in the world.

## THE UNIFICATION CHURCH

The Unification Church, founded in 1954 in Korea by Sun Myung Moon, decided on Manhattan as its base. In 1982, in Madison Square Garden ▲ 249, the Reverend Moon made a great show of his church's impressive number of disciples (the Moonies) by celebrating a mass marriage which joined 2,075 couples in matrimony.

## THE BLACK CHRISTIAN COMMUNITIES

At the end of the 18th century, in response to discrimination and racial segregation, a group of Black New Yorkers formed their own denomination, the African Methodist Episcopal Zion Church. Today most of the Black churches in New York, including the famous Abyssinian Baptist Church ▲ 359, can be found in Harlem. The largest Black denominations are the Baptists, the Methodists and the Pentecostalists.

Since the 18th century, Manhattan has hosted countless political, civic, religious and military events. These celebrations, most of which are annual but in some cases one-time events, reflect New York City's fundamental concerns. The first well-known festival took place in 1788; it celebrated the ratification of the American Constitution with a huge parade and a banquet for five thousand guests.

**DISTINGUISHED GUESTS**
These have included the French hero of the American Revolution the Marquis de Lafayette, who was received in 1824 with a profusion of speeches and parades. A lavish ball was held in his honor.

**THE CIVIL WAR**
The armed forces have often been involved in noteworthy festivals in the city's history. In 1865 thousands of soldiers marched through Manhattan to celebrate the end of the Civil War.

**TICKER TAPE PARADES**
At the end of the 19th century, in the Financial District ▲ *158*, official guests used to be bombarded with ticker tape thrown from the office buildings. Despite the fact that the practice of holding these parades has declined somewhat, due to the traffic and prohibitive cleaning costs, it nevertheless continues to this day, only now with shredded computer paper. The most recent ticker tape parade took place in 1991 to celebrate the return of the troops from the Gulf War.

### ST. PATRICK'S DAY PARADE
The St. Patrick's Day Parade takes place unfailingly every year on March 17th. This cultural event was organized for the first time in the 1760's by Irish soldiers stationed in New York. Since 1838, the parade has been sponsored by the Ancient Order of Hibernians, an Irish Catholic brotherhood. This major festival, which has become extremely popular, symbolizes the solidarity of the Irish community.

### FEAST OF SAN GENNARO
In September, Mulberry St., in Little Italy ▲ 196, hosts the parade for the patron saint of Naples.

### MACY'S THANKSGIVING DAY PARADE
This parade, which has taken place since the 1920's, has numerous floats, giant balloons of cartoon characters and brass bands. It is sponsored by Macy's ▲ 249, the city's largest department store.

### GAY AND LESBIAN PRIDE MARCH
This annual march commemorates the first major protest in favor of gay rights, the Stonewall Inn Riots ▲ 212, which broke out in Greenwich Village on June 30, 1969. As many as 10,000 people have attended this event over the past few years.

### CHINESE NEW YEAR
A fireworks display is one of the attractions of this lavish celebration that takes place in late winter in Chinatown ▲ 190. For thirty-six hours, traditional dragon figures weave their way through the quarter.

### GREENWICH VILLAGE HALLOWEEN PARADE
Several thousand people don elaborate costumes for this immensely popular Halloween celebration.

53

**THE "PENNY PRESS"**
The first mass-circulation newspapers emerged in the early 1830's and early 1840's with the founding of the *New York Sun*, the *New York Herald* and the *New York Tribune*.

# The New

Copyright 1901, by

*and as Second-Class Matter,*
*at New York, N. Y.*

NEW YORK MC

For more than 250 years, New York's vibrant and occasionally unruly press has played a central role in the life of the nation. One of the earliest battles over press freedom was fought, and won, by a New York printer, and the city has long been the home of many of the most influential newspapers and magazines. The New York press's robust contribution to the uniquely American cultural milieu, as well as to the nation's continuing impulse for political and social reform, endows it with a rich and varied history.

**"YELLOW JOURNALISM"**
In the 1890's, intense competition for readers between William Randolph Hearst's *New York Journal* and Joseph Pulitzer's *New York World* led to unparalleled levels of journalistic sensationalism and chauvinism. The featured sex, sin and violence came to be termed "yellow journalism", a name derived from the Yellow Kid, a popular character in Richard F. Outcault's *Sunday World* comic strip "Hogan's Alley", about life in tenements.

**THE ZENGER TRIAL**
Charged by New York's colonial governor with spreading "Scandalous, Virulent, False and Seditious Reflections upon the Government" in his *New York Weekly Journal*, colonial printer John Peter Zenger's acquittal in 1735 helped to establish a central tenet of the freedom of the press: the right to publish criticism of government officials.

**THE TABLOID NEWSPAPERS**
The *New York Post* and the *New York Daily News*, direct descendants of the Penny Press, did not merely deal with the most sordid aspects of life in the city; they also tackled political issues of national concern.

# ork Times.

York Times Company;

## DECEMBER 8, 1941.

### THE POWER AND THE GLORY

In most countries, one newspaper, published in the capital city, serves as the "journal of record", defining much of the nation's public agenda. Only *The Washington Post* – particularly during Watergate – has come close to challenging the role of *The New York Times* as the most influential national newspaper since World War Two.

### THE "MUCKRAKERS"

For the first dozen years of the 20th century, *McClure's* and other crusading magazines exposed many of society's ills. Called "muckrakers" by Theodore Roosevelt (after the Man with the Muckrake in *Pilgrim's Progress*), Ida Tarbells' *History of Standard Oil*, Lincoln Steffen's *The Shame of the Cities*, and Ray Stannard Baker's reports on working conditions shaped much of the Progressive agenda of the period and fostered needed urban and industrial reforms.

### THE NEW YORKER

For nearly seventy years, this urbane, intellectual, weekly magazine has focused on society and culture in the city. Its contributors have included such well-known writers as James Thurber, Dorothy Parker, Kenneth Tynan and John Updike as well as the artist Saul Steinberg.

### MAGAZINES

The United States' most famous magazines, which are read throughout the country and abroad, include *Time*, *Vogue*, *Harper's Bazaar*, *Esquire*, *Vanity Fair*, *People*, *Ebony* and *Rolling Stone*.

# ● RADIO AND TELEVISION

In 1907 Lee De Forest patented the Audion, an amplifier that was the precursor of the cathode ray tube. This invention heralded the advent of the crystal set, which was sold during the 1920's in Manhattan by mail order and in kit form. A decade later, people in New York witnessed the beginnings of television. Today, Manhattan is home to three major national private networks (ABC, CBS and NBC) and receives more than 75 other stations and cable channels.

**LEE DE FOREST'S AUDION**
Lee De Forest used this device to broadcast the voice of the famous tenor Enrico Caruso from the stage of the old Metropolitan Opera House. This feat of technology amazed the world. De Forest started the first amateur radio station at his home in the Bronx.

**DAVID SARNOFF**
Sarnoff saw the potential of radio as big business. As early as 1916 he stated that this "music box" would rapidly become useful around the home. In 1921 he became general manager and later president of RCA, parent of NBC (the National Broadcasting Company).

**FELIX THE CAT**
Following the invention of the electronic movie camera by Vladimir Zworykin and of the cathode ray tube, RCA (the Radio Corporation of America) decided, in 1923, to use the famous comic strip hero Felix the Cat for their first experiments in animation.

**GEORGE BURNS AND GRACIE ALLEN**
For seventeen years this pair of vaudeville actors were a great success in a popular comedy broadcast on the NBC radio network. In 1950 the program was transferred to television.

**WALTER CRONKITE**
A newscaster of the evening news at CBS (the Columbia Broadcasting System) from 1962 to 1981, Cronkite ended all of his programs with his own distinctive catchphrase, "And that's the way it was."

## "SESAME STREET"
Since 1969, this program and its star, Big Bird, have taught innumerable children how to read and count.

## IMPORTANT DEBATES
In 1960 John F. Kennedy and Richard M. Nixon, both presidential candidates, took part in the first series of televised election debates. After the last one, which took place in New York, Kennedy was elected president. Since then, television has become a key platform for political confrontations.

## SPORTS PROMOTION THROUGH THE MEDIA
In the 1960's and 1970's, ABC sportscaster Howard Cosell broadcast games live and interviewed sports personalities in their locker rooms. He brought sports into everyone's home, sharing his boisterous enthusiasm with his viewers.

## HOME BOX OFFICE AND MUSIC TELEVISION
HBO was the first pay cable network and the first to make use of satellite broadcasting.

MTV gave the music industry a means to plug in to cutting edge America, with its music videos and its "Beavis and Butthead".

## BARBARA WALTERS
In 1964 Barbara Walters made her debut as an interviewer on the *Today Show* for NBC; she was then co-anchor of the ABC evening news broadcast before finally becoming a star with her own television specials. Her success helped to promote women in the profession.

## "THE WAR OF THE WORLDS"
"Poisonous black smoke, death rays, an army wiped out, people dropping like flies. Monstrous Martians landing all over the country . . ." In 1938 a tidal wave of panic swept New York when Orson Welles broadcast, on CBS, his hyper-realistic description of a Martian invasion, inspired by H. G. Wells's famous novel *The War of the Worlds*.

The musical – the form of theater that best evokes Broadway – derives from operetta, which was introduced to New York by European composers in the early 20th century. These light operas caused some lovers of vaudeville and burlesque sketches to develop a taste for more refined entertainment.

### SHOW BOAT

**"SHOW BOAT"**
*Show Boat* (1927), based on the novel by Edna Ferber with music and lyrics by Jerome Kern and Oscar Hammerstein II, is an outstanding example of the Broadway musical that was revived in 1994, 67 years after its debut. "Old Man River" and "Only Make Believe" are just two of the songs that have made this love story, set in the deep South, an enduring American classic.

**GEORGE AND IRA GERSHWIN**
The two brothers, Ira, the lyricist (top), and George, the composer, born into a humble Jewish family, together created some of Broadway's greatest hits, including: *Lady Be Good*, *Funny Face*, and *Girl Crazy*.

**"OKLAHOMA!"**
This musical by Rodgers and Hammerstein broke away from the traditional chorus lines with Agnes de Mille's innovative choreography. The show, which opened in 1943, ran for 2,248 performances.

**"KISS ME KATE"**
Cole Porter composed some of Broadway's greatest songs, including "Kiss Me Kate", "Anything Goes", "Night and Day" and "Can Can".

> "NEW YORK WAS A YUKON–SALEM WHERE YOU COULD GET
> SPIRITUAL RICHES, SAVE YOURSELF, AND FLEE, ONE WAY OR
> ANOTHER, A KIND OF POVERTY AND DEATH."
>
> JANET HOBHOUSE

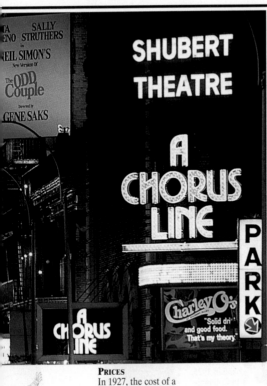

**"A CHORUS LINE"**
Directed by Michael
Bennett, *A Chorus
Line* holds the record
for the longest
running show on
Broadway, with 6,137
performances. Set in
modern-day New
York, and about show
business itself, its
main characters are a
producer and a
choreographer.

**PRICES**
In 1927, the cost of a
ticket for *Show Boat*
was $4.50. Today,
one can often
pay as much as
$65 to see a hit
Broadway musical.

**BOB FOSSE**
Fosse was one of
the rare Broadway
choreographers to
make movies as
well. In addition to
his resounding
stage success of
*Dancin',* he
directed the movies
*Cabaret, Lenny*
and the
autobiographical
*All That Jazz.*

**LAVISH
PRODUCTIONS**
Sophisticated
machinery,
lighting, sets and
eye-catching
costumes are now
integral parts of
the musical. In *Les
Misérables*, a
barricade is built
(center); in *Cats*, a
spaceship appears; in
*Phantom of the Opera*,
a huge chandelier
comes crashing down;
in *Miss Saigon*, a
helicopter lands and
takes off.

59

# THIRD EDITION
# COTTON CLUB PARADE

Although jazz was born in New Orleans, it came of age in New York. During the 1920's, Harlem was the capital of the African-American world, a mecca for the Black intelligentsia. In the prevailing climate of creative activity – both intellectual and financial – many new clubs sprang up, providing more opportunities for jazz musicians. They flocked to Harlem, and new styles of jazz were created by the many bands formed in this period.

**BIG BANDS**

### DUKE ELLINGTON

Duke Ellington was one of the great jazz composers of this century. As a star attraction at the Cotton Club, between 1927 and 1931, he developed "jungle music", an exotic style of jazz to accompany the sinuous dancing of chorus girls.

### COTTON CLUB

The Cotton Club opened in Harlem in 1922. Blacks were barred from the audience, as its gangster owners wanted the club to be a gathering place for the city's white *glitterati*. However all the bands and acts performing there were Black.

The popularity of the big bands, which were aimed primarily at dance audiences, hit an all-time high between the two world wars. Above, the Fletcher Henderson band in 1925, with Coleman Hawkins on tenor saxophone (bottom, second left) and Louis Armstrong on cornet (top, third left).

Duke Ellington

### SMALL BANDS: BEBOP

This provocative style with its insistent, fiendish beat and piercing dissonances, was well suited to small bands. It was very popular during the 1940's with young jazz "intellectuals", including saxophonist Charlie Parker, trumpeter Dizzy Gillespie, and pianist Thelonius Monk. Their younger colleague, trumpeter Miles Davis, created "cool", an introverted style in marked contrast to the aggressive exuberance of bebop. From left to right, Tommy Potter, Charlie Parker, Dizzy Gillespie and John Coltrane at Birdland in 1951.

> ## "FREEDOM AND JAZZ GO HAND IN HAND."
> THELONIUS MONK

### CAB CALLOWAY
The dancer-singer-conductor, who with his swinging jazz orchestra used to perform in Harlem, was nicknamed the "Hi-De-Ho Man" because of his strange way of mixing slang and yodeling in performance. In the 1930's, he wrote the *Hipster's Dictionary*, a work that revealed the secrets of his new mode of expression.

### APOLLO THEATER ▲ 358
Ella Fitzgerald and Sarah Vaughan (opposite) made their debut performing in the Apollo Theater's "amateur nights". Fitzgerald carried off first prize at the Apollo in 1934. Four years later she had her first hit with *A Tisket a Tasket*. Vaughan was discovered in 1942.

### SUN RA
At the end of the 1970's a frenzied, expressionistic style of music emerged. The conductor Sun Ra, headed a carnivalesque big band that included singers and dancers as well as instrumentalists. Among the latter was saxophonist John Gilmore.

## ● DANCE

In the 20th century New York has been a fertile breeding ground for daring essays in choreography. Ballet has explored new dimensions and the city has witnessed the birth of many companies. Three great pioneers of modern dance, Isadora Duncan, Ruth St. Denis

**MARTHA GRAHAM**
Her powerful, abrupt, angular style was resolutely innovative. After her debut as a soloist in 1926 she stated, "My dance is urban, not pastoral".

and Martha Graham, began their careers in New York. Martha Graham, the only one to remain here, stimulated and influenced this art, both in the works she created and through her teaching methods.

### THE NEW YORK CITY BALLET
In 1934, in response to a request by Lincoln Kirstein, George Balanchine (1904–83) founded the School of American Ballet. Realizing that the classical ballet he had been performing in St. Petersburg was in need of fresh inspiration, he then formed the New York City Ballet.

### PAUL TAYLOR
This former swimmer formed his own company which first performed in 1957. His bold, flowing choreography is often informed by a sense of humor.

### MERCE CUNNINGHAM
Cunningham founded his troupe in 1953 and soon became famous for his avant-garde creations. For some forty years he collaborated with the composer John Cage, as well as contemporary American artists Jasper Johns, Robert Rauschenberg and Andy Warhol. The company's work profoundly influenced young choreographers such as Trisha Brown, Douglas Dunn and Randy Warshaw.

## "THE NUTCRACKER"
In 1954, George Balanchine created a new version of this great classical ballet. Since then, *The Nutcracker* has become an American tradition. During the Christmas season, the New York City Ballet gives as many as thirty-two performances.

## "GISELLE"
The multi-ethnic Dance Theater of Harlem set the action of this classical ballet in New Orleans, while preserving the original choreography. The company was founded in 1969 in the crypt of a Harlem church by Arthur Mitchell, the first Black dancer to perform with the New York City Ballet.

## DANCE AT ALL LEVELS
The Broadway Dance Center located on Broadway between 55th and 56th sts., offers classes in all styles of dance.

## "REVELATIONS"
This is the best-known creation by the Alvin Ailey American Dance Theater, a mainly Black company formed in 1958. The exciting work produced by this troupe draws its inspiration from Black American tradition, Alvin Ailey's own roots, and traditional gospel music.

## THE SIXTIES
This turbulent decade produced many talented dancers. Two names in particular stand out: Twyla Tharp, whose style has breathed new life into the repertoire of many companies, and Meredith Monk (opposite) who has acquired a wide following.

63

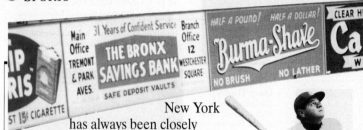

New York has always been closely associated with the world of sports. On June 19, 1845, the first baseball game was played just across the Hudson River in Hoboken. New York also boasts two of the country's most famous stadiums: Yankee and Shea.

### ALEXANDER JOY CARTWRIGHT (1820–92)

Although Abner Doubleday was long regarded as the father of baseball, credit was subsequently given to Cartwright; he adapted the rules of cricket, designed a new field and organized the first game in America.

### BABE RUTH (1895–1948)

Babe Ruth, considered the greatest of all baseball players, moved from the Baltimore Orioles, where he started in 1914, to the Boston Red Sox to the Yankees. With the Yankees, in 1927 he set the existing record of 60 home runs for one season. He hit 714 home runs in major league play, a record that held until 1974. He also led the Yankees to seven pennants (1921–3, 1926–8, 1932).

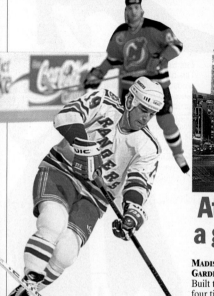

## At any moment, a great moment.

### MADISON SQUARE GARDEN

Built then rebuilt four times between 1879 and 1968, the most famous sports complex in New York has virtually never been closed. Among the many celebrities

BETTING PROHIBITED

THE YANKEES USE
LIFEBUOY
PROTECTS HEALTH
— STOPS B O

### NEW YORK YACHT CLUB

The New York Yacht Club, one of the oldest sailing clubs in the world, is situated in the heart of Manhattan ● 93, ▲ 251. This venerable institution manned the *America*, the first holder of the cup of that name. This trophy, which is competed for every three years, left the premises of the New York Yacht Club only in 1983, after 132 years of American invincibility.

### JOE NAMATH

His amazing skill as a quarterback at the University of Alabama earned him a three-year no-cut contract of over $400,000 from the New York Jets before he had ever played as a professional. Years before carrying off the Super Bowl in 1969, this high-spirited, charismatic player was the subject of gossip in the New York tabloids as well as being the idol of football fans.

### JOHN MCENROE

Raised in Queens, trained on Long Island, and now a Manhattan resident, John McEnroe is more closely associated

who have appeared in the Garden are Sarah Bernhardt, Marilyn Monroe, player Jimmy Connors and Muhammad Ali. The Garden's home teams are the Knicks ▲ 249 (above) and the Rangers (below, left).

### NEW YORK MARATHON

The New York Marathon, which usually takes place at the end of October, was first organized in 1970, when the vogue for jogging was at its peak. In the space of only a few years, this race has acquired an international reputation, due not only to its setting, but to the caliber of its participants and its generous prizes.

with New York than any other sports personality. Having won the U.S. Open four times between 1979 and 1984, McEnroe has helped to make the two weeks at Flushing Meadows a highlight of international tennis.

65

# ● INTERIOR DESIGN AND FURNITURE

**TIFFANY LAMPS**
These lamps, with brightly colored shades made of iridescent glass, set in lead like stained glass windows, are among the most eye-catching creations of Louis Comfort Tiffany, son of the jeweler Charles Lewis Tiffany, founder of the famous Tiffany & Co.

At the end of the 18th century, New York's master craftsmen – mainly European-born – satisfied their customers' desire for the latest fashions by copying and adapting the styles of the Old World. In the last few years of the 19th century, they adopted a showy, luxurious style of interior design which corresponded to the city's extraordinary growth. The single-story mansion on Fifth Avenue belonging to multi-millionaire William H. Vanderbilt was a perfect example of these excesses: its decoration cost $1,800,000.

**640 FIFTH AVENUE**

Above: a detail of the Vanderbilt house ▲ 284. The dining room was decorated in the so-called "aesthetic" style, which was then all the rage. Parisian interior designer Pierre Victor Galland created the *trompe l'œil* ceiling in this room, combining an unusually rich blend of Chinese, Japanese and Turkish influences. The house was crammed with works of art which, for the most part, reflected the tastes of the time. Once a week, Vanderbilt opened his art gallery to the public, showing off his collection of 19th-century European painting. The house was demolished in 1925.

66

### GOTHIC REVIVAL STYLE

Style followed style in the 19th century, each more eclectic than the last. This piece by A. J. Davis reveals the considerable influence of architecture ● *86* on furniture design. The chair's pointed arches romantically suggest the ogive windows of medieval cathedrals.

### THE CLASSICAL PERIOD

A neo-classical style, which emphasized harmony and symmetry, prevailed between the end of the American Revolution and the beginning of the 19th century. The carved eagle on the back of this dining room chair symbolizes the new American republic.

### "SKYSCRAPER" BOOKCASE

The rising set-back design of this work by Paul Frankl reflects the silhouette of 1920's skyscraper architecture in New York ● *97*.

### CHIPPENDALE-STYLE CARD TABLE

This table displays three features of furniture made in New York: the fifth leg, which permits the extension of the table-leaf, the ornamental design of the legs and the gadrooning just below the table top.

### ROCOCO REVIVAL STYLE

This style is distinguished by its luxuriant floral ornamentation. A typical example is the dining room table, by John Henry Belter, which is encrusted with a tangle of branches, leaves and bunches of grapes.

# ● CHEESECAKE

Founded in New York in 1921, *Lindy's* restaurant is famous for its cheesecake.

The two recipes (Jewish and Italian) for the American cheesecake originated in New York at the turn of the century. What is now called New York cheesecake by out-of-towners is closer to the Jewish recipe. It is heavier than the Italian recipe, whose main ingredient is *ricotta* cheese, and has a smooth texture which comes from the cream and cream cheese used.

**2.** Melt the butter then mix in a bowl with the graham crackers. Place the mixture in a mold lined with waxed paper.

**3.** Press down with a glass to obtain a base a scant ½ inch thick. Place in the refrigerator for about 45 minutes.

**6.** Gradually add the cream cheese to the mixture.

**7.** Then pour in the heavy cream and add the vanilla and the orange zest.

**11.** Leave to rest for an hour and a half, then unmold and decorate with the strawberries.

**12.** To make the syrup cook the strawberries the sugar and the water over a low heat.

## INGREDIENTS

*Topping:* 1 cup sugar, 3 tbsp/4½ tbsp cornstarch, 3½ cups cream cheese, 2 eggs, ½ cup heavy cream, 1 sachet of vanilla, orange zest, 18 oz strawberries.
*Syrup:* ¼ lb strawberries, ¼ cup sugar, 1½ tbsp water.
8½-inch mold.

Base: 4 tbsp butter, 9 oz graham crackers.

**1.** To make the base, first crush the graham crackers.

**4.** Cream the sugar and the cornstarch.

**5.** Add the whole eggs.

**8.** Mix the ingredients well.

**9.** Pour the topping into the mold.

**10.** Cook in a hot oven (400°–450°F) for 45 minutes.

**13.** Strain the mixture and use to glaze the cheesecake.

### BAGELS
These ring-shaped rolls, often served with smoked salmon and cream cheese, are a Jewish specialty.

You can buy large, chewy pretzels, hot and salted, from sidewalk vendors (above, a pretzel vendor in the 1940's).

A placemat depicting the presidents of the U.S.; a coffee cup illustrating a New York deli's ideals of service; in a more exotic vein, the spices sold on 9th Ave. at International Food.

The traditional doggy bag in which customers at some restaurants take home their leftovers. They are given to customers at the Carnegie Delicatessen, a typical New York establishment specializing in Jewish food from Central Europe, famous for its gargantuan servings of pastrami.

### WALDORF SALAD
The ingredients of this dish, created in the 1930's at the Waldorf-Astoria Hotel, include apples, walnuts and celery.

Certain pubs – New York institutions such as McSorley's Old Ale House, Pete's Tavern and the Peculiar Pub – serve locally brewed beer.

Jigsaw puzzles and ties are among New York's souvenirs.

# ARCHITECTURE

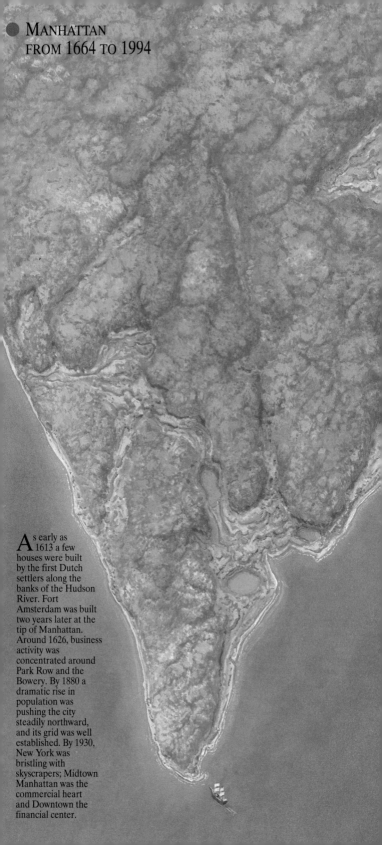

# MANHATTAN
## FROM 1664 TO 1994

As early as 1613 a few houses were built by the first Dutch settlers along the banks of the Hudson River. Fort Amsterdam was built two years later at the tip of Manhattan. Around 1626, business activity was concentrated around Park Row and the Bowery. By 1880 a dramatic rise in population was pushing the city steadily northward, and its grid was well established. By 1930, New York was bristling with skyscrapers; Midtown Manhattan was the commercial heart and Downtown the financial center.

1664

1664

1774

1774

1930

"New York City, the incomparable, the brilliant star city of cities, the forty-ninth state, a law unto itself, the Cyclopean paradox, the inferno with no out-of-bound, the supreme expression of both the miseries and the splendors of contemporary civilization, the Macedonia of the United States. It meets the most severe test that may be applied to definition of a metropolis – stays up all night. But also it becomes a small town when it rains."

John Gunther,
*Inside U.S.A.*

# ● COLONIAL STYLE AND FEDERAL STYLE

Vestiges of colonial New York, whether Dutch or English, are few and far between, although several remaining old Colonial houses in Manhattan hint at the look of the city in the late 18th century. Much more common are the early 19th-century houses built in the Georgian style dubbed "Federal" which developed in the early years of Independence.

**DYCKMAN HOUSE, 1783 (204th St. and Broadway)** ▲ *361*
Dyckman House is the only surviving example of the type of farmhouse built in Manhattan up until the mid-19th century by settlers of Dutch origin. Its double-sloped gambrel, or mansard, roof is typical of Dutch colonial houses.

Splayed stone lintels above windows, with or without keystone, are typical features of the Georgian style.

**MORRIS-JUMEL MANSION, 1765 (W. 160th St. and Jumel Terrace)** ▲ *361*
This is the only Georgian country house remaining in New York from the English colonial period. The grand Corinthian portico and corner quoins are reminiscent of the English Palladian style, which was widely adopted by wealthy Americans in the mid-18th century. The carved balustrade on the crest of the roof is a more typically American feature.

"Birdcages" decorate the wrought-iron railings of some Federal-style staircases.

### THE ROOF
Some Federal-style houses have pitched roofs pierced with dormer windows.

### THE ENTRANCE
The most striking feature of Federal-style houses is the main entrance. The doorway of 59 Morton Street, with its engaged colonettes, is crowned with a fanlight and flanked by sidelights.

Typical Federal-style lintels.

### EDWARD MOONEY HOUSE, 1785–9 (18 Bowery).
The Edward Mooney House is an example of transitional architecture. Its façade, overlooking the Bowery, displays Georgian elements, while the gable end (on Pell Street), with its top-story quarter round windows, anticipates the Federal style.

### ROMAN CATHOLIC ORPHAN ASYLUM, 1825–86 (32 Prince St.)
This former Catholic orphanage, a typical structure from the Federal period, now houses a convent and a school. Its features – so-called Flemish bond brickwork, dormer sash windows and fanlight – are reminiscent of domestic architecture.

The cast-iron railings of 10 Washington Square display a combination of Grecian geometric and floral motifs and classical scrolls.

The 1830's were prosperous years for New York. They witnessed the flowering of the Greek Revival style, which was widely applied to large civic, religious and commercial buildings, as well as houses. Although a development of late 18th-century European neo-classicism, the Greek Revival style also represented a tribute by an idealistic America to ancient Greek democracy.

**COLONNADE ROW, 1833, Seth Greer (428–34 Lafayette St.) ▲ 227**
Four houses remain out of the nine that originally made up LaGrange Terrace (the name was derived from the French country home of the Marquis de Lafayette). The Greek architectural features of this residential structure were modified to suit domestic typology: from the restrained decoration to the giant Corinthian-order portico.

**VILLAGE COMMUNITY CHURCH, 1847, Samuel Thomson (143 West 13th St.) ▲ 219**
In the 19th century many New York parishes commissioned new buildings modeled on the classical Greek temple. A typical example is this old church in Greenwich Village. Such buildings were constructed of brick, granite, polished marble or limestone; softer materials, such as sandstone or wood, were used for the columns. These austere exteriors often conceal richly decorated interiors.

An attic story is a characteristic feature of Greek Revival houses, like this one in Cushman Row, with its regular small square windows surrounded by laurel wreaths.

**FEDERAL HALL, 1834–42, Town & Davis (28 Wall St.) ▲ 162**
The most imposing examples of Greek Revival style in Manhattan are public buildings, and among these the most eye-catching is the former Federal Customs House. The restraint of its marble Doric exterior, modeled on the Parthenon, belies the sumptuous interior, which boasts a domed, coffered ceiling resting on marble Corinthian columns and adorned with elegant classical ironwork.

**WAREHOUSES**
After the fire of December 1835, many warehouses were built to the same basic design: granite ground floor, brick upper stories and a façade sometimes totally made of granite, as here, at 170–6 John Street.

**PORCHES**
Porches were set back within the façade so as not to encroach on the narrow New York streets. The main entrance, typically framed in solid granite, was illuminated by side lights and a fanlight.

The bays and the cornice are the only form of decoration. Here, wealth goes hand in hand with austerity.

**CUSHMAN ROW, 1840 (406–418 W. 20th St.) ▲ 220**
This is a group of identical row houses. The two most characteristic features of this style of house are the cornices and the attic story, concealing a flat roof.

# GOTHIC REVIVAL AND HIGH VICTORIAN GOTHIC STYLES

The arches of Grace Church, ▲ 224, on Broadway, are adorned with figurative reliefs.

The Gothic Revival style appeared in New York in the 1830's. Although it was applied primarily to religious structures, elements found their way into civic architecture. The early form of Gothic Revival, with its rural medieval architecture gave way, in the 1860's, to a more complex style, High Victorian Gothic, and later, at the end of the century, to Neo-Gothic, whose idiom was closer to that of 14th-century Gothic; St Thomas's, on Fifth Avenue, is an outstanding example.

When building the Church of the Holy Communion, Upjohn made every effort to reproduce the appearance of English rural churches down to the smallest detail, even to the point of choosing uneven blocks of stone, in different shades, to give the church the weathered look of old stone.

The Church of the Holy Communion is typical of American parishes in combining the place of worship with a building devoted to social activities.

**CHURCH OF THE HOLY COMMUNION, 1846, Richard Upjohn (6th Ave at 20th St.)** ▲ 220
In 1846, Upjohn, the architect of Trinity Church ▲ 154, designed the first asymmetrical Gothic Revival church in America, similar to those built in the English countryside. This church became the model for many others in the United States.

The Gothic Revival grillwork of
Grace Church on Broadway.

High Victorian Gothic, inspired by Italian and
French Gothic architecture, showed the
influence of John Ruskin's theories. It became
very fashionable in New York in the 1860's.

For a short time
during the 1840's the
property developers
of rowhouses applied
Gothic elements to
their buildings, as can
be seen on the doors
of 135 E. 12th Street
▲ 85.

**THOMAS STREET INN, 1875, J. Morgan Slade
(8 Thomas St.)** ▲ 209
This is an example of High Victorian Gothic
as applied to a commercial building. The
rational use of the materials – brick
and stone – and the polychrome
decoration are distinctive features
of this style.

A decorative arcade on
Governor Tilden's house.

**DECORATIVE
IRONWORK**
One of the most
striking features of
neo-Gothic style is
the use of cast iron
for screens and
balconies, which
boasted pointed
quatrefoil and trefoil
motifs.
**MEDIEVAL
INSPIRATION**
Some granite façades
had medieval features
such as lancet arch
doorways and ogee
arches.

**NATIONAL ARTS CLUB,
formerly GOVERNOR
TILDEN'S HOUSE,
1884, Calvert Vaux
(15 Gramercy Park
South)** ▲ 230
Here the architects
combined sculpture
and polychrome
decoration in the
purest Ruskinian
tradition. Note the
stringcourses under
the windows and the
curved arcading,
suggestive of
northern Italian
Gothic architecture.

# Italianate and Second Empire styles

The doorway of the Salmagundi Club (47 5th Avenue), crowned with a semicircular fanlight, has double doors. The lavishly carved architrave is topped with a pediment.

As early as 1845, but primarily in the 1850's and 1860's, two new styles took Manhattan by storm – one inspired by the Italian Renaissance and the other by Second Empire French architecture. The two styles could be combined, crowning "Florentine" façades with mansard roofs. It was during these years of heady economic and urban growth that architects began to make use of new materials such as cast iron.

## THE ITALIANATE CORNICE
The Italianate façade is articulated by deeply recessed windows with ledges. The building is crowned by a projecting cornice supported by corbels, often made of galvanized iron.

**CARY BUILDING, 1857, King and Kellum (105–107 Chambers St.)** ▲ *209*
Italianate-style commercial buildings were often constructed of cast-iron elements, bolted onto conventional brick or wooden structures. The façades of these cast-iron buildings were painted to resemble stone – which was too expensive – as on the Haughwout Building ● 94, ▲ *204*, or here, on the Cary Building.

**ANALOGY**
Features common to both Italianate and Second Empire styles are strong horizontal divisions, grouped columns, deeply recessed window arches and projecting cornices, as seen on the Cary Building (left) and Gilsey House (above, right).

## BROWNSTONES
Thousands of Italianate-style rowhouses were constructed between 1845 and 1870, a period of great economic growth. They were built of brownstone, a type of rich brown sandstone quarried in Connecticut and New Jersey. This material became so popular that New Yorkers still call these houses "brownstones". This (right) is the Langston Hughes House, at 20 E. 127th Street, in Harlem.

Italianate-style rowhouses were simple three-story structures (right) resting on a rugged rusticated basement. They have segmental arch bay windows (left) with very large windowpanes.

The ironwork on the roof of 881 Broadway is reminiscent of that on Napoleon III's addition to the Louvre.

**GILSEY HOUSE, 1871 (1200 Broadway)** ▲ 234

Several New York buildings, such as the Gilsey House, with its cast-iron façade, built by Stephen Decatur Hatch, were directly inspired by Haussmann's neo-Baroque style. The double-slope, so-called mansard roof, a key feature of this style, marks the first significant influence of French architecture in New York.

The Gilsey House's façade (below) overlooking Broadway, and a detail (left) of the pyramidal pavilion roof at the corner. Geometric and scattered polychrome patterns are created by the slates.

Another example of slate patterns at 19 Gramercy Park ▲ 230.

**70 PERRY ST., 1867**

The popular mansard roof had begun to replace flat roofs in the 1830's. Adding a mansard roof to an Italianate façade gave the owner an additional story to rent out.

# Queen Anne Style and Romanesque Revival

A stylistic change took place in the years following the depression of the 1870's. The Italianate style was replaced by two picturesque modes: Queen Anne and Romanesque Revival. The first combined Medieval, Renaissance, classical and even Japanese features to create an occasionally eccentric architecture. The second, a pragmatic, weighty style introduced by H. H. Richardson, combined Romanesque and Byzantine influences.

Brick was commonly used in the Queen Anne style for its formal and decorative potential, in combination with other materials. This varied effect is seen to good advantage in the Potter Building, Park Row ▲ 170.

The Japanese-style glazing bars of the Century Building ▲ 223 and the floral-motif ironwork of the Chelsea Hotel ▲ 220 – are typical of the Queen Anne style.

The sunflower became the archetypal motif of Queen Anne decoration.

Most Queen Anne structures in New York are polychromatic, with brick façades enhanced with stone and terracotta trimmings.

**QUEEN ANNE-STYLE ROW HOUSES, 1894, W. Holman Smith (35–45 W. 94th St.)**
These houses still have their eccentric gables, a galvanized metal cornice, punctuated alternately by small triangular pediments and scrolled pediments, decorated with pinecones. The regularity of the façades is interrupted by picturesque bow windows.

Stone, terracotta and brick used together in a Romanesque Revival lintel.

## GILBERT KIAMIE HOUSE formerly the Grolier Club, 1895 (29 E. 32nd St.)

Romanesque Revival façades are typically articulated by bold semicircular bays, divided by thick mullions and transoms, occasionally embellished with leaded glass panes. The bonding is richly varied, incorporating rubble stone, terracotta and reliefs featuring carved plant forms, strapwork and grotesque motifs.

**WALLACE BUILDING, 1893–4, Oscar Wirz (56–8 Pine St.).** This is one of the few examples of Romanesque Revival being applied to skyscraper architecture. Note the intricate Byzantine detailing of the semicircular bays (opposite).

On the Wallace Building Romanesque Revival decoration has been adapted to suit the proportions of the skyscraper.

The juxtaposition of rustication and dressed stone is typical of Romanesque Revival (seen here at 112 E. 17th St.). The contrast is accentuated by the use of bas-relief elements.

The grilles of the DeVinne Press Building employ a motif similar to those used on Rouen Cathedral in France.

**DEVINNE PRESS BUILDING, 1885–6, Babb, Cook and Willard (393–9 Lafayette St.) ▲ 227** In the prosperous 1880's, many Romanesque Revival factories and warehouses, including this printing works, were built in New York. Tall round-arched bays such as these were to influence commercial architecture at the end of the century.

Between 1846 and 1914, more than four hundred American architects studied in Paris at the École des Beaux-Arts. In fact, the United States had no architectural school until 1867. The prestige enjoyed by Paris-trained architects prompted their younger colleagues to follow in their footsteps, and nearly half of these graduates practised in New York. "Beaux-Arts"-style buildings are now coming back into favor among certain Postmodern architects.

**NEW YORK PUBLIC LIBRARY, 1911, Carrère & Hastings** (5th Ave., between 40th and 42nd sts.) ▲ 252. The key feature of this monumental building is the clearly organized and balanced plan (left), a fundamental lesson of Beaux-Arts training found in major public commissions. The wide corridors, punctuated by columns, are conducive to circulation and make every department of the New York Public Library easily accessible. The triple arcade, accentuated by columns and surmounted by groups of carved figures (above), gives the main entrance the status of a triumphal arch.

**HENRY VILLARD HOUSES, 1884, McKim, Mead and White** (451–5 Madison Ave., between 50th and 51st sts.) ▲ 284. This group of six private residences, arranged around a central courtyard, is a replica of a traditional Italian palazzo. The south wing was intended for Henry Villard, one of America's wealthiest railway magnates, who commissioned the project. The houses now form part of a hotel.

The main source of inspiration for the Henry Villard Houses was the Palazzo della Cancelleria in Rome, whose decoration was simplified and limited to the window frames, the balconies and the quoins.

**THE PIERPONT MORGAN LIBRARY, 1906, McKim, Mead & White (33 E. 36th St.)** ▲ 241
"I want a gem": these were the words of the financier J. Pierpont Morgan, an ardent admirer of Italian Renaissance architecture, when he commissioned a private library-cum-museum from McKim. The three rooms are linked by a vestibule extended by an apse. The allegorical paintings on the walls are adapted from Raphaël's frescoes in the Vatican.

The decoration of the cornice on the Racquet and Tennis Club of New York ▲ 286 sets up a subtle balance between picturesque and monumental elements.

**NEW YORK YACHT CLUB, 1900, Warren and Wetmore (37 W. 44th St.)** ▲ 251
The architects of this sailing club turned the narrow site to account by devising three classical bays decorated with galleon sterns, which could have come straight out of *Peter Pan*; they overhang 44th Street, bringing dolphins, seaweed and shells in their wake.

**LOW MEMORIAL LIBRARY, 1897, McKim, Mead & White (Columbia University)** ▲ 352
Between 1894 and 1903 Charles McKim designed the general plan for the Columbia campus, located between West 116th and 120th streets. The overall scheme, dense and homogeneous, is one of the most characteristic examples of the "City Beautiful" movement, the urban design equivalent of the "Beaux-Arts" style. The focal point of the composition is this library, with its awe-inspiring peristyle and dome. However, the proportions remain on a human scale and the steps, which serve as a podium, have become a popular student gathering place.

# THE BIRTH OF THE SKYSCRAPER

The birth of the skyscraper, in the 1860's, was a response to the spatial constraints imposed by the tight urban fabric of Lower Manhattan. It was made possible by the design of light steel frames, the invention of the electric passenger elevator and the fact that the rocky terrain lent itself to the laying of foundations. But there was another reason: the desire to go one better than the competition. However, although the techniques were new, the forms and the decoration remained eclectic.

In 1913 the Woolworth Building, dubbed the "eighth wonder of the world", was its tallest building at 792 feet ▲ *180*.

Decorative elements were cast in factories and then bolted onto the structure.

**HAUGHWOUT BUILDING, 1857, J. P. Gaynor (488 Broadway, at Broome St.) ▲** *204*. This forebear of the skyscraper was built by Daniel D. Badger, to plans by Gaynor, with prefabricated cast-iron elements which made it possible to incorporate large areas of glass. The Haughwout Building was originally a department store selling glass, china, clocks and watches.

**CAST-IRON ASSEMBLY**
Standardized cast-iron parts were assembled and bolted on at the construction site. This job did not require skilled workmen and the process was cheaper than stone construction. But the cast iron was not initially strong enough to be used for buildings with a large number of stories; in addition, its low resistance to fire represented a very real danger for the building's occupants. Behind the metal façade, the load-bearing structures continued to be made of wood or conventional masonry: it was not until the invention of the Bessemer process (1856) and the popularization of high-resistance steel, that a homogeneous frame was developed ▲ *203*.

**BAYARD BUILDING, formerly CONDICT BUILDING, 1898, Louis Sullivan and Lyndon P. Smith (65 Bleecker St.)** ▲ *209*
This is the only building in New York designed by the master of the Chicago School. A projecting cornice stabilizes the rhythm of the decorative pilasters, alternately thick and thin, and achieves an innovative balance between horizontal and vertical elements.

Detail from the terracotta decoration of the Bayard Building. Here Sullivan was exploiting the geometrical interlaced motifs which were a hallmark of his style.

In 1857, in the Haughwout Store, Elisha Otis installed the first passenger elevator fitted with a safety device.

**ANSONIA HOTEL, 1904, Paul E. M. Duboy and Michael Graves (2109 Broadway)** ▲ *347*. The French-born architect endeavored to give this apartment building a Parisian look. This was no easy task, as it entailed maintaining a harmonious sense of proportion in a huge apartment building with disparate façades, combining a whole spectrum of materials, whose height was three times that of its Parisian counterparts.

# THE ECLECTICISM OF THE FIRST SKYSCRAPERS

Diagram showing the assembly of a terracotta facing.

At the turn of the 20th century the technology necessary for erecting tall buildings came of age; the number of stories multiplied and skyscrapers shot up all over Manhattan. But these skyscrapers still needed to find their own aesthetic, instead of wavering between neo-Classicism and neo-Gothic.

**MUNICIPAL BUILDING, 1914, McKim, Mead & White (1 Centre St.) ▲ 182**
Designed by prominent champions of classicism, this skyscraper evokes a classical column in its tripartite composition, distinct base, shaft and capital. The Stalinist-era skyscrapers of Moscow, which also sport Corinthian pilasters and engaged columns, were inspired by this style.

**FLATIRON BUILDING, formerly FULLER BUILDING, 1902, Daniel H. Burnham & Co. (175 5th Ave.) ▲ 233**
Equipped with a system to prevent the spread of fire, this was the first self-sufficient skyscraper. It had an electric generator providing all its electricity and heating.

The tops of the Bankers Trust ▲ *163*, Woolworth ▲ *180* and Metropolitan Life Insurance Company ▲ *234* buildings were inspired respectively by classical mausoleums, Gothic steeples and the campanile in Saint Mark's square in Venice. This was not for ideological reasons but served, rather, to give each building a distinctive identity on the Manhattan skyline.

The plans drawn up in 1922 by the Viennese architect Adolf Loos for the headquarters of the *Chicago Tribune* (left) were a literal reference to the tripartite division of the skyscraper and suggest a giant Doric column.

**ZONING RESOLUTION**
In 1916 a set of building regulations was passed to prevent the "canyon" effect ■ *16*. Skyscrapers could be built with a height relative to the width of the street. Successive setbacks were then employed to make them narrower and allow light into the street. When the building size had been reduced to a quarter of the site at street level, the tower could continue to rise ad infinitum.

**EQUITABLE BUILDING, 1912–15 (120 Broadway)** ▲ *153*
Designed before the zoning law, the Equitable Building (left) should, according to its criteria, have been built in the shape of a pyramid (right).

97

During the property boom of the 1920's, New York architects drew their inspiration from European movements – Viennese Secession, German Expressionism, French Art Deco – and even transcended them. The Chrysler Building ▲ *266* is one of the most striking examples of this trend. The geometric, streamlined aesthetic of Art Deco was ideally suited to the tapering shape of the new skyscrapers.

**FRIEZES IN ABUNDANCE**
An abundance of decorative friezes appeared during the Art Deco period. Here, a detail of one at 2 Park Ave. built by Ely Jacques Kahn.

**THE FIRST ART DECO SKYSCRAPER**
The main entrance of the Barclay-Vesey Building, 1923–6 ▲ *140* (140 West St.) is decorated with bells, the logo of the Bell Telephone Company.

**GENERAL ELECTRIC BUILDING, formerly the RCA VICTOR BUILDING, 1930–1, Cross & Cross (570 Lexington Ave. at 51st St.) ▲ *286***
The summit of this spire is stunning in its originality and exuberance. The lacy ornamental stonework, brickwork and glazed ceramic veneer, gilded in places, suggest Flamboyant Gothic; yet, apart from the stylized pinnacles, none of these varied motifs had any precedents; the chevrons and bolts of lightning symbolize the Hertzian waves broadcast by the Radio Corporation of America, the original owner of this tower.

**DYNAMIC COMPOSITIONS**
The radiator grills in the Chanin Building, 1929 (122 E. 42nd St.) ▲ *272*. These grills, the work of the sculptor René Chambellan, combine rays and chevrons, spirals and ripples.

## THE SKYLINE

In 1929 the Multiple Dwelling Act authorized the construction of very tall apartment houses and hotels. Central Park West was subsequently endowed with a number of soaring residences, some with twin towers. On the East Side, the towers of the Waldorf-Astoria Hotel (1930–1, Schultze & Weaver) joined the Chrysler and General Electric buildings on the Midtown skyline.

**AMERICAN STANDARD BUILDING, formerly AMERICAN RADIATOR BUILDING, 1924, Hood & Fouilhoux (40 W. 40th St.)** ▲ *254.* This has one of the earliest pyramidal silhouettes. The black brick facing employed by Raymond Hood, a former pupil at the École des Beaux-Arts, was an innovative step. It enabled him to minimize the contrast between the building's solid masses and the windows.

**FILM CENTER BUILDING, 1928–9, Buchman & Kahn (630 9th Ave.)** ▲ *256*
The lobby of this building, designed by one of the masters of the Modern Jazz style, is a prime illustration of this style's typical features. Certain motifs, like those of the mosaics, were directly inspired by Mayan art.

The Gothic pinnacles on the setbacks of the American Standard Building are enhanced with gold.

**TWO NEW DECORATIVE ELEMENTS**
The horizontal bands of blue-green glazed terracotta and the giant stylized letters, which form part of the decoration of the entrance and the top of the McGraw-Hill Building, were introduced by the architect Raymond Hood.

**Former MCGRAW-HILL BUILDING, 1930–1, Hood, Godley & Fouilhoux (330 W. 42nd St.)** ▲ *256.* This skyscraper, whose use of horizontal lines and rounded corners at the top creates a dynamic effect, doubled as headquarters and printing works for a large publishing company. An early example of streamlining, this building displays a functionalism akin to that of the International Style.

The term "international style" was first used, in 1932, by the architect Philip Johnson and the art historian Henry-Russell Hitchcock to describe the exhibition of modern European architecture held at MOMA in the same year. However, New York architects were not ready to embrace European modernism and the city did not become a testing ground for modern architecture until around 1950.

**W. LESCAZE HOUSE, 1934 (211 E. 48th St.) ▲ 262**
This townhouse was the architect's home and place of work and one of the first International Style buildings in New York. It contrasts sharply with the neighboring brownstone residences. Ribbon windows and glass block panes let the light filter in while maintaining privacy.

**MOMA ▲ 290**, reconstruction of the original façade, 1939, Philip Goodwin and Edward Durell Stone (11 W. 53rd St.)
The original building to house the Museum of Modern Art formed a marked contrast with the adjacent rowhouses.

**THE INITIAL COMPOSITION**
The emphasis is on horizontal and vertical lines. The façade expresses the building's various functions: a welcoming, glazed ground floor, two levels of windowless exhibition rooms, two office stories and a roof terrace. The geometric severity of the building is tempered by the curve of the canopy and the round openings in the roof.

**LEVER HOUSE, 1952, Skidmore, Owing & Merrill (390 Park Ave.) ▲ 286.** The generation of "minimalist" skyscrapers, with their pared down lines, came of age with this building. It uses only a quarter of the available area and its main vertical structure is set at right angles to Park Avenue. Under threat in 1983, Lever House is now listed as a landmark.

**A NEW APPROACH TO PUBLIC OPEN SPACES.** Because Lever House rests on stilts, a pedestrian area opens up at street level. Trees grow up through the opening in the roof terrace (left). The airy effect breaks the uniformity of the avenue.

Narrow decorative bronze I-beams punctuate the windows of the Seagram Building and accentuate the vertical thrust of the metal frame.

**SEAGRAM BUILDING, 1958, Ludwig Mies van der Rohe in collaboration with Philip Johnson (375 Park Ave.)** ▲ *286*
The German-born architect was already an established name in Chicago when he received the commisssion for this building. A 38-story-high rectangle composed of three major bays, it is proportioned according to classical canons. The building is set back from Park Avenue, creating space for a deep plaza from which this minimalist skyscraper can be admired. Its austere lines were realized in rich materials and the Seagram Building topped all records for cost per square meter.

**DECORATIVE BRONZE**
The vertical structure is accentuated by decorative bronze I-beams; the corner posts are also clad in bronze.

The top is sliced off at a 45° angle, making Citicorp easy to distinguish on the Manhattan skyline.

**CITICORP CENTER, 1978, Hugh Stubbins & Assoc. (Lexington Ave., between 53rd and 54th Sts.)** ▲ *286*
This 46-story tower, sheathed in aluminum panels, sits on four pillars and a central column. A sunken plaza occupies the area which has been liberated at ground level.

**FORD FOUNDATION, 1967, Kevin Roche, John Dinkeloo & Assocs. (321 E. 42nd St.)** ▲ *264*. The technical and stylistic innovation of this building is its brick and glass façade. It was built using girders made of exposed steel (Cor-ten) which is resistant to atmospheric corrosion.

**BETTER BALANCE BETWEEN PUBLIC AND PRIVATE SPACES**
At the end of the 1960's, architects endeavored to improve the relationship between public and private spaces. The Ford Foundation is one successful example: two office wings open onto an immense enclosed atrium-garden which can be seen from the street.

# ● POSTMODERNISM

Detail of the polished steel elevator door-plaques inside the Sony Building.

In the 1980's, the prosperity enjoyed by big business gave the skyscraper a new lease on life. In New York, one of the hotbeds of Postmodernism since the 1970's, architects and real estate developers viewed the revival of past forms as an antidote to the International Style, and a means of restoring to larger corporate buildings a symbolic dimension.

**SONY BUILDING formerly AT&T BUILDING, 1979–83, Philip Johnson and John Burgee (550 Madison Ave.)**
The era of the Postmodern skyscraper dawned with this building. To make his "small" 37-story building more monumental, Johnson revived tripartite composition. His Chippendale-style pediment aroused great controversy.

**THE RISE OF POSTMODERNISM**
With its AT&T headquarters (now the Sony Building), which appeared on the covers of *Time* and *The New Yorker*, Johnson's firm launched a new fashion; and Johnson – once an exponent of the International Style – maintained his position as an arbiter of taste in New York.
The place of honor in the main lobby was held by a statue, the *Spirit of Communication*, brought from the previous headquarters.

**WASHINGTON COURT, 1986, James Stewart Polskek & Partners ▲ 212 (6th Ave., between Waverly Place and Washington Square)**
Postmodernism has also had its effect on residential architecture: these rowhouses, with their harmonious façades, reflect the spirit of Greenwich Village.

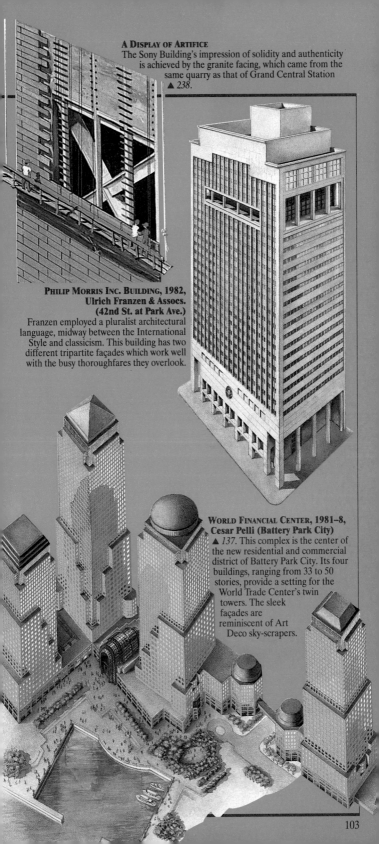

**A DISPLAY OF ARTIFICE**
The Sony Building's impression of solidity and authenticity is achieved by the granite facing, which came from the same quarry as that of Grand Central Station ▲ *238*.

**PHILIP MORRIS INC. BUILDING, 1982, Ulrich Franzen & Assocs. (42nd St. at Park Ave.)**
Franzen employed a pluralist architectural language, midway between the International Style and classicism. This building has two different tripartite façades which work well with the busy thoroughfares they overlook.

**WORLD FINANCIAL CENTER, 1981–8, Cesar Pelli (Battery Park City)**
▲ *137*. This complex is the center of the new residential and commercial district of Battery Park City. Its four buildings, ranging from 33 to 50 stories, provide a setting for the World Trade Center's twin towers. The sleek façades are reminiscent of Art Deco sky-scrapers.

Because of the recession, some projects designed in the 1980's never saw the light of day. Neither the skyscrapers scheduled to be built on Columbus Circle nor Donald Trump's 150-story dream tower were realized. However, on the West Side, the redevelopment of the banks of the Hudson reveals a new approach to urban design.

**WHITNEY MUSEUM, 1966, Marcel Breuer & Assocs.
(Madison Ave. at 75th St.) ▲ 326**

This building, built by a former professor at the Weimar Bauhaus to house a collection of modern American art, quickly became too cramped. The plans for enlarging it, designed in 1986 by Michael Graves, rekindled the "quarrel of the Moderns and the Postmoderns". In order to treble the effective area, Graves planned to demolish some apartment buildings on Madison Avenue and to build on top of the existing museum and a new red granite base. Ignoring the style of the original building he planned a huge exhibition hall illuminated by a lunette, with a colonnaded restaurant on top.

Plans for a tower by Pederson and Fox at 383 Madison Avenue were abandoned.

**WHITEHALL FERRY TERMINAL**
In 1992 the Postmodernist architect Robert Venturi was commissioned to build a new maritime terminal on the tip of Manhattan. He reproduced the proportions of the façade from the neighboring Battery Maritime Terminal and topped the building with a startling clock over 98 feet in diameter, which called to mind the slogan "Time is Money". This approach follows the tradition of large American neo-Classical railroad stations.

# NEW YORK
## AS SEEN BY PAINTERS

### JONATHAN WEINBERG

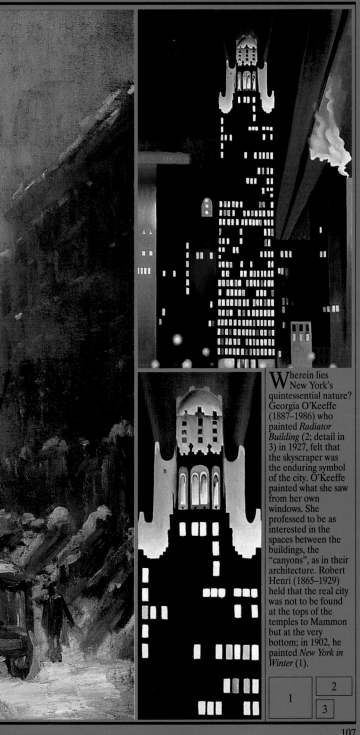

"WHAT A SIGHT THESE TOWERS OF MANHATTAN ARE, GLITTERING WITH MILLIONS OF GOLDEN SPECKS, SOARING ENDLESSLY, AS IF THEY WERE GOING TO TOUCH THE SKY!"

LANGSTON HUGHES

Wherein lies New York's quintessential nature? Georgia O'Keeffe (1887–1986) who painted *Radiator Building* (2; detail in 3) in 1927, felt that the skyscraper was the enduring symbol of the city. O'Keeffe painted what she saw from her own windows. She professed to be as interested in the spaces between the buildings, the "canyons", as in their architecture. Robert Henri (1865–1929) held that the real city was not to be found at the tops of the temples to Mammon but at the very bottom; in 1902, he painted *New York in Winter* (1).

| | 2 |
| 1 | 3 |

107

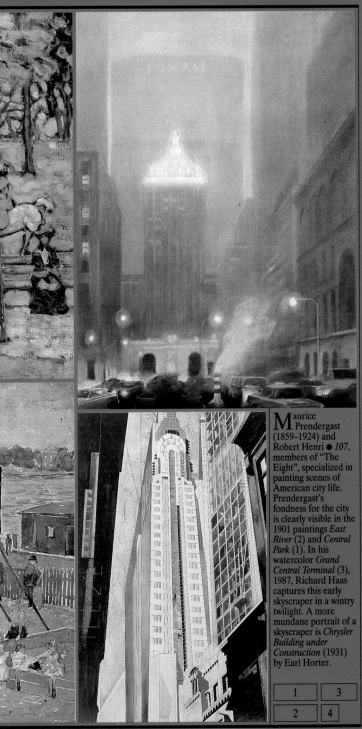

"A LOVE OF ART IS NOT ENOUGH TO PERCEIVE THE STRENGTH, MEANING AND SPARK OF BEAUTY IN A GANG OF URCHINS FROM THE EAST SIDE."

ROBERT HENRI

Maurice Prendergast (1859–1924) and Robert Henri ● *107*, members of "The Eight", specialized in painting scenes of American city life. Prendergast's fondness for the city is clearly visible in the 1901 paintings *East River* (2) and *Central Park* (1). In his watercolor *Grand Central Terminal* (3), 1987, Richard Haas captures this early skyscraper in a wintry twilight. A more mundane portrait of a skyscraper is *Chrysler Building under Construction* (1931) by Earl Horter.

| 1 | 3 |
| 2 | 4 |

"I REGARDED THIS MODERN CITY AS A SORT OF HELL. THE SUBWAY, HIDDEN IN THE BOWELS OF THE EARTH, SEEMED TO YMBOLIZE AN ENVIRONMENT THAT CONFOUNDS THE SENSES AND DESTROYS LIFE."

GEORGE TOOKER

Edward Hopper (1882–1967; below), the most outstanding of Robert Henri's pupils, visited Paris where he began his career by painting in an impressionist style. He returned to New York in 1910, to devote himself to

more familiar American subjects. The works for which he became famous depicted lonely figures in such urban settings as cinemas, service stations, and hotel rooms. Hopper stated that his favorite subject was "sunlight striking the wall of a house". *Roofs of Washington Square*, 1926 (1), is the view from the roof of his studio. This canvas, a dazzling composition of light and airy distances, seems to offer an escape from the artificial lighting of the New York subway system, depicted in George Tooker's painting *Subway* (2; detail in 3). In this oppressively claustrophobic canvas, completed in 1950, the characters are lost in the alienating maze of technology. Hopper and Tooker both evoked a stark and lonely American landscape.

| 1 |
|---|

| 2 | 3 |
|---|---|

These two paintings, *View of Manhattan West from Philip Morris at Par...*
*Avenue and 41st Street* (1982), by Richard Haas, with its jumble ...
buildings and erratic spaces, and – even more so – Joseph Stella ...
*Brooklyn Bridge, Variation on an Old Theme* (1939), with its Gothic arche...
rigid steel cables and heavy traffic, enshrine the city in its own mytholog...

# NEW YORK
## AS SEEN BY WRITERS

## NEW YORKERS

### TALENT

*Does the character of a city come principally from its buildings or its people? According to Timothy Dwight (1752–1817), writing in 1811, the city acts as a magnet for people of talent and is thus shaped by them.*

❝In every large city there will always be found a considerable number of persons who possess superior talents and information; and who, if not natives, are drawn to it by the peculiar encouragement which it holds out to their exertions. The field of effort is here more splendid, and the talents are more needed, honored, and rewarded than in smaller towns. New York has its share of persons sustaining this character: men really possessing superior minds and deserving high esteem. Together with these, there is not a small number, here as elsewhere, who arrogate this character to themselves, and some of whom occasionally acquire and lose it: men accounted great through the favorable influence of some accident, the attachment of some religious or political party during a fortunate breeze of popularity, or the lucky prevalence of some incidental sympathy, or the ardent pursuit of some favorite public object in which they have happened to act with success. These meteors, though some of them shine for a period with considerable luster, soon pass over the horizon, and are seen no more.

The citizens at large are distinguished as to their intelligence in the manner alluded to above. To this place they have come with the advantages and disadvantages of education found in their several native countries. Some of them are well informed, read, converse, and investigate. Others scarcely do either, and not a small number are unable to read at all. Most of these are, however, Europeans.❞

TIMOTHY DWIGHT, *TRAVELS IN NEW ENGLAND AND NEW YORK*,
HARVARD UNIVERSITY PRESS, 1969

### GILDED YOUTH

*F. Scott Fitzgerald (1896–1940) glamorized the 1920's as a decade belonging to "gilded youth". In this autobiographical piece, he feels like an observer of the city rather than a participant because his future wife, Zelda, is in Alabama.*

❝New York had all the iridescence of the beginning of the world. The returning troops marched up Fifth Avenue and the girls were instinctively drawn East and North toward them – this was the greatest nation and there was gala in the air. As I hovered ghost-like in the Plaza Red Room of a Saturday afternoon, or went to lush and liquid garden parties in the East Sixties or tippled with Princetonians in the Biltmore Bar I was haunted always by my other life – my drab room in the Bronx, my square foot of the subway, my fixation upon the day's letter from Alabama – would it come and what would it say? – my shabby suits, my poverty, and love. While my friends were launching decently into life I had muscled my inadequate bark into midstream. The gilded youth circling around young Constance Bennett in the Club de Vingt, the classmates in the Yale-Princeton Club whooping up our first after-the-war reunion, the atmosphere of the millionaires' houses that I sometimes frequented – these things were empty for me, though I recognized them as impressive scenery and regretted that I was committed to other romance. 99

F. SCOTT FITZGERALD, *THE CRACK UP*, © FITZGERALD ESTATE, 1932

### STRANGERS AND NEIGHBORS

*Edmund B. White (1899–1985), an American journalist, was very conscious of the city's previous illustrious inhabitants.*

66On any person who desires such queer prizes, New York will bestow the gift of loneliness and the gift of privacy. It is this largess that accounts for the presence within the city's walls of a considerable section of the population; for the residents of Manhattan are to a large extent strangers who have pulled up stakes somewhere and come to town, seeking sanctuary or fulfillment or some greater or lesser grail. The capacity to make such dubious gifts is a mysterious quality of New York. It can destroy an individual, or it can fulfill him, depending a good deal on luck. No one should come to New York to live unless he is willing to be lucky.

New York is the concentrate of art and commerce and sport and religion and entertainment and finance, bringing to a single compact arena the gladiator, the evangelist, the promoter, the actor, the trader and the merchant. It carries on its lapel the unexpungeable odor of the long past, so that no matter where you sit in New York you feel the vibrations of great times and tall deeds, of queer people and events and undertakings. . . . I am twenty-two blocks from where Rudolph Valentino lay in state, eight blocks from where Nathan Hale was executed, five blocks from the publisher's office where Ernest Hemingway hit Max Eastman on the nose, four miles from where Walt Whitman sat sweating out editorials for the Brooklyn Eagle, thirty-four blocks from the street Willa Cather lived in when she came to New York to write books about Nebraska, one block from where Marceline used to clown on the boards of the Hippodrome . . . and for that matter I am probably occupying the very room that any number of exalted and somewise memorable characters sat in, some of them on hot, breathless afternoons, lonely and private and full of their own sense of emanations from without. 99

E. B. WHITE, *HERE IS NEW YORK*, HARPER BROS., 1949

### LABORERS

*First-generation immigrants add color and diversity to the masses thronging the streets of the city. Charles Dickens (1812–70) described some Irish laborers.*

66 . . . let us see what kind of men . . . are . . . those two labourers in holiday clothes, of whom one carries in his hand a crumpled scrap of paper from which he tries to spell out a hard name, while the other looks about for it on all the doors and windows.

Irishmen both! You might know them, if they were masked, by their long-tailed blue coats and bright buttons, and their drab trousers, which they wear like men well used to working dresses, who are easy in no others. It would be hard to keep your model republics going, without the countrymen and countrywomen of those two labourers. For who else would dig, and delve, and drudge, and do domestic work, and make canals and roads, and execute great lines of Internal Improvement! Irishmen both, and sorely puzzled too, to find out what they seek. Let us go down, and help them for the love of home, and that spirit of liberty which admits of honest service to honest men, and honest work for honest bread, no matter what it be.

That's well! We have got at the right address at last, though it is written in strange characters truly, and might have been scrawled with the blunt handle of the spade the writer better knows the use of, than a pen. Their way lies yonder, but what business takes them there? They carry savings: to hoard up? No. They are brothers, those men. One crossed the sea alone, and working very hard for one half year, and living harder, saved funds enough to bring the other out. That done, they worked together side by side, contentedly sharing hard labour and hard living for another term, and then their sisters came, and then another brother, and lastly, their old mother. And what now? Why, the poor old crone is restless in a strange land, and yearns to lay her bones, she says, among her people in the old graveyard at home: and so they go to pay her passage back: and God help her and them, and every simple heart, and all who turn to the Jerusalem of their younger days, and have an altar-fire upon the cold hearth of their fathers. 99

CHARLES DICKENS, *AMERICAN NOTES*,
LONDON, 1842

### RAGING TORRENTS

*Theodore Dreiser (1871–1945), the American novelist, writes here of the sheer masses of people going about their business in the city.*

66Take your place on Williamsburg Bridge some morning, for instance, at say three or four o'clock, and watch the long, the quite unbroken line of Jews trundling pushcarts eastward to the great Wall-about Market over the bridge. A procession out of Assyria or Egypt or Chaldea, you might suppose, Biblical in quality; or, better yet, a huge chorus in some operatic dawn scene laid in Paris or Petrograd or here. A vast, silent mass it is, marching to the music of necessity . . . And they are New York, too – Bucharest and Lemberg and Odessa come to the Bowery, and adding rich, dark, colorful threads to the rug or tapestry which is New York.

Since these are but a portion, think of those other masses that come from the surrounding territory, north, south, east and west. The ferries – have you ever observed them in the morning? Or the bridges, railway terminals, and every elevated and subway exit?

Already at six and six-thirty in the morning they have begun to trickle small streams of human beings Manhattan or cityward, and by seven and seven-fifteen these streams have become sizable affairs. By seven-thirty and eight they have changed into heavy, turbulent rivers, and by eight-fifteen and eight-thirty and nine they are raging torrents, no less. They overflow all the streets and avenues and every available means of conveyance. They are pouring into all available doorways, shops, factories, office-buildings – those huge affairs towering so significantly above them. Here they stay all day long, causing those great hives and their adjacent streets to flush with a softness of color not indigenous to them, and then at night, between five and six, they are going again, pouring forth over the bridges and through the subways and across the ferries and out on the trains, until the last drop of them appears to have been exuded, and they are pocketed in some outlying side-street or village or metropolitan hall-room – and the great, turbulent night of the city is on once more. 99

THEODORE DREISER,
*THE COLOR OF A GREAT CITY*,
THE DREISER TRUST, 1923 © 1923 BY
BONI & LIVERIGHT, INC.

116

## A TRANSIENT POPULATION

*Don DeLillo (b. 1936) picks some individuals out of the crowd – not celebrities but anonymous characters or people on the streets.*

❝Harbors reveal a city's power, its lust for money and filth, but strangely through the haze what I distinguished first was the lone mellow promise of an island, tender retreat from straight lines, an answering sea-mound. This was the mist's illusion and the harbor's pound of flesh. Skippy tugged at licorice with her teeth, the black strands expanding between hand and jaw. She had a shaded face and she was ageless, a wanderer in cities, one of those children found after every war, picking in the rubble for scraps of food the gaunt dogs have missed. Such minds are unreclaimable but at the same time hardly dangerous and governments acknowledge this fact by providing millions of acres of postwar rubble. On our way to find a bus stop we saw the subway crowds drop into openings in the earth, on their way up the length of Manhattan or under rivers to the bourns and orchards, there to be educated in false innocence, in the rites of isolation. Perhaps the only ore of truth their lives possessed was buried in this central rock. Beyond its limits was their one escape, a

dreamless sleep, no need to fear the dare to be exceptional. Dozens of pigeons swarmed around a woman tossing bread crumbs. She was in a wheelchair held at rest by a young boy, both on fire with birds, the pigeons skidding on the air, tracing the upward curve of the old woman's arm. I watched her eyes climb with the birds, all her losses made a blessing in a hand's worth of bread. Pigeons and meningitis. Chocolate and mouse droppings. Licorice and roach hairs. Vermin on the bus we took uptown. I wondered how long I'd choose to dwell in these middle ages of plague and usury, living among traceless men and women, those whose only peace was in shouting ever more loudly. Nothing tempted them more than voicelessness. But they shouted. Transient population of thunderers and hags. They dragged through wet streets speaking in languages older than the stones of cities buried in sand. Beds and bedbugs. Men and lice. Gonococcus curling in the lap of love. We rode past an urban redevelopment project. Machine-tooth shovels clawed past half-finished buildings stuck in mud, tiny balconies stapled on. All spawned by realtor-kings who live in the sewers. Skippy coughed blood onto the back of her hand. The bus panted over cobblestones and I studied words drawn in fading paint on the sides of buildings. Brake and front end service. Wheel alignment. Chain and belt. Pulleys, motors, gears. Sheet-metal machinery. Leather remnants. Die cutting and precision measuring. Cuttings and job lots. Business machines. Threads, woolens, laces. Libros en español. We left by the back door and Skippy went back to whatever she was doing (or dealing) in that hotel. Rain blew across the old streets. The toothless man was still at his cart, a visitation from sunken regions, not caring who listened or passed, his cries no less cadenced than the natural rain. YOU'RE BUYING I'M SELLING YAPPLES YAPPLES YAPPLES.❞

DON DELILLO, *GREAT JONES STREET*,
RANDOM HOUSE INC., NEW YORK, 1989

## "TALL BUILDINGS"

### AMERICAN BEAUTY

*In "The American Scene", Henry James (1843–1916) wrote of his impressions of a visit in 1906 after an absence of almost twenty years.*

❝Memory and the actual impression keep investing New York with the tone, predominantly, of summer dawns and winter frosts, of sea-foam, of bleached sails and stretched awnings, of blanched hulls, of scoured decks, of new ropes, of

polished brasses, of streamers clear in the blue air; and it is by this harmony, doubtless, that the projection of the individual character of the place, of the candour of its avidity and the freshness of its audacity, is most conveyed. The "tall buildings," which have so promptly usurped a glory that affects you as rather surprised, as yet, at itself, the multitudinous sky-scrapers standing up to the view, from the water, like extravagant pins in a cushion already overplanted, and stuck in as in the dark, anywhere and anyhow, have at least the felicity of carrying out the fairness of tone, of taking the sun and the shade in the manner of towers of marble. They are not all of marble, I believe, by any means, even if some may be, but they are impudently new and still more impudently "novel" – this in common with so many other terrible things in America – and they are triumphant payers of dividends; all of which uncontested and unabashed pride, with flash of innumerable windows and flicker of subordinate gilt attributions, is like the flare, up and down their long, narrow faces, of the lamps of some general permanent "celebration".
You see the pin-cushion in profile, so to speak, on passing between Jersey City and Twenty-third Street, but you get it broadside on, this loose nosegay of architectural flowers, if you skirt the Battery, well out, and embrace the whole plantation. Then the "American beauty," the rose of interminable stem, becomes the token of the cluster at large – – to the degree that, positively, this is all that is wanted for emphasis of your final impression. Such growths, you feel, have confessedly arisen but to be "picked," in time, with a shears; nipped short off, by waiting fate, as soon as "science," applied to gain, has put upon the table, from far up its sleeve, some more winning card. Crowned not only with no history, but with no credible possibility of time for history, and consecrated by no uses save the commercial at any cost, they are simply the most piercing notes in that concert of the expensively provisional into which your supreme sense of New York resolves itself. They never begin to speak to you, in the manner of the builded majesties of the world as we have heretofore known such – towers or temples or fortresses or palaces – with the authority of things of permanence or even of things of long duration. One story is good only till another is told, and sky-scrapers are the last word of economic ingenuity only till another word be written. **99**

HENRY JAMES, *THE AMERICAN SCENE*,
INDIANA UNIVERSITY PRESS, BLOOMINGTON
AND LONDON, 1968

### RAPID RUINS

*G.K. Chesterton (1874–1936), the English journalist, novelist and short-story writer, was impressed by the industry of the city's builders.*

**66**There is one point, almost to be called a paradox, to be noted about New York; and that is that in one sense it is really new. The term very seldom has any relevance to the reality. . . . But there is a sense in which New York is always new; in the sense that it is always being renewed. A stranger might well say that the chief industry of the citizens consists of destroying their city; but he soon realises that they always start it all over again

> **"A HAVEN AS COSY AS TOAST, COOL AS AN ICEBOX
> AND SAFE AS SKYSCRAPERS."**
>
> DYLAN THOMAS

with undiminished energy and hope. At first I had a fancy that they never quite finished putting up a big building without feeling that it was time to pull it down again; and that somebody began to dig up the first foundations while somebody else was putting on the last tiles. This fills the whole of this brilliant and bewildering place with a quite unique and unparalleled air of rapid ruin. Ruins spring up so suddenly like mushrooms, which with us are the growth of age like mosses, that one half expects to see ivy climbing quickly up the broken walls as in the nightmare of the Time Machine, or in some incredibly accelerated cinema. There is no sight in any country that raises my own spirits so much as a scaffolding. It is a tragedy that they always take the scaffolding away, and leave us nothing but a mere building. If they would only take the building away and leave us a beautiful scaffolding, it would in most cases be a gain to the loveliness of earth. If I could analyse what it is that lifts the heart about the lightness and clarity of such a white and wooden skeleton, I could explain what it is that is really charming about New York; in spite of its suffering from the curse of cosmopolitanism and even the provincial superstition of progress. It is partly that all this destruction and reconstruction is an unexhausted artistic energy; but it is partly also that it is an artistic energy that does not take itself too seriously. It is first because he is a stage carpenter. Indeed there is about the whole scene the spirit of scene-shifting. It therefore touches whatever nerve in us has since childhood thrilled at all theatrical things.**99**

G. K. CHESTERTON, *WHAT I SAW IN AMERICA*,
HODDER AND STOUGHTON, LONDON, 1922

### A DELIGHTFUL WALK

*George Templeton Strong (1820–75) wrote in his diary for June 11, 1859, about the development of Central Park in the midst of the city.*

**66**Improved the day by leaving Wall Street early and set off with George Anthon and Johnny to explore the Central Park, which will be a feature of the city within five years and a lovely place in A.D. 1900, when its trees will have acquired dignity and appreciable diameters. Perhaps the city itself will perish before then, by growing too big to live under faulty institutions corruptly administered. Reached the park a little before four, just as the red flag was hoisted – the signal for the blasts of the day. They were all around us for some twenty minutes, now booming far off to the north, now quite near, now distant again, like a desultory "affair" between advanced posts of two great armies. We entered the park at Seventy-first Street, on its east side, and made for "The Ramble," a patch just below the upper reservoir. Its footpaths and plantations are finished, more or less, and it is the first section of the ground that has been polished off and made presentable. It promises very well. So does all the lower park, though now in most ragged condition: long lines of incomplete macadamization, "lakes" without water, mounds of compost, piles of blasted stone, acres of what may be greensward hereafter but is now mere brown earth; groves of slender young transplanted maples and locusts, undecided between life and death, with here and there an arboricultural experiment that has failed utterly and is a mere broomstick with ramifications. Celts caravans of dirt carts, derricks, steam engines, are the elements out of which our future Pleasaunce is rapidly developing. The work seems pushed with vigor and system, and as far as it has gone, looks thorough and substantial. A small army of Hibernians is distributed over the ground. Narrowness is its chief drawback. One sees quite across this *Rus in Urbe* at many points. This will be less felt as the trees grow. The tract seems to have been judiciously laid out. Roads and paths twist about in curves of artistic tortuosity. A broad avenue, exceptionally straight (at the lower end of the park) with a quadruple row of elms, will look Versailles-y by A.D. 1950. On the Fifth Avenue side, the hideous State Arsenal building stares at students of the picturesque, an eyesore that no landscape gardening can alleviate. Let us hope it will soon be destroyed by an accidental fire. From the summit of the rock mount in which "The Ramble" culminates, and from the little wooden framework of an observatory or signal flag tower thereon erected, the upper reservoir (lying on the north) is an agreeable object, notwithstanding the formalism of its straight lines. Johnny was delighted with his walk . . . **99**

*THE DIARY OF GEORGE TEMPLETON STRONG*
THE MACMILLAN PUBLISHING COMPANY, NEW YORK, 1952

### BROADWAY

*The Russian futurist poet Vladimir Mayakovsky (1893–1930) was often out of favor with government regimes in his homeland but after his suicide, he was acclaimed by Stalin as "the best and most talented poet of our Soviet epoch".*

**66**Tarmac like glass.
                A clang with each step.
Trees,
       and blades of grass,
                 with crew-cuts.
Avenues
       run
           from North to South,
and streets
       from East to West.
Between –
       who could have stretched them that far! –
buildings
       a good mile high.
Some houses seem to touch
              the stars,
while others
       reach for the sky.
Most Yanks are too idle
           to go out walking.
They ride express
       elevators
             throughout.

"IF PARIS IS THE SETTING FOR A ROMANCE, NEW YORK IS THE PERFECT CITY IN WHICH TO GET OVER ONE, TO GET OVER ANYTHING. HERE THE LOST *DOUCEUR DE VIVRE* IS FORGOTTEN AND THE INTOXICATION OF LIVING TAKES OVER." CYRIL CONNOLLY

At seven hundred hours
                    the human tide rolls in.
And at seventeen hundred
                    rolls out.
Machines
        rattle
            clatter
                chink
pedestrians
        go deaf and dumb,
while past them more
                    dumb people sprint
only stopping
            to spit out their chewing gum.
Yelling at a friend:
            'Make money!'
A mother suckles her child:
                    'Don't holler!'
And the kid,
        with its nostrils runny
looks less like it sucks a breast than
                            a dollar
and like everyone else,
                in a hurry.
The workday done,
            now all around
you're battered by
                electric hurricanes.
You take the subway,
                vanish underground,
or climb
        on the elevated
                train.
You can ride as high
                as a chimney stack
or dart
        between the feet of a house.
On Brooklyn Bridge, a tram
                    snakes its back
or under the Hudson,
            sneaks like a mouse."

VLADIMIR MAYAKOVSKY, *BROADWAY*

### THE VILLAGE
*The development of Greenwich Village is described by Edmund Wilson (1895–1972) in his novel "I Thought of Daisy".*

"Among those tangled irregular streets to the west of Washington Square, I caught occasionally, from the taxi, a glimpse, almost eighteenth-century, of a lampless, black-windowed street-end where the street-urchins, shrieking in the silence, were stacking up bonfires in the snow – those lost corners of the old provincial city, where the traffic of the upper metropolis no longer gnashed iron teeth, no longer oppressed the pavements with its grindings and its groans – where those soft moans and hoots of the shipping washed the island from the western shore. There they had come, those heroes of my youth, the artists and the prophets

121

of the Village, from the American factories and farms, from the farthest towns and prairies – there they had found it possible to leave behind them the constraints and self-consciousness of their homes, the shame of not making money – there they had lived with their own imaginations and followed their own thought. I did not know that, with the coming of a second race, of which Ray Coleman, without my divining it, had already appeared as one of the forerunners – a mere miscellaneous hiving of New Yorkers like those in any other part of town, with no leisure and no beliefs – I did not know that I was soon to see the whole quarter fall a victim to the landlords and the real-estate speculators, who would raise the rents and wreck the old houses – till the sooty peeling fronts of the south side of Washington Square, to whose mysterious studios, when I had first come to live in the Village, I had so much longed some day to be admitted, should be replaced by fresh arty pinks – till the very guardian façades of the north side should be gutted of their ancient grandeurs and crammed tight with economized cells – till the very configuration of the streets should be wiped out, during a few summer months when I had been out of New York on vacation, by the obliteration of whole blocks, whole familiar neighborhoods – and till finally the beauty of the Square, the pattern of the park and the arch, the proportions of everything, should be spoiled by the first peaks of a mountain-range of modern apartment-houses (with electric refrigerators, uniformed elevator boys and, on the street-level, those smartly furnished restaurants in which Hugo was soon to be horrified at finding copies of *Town and Country*), dominating and crushing the Village, so that at last it seemed to survive as a base for those gigantic featureless mounds, swollen, clumsy, blunt, bleaching dismally with sandy yellow walls that sunlight which once, in the autumn, on the old fronts of the northern side, still the masters of their open plaza – when the shadows of the leafless trees seemed to drift across them like clouds – had warmed their roses to red.**"**

Edmund Wilson, *I Thought of Daisy*,
W. H. Allen, London, 1920

### Ferryboat ride

*The novel "Manhattan Transfer" by John dos Passos (1896–1970) is a collection of hundreds of fictional and atmospheric episodes that take place in New York. The following extract describes a trip on the Ellis Island Ferry.*

**"**It was blowing cold in his face and he was sitting on the front of a ferryboat when he came to. His teeth were chattering, he was shivering . . . .

Across the zinc water the tall walls, the birchlike cluster of downtown buildings shimmered up the rosy morning like a sound of horns through a chocolatebrown haze. As the boat drew near the buildings densened to a granite mountain split with knifecut canyons. The ferry passed close to a tubby steamer that rode at anchor listing towards Stan so that he could see all the decks. An Ellis Island tug was alongside. A stale smell came from the decks packed with upturned faces like a load of melons. Three gulls wheeled complaining. A gull soared in a spiral, white wings caught the sun, the gull skimmed motionless in whitegold light. The rim of the sun had risen above the plumcolored band of clouds behind East New York. A million windows flashed with light. A rasp and a humming came from the city. . . .

In the whitening light tinfoil gulls wheeled above broken boxes, spoiled cabbageheads, orangerinds heaving slowly between the splintered plank walls, the green spumed under the round bow as the ferry skidding on the tide, gulped the broken water, crashed, slid, settled slowly into the slip. Handwinches whirled with jingle of chains, gates folded upward. Stan stepped across the crack, staggered up the manuresmelling wooden tunnel of the ferryhouse out into the sunny glass and benches of the Battery. He sat down on a bench, clasped his hands round his knees to keep them from shaking so. His mind went on jingling like a mechanical piano.

There was Babylon and Nineveh, they were built of brick. Athens was goldmarble columns. Rome was held up on broad arches of rubble. In Constantinople the minarets flame like great candles round the Golden Horn. . . . O there's one more river to cross. Steel, glass, tile, concrete will be the materials of the skyscrapers. Crammed on the narrow island the millionwindowed buildings will jut, glittering pyramid on pyramid, white cloudsheads piled above a thunder storm . . . Kerist I wish I was a skyscraper.❞

JOHN DOS PASSOS, *MANHATTAN TRANSFER*,
HARPER AND BROTHERS, NEW YORK AND LONDON, 1925

### RAMSHACKLE STREETS

*Joseph Heller, the novelist, was born in New York in 1923. His novel "Good As Gold" satirizes the politics of the city and this particular extract describes a drive along the southern rim of Brooklyn.*

❞Following the smooth parkway as it curved with the shoreline to the east, he soon saw in the distance on his right the gaunt structure of the defunct Parachute Jump standing on the narrow spit of land across Gravesend Bay and recalled, with some pride in his upbringing, how that Parachute Jump, the hit of the World's Fair in New York in 1939 or '40, was moved to the Steeplechase boardwalk afterward but had never proved adequately perilous for success to an indigenous population trained on the Cyclone and the Thunderbolt and on the Mile Sky Chaser in Luna Park. Now it looked forlorn: no one owned it and no one would take it away. Like those haunted, half-completed luxury apartment houses in Manhattan whose builders had run out of money and whose banks would not supply more, gaping with dismal failure and aging already into blackest decrepitude before they ever shone spanking new. A moment later came the skeletal outline of the giant Wonder Wheel, idled for the year by the chilly season, the only Ferris wheel left in Coney Island now that Steeplechase, the Funny Place, was bankrupt and gone. Hard times had descended there as in other places. Where Luna Park had last whirred in bright lights on summer evenings over thirty years earlier there now rose a complex of

high, honeycombed brick dwellings that looked drabber than ordinary against the lackluster sky. On the overpass spanning Ocean Parkway Gold turned his head for a speeding glimpse of Abraham Lincoln High School and bemoaned for the thousandth time the vile chance that had located him in classes there the same time as Belle and gulled him into a mismanaged destiny of three dependent children and a wife so steadfast. If a man marries young, he reasoned aristocratically in the self-conscious mode of a Lord Chesterfield or a Benjamin Franklin, as Gold himself had been minded to do, it will likely be to someone near him in age; and just about the time he learns really to enjoy living with a young girl and soars into his prime, she will be getting old. He would pass that precious homiletic intelligence on to both sons, if he remembered. If only Belle were fickle, mercenary, deceitful. Even her health was good.

He turned off the parkway past Brighton at the exit leading toward Sheepshead Bay and Manhattan Beach. The slender crescent on the southern rim of Brooklyn through which he'd driven was just about the only section of the area with which he was familiar. Almost all of the rest was foreign to him and forbidding. His thoughts went back to a ramshackle street he'd passed minutes before on which stood the same moldering antique police station to which he'd been brought as a small child the day Sid had abandoned him and gone off with his friends. What a heartless thing to have done. Gold must have been numb as he waited in the precinct house. If they asked him his address he might not have known it. The nearest telephone to his house then was in a candy store at the trolley stop on the corner of Railroad Avenue. Just a few years later he was earning two-cent tips for summoning girls from the flats for calls from boys phoning for dates. Brooklyn was a big fucking borough. **99**

JOSEPH HELLER, *GOOD AS GOLD*, JONATHAN CAPE, LONDON, 1979

**BAYMEN**

*Joseph Mitchell (b. 1908) reminds us that New York is situated on the ocean and many make their living from fishing.*

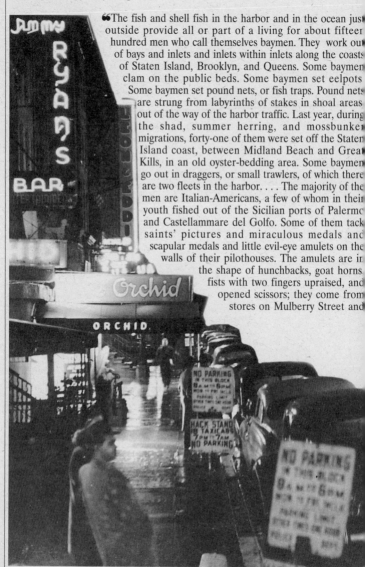

**66**The fish and shell fish in the harbor and in the ocean just outside provide all or part of a living for about fifteen hundred men who call themselves baymen. They work out of bays and inlets and inlets within inlets along the coasts of Staten Island, Brooklyn, and Queens. Some baymen clam on the public beds. Some baymen set eelpots. Some baymen set pound nets, or fish traps. Pound nets are strung from labyrinths of stakes in shoal areas out of the way of the harbor traffic. Last year, during the shad, summer herring, and mossbunker migrations, forty-one of them were set off the Staten Island coast, between Midland Beach and Great Kills, in an old oyster-bedding area. Some baymen go out in draggers, or small trawlers, of which there are two fleets in the harbor. . . . The majority of the men are Italian-Americans, a few of whom in their youth fished out of the Sicilian ports of Palermo and Castellammare del Golfo. Some of them tack saints' pictures and miraculous medals and scapular medals and little evil-eye amulets on the walls of their pilothouses. The amulets are in the shape of hunchbacks, goat horns, fists with two fingers upraised, and opened scissors; they come from stores on Mulberry Street and are made of plastic. The harbor draggers range from thirty to fifty feet and carry two to five men. According to the weather and the season, they drag their baglike nets in the Lower Bay or in a fishing ground called the Mud Hole, which lies south of Scotland and Ambrose lightships and is about fifteen miles long and five to ten miles wide. The Mud Hole is the upper part of the Old Hudson River Canyon, which was the bed of the river twenty thousand years ago, when the river flowed a hundred and twenty-five miles past what is now Sandy Hook before it reached the ocean. The draggers catch lower-depth and bottom feeders, chiefly whiting, butterfish, ling, cod, porgy, fluke, and flounder. They go out around 4 A.M. and return around 4 P.M., and their catches are picked up by trucks and taken to Fulton Market.**99**

JOSEPH MITCHELL, *UP IN THE OLD HOTEL*, PANTHEON BOOKS, NEW YORK, 1992

## LIFE IN THE CITY

### WALKING ON MIRRORS

*Wallace Stevens (1879–1955), the American poet, made the following entries in his journal in the year 1900, during a visit to New York.*

**66**Took dinner in a little restaurant – poached eggs, coffee and three crusts of bread – a week ago my belly was swagging with strawberries. Bought a couple of newspapers from a little fellow with blue eyes who was selling *Journals* and *Worlds* & who had to ransack the neighborhood for the ones I wanted. As I came back to my room the steps of the street for squares were covered with boarders etc. leaning on railings and picking their teeth. The end of the street was ablaze with a cloud of dust lit by the sun. All around me were tall office buildings closed up for the night. The curtains were drawn and the faces of the buildings looked hard and cruel and lifeless. This street of mine is a wonderful thing. Just now the voices of children manage to come through my window from out it, over the roofs and through the walls.

All New York, as I have seen it, is for sale – and I think the parts I have seen are the parts that make New York what it is. It is dominated by necessity. Everything has its price – from Vice to Virtue. I do not like it and unless I get some position that is unusually attractive I shall not stay. What is there to keep me, for example, in a place where all Beauty is on exhibition, all Power a tool of Selfishness, and all Generosity a source of Vanity? New York is a field of tireless and antagonistic interests – undoubtedly fascinating but horribly unreal. Everybody is looking at everybody else – a foolish crowd walking on mirrors. I am rather glad to be here for the short time that I intend to stay – it makes me appreciate the opposite of it all.

Thank Heaven the winds are not generated in Yorkville, or the clouds manufactured in Harlem. What a price they would bring!

The carpet on the floor of my room is gray set off with pink roses. In the bathroom is a rug with the figure of a peacock woven in it – blue and scarlet, and black, and green, and gold. And on the paper on my wall are designs of fleur-de-lis and forget-me-not. Flowers and birds enough of rags and paper – but no more. In this Eden, made spicey with the smoke of my pipe which hangs heavy in the ceiling in this Paradise ringing with the bells of streetcars and the bustle of fellow boarders heard through the thin partitions, in this Elysium of Elysiums I now shall lay me down.**99**

**66**June 17, Sunday.

Last night I sat in an open square near the Washington Arch. A man passed me with his coat tightly buttoned, his hands in his

125

trousers pockets, his head bent and his hat well pulled-down. His clothes were in rags. As he started to cross Fifth Avenue a 'bus drove by and he stopped to let it pass. On the top of the 'bus was a group of girls in neat Spring jackets and bonnets covered with cherries and roses.

This morning the church bells are ringing.

New York is the most egotistical place in the world. **99**

FROM HOLLY STEVENS, *SOUVENIRS AND PROPHECIES*,
ALFRED A. KNOPF INC., NEW YORK, 1977

### THE JANITOR

*The Russian politician Lev Trotsky (1879–1940) was expelled from his homeland in 1924. He and his family wandered from country to country for a while before settling in Mexico. The following extract from his autobiography describes a spell in New York.*

**66**We rented an apartment in a workers' district, and furnished it on the instalment plan. That apartment, at eighteen dollars a month, was equipped with all sorts of conveniences that we Europeans were quite unused to: electric lights, gas cooking-range, bath, telephone, automatic service-elevator, and even a chute for the garbage. These things completely won the boys over to New York. For a time the telephone was their main interest; we had not had this mysterious instrument either in Vienna or Paris.

The janitor of the house was a negro. My wife paid him three months' rent in advance, but he gave her no receipt because the landlord had taken the receipt-book away the day before, to verify the accounts. When we moved into the house two days later, we discovered that the negro had absconded with the rent of several of the tenants. Besides the money, we had intrusted to him the storage of some of our belongings. The whole incident upset us; it was such a bad beginning. But we found our property after all, and when we opened the wooden box that contained our crockery, we were surprised to find our money hidden away in it, carefully wrapped up in paper. The janitor had taken the money of the tenants who had already received their receipts; he did not mind robbing the landlord, but he was considerate enough not to rob the tenants. A delicate fellow indeed. My wife and I were deeply touched by his consideration and we always think of him gratefully. This little incident took on a symptomatic significance for me – it seemed as if a corner of the veil that concealed the "black" problem in the United States had lifted. **99**

LEV TROTSKY, *MY LIFE*, CHARLES SCRIBNER'S SONS, NEW YORK, 1930

### BEAUTIFUL GIRLS

*Ogden Nash (1902–71) was famous for his light verse, of which the following is a good example.*

**66**In New York beautiful girls can become more beautiful
by going to Elizabeth Arden,

> **"A HUNDRED TIMES I HAVE THOUGHT, NEW YORK IS
> A CATASTROPHE, AND FIFTY TIMES: IT IS A
> BEAUTIFUL CATASTROPHE."**
>
> LE CORBUSIER

And getting stuff to put on their faces and waiting for
    it to harden,
And poor girls with nothing to their names but a letter
    or two can get rich and joyous
From a brief trip to their loyous.
So I can say with impunity
That New York is a land of opportunity.
It also has many fine theatres and hotels,
And a lot of taxis, buses, subways and els,
Best of all, if you don't show up at the office or at a
    tea nobody will bother their head,
They will just think you are dead.
That's why I really think New York is exquisite.
And someday I'm going to pay it a visit. **"**

OGDEN NASH, *A BRIEF GUIDE TO NEW YORK*,
FROM *"VERSES FROM 1929 ON"*, 1940

### THE HARLEM RENAISSANCE

*Langston Hughes (1902–67) was one of the most impor-
tant figures of the Harlem Renaissance. Discovered by
the poet Vachel Lindsay, he wrote poetry, plays,
and novels whose language resonated with
dialect and jazz rhythms. In "The Big Sea"
(1940), his autobiography, Hughes
recounts a fascinating life in Paris
and Harlem when "the
Negro was in vogue".*

**"**White people began to come to
Harlem in droves. For several years they
packed the expensive Cotton Club on Lenox
Avenue. But I was never there, because the Cotton Club
was a Jim Crow club for gangsters and monied whites. They were
not cordial to Negro patronage, unless you were a celebrity like
Bojangles. So Harlem Negroes did not like the Cotton Club and never
appreciated its Jim Crow policy in the very heart of their dark community. Nor did
ordinary Negroes like the growing influx of whites toward Harlem after sundown,
flooding the little caberets and bars where formerly only colored people laughed
and sang, and where now the strangers were given the best ringside tables to sit and
stare at the Negro customers – like amusing animals in a zoo.
The Negroes said: 'We can't go downtown and sit and stare at you in your clubs.
You won't even let us in your clubs.' But they didn't say it out loud – for Negroes
are practically never rude to white people. So thousands of whites came to Harlem
night after night, thinking the Negroes loved to have them there, and firmly
believing that all Harlemites left their houses at sundown to sing and dance in
cabarets, because most of the whites saw nothing but the cabarets, not the houses.
Some of the owners of Harlem clubs, delighted at the flood of white patronage,
made the grievous error of barring their own race, after the manner of the famous
Cotton Club. But most of these quickly lost business and folded up, because they
failed to realize that a large part of the Harlem attraction for downtown New
Yorkers lay in simply watching the colored customers amuse themselves. And the
smaller clubs, of course, had no big floor shows or a name band like the Cotton
Club, where Duke Ellington usually held forth, so, without black patronage, they
were not amusing at all.**"**

LANGSTON HUGHES, *THE BIG SEA*, 1940

### A COLLAPSING CITY

*The following piece by John Updike (1932– ), the American novelist, short-story writer
and poet, comes from an essay entitled "Is New York City Inhabitable?"*

❝New York is of course many cities, and an exile does not return to the one he left. I left, in April of 1957, a floor-through apartment on West Thirteenth Street, and return, when I do, to midtown hotels and the Upper East Side apartments of obliging friends. The Village, with its bookstores and framer's shops, its bricked-in literary memories and lingering bohemian redolence, is off the track of a professional visit – an elevator-propelled whirl in and out of high-rise offices and prix-fixe restaurants. Nevertheless, I feel confident in saying that the disadvantages of New York life which led me to leave have intensified rather than abated, and that the city which Le Corbusier described as a magnificent disaster is less and less magnificent. Always, as one arrives, there is the old acceleration of the pulse – the mountainous gray skyline glimpsed from the Triboro Bridge, the cheerful games of basketball and handball being played on the recreational asphalt beside the FDR Drive, the startling, steamy, rain-splotched intimacy of the side streets where one's taxi slows to a crawl, the careless flung beauty of the pedestrians clumped at the street corners. So many faces, costumes, packages, errands! So many preoccupations, hopes, passions, lives in progress! So much human stuff, clustering and streaming with a languid colorful impatience like the pheromone-coded mass maneuvers of bees! But soon the faces and their individual expressions merge and vanish under a dulling insistent pressure, the thrum and push of congestion. As ever more office buildings are heaped upon the East Fifties – the hugest of them, the slant-topped white Citicorp building, clearly about to fall off its stilts onto your head – and an ever-greater number of impromptu merchants spread their dubiously legal wares on the sidewalks, even pedestrian traffic jams. One is tripped, hassled, detoured. Buskers and beggars cram every available niche. The sidewalks and subway platforms, generously designed in the last century, have been overwhelmed on both the minor and major entrepreneurial scales. The Manhattan grid, that fine old machine for living, now sticks and grinds at every intersection and the discreet brownstones of the side streets look down upon a clogged nightmare of perpetual reconstruction and insolent double parking. Even a sunny day feels like a tornado of confusion one is hurrying to get out of, into the sanctum of the hotel room, the office, the friendly apartment. New York is a city with virtually no habitable public space – only private spaces expensively maintained within the general disaster. While popular journalism focuses on the possible collapse of Los Angeles and San Francisco into chasms opened by earthquakes, here on the East Coast, on its oblong of solid granite, the country's greatest city is sinking into the chasm of itself.❞

John Updike, *Odd Jobs*, Alfred A. Knopf Inc.,
New York, 1991

# NEW YORK
## ITINERARIES

▲ The World Trade Center  90 West St., with the World Trade Center in the background

The Fuller Building ▲

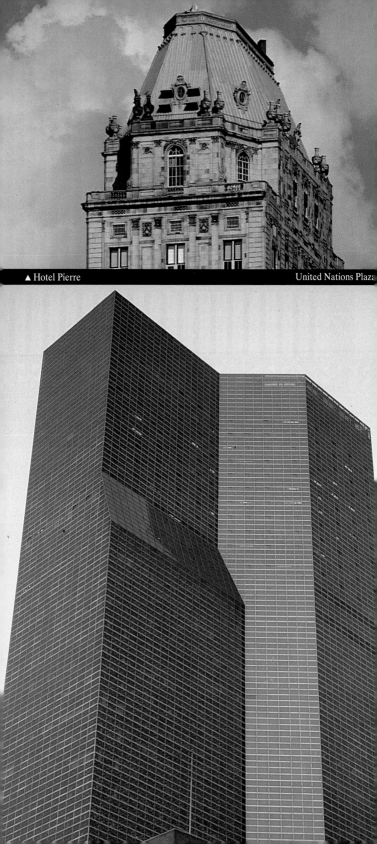

▲ Hotel Pierre                    United Nations Plaza

World Financial Center

The American Standard Building ▼

▲ 3 Park Ave.

The Waldorf-Astoria Hotel ▼

# AROUND THE
# WORLD TRADE CENTER

*0*

# ▲ WORLD TRADE CENTER

1 CASTLE CLINTON
2 PIER A
3 MARINE MEMORIAL
4 1 BROADWAY
5 BROOKLYN TUNNEL
ENTRANCE
6 DOWNTOWN
ATHLETIC CLUB
7 CUNARD BLDG.
8 29 BROADWAY
9 TRINITY CHURCH
10 90 WEST ST.
11 THAMES TWINS
12 1 LIBERTY PLAZA

13 EAST RIVER SAVINGS
BANK
14 WORLD FINANCIAL
CENTER
15 WORLD TRADE
CENTER
16 ROCKEFELLER BLDG.
17 EMPIRE STATE BLDG.
18 WOOLWORTH BLDG.
19 BATTERY MARITIME
BLDG.
20 U.S. CUSTOM HOUSE
21 FRAUNCES TAVERN
22 BOWLING GREEN

23 85 BROAD ST.
24 26 BROADWAY
25 67 BROAD ST.
26 INDIA HOUSE
27 N.Y. STOCK
EXCHANGE
28 55 WALL ST.

BROOKLYN BRIDGE

EAST RIVER

HELIPORT

**32** 40 WALL ST.
**33** 60 WALL ST.
**34** SOUTH STREET
SEAPORT
**35** EQUITABLE BLDG.
**36** FEDERAL RESERVE
BANK
**37** 70 PINE ST.
**38** CHASE MANHATTAN
BANK
**39** LIBERTY TOWER
**40** FEDERAL HALL
**41** DELMONICO'S
**42** MUNICIPAL BLDG.

**29** 20 EXCHANGE
PLACE
**30** 63 WALL ST.
**31** 48 WALL ST.

**THE SITE**
The site of the World Trade Center was originally occupied by twelve dilapidated blocks called "Radio Row", a paradise for

radio and photography enthusiasts. The construction of the Center necessitated digging foundations to a depth of 69 feet; the 1.2 million cubic yards of excavated earth served as landfill for the future Battery Park City. It was also necessary to destroy many piers and warehouses along the Hudson (below, former cargo loading stations along the Hudson on the site of the World Trade Center). Traffic on the Hudson River was very heavy until cargo was able to be delivered by air or truck. Goods arrived in New Jersey by rail, then were shipped by ferry to Manhattan.

Downtown Manhattan, the southern tip of the island, includes the Financial District, the World Trade Center, Battery Park and Battery Park City. Its early settlers – first the Dutch then the English – laid out narrow, winding streets here. The oldest of these, whose names date back to the 17th century, as well as their configuration – borrowed from that of Amsterdam – testify to this initial occupation. And, as was the case in the parent city, some of these streets, notably Broad Street, were originally canals ● *32*. Others, built later, reflect the well-known Dutch practice of reclaiming land from the sea by drainage; in fact, over the centuries, Manhattan has expanded well beyond its original boundaries ■ *18*, ● *72*. At the time of the Dutch settlements, the shape of the shoreline differed greatly from its present one. It ran alongside WATER STREET to the east, along GREENWICH STREET to the west and along STATE STREET to the south. The acres of land that were gradually gained – due to a buildup of abandoned ships, detritus, earth from excavation work for the construction of buildings and subway lines – are now some of the most expensive in the world. Among the few remaining traces of the English colonial period is the cemetery of TRINITY CHURCH, where some of the most famous names in American colonial history are buried. Just opposite, on the other side of Broadway, is Wall Street, the heart of the Financial District, which bankers and stockbrokers call simply "The Street". A harbor city, New York has grown through trade and shipping. Offshore in the distance stand the Statue of Liberty ▲ *144* and Ellis Island ▲ *148*, witnesses to the arrival of immigrants in their thousands. Over the centuries architects have ceaselessly rebuilt the city on top of this piece of original territory, where all the different layers of its history are now superimposed. The best time to visit Lower Manhattan is during the week; on weekends it is deserted.

## AROUND THE WORLD TRADE CENTER

**WORLD TRADE CENTER.** BETWEEN CHURCH, LIBERTY, WEST AND VESEY STS. (1976, arch. Minoru Yamasaki & Assocs.; Emery Roth & Son). The World Trade Center is a complex of seven buildings grouped around a vast PLAZA, dominated by the 110-story TWIN TOWERS ★. It is the property of the port authorities of the states of New York and New Jersey and was designed to attract international companies to Lower Manhattan, which was experiencing a massive exodus of offices to Midtown. The beginnings of the complex were problematic, and in order to avoid financial disaster, the State of New York rented out most of the buildings. Today it is a flourishing business center, a base for five hundred international companies which provide jobs for 50,000 people. The Center has

"THE WORLD TRADE CENTER LIKE AN ILLUMINATED COMPUTER, WITH ITS TWO TOWERS LIKE TALL VISUAL DISPLAY UNITS..."

PHILIPPE SOLLERS

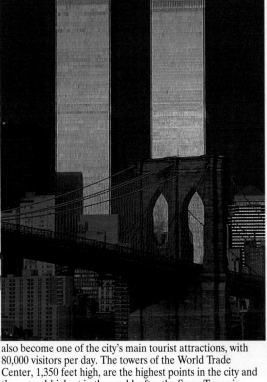

**"KING KONG"**
Unlike the original legendary movie by Merian Cooper and Ernest B. Schoedsack (1933), in which the giant gorilla takes refuge at the top of the Empire State

Building ▲ *242*, the 1976 remake by John Guillermin uses the even-dizzier heights of the World Trade Center as the backdrop for the gorilla-hero's escape and death.

The World Trade Center seen from Brooklyn.

**LOBBY OF THE WORLD TRADE CENTER**
Thanks to a new structural design, the exterior walls of the towers bear most of the load, creating vast interior spaces. The lobby, on two levels, serves as a transition between the plaza and the lower street level.

also become one of the city's main tourist attractions, with 80,000 visitors per day. The towers of the World Trade Center, 1,350 feet high, are the highest points in the city and the second-highest in the world, after the Sears Tower in Chicago. The view over Manhattan from the top is not to be missed; it can be enjoyed from the observation deck of Tower Two. (The restaurant Windows on the World, at the top of Tower One, is closed at least until December 1995.) From either vantage point you can see Manhattan spreading off to the north, cradled in the arms of the Hudson and the East River. The most famous skyscrapers can easily be pinpointed: in the distance, the graceful spire of the Empire State Building and the playful Chrysler Building are easily distinguished. Farther into the distance you have a panoramic view over the bay, the four other boroughs of New York and the surrounding countryside. On a clear day, you can even discern the curvature of the Earth! Looking downward, you plumb the depths of the "canyons" of the Financial District, with its own idiosyncratic building tops. In 1974 the French tightrope walker Philippe Petit crossed the gap between the towers on a high wire without a safety net. The following year the mountaineer George Willig scaled these giants, by designing a special tool that fit into the window washing tracks. In 1993 the parking garage and the lower ground floor, which has its own subway station and a shopping concourse including 70 stores, were badly damaged by a bomb attack which claimed six lives.

Because 90 West St. was designed to be seen from a distance, its crown is dramatically illuminated at night.

Interior of the New York Telephone Building.

**SAINT NICHOLAS PROCESSION**
On January 6 (the feast of Epiphany), Greek Orthodox parishioners of St. Nicholas' Church proceed to Battery Park, where divers perform the ritual of searching for a wooden cross in the harbor waters.

**BARCLAY–VESEY/NEW YORK TELEPHONE CO. BUILDING** ★. 140 WEST ST., BETWEEN BARCLAY AND VESEY STS. (1923–6, arch. Ralph Walker, McKenzie, Voorhees & Gmelin) ● *98*. When this Art Deco building, located north of the World Trade Center, was completed, it was considered so striking an expression of the new industrial age that its designers were awarded the Architectural League of New York's gold medal of honor for 1927. The lobby, which runs the length of the building and which can be entered via Washington Street, is well worth a visit. The lobby floor is covered with bronze plates, which depict the workers laying the New York telephone system and the ceiling frescoes retrace the history of communication. To see the whole building at its best, you need only walk back to West Street then head toward the Hudson.

**90 WEST STREET** ★. (1905, arch. Cass Gilbert). This 23-story building was one of the first New York skyscrapers constructed using a fire-resistant frame. The lavish decoration of the neo-Gothic façade becomes increasingly more intricate as the building rises, culminating in an extravaganza of stalactites dripping from a cornice supported by consoles.

**ST. NICHOLAS GREEK ORTHODOX CHURCH.** 155 CEDAR ST. (1832). This Greek Orthodox chapel is a reminder that the district was once home to a Greek community. In 1920, the Hellenic Orthodox Church of Saint Nicholas bought this building, which was originally a private house, then a bar. Its upkeep is now seen to by a handful of parishioners, who stubbornly reject repeated offers from real estate developers. The fact that it sits in the middle of a parking lot, in close proximity to the Twin Towers, makes it one of the most incongruous sights in Downtown Manhattan.

West St., looking toward Liberty St., in 1900.

# BATTERY PARK CITY

**BATTERY PARK CITY.** (1979, arch. Cooper Eckstut Associates). This vast complex of 112 acres, comprising offices, apartment buildings and open spaces, is located west of WEST STREET between BATTERY PARK to the south and CHAMBERS STREET to the north. It was built on landfill ■ *19* which was supplied partly by excavation work when the foundations of the World Trade Center were laid. The architects at Cooper Eckstut, who designed Battery Park City, did their utmost to respect the surrounding architecture and the natural environment. The World Financial Center consists of four stocky polished granite and glass towers, crowned with geometrically shaped roofs which identify their owners: a stepped pyramid (Merrill Lynch), a solid pyramid (American Express), a mastaba (Dow Jones and Oppenheimer). The luxurious, showy lobbies of the Center, with their wealth of materials, including polychromatic marble flooring and shiny black columns, are connected to the World Trade Center by two walkways, called North Bridge and South Bridge which cross West Street. The WINTER GARDEN, a pavilion that sits at the entrance to the World Financial Center, is surrounded by the groups of buildings and thoroughfares that make up the Battery Park City complex. This building is like a huge greenhouse planted with giant Washingtonia Palms.

**THE WORLD FINANCIAL CENTER.** (1985, design arch. Cesar Pelli) ● *103*. The center consists of four towers which surround NORTH COVE MARINA, forming what one critic has enthusiastically described as a "Saint Mark's Square on the Hudson". The guardrail along the marina's esplanade is engraved with quotations from WALT WHITMAN and THOMAS O'HARA, former inhabitants of Lower Manhattan, celebrating the history and beauty of this site.

**THE HOBOKEN FERRY.** The landing stage for the ferry – whose nickname, the "Penguin Boat", is derived from the number of sober-suited executives ferried daily between the Financial District and Hoboken – is situated at the northernmost tip of North Cove. The crossing affords a wonderful view of Manhattan. Hoboken, which served as the setting for Elia Kazan's film *On the Waterfront* (1954) starring Marlon Brando, is also the birthplace of Frank Sinatra.

**A UTOPIAN PROJECT**
An extensive redevelopment program for Manhattan's West Side waterfront proposed to cover the riverside walkway with a vast park which would have run alongside the Hudson from Battery Park to the George Washington Bridge. The then governor of New York, Nelson Rockefeller, talked of swimming once again in the "purified" waters of the river and of a reduction in the levels of air pollution in Manhattan. Battery Park City is a later manifestation of this aborted project.

**ON THE WATERFRONT**
Marlon Brando in a scene (below) from Elia Kazan's movie *On the Waterfront*. New York Harbor provides a realistic backdrop for a story of union corruption and for the private drama of a weak man who, in his search for happiness, is plagued by his conscience.

*On The Waterfront*

View of New York Harbor in 1878.

**COMMEMORATIVE MONUMENTS**
A number of memorials have been built in the vicinity of Battery Park. The American Merchant Mariners' Memorial. This sculpture (1991) by Marisol, inspired by a news photo from World War Two, is southeast of Pier A. In the park there is

the John Ericsson Memorial, dedicated to the designer of the *Monitor* ▲ *174*, the Netherlands Memorial Monument, commemorating the purchase of Manhattan from the Indians, and the Verrazano Memorial in honor of the first European to sail into the bay.

**STUYVESANT HIGH SCHOOL.** 345 CHAMBERS ST. (1992, arch. Gruzen Stanton Steinglass). This high school (not shown on the map) is situated just north of Battery Park City. Founded in 1904, it is a still-thriving institution, with a sterling reputation which enables it to recruit 3,000 of the brightest students in the city by means of extremely competitive examinations. The school has recently taken up residence in this monumental Postmodern building.

**ESPLANADE AND SOUTH COVE ★.** The esplanade (built in 1983) was the first seafront park project to be created in New York since that of Brooklyn Heights ▲ *366*. It affords magnificent views of the harbor. South Cove, with its rocks, wooden piers and wild grasses, evokes Manhattan's shoreline at the beginning of the colonial period. The OBSERVATION DECK is an abstract replica of the crown worn by the Statue of Liberty, which it faces.

**DOWNTOWN ATHLETIC CLUB.** 19 WEST ST. (1930, arch. Starrett & Van Vleck). The architects of this building were members of a very exclusive club for male WASPs (White Anglo-Saxon Protestants). With a height of 535 feet, this 36-story building was one of the tallest in Manhattan for its time. Its glazed-tile and glass Art Deco ● *98–9* ornamentation is greatly admired. Every year the club awards the Heisman Trophy for the best college football player in the nation. To visit the Trophy Hall, lined with the portraits of prizewinners since 1935, take the elevator; press the button marked "H".

## BATTERY PARK

The southern tip of Manhattan, once of paramount strategic importance, was until the early 1800's the site of batteries of artillery. Today the public gardens of Battery Park are now arranged around Castle Clinton, the old fort where tickets for Ellis Island and the Statue of Liberty ▲ *144* are sold.

**A "NEW" FORT.** In 1635, on the site of what is now the U.S. Custom House, the Dutch built FORT AMSTERDAM later re-named FORT GEORGE by the British. In addition, the British built another fort on a man-made island 295 feet offshore. Between 1807 and 1811, in anticipation of war with Britain, a new fort, designed by JOHN McCOMB was erected on the island. This fortification, called West Battery, formed a pair with East Battery on Governor's Island at the entrance to the East River. In 1815 West Battery was demilitarized and renamed CASTLE CLINTON, in honor of the mayor of New York,

De Witt Clinton, who later as governor of the state instigated the construction of the Erie Canal ● 27. Foreign dignitaries visiting New York were officially welcomed at Castle Clinton; among them was Lafayette who received a warm reception in 1824. Earlier that year the fortress had been renamed Castle Garden and remodeled. Later, it became a concert hall seating 6,000 people. Here, New Yorkers could attend the opera for 50 cents. After it was declared bankrupt in 1855, Castle Garden was transformed into the main immigrant landing depot, where immigrants could obtain information, medical care, currency and job offers. By the time the center was transferred to Ellis Island ▲ 148, in 1892, eight million people had already passed through its doors. The land between Castle Clinton's island and Manhattan was gradually filled in, and in 1896 the fort was transformed into the New York Aquarium, which attracted millions of visitors. The aquarium was closed in 1941 to permit the construction of the BROOKLYN-BATTERY TUNNEL, then was moved to Coney Island. The fort was saved from demolition by ELEANOR ROOSEVELT, restored and listed as a National Historic Monument in 1946.

**PIER A ★.** S. W. CORNER OF WEST ST. AND BATTERY PLACE (1886, eng. George Sears Green, Jr.). This is the oldest pier in Manhattan. In 1919, in homage to the victims of World War One, a clock tower was added. Its bells used to signal the watches that were kept on shipboard. Until 1959 the pier was used as a headquarters for the harbor police and the maritime fire department – whose flotilla used to greet steamships landing for the first time with fantastic volleys of water.

**A PLUCKED NIGHTINGALE**
On September 11, 1850, Jenny Lind, the "Swedish Nightingale", made her American debut at Castle Garden, promoted by P. T. Barnum. The latter caused a controversy in the New York press by praising the diva in public while panning her singing performance in print using various pseudonyms. This ruse pushed the ticket price up to $25 for her first night. Several years later, the soprano was just a memory.

**A FORT-AQUARIUM**
The aquarium had numerous species on display to the public. It also served as a breeding farm for fish which were later released into the state's rivers.

Tip of Lower Manhattan (below) with Battery Park.

# ▲ THE STATUE OF LIBERTY

In 1886, the people of France presented the people of the United States with a huge statue, "Liberty Enlightening the World". The idea for the monument was conceived by Edouard-René Laboulaye, the champion of liberalism, as a symbol of Franco-American friendship. In discussion with the statue's sculptor, Bartholdi, Laboulaye declared: "This will not be the revolutionary Liberty wearing a red bonnet and carrying a pike but the American Liberty, who brandishes not an incendiary torch, but one that lights the way." Erected in New York Harbor the statue has become a symbol of both freedom and the United States itself.

## A TRIP THROUGH THE BODY OF A GIANT

The Statue of Liberty's colossal heel is the first sight to greet the visitor's eye. Once inside the base, you can visit a museum (renovated in 1986), that relates the statue's history. An elevator will take you to the top of the pedestal, then a metal spiral staircase leads to the crown with a view out over the ocean. Entrance to the torch is now prohibited for reasons of safety. The cartoon (right) from *The World*, May 16, 1885, shows Uncle Sam congratulating Miss Liberty.

## BARTHOLDI: A SCULPTOR'S APPRENTICESHIP

Frédéric Auguste Bartholdi was born on April 2, 1834, in Colmar, Alsace. Family connections introduced the sculptor to a network of influential republican contacts.

The statue's stern facial features have been likened to the portrait of Mme Bartholdi, the sculptor's mother, by Ary Scheffer. Although the sculptor may have used his mother as a model, there is no reference to this in the exchange of letters between them.

### EIFFEL TO THE RESCUE OF LIBERTY
At a height of 145 feet, the statue was vulnerable to high winds. The engineer Gustave Eiffel was hired to solve this

problem. The 1/10-inch-thick copper gown is riveted onto a flexible steel frame, which allows the statue a measure of give.

### "LIBERTY" EXHIBITED IN PARIS
At the Paris Universal Exposition of 1878, visitors could climb inside a life-size model of the statue's head. For a time it towered above the roofs of Paris; for 50 centimes, one could climb as far as the crown and the torch. Although the Parisians, led by Victor Hugo, did not want to allow "their" statue of Liberty to leave Paris, it was nevertheless dismantled, packed in 214 crates, and shipped to America on the frigate *Isère*.

### RICHARD MORRIS HUNT, ARCHITECT OF THE PEDESTAL
Hunt designed a high pedestal, a Doric base topped with a neo-classical loggia made of reinforced concrete and granite, to accentuate the size of the statue. The first stone was laid – following Masonic rites – in spring 1884.

The statue, which has been administered by the National Park Service since 1937, was given a facelift for her centennial in 1986. A Franco-American team was given the task of correcting the right arm and the head, which were slightly askew due to an error made when the statue was originally assembled. With a

new torch, its flame gilded in gold leaf, and her freshly cleaned gown, Miss Liberty was ready to take up her duties again for another century. Many people forget her French origins – so thoroughly has she come to symbolize the United States.

## DEDICATION

On October 28, 1886, the statue, her face veiled by the Tricolor, was dedicated (above). Apart from her symbolic role at the entrance to New York, she has become a universally recognized figure, the subject of all sorts of products, from jam to pasta (top); she has "posed" for painters (Andy Warhol made multiple portraits of her) and appeared in films, such as Hitchcock's *Saboteur* (1942) and Schaffner's *Planet of the Apes* (1968).

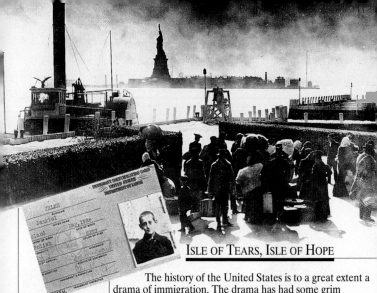

Arrival of immigrants at Ellis Island circa 1900.

Immigrants arriving in New York harbor during the era of the great sailing ships (opposite). Painting by Samuel Waugh.

"Rumour had it . . . that some of us would be refused entry into the United States and would be sent back to Europe. The very thought brought me out in a cold sweat . . . Later, having mastered these anxieties, I was gripped by the fear that I would catch the mumps, smallpox, or some other disease . . . I didn't sleep a wink. I shook all night, listening to all those passengers snoring and dreaming aloud in a dozen different languages."
Louis Adamic, describing his crossing in 1913

## ISLE OF TEARS, ISLE OF HOPE

The history of the United States is to a great extent a drama of immigration. The drama has had some grim moments. By the end of the 19th century, immigrants were being attacked, even murdered, due to a rising tide of xenophobia in American society. Public opinion, which had turned against Central and Southern European nationals, forced the Federal Government to assume responsibility for immigration, which had hitherto been left to the discretion of individual states. Institutions were restructured and centralized, various central committees were set up, strict immigration quotas were imposed. In 1892 the United States Immigration Station was established on Ellis Island. For millions of immigrants this was the waiting room for the Promised Land.

**HOW TO GET THERE.** To get to Ellis Island from Manhattan, take the ferry from Castle Garden Dock (Battery Park ▲ 142). After a crossing lasting some twenty minutes you will alight at the impressive redbrick landing stage, topped by a glass canopy, which leads to the Main Building.

**MUSEUM OF IMMIGRATION.** Within the building's precincts,

facing the sea, a wall of honor has been erected. It is some 98 feet long and is covered with a sheet of engraved copper bearing the names of 200,000 immigrants. A museum has recently been opened inside the building. The BAGGAGE ROOM on the ground floor, with its collection of trunks, suitcases, baskets and assorted belongings, all of which accompanied the immigrants on their journey, has been reconstructed on the ground floor, where various signboards indicate the route to follow. If you are in a hurry, you can take the elevator directly to the second story; but visitors with plenty of time may wish to begin their visit with an overview of the history of American immigration, which is provided in the main hall on the ground floor. This exhibition takes the form of individual

profiles and family trees. There are also
documentaries about Ellis Island (tickets can be
obtained in the entrance hall). On the second story, two
semicircular galleries, west and east of the large Registry Hall,
or Great Hall, document the lengthy process immigrants had
to endure before being admitted to the United States
(medical examinations, literacy tests) and list the marriages
contracted in Manhattan in cases where the name of one of
the spouses was registered on Ellis Island. This room also
contains testimonies supplied by immigrants and their
children. These statements bear witness to the new arrivals'
gradual integration into American society with the support of

**IMMIGRATION CENTER**
Between 1892 and
1954 nearly seventeen
million people passed
through this
building's vast waiting
rooms, dormitories,
offices and medical
examination rooms.

149

# ▲ ELLIS ISLAND

Main entrance to
Ellis Island.

**THE MEDICAL EXAMINATION**
All the immigrants to the United States (below in the 19th century and in 1914) had to undergo a medical examination. Those suffering from contagious diseases such as trachoma (inflammation of the eyes), were rejected. Between 6 and 11 percent were deported for health reasons.

networks that helped them find jobs and acquire new skills and facilitated their children's rapid assimilation into American life. There is a second movie theater for visitors wanting further information. The third story is probably the most fascinating part of the museum; its east gallery displays a collection of objects, both valuable and everyday, that shared the immigrants' odyssey. They illustrate the wide-ranging origins of their owners – a Scottish teapot, an Austrian pipe – and their hopes and dreams – wedding shoes, religious books, a sewing machine, a typewriter, flatirons, tools for a new life in a new land. The room of "Forgotten Voices", which is just as moving, focuses on the abandoned objects found before Ellis Island was restored. This leads to the west gallery where display cases detail the entry procedures for the United States, via the dormitories. Another doorway leads into a room devoted to small temporary exhibitions of works by contemporary artists depicting Ellis Island.

## A HISTORICAL SITE, THE HISTORY OF A SITE

**THE COST OF ASYLUM.** Immigration laws were successively tightened to prohibit entry into the United States by anyone suffering from contagious diseases, by polygamists, prostitutes, the indigent,

anarchists, the Chinese (1882), the Japanese (1907) and the illiterate (1917). Despite being a narrow strip of land (it was soon doubled in size) Ellis Island was the ideal site for weeding out, detaining and deporting possible candidates for immigration. The original structure, which was far too small and was destroyed by a fire in 1897, was ultimately replaced by thirty-five buildings. In 1907, a record year, the Island processed a total of one million people. The majority of these hopeful candidates, who had often reached their destination after a grueling voyage, had only to endure another five or six hours of examination and interviews before

reaching freedom, but approximately 20 percent were held in dormitories to await money from relatives or further medical examination. Each dormitory probably slept about three hundred immigrants and the hospital had room for as many as five hundred patients. About half of the detained were ultimately deported.

Some 3,500 people died on Ellis Island, and 350 were born there.

**AT THE GATES OF OBLIVION.** The 1924 laws regarding immigration quotas were the start of Ellis Island's slow decline. In 1933, for the first time, immigrants returning to their homeland outnumbered those who were just arriving. In 1937 the center

❝A stranger who greeted us,
a hard man, asked:
'And how's your health?'
He examined us. His eyes
Like a dog's scrutinized us ...
One thing is certain,
If he could have plumbed
the depths of our hearts
He would have seen–
the wound.❞
Avrom Reisen

**SORTING IMMIGRATION CANDIDATES**
This room (left) is where the immigrants were divided into categories based on criteria laid down in American legislation. This process often lasted for five hours and 400–500 hundred people were dealt with every day.

"New York is an ugly city, a dirty city. Its climate is a scandal, its politics are used to frighten children, its traffic is madness, its competition is murderous. But there is one thing about it – once you have lived in New York and it has become your home, no place else is good enough!"

John Steinbeck
*The Making of New York*

dealt with only 160 deportees and thirty prisoners. During World War Two Ellis Island became a detention center for "enemies of the United States". The occasional Jewish refugee rubbed shoulders with Nazis and Communists from all over America. Finally, as Ellis Island was no longer

Ellis Island at the turn of the century.

cost-effective, given the meager service it provided, it was permanently closed in 1954.

**THE RESTORATION OF ELLIS ISLAND.** Neglect brought decay: the decorated buildings, the historic objects left in storage there, the surrounding land were all left to the mercy of vandals, looters and the elements. Nature reclaimed the rooms that once had thronged with countless immigrants; all that remained were walls decayed by damp, gaping roofs, crumbling ceilings and parquet floors. In 1965 President Johnson's administration took action, making Ellis Island a National Monument, affiliated with the Statue of Liberty. The sea wall was strengthened and rebuilt in places. From 1976, when it was opened to the public, fifty thousand people have visited this site every year. In 1982, a campaign alerted public opinion to the dilapidated condition of the monument. Donations flooded in from all over the nation to save this part of its cherished heritage. The site was closed in 1983 for restoration. A detailed inventory was drawn up of everything worth salvaging: the registry hall ceiling, which had been constructed and covered with terracotta tiling in 1918, using Catalan technique, was restored; the walls were repaired, saving some of the messages that had been carved into the plaster at the turn of the century – moving testimonies of the immigrants' hopes and fears. The restoration of Ellis Island has been the most expensive project of its kind ever undertaken in the history of the United States ($156 million). However, the museum, opened on September 10, 1990, receives two million visitors every year.

**AN ERUDITE IMMIGRANT**
Albert Einstein on his arrival in New York on October 27, 1933.

**MOVING MEMORIES**
For one hundred million Americans these buildings are evocative of memories of parents, grandparents and other family members. Ellis Island was the point of entry to the New World for some twelve million immigrants.

**HYPER–REALISM**
In fine weather,
bankers and
stockbrokers sit on
the steps of Liberty
Plaza, their ties
flicked over their
shoulders, eating
sandwiches bought in
one of the Broadway
delis. One of them,

seated on a bench, is
checking the contents
of his briefcase,
sifting through
documents from the
Merrill Lynch
brokerage firm. This
is actually a startlingly
lifelike statue,
entitled *Double
Check* (J. Seward
Johnson Jr., 1982);
the documents are
perfectly legible.
Another interesting
sight is the clock set
in the sidewalk at 174
Broadway. This
belongs to a nearby
jewelry store, William
Barthman Jewelers.

**LANDMARKS
PRESERVATION LAW**
The Singer Building
(right), destroyed in
1970, is one of New
York's most sorely
missed masterpieces.
Since then, the New
York Landmarks
Preservation
Commission has
consolidated its
power of veto and
widened its sphere of
influence: it also has
the right to preserve
building interiors that
are open to the
public. There are
more than 50
designated landmarks
in New York today.

This route runs from the World Trade Center down
Broadway, the most famous thoroughfare in Manhattan,
which crosses the island from north to south. It was originally
an old Indian trail that curved around forests and hills.
During the building of Fort Amsterdam the Dutch widened it
south of what is now Bowling Green and named it "Breede
Wegh" (Broadway). "Lower Broadway" is now so densely
lined with buildings that you cannot see their tops from street
level: the disorderly layout of old New York and the heavy
traffic hem you in. Many of the buildings have
spacious lobbies covering an entire block.

## AROUND LIBERTY PLAZA

**EAST RIVER SAVINGS BANK BUILDING.** 26
CORTLANDT ST., BETWEEN CHURCH, DEY
AND CORTLANDT STS. (1934, arch. Walker
& Gillette). The East River Savings
Bank Building, which now houses a
large store and leads from Cortlandt
Street to Dey Street, is an Art Deco
gem. The breathtaking scale of the red,
black and brown marble former banking
hall, with its barrel-vaulted ceiling and
its floor patterned with optical
geometrical motifs, makes the building
well worth a visit.
**1 LIBERTY PLAZA/165 BROADWAY.** (1974,
arch. Skidmore, Owings & Merrill). The
construction of this glass box, which
occupies the block bounded by
Broadway, Church, Cortlandt and
Liberty streets, was to blame for the
demolition, in 1970 of the Singer
Building – doomed because its usable
floor space was five times smaller than
that of the proposed new building. A
Beaux Arts masterpiece, designed by
ERNEST FLAGG, the Singer Building was
the world's tallest building at the
time of its completion
(1908). Sixty years
later it was the

The circular brass seal of the East River Savings Bank, flanked by two eagles, used to adorn the parapet overhanging the side entrances.

The Sky Lobby (left) of the Equitable Building.

> "Before me stretches an avenue which would have looked wide if it had been lined with European houses; but it seems little more than a lane, dominated by buildings thirty and forty stories high. The sun only slants in fleetingly when it is at its zenith . . . These massive pieces of architecture weigh down on passersby, very nearly crushing them. These skyscrapers, who belong to a brotherhood of giants, help each other to rise, to prop each other up, to soar until all sense of perspective disappears. You try to count the stories one by one, then your weary gaze starts to climb in tens; you tilt your head, you crane your neck, and you realize that the topmost story is actually no more than the first of a sequence of set-back terraces, that can only be seen only from the side, or from the air."
>
> Paul Morand,
> *New York*

tallest building ever to be pulled down. It could withstand wind pressure of 350 tons. It also anticipated the Zoning Resolution of 1916 ● *97* for its slender, elegant tower formed a setback in relation to the larger mass below, thereby allowing sunlight to reach the street. At the time of its demolition, the New York City Landmarks Commission, only five years old, was not sure enough of its powers to halt the plans of the new landlord, U.S. Steel.

**MARINE MIDLAND BANK.** 140 BROADWAY, BETWEEN LIBERTY AND CEDAR STS. (1967, arch. Skidmore, Owings & Merrill). This flat-roofed monolith, a typical example of the International Style ● *100*, is devoid of all decoration. Conventional ornamentation has taken the form of a separate work of art: the red cube sculpture (below) by Isamu Noguchi (1973).

**EQUITABLE BUILDING** ● *97* ★. 120 BROADWAY (1915, arch.

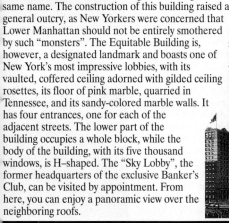

Ernest R. Graham of Graham, Anderson, Probst & White). Stone eagles and lions adorn the lower part of the façade of this neo-Renaissance building which covers a surface area thirty times larger than that of the original building of the same name. The construction of this building raised a general outcry, as New Yorkers were concerned that Lower Manhattan should not be entirely smothered by such "monsters". The Equitable Building is, however, a designated landmark and boasts one of New York's most impressive lobbies, with its vaulted, coffered ceiling adorned with gilded ceiling rosettes, its floor of pink marble, quarried in Tennessee, and its sandy-colored marble walls. It has four entrances, one for each of the adjacent streets. The lower part of the building occupies a whole block, while the body of the building, with its five thousand windows, is H–shaped. The "Sky Lobby", the former headquarters of the exclusive Banker's Club, can be visited by appointment. From here, you can enjoy a panoramic view over the neighboring roofs.

The Equitable Building in 1914.

The Trinity Building, as seen by a reveler, takes on a strange appearance. . . .

**THAMES TWINS/TRINITY AND REALTY BUILDINGS** ★. 111–115 BROADWAY (1905 and 1907, arch. Francis H. Kimball). These twin buildings, linked by a walkway that straddles Thames Street, are one of New York's architectural gems and make for a pleasant surprise deep in the heart of the bustling Financial District. The façades call to mind the Gothic lines of Trinity Church, and the interiors are treated in a similar style, with stained glass windows and gilded elevator doors, grotesques and gilded ornaments.

## AROUND TRINITY CHURCH

**BANK OF NEW YORK, FORMERLY IRVING TRUST BUILDING** ★. 1 WALL ST., S. E. CORNER OF BROADWAY (1932, arch. Voorhees, Gmelin & Walker). The Greek practice of fluting columns to enhance the illusion of height and delicacy was adapted for the walls of this building. The plain limestone cladding and the abstract Art Deco motif of the façade enhance the building's monolithic appearance. Although built during the Great Depression, the Irving Trust Building, exudes a feeling of confidence. The company's name is derived from the American author, Washington Irving, who used to live at 3 Wall Street. To view the building as a whole, walk back to Rector Street.

**TRINITY CHURCH** ★. BROADWAY AT WALL ST. (1846, arch. Richard Upjohn). Trinity Parish, founded by a charter granted by William III in 1697, was given extensive pasture lands in Manhattan, which made it eventually the richest church in the United States. This is the third building of the same name to be built on this site; the first church, built in 1698, was destroyed by a fire in 1776 and the second was demolished in 1839 due to a defective roof frame. Completed in 1846, the present Gothic Revival church is clad in brownstone and boasts a bell tower whose slender spire soars to 280 feet. Until the end of the 19th century Trinity Church was the tallest building in New York; it used to serve as a landmark for ships. The stained glass window over the choir is one of the earliest made in the United States. The three bronze porch doors, designed by Richard Morris Hunt and constructed by Karl Bitter, Charles Niehaus, and J. Massey Rhind illustrate Adam and Eve's expulsion from Paradise. The hundred-year-old oak trees in the church burial ground shelter the graves of Alexander Hamilton, the first Secretary of the Treasury, Robert Fulton, inventor of the steam warship ▲ *174*, Captain

**IRVING TRUST BUILDING**
The ground-floor banking hall of this building glows with red and gold mosaics.

**AN ENGLISH CHURCH**
Trinity Church (right, as rebuilt in 1846) was the first Manhattan parish established by the Church of England. When it was built, in the 1690's, all residents, whatever their religion, had to pay a tax for its construction.

James Lawrence, a hero of the War of 1812, William Bradford, the founder of the first newspaper in New York, and Albert Gallatin, statesman and a founder of New York University ▲ *200*. The oldest tombstone dates from 1681. An ossuary contains the ashes of two thousand prisoners who died during the War of Independence.

**29 BROADWAY.** (1931, arch. Sloan & Robertson). This Art Deco building has several interesting features, notably the stringcourses that coil around its gable, creating the effect of a console. The lobby, with its wealth of jade marble, engraved glass doors and radiator grills, is a perfect example of Art Deco style. Cross the street to appreciate the overall design of the building.

## AROUND BOWLING GREEN

**FORMER CUNARD BUILDING.** 25 BROADWAY (1921, arch. Benjamin Wistar Morris; Carrère and Hastings). In the 1920's, after its merger with the White Star Line, Cunard became the leading steamship company to provide a passenger service. With the exception of the luxury liners, QUEEN MARY, QUEEN ELIZABETH and QUEEN ELIZABETH II, most of their ships had names ending in "ia" (MAURETANIA, for example) – as did the company's first ship, BRITANNIA, which berthed in New York on July 4, 1840. A post office now occupies part of Cunard's former headquarters. The sumptuous main entrance, set in a neo-Renaissance façade, leads into an immense lobby, illuminated by antique chandeliers, with a vaulted ceiling and walls lined with polychromatic terracotta.

**AN AMERICAN CHURCH**
After the fire of 1776 the original Trinity Church (above) remained in ruins throughout the War of Independence. A second church was built after the war. Like other Anglican Churches in the United States, it became part of the new, independent Episcopal Church.

**LOBBY OF THE CUNARD BUILDING**
The octagonal main hall, 65 feet high, is surmounted by three domes. The interior walls of the building are decorated with charts showing Cunard's lines and illustrated by flags from former French and English colonial empires (by the artist Ezra Winters). The pendentives supporting the main dome are decorated with paintings of the ships of four famous sailors: Christopher Columbus, Leif Eriksson, John Cabot and Sir Francis Drake.

Government House in 1797, on the site of the future U.S. Custom House.

**STEAMSHIP ROW**
At the beginning of this century, during the heyday of maritime transportation, the major shipping companies built their head offices around Bowling Green and along "Steamship Row", on Lower Broadway. This enabled them to keep an eye on the comings and goings of their own ships and those of their competitors.

**1 BROADWAY.** This was the first office building to be built (in 1884), along the longest and most famous street in New York. It was originally called the Washington Building. In 1922 it was refurbished to house the headquarters of the United States Line, one of the many shipping companies based on Steamship Row. The reservation and ticket sales office (now converted into a bank) was on the ground floor. Note the compass dial set in the floor and the words "First-Class tickets" which still appear outside.

**FORMER STANDARD OIL BUILDING.** 26 BROADWAY (1922, arch. Carrère & Hastings and Shreve, Lamb & Blake). The neo-Renaissance façade of the former Standard Oil Building (left) cunningly curves here in a fan shape to follow the contour of Broadway. The names of the founders of the oil company, including John D. Rockefeller, grace the lobby which is lined with pilasters and columns. Note the STANDARD OIL CLOCK, on which the "S" indicates the minutes and the "O" the hours. As you approach Bowling Green, you can see the top of the building's pyramidal tower, whose main axis is aligned east-west, at an oblique angle to the main part of the building. This building now houses THE MUSEUM OF AMERICAN FINANCIAL HISTORY.

**BOWLING GREEN.** (rest. 1978, landscape architect, Paul Friedberg). Created in 1733, Bowling Green is the oldest park in the city. It occupies the site of a former Dutch parade ground, which had originally been adjacent to a cattle market. The new park consisted of a green where gentlemen could bowl (hence its name) for an annual fee of one peppercorn, paid to the municipal government. It was here that PETER MINUIT bought Manhattan from the Indians ● *30*. At the center of the green, in 1766, New Yorkers raised a gilded statue of George III to show their gratitude for the repeal of the Stamp Act, which had placed a tax on all written documents. Although the 18th-century railings that surrounded the park are still there, the statue was melted down for making bullets during the War of Independence. In 1842 a fountain was built in the park. It was supplied with fresh water from the Croton Reservoir, thus giving New Yorkers, for the first time, access to clean water, unlike the well water that caused so many epidemics ● *34* in the city.

**"BOWLING GREEN BULL".** This enormous bronze bull (Arturo di Modica, 1989), stands for the time being at the entrance to the Financial District ▲ *158*, at the northernmost end of Bowling Green. The bull and the bear represent the two trends of the stock market: rising and declining.

**❝**The bull strives to crush the bear, which is waiting for the best time to throttle it. **❞**
André Kostolamy, *Si la Bourse m'était contée*

**U.S. Custom House ★.** 1 Bowling Green (1907, arch. Cass Gilbert). The U.S. Custom House was established in 1842 at 28 Wall Street, the building now housing the present Federal Hall National Memorial. Twenty years later it was moved to 55 Wall Street, within the walls of the former Merchants' Exchange, and then in 1907 to 1 Bowling Green. When this Beaux Arts style ● 92 building was completed, there was no income tax, so customs duties were the

Federal Government's primary source of income. The lion's share of this revenue was provided by New York City, and therefore the U.S. Custom House accounted for most of the money vital to the American economy. Its importance is reflected in this imposing building. The marble hall leads into a sumptuous oval rotunda 48 feet high, illuminated by an elliptical skylight. The walls are decorated by eight frescoes (Reginald Marsh, 1937) depicting the arrival of a transatlantic steamship in New York Harbor. (One of them shows Greta Garbo disembarking and being met by the press.) In 1973 the Custom House moved to the World Trade Center. The National Museum of the American Indian took over these premises in 1994.

## Toward the Sea

**Church of Our Lady of the Rosary.** 7–8 State St. (1793–1806, arch. John McComb, rest. 1965, Shanley & Sturges). This church can be found in a house with a Georgian-style east wing (1793) and a Federal-style west wing (1806) ● 82. It belonged to shipowner James Watson who would spend long hours watching the harbor activity from his house; its columns were made from ships' masts.

**Battery Maritime Building.** 11 South St. (1909, arch. Walker & Gillette). Until 1938 the Municipal Ferry Piers served as landing stages for the various Brooklyn ferryboat lines. They are now used by the Governor's Island ferry. The inland side of this building, which gives access to the piers, has a colonnade and arches facing the water.

**Allegorical ornaments**
The steps of the main entrance to the U.S. Custom House are adorned with statues by Daniel Chester French, symbolizing four continents. The building's front-facing windows bear the heads of the eight races of mankind (Caucasian, Hindu, Latin, Celtic, Mongolian, Eskimo, Slavic and African); above the cornice are twelve statues representing the great commercial centers in Western history.

**Saint Elizabeth Ann Seton**
In 1809 Elizabeth Seton (1774–1821), who lived at 7–8 State St., founded the Sisters of Charity, the first American order of nuns. A member of the New York aristocracy, she was ostracized for her conversion to Catholicism. She was canonized in 1975, becoming the first female American saint ● 50. There is a statue of her in the Shrine of St. Elizabeth Ann Seton.

**THE FINANCIAL DISTRICT**
The Financial District, which dates back to 1792 with the creation of the first Stock Exchange, was once dominated by the spire of Trinity Church ▲ 154. With the advent of the skyscraper, the area's appearance changed radically.

**"ONCE UPON A TIME IN AMERICA"**
A scene (below) for the movie, *Once Upon a Time in America*, made in 1984 by Sergio Leone and filmed in the Federal Reserve

Bank. In this movie the director explores another face of the "American dream": the birth of great cities and the stranglehold of mob rule.

## AROUND THE FEDERAL RESERVE BANK

**JOHN STREET UNITED METHODIST CHURCH AND MUSEUM.** 44 JOHN ST. (1841, arch. William Hurry). This church (the third on this site) was the home of the first Methodist congregation in America. Founded by the Englishman JOHN WESLEY (1703–91), Methodism rejected the ecclesiastical authority of the English crown and it became very popular in the United States. This building, contemporary with the Greek Revival style ● 84, anticipates the Italianate style ● 88 in its central Venetian window, flanked by two other tall arched windows. The interior displays a refined elegance with its unostentatious stained glass windows and its horseshoe-shaped gallery. There is a MUSEUM on the lower ground floor.

**FEDERAL RESERVE BANK.** 33 LIBERTY ST. (1924, arch. York & Sawyer). The Federal Reserve Bank was founded in 1913 by President Woodrow Wilson to centralize the American banking system. The New York Reserve Bank, a key part of the Federal Reserve System, is where monetary policy is implemented for the Federal Reserve, influencing interest rates and economic activity throughout the nation.

**HOLIDAY PRESENTS,**
**$10, $15, $20, $25.**

Only Office in the United States, No. 78 Nassau Street, New York.

Advertisement in *Harper's Weekly* for the Watch Company, a Swiss company located at 78 Nassau St. in the Financial District.

The gold reserves from eighty countries and some foreign banks and international organizations, over one quarter of the world's stock, are stored 80 feet below ground in this massive rectangular fortress built of limestone and sandstone. Its impregnable appearance is modeled on Florentine Renaissance palaces. The strong rooms can be visited by appointment, and it used to be possible to watch old banknotes being destroyed. LOUISE NEVELSON PLAZA, farther east, at the intersection of Maiden Lane and Liberty and William streets, affords the best view of the crenelated turret that tops this building. This pedestrian area contains an abstract sculpture, *Shadows and Flags*, created by Louise Nevelson in 1977.

**CENTRAL BANK OF CHINA, FORMER NEW YORK CHAMBER OF COMMERCE.** 65 LIBERTY ST. (1901, arch. James B. Baker). This architectural gem is one of the finest Beaux Arts style ● *92* buildings in New York and a product of the "City Beautiful" movement. The three pedestals on the façade used to bear statues, which did not survive the ravages of pollution. The wonderful lobby is worth a visit.

**CHASE MANHATTAN BANK.** 1 CHASE MANHATTAN PLAZA (1960, arch. Skidmore, Owings & Merrill). This building marked a watershed in the postwar development of Lower Manhattan, being the first International Style ● *100* office building to be constructed in this part of the city. It expressed the confidence of the bank's president, David Rockefeller, in the future of Downtown, at a time when businesses were moving Uptown. The tower's plain rectangular shape contrasts markedly with the slender spires surrounding it. The Chase Manhattan Bank boasts a superb art collection and its huge plaza contains work by Isamu Noguchi – a sunken Japanese garden with an arrangement of seven rocks – as well as a sculpture by Dubuffet (above), *Group of Four Trees*, created in 1972. The plaza affords a spectacular view of the neighboring buildings, especially 70 Pine Street.

**AMERICAN INTERNATIONAL BUILDING ★.** 70 PINE ST. (1932, arch. Clinton and Russell; Holton and George). This Art Deco ● *98* skyscraper, which originally housed the CITIES SERVICE COMPANY, responsible for the

**LIBERTY TOWER**
Situated at 55 Liberty St., this neo-Gothic tower decorated with finials and gargoyles once housed the Standard Oil Company ▲ *156*. The frescoes in its lobby depict the building in 1909, as well as the Singer Building ▲ *152*, which stood on the site of the present Liberty Plaza.

159

The French franc, which was hard currency at the time, is carved on the pediment (above) of the main door of 20 Exchange Place.

**60 WALL STREET** Built in 1988, the Morgan Bank's new building, is a heavy Postmodern tower, contrasting sharply with its more graceful neighbors. However, the lower part of the building is composed of a colonnade, echoing the one at 55 Wall St., just opposite. It houses a

vast atrium (above), open to the public in accordance with city-planning regulations.

The deeply recessed main entrance to Citibank behind its colonnade.

city's substructural work, was designed to create an impression of power and wealth. The Chase Manhattan Plaza affords a good view of its Gothic tower, which is one of the Financial District's three most prestigious tops, along with 40 WALL STREET and 20 EXCHANGE PLACE. A limestone model of the building has been carved onto the central column of the entrance. The triangles that adorn the main doors are the agency's emblem. Of the two elevators, behind Egyptian-style doors in the lobby, one serves odd floors, one even floors.

## WALL STREET

The financial world's most famous street once marked the northernmost boundary of New Amsterdam. In 1653 the Dutch erected a wooden palisade as a form of protection, first against the Indians, then against the English ● *32*. From 1792, when the first stock exchange was organized in this neighborhood ▲ *164*, Wall Street began to establish its reputation as a financial center.

**WILLIAMSBURGH SAVINGS BANK, FORMERLY SEAMEN'S BANK FOR SAVINGS.** 72–74 WALL ST. (1926, arch. Benjamin Wistar Morris). The ships and anchors that adorn the ashlar façade are a reminder of this building's previous occupant. The lobby of no. 72, with its decorative brass grilles, paneled doors and gilded ceiling, is a masterpiece. The central door, opposite the elegant bank of elevators, is crowned with a brass bas-relief depicting a lighthouse.

**63 WALL STREET.** (1929, arch. Delano and Aldrich). The building rises in a series of setbacks to a top decorated with ornamental gargoyles, a better view of which can be obtained farther back up Wall Street. Note the coins adorning the façade and take a look at the corner lobby.

**22 WILLIAM STREET BETWEEN BEAVER STREET AND EXCHANGE STREET ★.** (1931, arch. Cross & Cross). Built for the CITY BANK FARMERS' TRUST COMPANY, this office tower fills a trapezoid-shaped block and has a façade with bevelled quoins. Take a look at the bronze doors decorated with trains, boats, planes and airships, typical Art Deco ● *98* motifs. On the cornice of the lower part of the building, huge helmeted centurions seem to watch the passersby. There is a better view of the lofty, slender tower farther west from William Street. The lobby offers a profusion of marble, mosaics, paintings and tin. Note the central dome, vaulted ceilings, elevator doors, floor and glass telephone booths.

**CITIBANK.** 55 WALL ST. (1836–42, arch. Isaiah Rogers; 1907, arch. McKim, Mead & White). This classical-inspired building, with its two-story colonnades, was built on the site of the first Merchants' Exchange, which had been destroyed by fire in 1835. The lower part of the building, which dates from 1836, served as the U.S. Custom House from 1863 ▲ *157* until 1899. After the departure of that tenant, "55 Wall Street" was enlarged to house Citibank (then called the First National City Bank). A Corinthian-order colonnade was added to the Ionic one by the architects McKim, Mead & White. The huge lobby measures 198 by 132 feet in height. The building now stands empty; it has been closed to the public since 1992.

**BANK OF NEW YORK BUILDING.** 48 WALL ST. (1927, arch. Benjamin Wistar Morris III). Cross the street to appreciate the setbacks of this skyscraper which draws its inspiration from the Italian Renaissance and whose topmost aedicula is crowned with an eagle. The Bank of New York, the first bank in the newly independant state, was founded in 1784 by Alexander Hamilton ▲ *154*, Washington's former aide-de-camp and first Secretary of the Treasury. Alexander Hamilton died after being shot in a duel on July 11, 1804 by Aaron Burr, a rival in politics as well as in business.

**MANUFACTURERS' HANOVER TRUST, FORMERLY BANK OF MANHATTAN CO. BUILDING ★.** 40 WALL ST. (1929, arch. H. Craig Severance and Yasuo Matsui). This 69-story skyscraper (left) bears a certain resemblance to the Empire State Building ▲ *242* (like the latter, it was even hit by a plane in the 1940's). It was the tallest

building in the world for just a few days before it was overtaken by the Chrysler Building ▲ *266*. The top, a Gothic Revival green pyramid, similar to the top of the Woolworth Building ▲ *180*, can easily be recognized on the Lower Manhattan skyline. The northeast corner of Broad and Beaver streets provides a good vantage point. The Bank of Manhattan Company, which was initially called the Manhattan Water Company, was New York's first public services company; it was founded by Aaron Burr in 1799 to supply drinking water. In 1842, when the Croton Aqueduct was opened, the company, which had also engaged in banking activities, dropped its water supply function and officially took the name of the Bank of Manhattan.

**SEAMEN'S BANK FOR SAVINGS.** 30 WALL ST. (1919, arch. York and Sawyer). This building was built on the site of the United States Assay Office which was designed by Martin E. Thompson and completed in 1823; it was demolished in 1915. Its façade is displayed in the American Wing of the Metropolitan Museum of Art.

Former subtreasury vaults.

In 1883, a statue of George Washington by John Quincy Adams Ward was placed outside the entrance Federal Hall, at the approximate spot where he took his oath of office and where (right) President Benjamin Harrison made a speech.

**26 WALL STREET**
Built in 1842, the U.S. Custom House displays a Doric austerity contrasting with the Stock Exchange (1903) façade, with its profusion of

figures and Corinthian opulence. Here, architecture mirrors the development of the United States, showing how the nation had evolved in sixty years from a modest, idealistic infancy to powerful and affluent maturity.

**FEDERAL HALL NATIONAL MEMORIAL ★.** 26 WALL ST. (1834–42, arch. Town & Davis). In 1701, the second New York CITY HALL was built on this site ▲ *176*. Remodeled in 1788 by Pierre-Charles L'Enfant (architect and city-planner for Washington, D. C.), the building, now renamed Federal Hall, served briefly as the headquarters of the American government until the capital was moved to Philadelphia in 1790. This building, later demolished, housed the first meeting, in March 1789, of the new Congress, and was the site of George Washington's inauguration as the first president of the United States, on April 30 of that year. The present Greek Revival ● *84* building was built in 1842 to house the first U.S. Custom House ▲ *157,* then, between 1862 and 1920, it became the headquarters of a U.S. subtreasury. Exhibits in the museum retrace the origins and history of the United States.

**MORGAN GUARANTY TRUST COMPANY.** 23 WALL ST. AT S. E. CORNER OF BROAD ST. (1913, arch. Trowbridge & Livingston). In 1907, financier and businessman J. Pierpont Morgan managed to stem the tide of panic then threatening Wall Street by locking the leading city bankers in his 5th Avenue home and forcing them to come up with a plan to rebuild people's confidence. While the "prisoners" were working, Morgan played solitaire – which indicates his status

> "ALL THE MAJOR FINANCIAL MARKETS HAVE GROWN UP IN THE HEART OF A CAPITAL CITY. THE AMERICAN STOCK EXCHANGE IS AN EXCEPTION: IT WAS CREATED IN A PORT, ON THE OUTSKIRTS OF A CITY WHICH IS NOT EVEN THE CAPITAL."
>
> M. T...

among them. His bank at 23 Wall Street was the last building to be built at this key intersection, around which were grouped the U.S. subtreasury (now the FEDERAL HALL NATIONAL MEMORIAL), to the north: the NEW YORK STOCK EXCHANGE, to the west; and, opposite, BANKE... rival occupying, in 1912, th...

By buildin... ...organ intended ...ying sign – the Morgan establishment did not need one! The Morgan family's highly reactionary stance brought them many enemies: a bomb exploded outside the building on September 16, 1920, killing thirty-three people and wounding hundreds of others. Those responsible were never traced.

## BROAD STREET AND NEW YORK STOCK EXCHANGE

**BROAD STREET.** This street, which runs from Wall Street down to the tip of Manhattan, was originally a canal dug by the Dutch in 1660. In 1676, it was filled in ● 76. Although "Wall Street" is famous the world over as shorthand for the U.S. stock market, the New York Stock Exchange, the focal point for most of the district's financial activity, is actually on Broad Street.

**NEW YORK STOCK EXCHANGE ★.** 8 BROAD ST. (1903, arch. George B. Post). The largest stock exchange in the world opened on May 17, 1792 under a buttonwood tree, near the intersection of Wall and William streets. Here twenty-four American brokers met to impose some sort of order on a chaotic market and signed the "Buttonwood Agreement". The tree was felled in 1865 by a storm, but a commemorative plaque was laid in front of 8 Broad Street. On March 8, 1817, the market adopted a constitution and a name, the New York Stock and Exchange Board, and moved into 40 Wall Street. In 1863, the Board shortened its name to ... ...moved ... Street. Thirty-five years la... settled in its present home at 8 Broad Street. The history of the New York Stock Exchange is filled with eccentric figures. One of the most famous was Hetty Green, nicknamed the "Witch of Wall Street", who, in the 1880's, transformed her inheritance into a fortune worth more than $100 million. She achieved this without ever showing her face in the stockbroker central enclosure. The classical façade of the New York Stock Exchange conceals a vast and highly sophisticated trading floor, which can be visited during the week. Don't miss the opportunity to view this frenetic spectacle, with its hundreds of shouting stockbrokers and flashing annunciator boards.

**"WALL S...** The fac... ...the New... ...tock ...bears a ...nt enlivened ...th a group of sculpted figures entitled *Integrity Protecting the Works of Man* (John Quincy Adams Ward). In the center, the winged figure of Integrity looms over Science, Industry and Invention on the right, Agriculture and on the left, the Mining Industry.

The pyramid that tops the Bankers Trust (14–16 Wall St.) is one of the most distinctive sights on the Manhattan skyline and the only sign of eccentricity in the architecture of this building.

A hard currency – the dollar – a buoyant economy and a well-established banking system have made the New York Stock Exchange the leading money market in the world. Since its founding in 1792 it has survived many crises, including the crash of 1929. "Wall Street" has been instrumental in generating many of the technical innovations and new financial products used in trading halls since the beginning of the 20th century. It has created a new generation of stockbrokers.

**"BLACK FRIDAY" AT THE NEW YORK STOCK EXCHANGE**
On September 24, Jay Gould's attempt to corner the market having collapsed, the price of gold dropped nearly 20 percent. A panic in the securities market quickly followed.

**"CURB EXCHANGE"**
Early in this century small-scale stockholders carried out transactions at cash desks in stockbrokers' offices located along Broad St., and even in the street itself (below, in 1918).

**ON TICKER TAPE**
In order to send the rates on the Stock Exchange's Big Board to stockbrokers all over the country, Wall St. began, in 1867, to use teletype.

After World War Two, while European stockbrokers waited for the recovery, on the other side of the Atlantic, records were being broken! However, in New York, people were wary of a new tool that had just appeared on the stockmarket: information technology.

# 12,894,650-

"On the Stock Exchange's coat of arms, the bull and the bear, hostile brothers, face each other." This animal metaphor, which originated in America, is now used to describe speculators' activity. The behavior of the "bears" – who sell stocks and shares because they believe the market is falling – and of the bulls – who buy stocks and shares at a certain price because they are gambling on a rising market – generate the Stock Market prices ▲ 156.

## The New York Times.

WORST STOCK CRASH STEMMED BY BANKS; 12,894,650-SHARE DAY SWAMPS MARKET; LEADERS CONFER, FIND CONDITIONS SOUND

### PANIC ON WALL STREET

"Worst Stock Crash Stemmed By Banks" ran the headline in *The New York Times* on Friday October 25, 1929. The day before, the share prices of the big names in American industry had plummeted and 12,894,650 stocks and shares had changed hands. America was about to plunge into the Great Depression. In 1934, to prevent a catastrophe of this scale from recurring, Congress instituted the Securities and Exchange Commission, which established strict regulations to prevent violent market fluctuations.

### MICHAEL MILKEN

The "Golden Boy", inventor of junk bonds, being sworn in, in 1987.

The aggressive climate of the 1980's led to a series of illegal schemes: there was a rise in hostile takeover bids – the targeted company would be shut and stripped of its assets – and junk bonds. Unscrupulous businessmen such as Michael Milken built up huge fortunes in this way. In 1990 he was imprisoned for fraud.

**VIETNAM WAR VETERANS' MEMORIAL**
The writings on the memorial (above) to soldiers who fought in the Vietnam War (Vietnam Veterans' Plaza, S.E. Water St.), include extracts from letters, military dispatches and newspaper clippings.

The sign in front of the Fraunces Tavern.

**INDIA HOUSE**
This building, at 1 Hanover Square, housed the Hanover Bank, the N.Y. Cotton Exchange and the W. R. Grace & Co., in quick succession. India House is a classic example of an Italianate-style ● *88* brownstone

residence. It is now occupied by a businessmen's club and contains a collection of art and naval objects.

**INTERNATIONAL TELEPHONE AND TELEGRAPH BUILDING.** 67 BROAD ST. (1928, arch. Buchman & Kahn). The best view of the spectacular verticality of this 35-story Gothic Revival ● *86* building is from the corner of Beaver Street and Broadway. The allegorical frescoes of the lobby, which take communication as their theme, depict mythological figures. The alcove of what used to be the main entrance, on the corner of William Street, is embellished with a mosaic (right).

**MARITIME EXCHANGE BUILDING.** 80 BROAD ST. (1930, arch. Sloan & Robertson). The entrance of this Art Deco ● *98* building, topped with four silver sea horses, leads into the lobby, whose ceiling is covered with paintings of ships, illustrating the history of ship-building. The building has Tiffany-style ● *66* stained glass windows, depicting cars, trains, boats and planes.

**85 BROAD STREET.** (1983, arch. Skidmore, Owings & Merrill). A brass plaque bearing a map of Lower Manhattan c. 1660 is placed below the archway leading into this building. The lobby follows the curve of the intersection with Stone Street. When the foundations were being laid, objects from the Dutch era were found; these are now exhibited in Pearl Street.

## FRAUNCES TAVERN BLOCK HISTORIC DISTRICT

The Fraunces Tavern Block, located between Broad, Pearl and Water streets and Coenties Slip, occupies land salvaged from the sea by the Dutch in 1689.

**FRAUNCES TAVERN.** 54 PEARL ST. This house is an architectural conjecture of one built in 1719 for a wealthy merchant, Étienne (or Stephen) de Lancey. It was bought in 1762 by Samuel Fraunces who opened a restaurant in it called Queen's Head Tavern. After Independence, he changed its royalist name to his own. The tavern was frequented by members of the New York élite. George Washington was one of the establishment's patrons, and it was here, in 1783, that he gave a farewell dinner for his officers. In 1785, his business on the wane, Fraunces sold the tavern and became Washington's steward. The building, in Georgian style, was bought in 1904 by the Sons of the Revolution and restored in 1907 by William Mersereau. It houses a museum on early New York history and American decorative arts.

**HANOVER SQUARE.** This square was originally called Printing House Square in homage to William Bradford ● *54*, who founded the first American printing works here in 1693. It was renamed "Hanover" by the English, in honor of the reigning dynasty. Many streets in the district followed suit, taking the names of members of the royal family. After Independence, only Hanover Square retained its name. A statue of Abraham De Peyster, Mayor of New York between 1691 and 1693, stands in this square.

**DELMONICO'S.** 56 BEAVER ST. (1891, arch. James Brown Lord). This restaurant was founded in 1827 by two Italian immigrants, the Delmonico brothers. It has a white marble portico, possibly an antique from Pompeii. The interior contains photos, engravings and tapestries of old New York.

# AROUND
# CITY HALL

Civic Center, New York City.

**CITY HALL**
In paying homage to the Georgian and Louis XVI styles, the architects who designed City Hall (above, in 1826) were deliberately rejecting the monumental form of neo-classicism favored for the new capital, Washington. On top of City Hall's clock tower (below) stands a statue of Justice.

Center, the cupola of City Hall.

The area now occupied by the Civic Center, the nation's second largest administrative center after that of Washington, employing 50,000 people, was a tranquil patch of countryside covered with fields and marsh lands. To the south stands City Hall, the offices of the mayor of New York since 1812, and Park Row, once the center of the theater district and also known as "Newspaper Row" because of the many newspapers based here. Farther southeast lies South Street Seaport, a remnant of the city's commercial, maritime past. To the west towers the Woolworth Building, while to the northeast administrative buildings and courthouses for the city and the State of New York are grouped around Foley Square.

## AROUND CITY HALL

**CITY HALL ★.** Between PARK ROW and BROADWAY (1803–12, arch. Joseph François Mangin and John McComb, Jr). This was New York's third City Hall. The first, built in 1641 during the Dutch occupation, was situated at about 71 Pearl Street, opposite the site where the Fraunces Tavern block ▲ 166 now stands. The second, built in 1701 on the corner of Broad and Wall streets, was demolished in 1812. On the same site, the U.S. CUSTOM HOUSE, now the

FEDERAL HALL NATIONAL MEMORIAL ▲ 162 was constructed. City Hall served as the seat of Manhattan's administrative offices until the creation of "Greater New York" in 1898, which brought together the five boroughs – the Bronx, Queens, Brooklyn, Staten Island and Manhattan – following which the MUNICIPAL BUILDING ▲ 182 was built. It still houses the Mayor's office and is used for official ceremonies. The courtrooms and the office (open to the public) used by "Hizzoner" (the traditional New York nickname for the mayor) are reached by the building's main staircase.

**CITY HALL PARK.** The apple trees of this former public grazing ground (1686) were once used as gallows by the British. JACOB LEISLER, a Dutch merchant who was proclaimed "leader of Free New York" during the city's rebellion against excessive taxation by JAMES II, was hanged here for treason in 1691. The statue of another legendary convict – although executed elsewhere – also stands in the park ▲ 262: NATHAN HALE, a hero of the American Revolution, was summarily hanged by the British for spying. His last words were, "I only regret that I have but one life to lose for my country." The

WORTH ST.

CHAMBERS ST.

LAFAYETTE ST.

CENTRE ST.

PARK ROW

BROOKLYN BRIDGE

SOUTH ST.

SOUTH ST. SEAPORT

FULTON FISH MARKET

🏃 Six hours

pole on the green commemorates the "Liberty Poles" raised
by New Yorkers in 1767 to mark the first anniversary of the
repeal of the STAMP ACT ● 27. This was also where a huge
crowd gathered on July 9, 1776 to hear a reading of the
Declaration of Independence, a document written mainly by
Thomas Jefferson (1743–1826) and adopted by the
Continental Congress in Philadelphia, on July 4, 1776.

**THE CROTON FOUNTAIN**
In 1842 a fountain was built on the site of the ornamental pond in City Hall Park (above) to celebrate the city's first supply of piped drinking water from the Croton Reservoir. The fountain was demolished in 1875.

**FORMER POST OFFICE**
This post office (opposite), which replaced the Croton Fountain, stood in front of City Hall. It was demolished in 1939 when the General Post Office was built on 8th Ave. ▲ 249.

**NEWSPAPER ROW**
In 1895 around fifteen daily newspapers were located near Park Row (below), including the *Times, World, Tribune, Sun, Post, Journal* and *Staats Zeitung*. Children used to sell

**BENJAMIN FRANKLIN.** PRINTING HOUSE SQUARE (1872, Ernst Plassman). In this square, east of City Hall, stands a statue of BENJAMIN FRANKLIN, printer, writer, scientist, statesman and signatory of the Declaration of Independence. From 1729 Franklin was editor of the *Pennsylvania Gazette*. Between 1732 and 1757 he published *Poor Richard's Almanack*.

## PARK ROW, FORMERLY "NEWSPAPER ROW"

This area was the center of journalism during the second half of the 19th century. The proximity of City Hall and of the theater district around Theater Alley, was ideal for the newspapers, which took advantage of the inexhaustible supply of scandal afforded by these establishments. Although some of the buildings are still standing, the newspapers and the theaters have moved uptown to the vicinity of Times Square.

**PACE UNIVERSITY, FORMERLY THE NEW YORK TIMES BUILDING.** 41 PARK ROW (1889, arch. George B. Post). This building, occupied by Pace University since 1952, has such sturdy foundations (to accommodate the printing presses) that it was able to bear the extra weight when the height of the building was raised in 1905. The *New York Times* moved in

1903 to offices on what became Times Square ▲ 255.

**POTTER BUILDING.** 38 PARK ROW (1883, arch. Nathan Starkweather). This replaced the NEW YORK WORLD BUILDING, which had been destroyed by a fire. It was said to be fireproof due to its terracotta construction. The ornamental treatment of the façade was a first for an office building. The *Daily News*, the *New York Press* and the *Daily Observer* subsequently occupied

the morning and evening editions on the street with the familiar shout "Extra! Read all about it!". The office buildings had cavernous basements which housed heavy printing presses.

this building in their turn.

**THE FORMER AMERICAN TRACT SOCIETY BUILDING.** 150 NASSAU ST. (1896, arch. R. H. Robertson). The COLONNADE on top is all that remains of a penthouse suite built on top of the sloping copper roof. It was demolished when the height of the TIMES BUILDING was raised, thereby blocking its view. Visit the semicircular lobby, with its original marble moldings and coffered ceiling. This building has some of the last manually operated elevators in New York.

**"THE MUSE WHO NOW RULES THE PRESS."**

ANTHONY TROLLOPE

The riot quelled by the police in front of the Tribune Building, July 11, 1863.

**PARK ROW BUILDING.** 15 PARK ROW (1899, arch. R. H. Robertson). This building was the tallest skyscraper in the world when it was opened. The twin-domed crown used to dominate the skyline. The balconies thrusting away from the façade at intervals seem to be secured by magnetization. Four stone goddesses watch over the entrance. Make sure to see the reception area and the lobby, with its semicircular elevators. The lobby still has its original decoration: solid brass ramps, delicate marble trim and coffered ceiling.

## TOWARD THE SOUTH STREET SEAPORT

**TITANIC MEMORIAL LIGHTHOUSE.** FULTON ST., between PEARL and WATER STS. This monument, erected in memory of those who went down with the *Titanic*, once sat on top of the Seamen's Church Institute Building (on State Street). The *Titanic* Memorial Lighthouse was moved to this site in 1976 and marks the entrance to South Street Seaport. Its clock is highly original: every day, at noon exactly, a black ball slides down from the top of a post.

**PECK SLIP ★.** PECK SLIP at FRONT ST.
In the 18th century this neighborhood boasted many Federal-style houses belonging to the élite. In 1973 the Con Edison company demolished several blocks to build a sub-station, despite the angry protests of residents. Its wall is decorated with a trompe l'oeil painting by Richard Haas, which depicts the demolished site, the arches of the South Street Viaduct and the Brooklyn Bridge ▲ 186.

**DRAFT RIOTS, JULY 11, 1863**
The protesters converged on City Hall. They also attacked certain newspapers, especially Horace Greeley's *New York Tribune*, which "dared" to print the comment that "a negro is worth as much as an Irishman". They attempted to charge Tribune Tower, but the riot was quelled by the police.

**JOURNALISM AND LITERATURE**
The press, which had been free from the beginning, tended to favor journalistic methods that appealed to a mass market. The Civil War (1861–5) confirmed this trend and, during the 19th century, many writers who published their work in the newspapers gave rise to a type of journalism that appropriated the techniques of literature.

Since 1967
South Street Seaport
Historic District, which
covers seven blocks in Lower
Manhattan and extends along three piers on the
East River, has managed to preserve some of the
last buildings to house shipowners' and merchants'
offices during the golden age of the clipper ships.
Schermerhorn Row, built in 1811 (opposite), was
preserved in this way. The old Fulton Ferry
Hotel, which faces the river,
dates back to the 1860's.
South of the block, the
A. A. Low warehouse
(1850) still stands.

*Lettie G. Howard*

*Pioneer*

*Peking*

*Wavertree*

A fleet of historic ships evokes the hustle and
bustle of this neighborhood during the 19th
century, when the long booms virtually
touched the façades of the buildings – and
when oysters (left) were cheap.

**PIER 15, PIER 16**
Along pier 15 (above right) lies the *Wavertree*, built in England in 1885. In the center is the *Peking* (made in Germany in 1911); to the left of Pier 16 is the *Ambrose* (1907), a bright red lightship serving at the entrance to the Ambrose Channel, excavated in 1899, which enabled New York Harbor to accommodate the giant transatlantic liners of the 20th century.

Behind the poop of the *Peking* are the *Pioneer*, the *Andrew Fletcher*, which offers excursions around the harbor in the summer, and the *Lettie G. Howard*, a fishing schooner of 1893 (moored between the prows of the two square-rigged schooners).

**FULTON FERRY HOTEL**
This establishment's varied clientele included captains of trading vessels, farmers with produce to sell at the local markets, traders and businessmen.

**A. LOW WAREHOUSE**
The warehouse, designed by A. A. Low, a clipper owner and merchant involved in the China trade, now houses an exhibit of maritime artifacts.

SOUTH STREET SEAPORT MUSEUM
BOAT BUILDING SHOP

173

During the 19th century New York was the
scene of several of the greatest technological
advances in shipbuilding made possible by the
industrial revolution. It was in New York in
1807 that Robert Fulton built the first profit-
making steamboat; in 1814 he designed and
launched the first steam battleship.

### SHIPBUILDING IN NEW YORK

During the era of steel shipbuilding, New
York's shipyards, in Brooklyn (above, in 1883)
launched several of the country's great
warships, including the *Maine* (above, left),
whose sinking in Havana harbor in 1898 was
one of the main causes of the Spanish-
American War.

### THE "MONITOR"

Built in 1862 by the Swedish engineer John
Ericsson, the *Monitor* was the first battleship
in the world to have its cannons housed in an
armor-plated turret. It is here shown in
battle with the Confederacy's own ironclad,
the *Virginia*.

The New York shipyards, which are
located in Brooklyn, Staten Island and
on the Jersey shore, still do a lively
business repairing and refitting all types of
ships including the ocean liners, small tugs
and barges that use the harbor.

Seafaring paraphernalia in local shop window (left) and fish signboard (right).

### FULTON FISH MARKET
This original market (for produce) opened in 1821; eventually benefiting from the busy harbor activity, it became the city's wholesale fish market.

### THE FISH MARKET
The flat-roofed Fulton Fish Market is located right on the East River front. The fish are no longer delivered by fishing boats; they arrive at night in refrigerated trucks from all over the country. Fish is for sale from midnight until 9 in the morning.

### NEW YORK CENTRAL NO. 31
The pilothouse on exhibit on pier 13 at the South Street Seaport Museum was taken from a steam tug boat built in 1923.

## OYSTERS And CLAMS

Oysters and clams are two of New York's natural resources and for a long time were a local tradition in the city. Here and there you can still find "oyster bars" ▲ 238, where you can savor the famous Manhattan clam chowder.

South Street Seaport's two oldest restaurants are on Schermerhorn Row: Sloppy Louie's (early 1900's) is opposite on South St., and Sweet's Restaurant (mid-19th century) is in the old Fulton Ferry Hotel.

### SOUTH STREET SEAPORT HISTORIC DISTRICT
Various temporary and permanent photographic exhibitions are mounted in the historic district, which is bounded by Fulton, Front, Beekman and Water sts. The Trans-Lux Seaport Theater (133 Beekman St.) shows films retracing the history of this area.

An exhibition of model ships (above) in the Fish Market.

SOUTH STREET SEAPORT MUSEUM

**The Invention of the Telephone**
AT&T was founded in 1877 to develop Alexander Graham Bell's patented invention of the telephone. One year later, Bell succeeded in talking to someone over a distance of 14 miles, from Boston to Essex, Massachusetts.

The huge cathedral of commerce that is Woolworth Building along with Saint Paul's Chapel, which in 1776 marked the city's northernmost boundary, are both situated to the west of the Civic Center. Another local landmark is the former AT&T Building.

**Former AT&T Building ★.** 195 Broadway (1915–22, arch. William Welles Bosworth). This building conveys a feeling of strength. The huge Doric columns, 40 feet high, with their purity of line, are echoed by those in the lobby (below, left). One element strikes a false note with the classical Greek decoration: the vertical joins of the columns reveal that the stone is merely a covering. Against the lobby's west wall a monument to the glory of communication trumpets the vocation of the building's previous occupant, AT&T: "Service to the Nation in peace and war". The lobby also boasts a statue of *Adonis*. Another sculpture, by E. B. Longman, was erected on the roof of the building. This statue, called *Spirit of Communication*, or more affectionately, *Golden Boy*, was moved in 1984 to the lobby of the new AT&T building at 550 Madison Avenue ▲ *289*, but was removed from there when Sony bought the building in 1993.

## St. Paul's Chapel ★

St. Paul's Chapel, at the intersection of Broadway and Fulton streets, is a part of Trinity parish. Having miraculously escaped unscathed from the many fires that

**Telecommunications**
For more than a century AT&T provided virtually all the telephone services in the United States. In the 1970's, the company, which still owns the *Bell Laboratories* for research and development facilities, was the largest privately owned company in the world. In 1981 AT&T had more than one million employees, a turnover of 60 billion dollars, and over three million shareholders. An AT&T investment was the archetypal "gilt-edged investment" – risk-free. In 1982 the company lost its monopoly.

"A BLACK MOONLESS NIGHT; JIMMMY HERF IS WALKING ALONE UP SOUTH STREET. BEHIND THE WHARFHOUSES SHIPS RAISE SHADOWY SKELETONS AGAINST THE NIGHT."

JOHN DOS PASSOS

evastated most of Lower Manhattan ● *38*, his building is the only monument in the eighborhood predating the War of Independence. Completed in 1766, it is the oldest church in New York. The building, designed by Thomas McBean, was constructed of regular-sized blocks of Manhattan schist. It resembles St. Martin's-in-the-Fields, in London, whose architect, James Gibbs, taught McBean. Entry to St. Paul's used to be through the churchyard on Church Street. Above the present-day entrance, on Broadway, there is a NICHE containing a statue of St. Paul armed with a sword. Just below, in the middle of the porch, there is the tomb and monument of Brigadier General Richard Montgomery, who died in 1775 during the American Revolution at the battle of Quebec. The interior, painted in pastel colors, is graced by a barrel vaulted ceiling and an exquisite organ loft. The church service following George Washington's inauguration as President, on April 30, 1789, was held here. His PEW, as well as that of New York State's first governor, George Clinton, can still be seen. Free concerts are given in the chapel twice a week at noon. Its churchyard is a true haven of peace for employees who come from the Financial District to unwind. Seen from City Hall Park, the church spire forms a marked contrast with the twin towers of the World Trade Center.

### GEORGE WASHINGTON IN ST. PAUL'S CHAPEL
Above George Washington's pew hangs the first oil painting of the Great Seal of the United States, designed in 1789, shortly after the election of the first president. George Washington's regimental flag is displayed at the rear of the nave.

*Saint Paul's Chapel* (center), a painting (1940) by Saul Berman.

### THE CHURCHYARD OF ST. PAUL'S CHAPEL
This churchyard is even more of an oasis than the one at Trinity Church. Its trees – a riot of blossom in spring – its squirrels and its tombstones, most of them dating back to

the 18th century, present a striking contrast with the surrounding neighborhood. It is no longer used as a cemetery.

## WEST OF BROADWAY

**NEW YORK COUNTY LAWYERS' ASSOCIATION.** 14 VESEY ST. (1930, arch. Cass Gilbert). This austere neo-Georgian building ● *82*, constructed of Vermont marble and limestone, was designed by the

**A POLITICAL JOURNAL**
Four allegorical
figures, representing
the spoken word, the
written word, the
printed word and the
newspaper were
carved on the façade
of 20 Vesey Street in
homage to Alexander
Hamilton. Thomas
Jefferson's victory in
the election of 1800
prompted his
opponents to found
the first politically
oriented newspaper in
New York.

Façade of the Federal
Office Building.

**"With an astonishing
sense of harmony,
[the city] crammed all
of them together, the
arched solid masses,
the square towers, the
terraces . . . and the
stepped levels . . ., the
pyramidal ziggurats,
creating an ever-
thickening forest of
spires, obelisks, cones
and turrets."**

Elie Faure,
*Mon Périple*

architect of the Woolworth Building ▲ *180*, the Custom House ▲ *157* and the U.S. Courthouse. It is the headquarters of the New York County Lawyers' Association and has been dubbed "the house of law". The retrospective style of this building, designed for a conservative body concerned with projecting a traditional image, made it conspicuous at a time when architecture in the United States was going through a more bold, forward-looking phase. Its large auditorium (which is open to the public on request) is modeled on the main hall of Philadelphia's Independence Hall.

**FORMER GARRISON BUILDING.** 20 Vesey St. (1906, arch. Robert D. Kohn, sculptor Gutzon Borglum). At one time, this building housed the *New York Evening Post*. In 1801 Alexander Hamilton, who is buried not far from here in Trinity churchyard, founded the newspaper which is now published as the *New York Post*, but was then a mouthpiece for conservative Federalist opinions. Later, another famous writer, William Cullen Bryant, who edited the *Post* from 1829 to 1878, gradually moved it toward a more working-class ethic. The building's façade is structured by limestone piers which rise in unbroken lines to the fine curb roof. The side walls were left plain, as future plans included other buildings on either side. Cross to the opposite side of the street to admire the ornamental Art Nouveau sculptures on top of the building, allegorical figures representing the "Four Periods of Publicity". They are the joint work of Estelle Rumbald Kohn (the architect's wife) and Gutzon Borglum. The latter also created the famous National Memorial in South Dakota where the gigantic heads of Presidents Washington, Jefferson, Lincoln and Roosevelt are carved into the side of Mount Rushmore.

**FEDERAL OFFICE BUILDING & U.S. POST OFFICE.** 90 Church St. (1935, arch. Cross & Cross, Pennington Lewis & Mills Inc., Lewis A. Simon). There is no doubt that this building, complete with majestic eagles and occupying the entire block, is the property of the federal government, even if the main entrance, rather than being a triumphal focus of attention, is minimized by the sides of the building. The architects of this building combined architectural forms alternating vertical and horizontal lines: the stocky twin towers rise from a setback which sits above a sturdy neo-classical temple, a desperate attempt to marry the characteristic verticality of New York with the horizontality of Washington. Enter the building on Church Street to discover one of the finest post office interiors in the city, with its intricately worked grilles and monumental black Doric columns echoing the ones on the façade. Be sure to make a detour to see the stunning Art Deco stained glass windows and the inlaid work of the floor and ceiling – from which light is diffused through square panels, creating the effect of coffering. The building also boasts a magnificent lobby.

**ST. PETER'S CHURCH.** 22 Barclay St. (1838, arch. John R. Haggerty and Thomas Thomas). This church was built on the site of an earlier St. Peter's Church, erected in 1785, the year after a ban on Roman Catholicism in New York was lifted. This was the parish church of the first Black American saint, Pierre Toussaint, whose ashes now lie in a crypt in St. Patrick's Cathedral on 5th Avenue ▲ *283*.

The eagle that adorns the entrances and façades of many New York buildings became the emblem of the United States on June 20, 1782, when, after six years of deliberation, Congress adopted the bald eagle, an American species with a dark body and white head and tail, as the central figure of the republic's Great Seal. A symbol of power and independence, suitable for the new nation's self-image, the eagle quickly became a very popular motif. From the War of Independence to the Civil War, scarcely any kind of everyday object escaped eventually being decorated with an eagle. Initially it was portrayed with a long neck and rather frog-like feet, following the style of English heraldry, but around the beginning of the 19th century, it began to reflect the influence of neo-classicism, inspired by ancient Greece and Rome. In the 20th century it has undergone another transformation, its characteristics being severely stylized (left) in the Art Deco style.

179

**A RECORD TO BEAT**
With its 60 stories and a height of 792 feet, this was the world's tallest building – 92 feet taller than the Metropolitan Life Tower. It was relegated to third place by the Chrysler Building ▲ *266* and 40 Wall St. in 1929.

In 1909 Frank Woolworth, the "king" of two hundred five-and-ten-cent stores, embarked on the creation of a headquarters for the company which had made him a household name. He bought a plot of land on Broadway. Cass Gilbert, the epitome of the eclectic architect, urged his client to build the tallest building in the world. The foundations of this "cathedral of commerce" were laid in August 1911 and work proceeded at the rate of one and a half stories a week. Woolworth paid for his skyscraper in cash: $15.5 million.

**SIGNED IN STONE**
Traces of the sort of humor sometimes found in cathedrals can be seen in the building's sculptures: one of the consoles (left) depicts Frank Woolworth counting the nickels and dimes that made his fortune.

**THE "EIGHTH WONDER OF THE WORLD"**
Official opening of the building took place in April 1913 with a gala for 800 people, during which President Woodrow Wilson switched on the building's lights from the White House.

**A COPPER PINNACLE ON TOP OF A "TERRACOTTA" CATHEDRAL**
Influenced by his travels in Europe, Woolworth insisted that his architect employ a Gothic style ● 86, reminiscent of French cathedrals and of London's Houses of Parliament.

*Labor*

**THE LOBBY**
The lobby, with entrances on Broadway, Barclay St. and Park Place, is a vast shopping arcade in the shape of a Latin cross. The walls are sheathed in marble and the vaulted ceilings in mosaics of Byzantine inspiration (above), which extol the virtues of labor and commerce. The Woolworth Building was one of the first buildings to provide direct access to the subway.

Most of the buildings of the Civic Center can be found to the north of the City Hall. They represent a host of architectural styles, their construction having spanned more than a century. Some of them were built in neo-classical styles inspired by Greco-Roman democratic tradition, frequently favored in the United States for government buildings. Architects and their clients, however, who were keen to build higher, often used neo-classical temples as bases on which to erect loftier structures. As the 20th century progressed, New York, whose architecture had been influenced previously by London, then Paris, began to create its own distinctive identity.

At the beginning of the 19th century, a new wave of immigrants in search of cheap accommodation settled on the intersection of Baxter, Park and Worth streets. This small triangular park, which was the setting for all kinds of entertainment, soon came to be called "Paradise Park". During the 1820's, the neighborhood began to deteriorate, becoming the haunt of gangsters and prostitutes. In 1845 the Five Points Mission (above) was set up.

❝Was there such a thing as an American style? Yes, if you saw it as an incredible juxtaposition of every architectural form imaginable. In one hundred metres, you could savour Renaissance-style columns with drums; Doric shafts; Corinthian capitals with peculiarly intricate designs, and even the odd allusion to the Egyptian Litiform Order. As for the buildings themselves, they fluctuate from gable to dome, from crenel to terrace roof, with relentless variety.❞
Victor Segalen,
*Journal des Îles*

The Municipal Building (right).

## FOLEY SQUARE

This square occupies the site of what was once COLLECT POND ● *74*, which had disappeared by 1811. Before Independence, a gallows stood on the island in the center. In 1854 the FIVE POINTS MISSION was founded in this section of New York to help the poor in the nearby slums of Five Points ● *191*, who were being decimated by cholera. Thomas Foley (1852–1923), whose name was given to the square in 1926, had run a bar in the neighborhood before going into politics: he became alderman and sheriff of the County of New York and played a key role in getting Al Smith elected governor. Foley used to say that he enjoyed being involved in political intrigue for its own sake. He attributed his success to the fact that he always told the truth, adding: "People don't like it, but they come back six months later."

**MUNICIPAL BUILDING ★.** 1 CENTRE ST. AT 4 CHAMBERS ST. (1914, arch. McKim, Mead & White) ● *96*. When the Bronx, Queens, Brooklyn and Staten Island were linked to Manhattan in 1898 to create Greater New York, it was decided that new administrative offices were needed. This building, which looks like a square-shouldered giant guarding City Hall, made such an impression on Stalin that the University of Moscow was later modeled on it. The architects, who were searching for a style of administrative architecture that best symbolized America and the 20th century, were influenced by the "City Beautiful" movement which sprang up after the 1893 World's Columbian Exposition in Chicago and which focused on the creation of grand public buildings in elegantly landscaped parks. Their building consists of a fourteen-story u-shaped block crowned with a "Renaissance palace" rising from a monumental base with a neo-classical colonnade. The building is topped with three tiered drums, the bottom of which is flanked by four pinnacle turrets symbolizing the four boroughs joined to Manhattan. On the top stands a statue, *Civic Fame*, by Adolph A. Weinman. The building straddles Chambers Street with a central arch, through which vehicles crossing the Brooklyn Bridge ▲ *186* could formerly pass; thus the building became known as the "Gate of the City". A pedestrian walkway, over the bridge, starts here and is well worth following, as it affords an extraordinary view over Manhattan and leads to Brooklyn Heights ▲ *366*.

**U.S. COURTHOUSE ★.** 40 CENTRE ST. AT S. E. CORNER OF PEARL ST. (1936, arch. Cass Gilbert and Cass Gilbert, Jr) This was the last of Cass Gilbert's New York buildings. Here neo-classicism seems to be played out: a marble platform supports a CLASSICAL TEMPLE, pierced by a modern twenty-four-story tower with a gold top. During the week, one can attend hearings in the various courtrooms. The basement houses a SHOOTING GALLERY for F.B.I. agents.

**NEW YORK COUNTY COURTHOUSE.** 60 CENTRE ST. (1913–27, arch. Guy Lowell). The New York County Courthouse is an imposing Corinthian temple approached by a monumental staircase. At the center this hexagon-shaped building is a domed circular area, which is linked to each of the six wings by corridors. Thirty years later, this layout was adapted by the architects of the Pentagon. This central area is decorated with fine murals and a polychrome marble floor inlaid with brass medallions representing the signs of the zodiac. Outside, statues entitled *Law, Truth and Equity* stand on the pediment of the main entrance.

**CRIMINAL COURTS BUILDING, FORMERLY THE DETENTION CENTER FOR MEN.** 100 CENTRE ST. BETWEEN WORTH AND LEONARD STS. (1939, arch. Harvey Wiley Corbett and Charles B. Meyers). This building houses the City of New York's Courthouse and, formerly, a men's prison. It is the third municipal prison: the esplanade opposite stands on the site of the two previous buildings. The first, dating from 1838, was built in the Egyptian Revival style, which gave the building its nickname of "The Tombs", a nickname also applied to its two successors. One of the most famous anecdotes relating to the original prison concerns John Colt. This man, sentenced to be hanged in 1842, was allowed to marry and enjoy an hour-long honeymoon. At the end of the allotted hour he was found dead, stabbed through the heart with a knife. A second,

"In New York, everyone is afraid of the burly Irish cop: he only has to blow on his whistle to commandeer vehicles or to obtain help from everyone. Like ambulances and fire engines, the police have right of way on the road and priority use of the telegraph system and the telephone. This peace force whose job is to send people to Sing-Sing", as described by Paul Morand in *New York*, was divided into different specialist squads concentrating on areas such as robbery or bootlegging.

**THE "TOMBS"**
In *Ragtime*, a novel based on real characters which takes place in New York at the turn of the century, the writer E. L. Doctorow tells the story of a multi millionaire in a cell in The "Tombs". Above, the first, Egyptian-style prison.

Bas-reliefs from the Paine St. façade of the N.Y.C. Department of Health.

**THE FIREHOUSES**
When horses were first used to pull fire engines, they were kept in stables on the ground floor of firehouses (above, Engine Company no. 31). The men, who slept on the second floor, above, protested violently, so it was decided to move the stables to the back of the building. However, the firemen soon changed their mind about this because by the time they had harnessed up the horses to the vehicles, the fire had, in many cases, destroyed everything. Many horses who had spent their early working lives with the fire department found it very hard to adjust to a more tranquil life as carriage horses: whenever they heard a fire engine's siren, they would gallop off, putting their new owner in grave danger.

French Renaissance-style prison was built on the ruins of the first which was demolished in 1893. This in turn was destroyed in 1947. The present building, in Art Deco style, no longer contains a prison (moved to Rikers Island in 1974), but its court attracts visitors who attend trials held here.

**DEPARTMENTS OF HEALTH, HOSPITAL AND SANITATION.** 125 WORTH ST. (1935, arch. Charles B. Meyers). This Art Deco ● 98 temple was built to celebrate the victory of medicine over cholera, smallpox and tuberculosis. Previously, the department had occupied run down premises, inadequate for the task of trying to control the health and hygiene of 6 million inhabitants. Note the bas-reliefs depicting the medical sciences (above) and the splendid torchères (below, right) that grace the south and east entrances.

**ENGINE COMPANY No. 31.** 87 LAFAYETTE ST. AT N. E. CORNER OF WHITE ST. (1895, arch. Napoleon Le Brun & Sons). The architect, who specialized in building firehouses, designed this building like a Loire Valley chateau, a style then very popular for the houses of the rich. Firemen used to live virtually full-time in the firehouse. This building, which is no longer used for its original purpose, is now a designated landmark.

**JACOB K. JAVITS FEDERAL BUILDING AND CUSTOMS COURTHOUSE.** 26 FEDERAL PLAZA (1967, arch. Alfred Easton Poor, Kahn & Jacobs, Eggers & Higgins). This International Style ● 100 building is clad in a facing whose motifs are designed to disguise its massive frame. Every day long lines of hopeful citizenship candidates stretch back from the checkpoint.

**CITY OF NEW YORK OFFICE BUILDING, former EMIGRANT INDUSTRIAL SAVINGS BANK.** 51 CHAMBERS ST. (1912, arch. Raymond F. Almirall). This precursor of the Municipal Building is a mixture of styles: its Renaissance Revival twin towers with Art Deco tops stand on a neo-classical base. It was once the headquarters of the Emigrant Savings Bank, founded in 1851 by the Irish to help their fellow countrymen who were living in the slums of Five Points ▲ 191. In time it became one of the most powerful banks in the country. Enter through the west door to admire the gilded elevator cages.

**"TWEED COURTHOUSE", OLD NEW YORK COUNTY COURTHOUSE.** 52 CHAMBERS ST. (1858–78, arch. John Kellum, Leopold Eidlitz). The former New York County courthouse stands as a monument to the heights of corruption reached by William Marcy, TAMMANY HALL'S "Boss" Tweed ● *40*. Until his arrest in 1871, Boss Tweed pocketed huge amounts of city funds. A total of $14 million was eventually spent on the construction of this building, which was completed twenty years later and whose original cost had been estimated at $250,000. The municipal government then paid for an order – which was never delivered – of enough carpeting to cover City Hall Park three times over. The campaign led by George Jones, editor of *The New York Times*, and Thomas Nast, the cartoonist, finally led to Tweed's downfall. He was tried and sentenced, and died behind bars in 1878. The building, which was completed without the dome or

marble facing originally planned, has a CENTRAL ROTUNDA (above).

**HALL OF RECORDS, SURROGATE'S COURT** ★. 31 CHAMBERS ST. AT N. W. CORNER OF CENTRE ST. (1899–1911, arch. John R. Thomas, Horgan & Slattery). This impressive building, which serves both as surrogate's court and a home for the city archives, was intended to be the Municipal Building, but was deemed too small for this purpose. Work on the building was stopped, only to be restarted to build the Hall of Records. The architect used the popular Beaux Arts style ● *92* to reproduce the affluence of the Paris Opera House.

Detail from the façade of the Emigrant Savings Bank.

**TWEED COURTHOUSE**
The scandal surrounding the construction of the old New York Courthouse (below left) clearly demonstrates the type of methods that "Boss" Tweed stooped to as early as 1852 when he was an alderman. He would inflate costs on orders issued by the municipal government and pocket the difference. No one ever knew just how much Tweed and his ring embezzled.

**UNDER THE HALL OF RECORDS**
This building occupies, in part, the site of an old cemetery for Blacks; recently discovered, it was designated a landmark. Several hundred bodies have been exhumed, some of them still wearing 18th-century British uniforms; the British offered freedom to slaves who fought on their side in the War of Independence.

The neo-Baroque rotunda (left) of the Hall of Records and Surrogate's Court, designed by John R. Thomas.

185

**FERRYBOATS REPLACED BY A BRIDGE**
In the mid-19th century, 50 million people a
year crossed the East River on the slow,
overcrowded ferryboats.

Manhattan, cut off from the mainland by a wide estuary and a
great river, the Hudson, needed bridges if it was to grow; but it
took many years before engineers
were able to construct bridges of
the required length. The oldest is
the Brooklyn Bridge, completed
in 1883.

**A COSMOPOLITAN BUILDING SITE**
The work force employed was a mixture of
old American stock and newly arrived
immigrants from Ireland, Germany and Italy.

TRY OUR CABLE SCREW WIRE BOOTS & SHOES

### A STEEL AND GRANITE MONSTER
This was the longest, highest bridge of the 19th century, with its two granite towers and steel cables and its metal roadway with a span of 1,595 feet, towering 148 feet above the water.

"A work whose towers will mark the entrance to the New World and whose roadway will point westwards, like Americans off to conquer the continent. . . ."    John Roebling

### GIANT CABLES
In 1867 the State of New York authorized the construction of the suspension bridge in line with plans drawn up by John Roebling (1806–69), who arrived from Germany in 1831.

k 14 years to build and 16 million, exceeding expectations.

### A FAMILY OF ENGINEERS
Due to an accident at work, Roebling developed tetanus and died in 1869. His son Washington took over but was

The Manhattan skyline seen from Brooklyn.

disabled by "caisson disease"; Washington's wife, Emily, then became a liaison between Washington and the crew.

The New Harlem Bridge over the Harlem River (here in 1868) linked Harlem and the Bronx.

**STATISTICS OF SOME NEW YORK BRIDGES**
(1) Brooklyn: span 1,595 feet
(2) Manhattan: span 1,470 feet
(3) Williamsburg: span 1,597 feet
(4) Queensboro: max. span 1,182 feet
(5) Verrazano: span 4,260 feet
(6) George Washington: span 3,500 feet

# THE BRIDGES OF MANHATTAN

For twenty years the Brooklyn Bridge remained the only link (apart from ferries) between Manhattan and Long Island, which – along with its beauty and virtuoso engineering – accounted for its popularity. Then, in the first decade of the 20th century, to satisfy the demands of a growing city, three other bridges were built over the East River.

**ACROSS THE EAST RIVER.** These were the Williamsburg Bridge in 1903, followed by the Queensboro bridge (commonly called the 59th Street Bridge) in 1909, and the Manhattan Bridge, in

1912. At the same time, the railroad and subway companies began to dig tunnels under the East River. In the 1930's, despite the Depression, a fifth bridge was built: the Triborough Bridge, a three-pronged bridge connecting the Bronx and Queens to Manhattan.

**ACROSS THE HUDSON.** The George Washington Bridge, designed by Othmar Ammann and completed in 1931, remains the city's only bridge over the Hudson River. It is a suspension bridge, linking Manhattan, at 178th Street, to Fort Lee in New Jersey. Its span is over 3,500 feet – twice as long as that of the Brooklyn Bridge. This was the first major project to be completed by the Port of New York Authority, an interstate body created in 1921 to coordinate transportation in the metropolitan region. Although originally conceived as a railroad bridge, it was finally designed for automobile traffic; a lower level was added in 1962.

**ACROSS THE NARROWS.** At one time the longest suspension bridge in the world, the Verrazano-

Narrows Bridge (1964) spans the strait dividing Brooklyn from Staten Island at the mouth of the Upper Bay. This bridge, also designed by Ammann, has a span of 4,260 feet and a total length of 13,700 feet. In addition to its practical value in easing traffic congestion in Manhattan by providing a direct route from New Jersey to Long Island and its airports, the bridge serves as a spectacular gateway to the city.

**ANNUAL TRAFFIC**
Number of people crossing the bridges each year:
(1) Brooklyn
(2) Manhattan
(3) Williamsburg
(4) Queensboro

(1) 178,000
(2) 360,000
(3) 240,000
(4) 248,000

**WILLIAMSBURG BRIDGE**
The Brooklyn Bridge (1883), then the Williamsburg Bridge (1903), shown (right) at the beginning of the century, made it much easier for New Yorkers who lived in Brooklyn to travel daily to their offices in Manhattan.

# LOWER EAST SIDE

*SETH KAMIL*

▲ LOWER EAST SIDE

1 COLUMBUS PARK  2 TRANSFIGURATION CATHOLIC CHURCH  3 QUONG YEUN SHING & CO.  4 KAOSHEN CLUB  5 ASSN. SUN WEI  6 HIP SING TONG  7 CHATHAM SQUARE  8 SHEARITH ISRAEL GRAVEYARD  9 ST. JAMES CHURCH  10 MARINERS' TEMPLE BAPTIST CHURCH

The Lower East Side is one of Manhattan's liveliest, most historical neighborhoods. From the city's very beginnings this has been an immigrant neighborhood. An astonishing variety of ethnic groups have chosen to live here: Dutch, Irish, Black, Jewish, Italian, Chinese, German and Latin American, to mention only a few. Each of these groups has tried to form a self-sufficient community, creating its own social organizations as a bulwark against the demands of city life. These mutual aid institutions have played a vital role in finding work and accommodation for new immigrants and introducing them to the ways of the "New World". Religious and ethnic subgroups were formed within each community, so that there were organizations not simply for Jews, but for Russian Jews, Romanian Jews and Hungarian Jews, for example. Similarly Italian immigrants settled on the Lower East Side not as Italians but as Neapolitans, Sicilians and Milanese. This continual influx of immigrants also imported its share of marvelous national recipes – some of the best and cheapest restaurants in New York can be found on the Lower East Side.

**"THE BIG ONION"**
During the 1870's, the Lower East Side was called "The Big Onion". Although at the time this was a pejorative term, it has now acquired a new significance. In a sense, this neighborhood does resemble an onion: every time a layer is peeled away, there is another underneath, each representing a part of the neighborhood or another ethnic group.

## CHINATOWN

**COLUMBUS PARK.** BAYARD AND MULBERRY (1892) was originally a patch of cultivated land belonging to the Bayard family, at the corner of Bayard Street and Mulberry Street. In the 19th century, the curved part of Mulberry Street was known as Mulberry Bend. This street led to Five Points, deep in the heart of the Sixth District, called by many

**1970, THE CHANGING FACE OF A NEIGHBORHOOD**
Above the modern sign for "New Jeannie's Restaurant", at 32 Mulberry St., there is still an old wooden sign for the establishment in its former Italian incarnation: "Moneta's". This exemplifies how the ethnic make-up of Mulberry St. has changed. Until the 1970's, this sector was exclusively Italian (right, at the beginning of the century) but it has now become almost exclusively Chinese: the restaurant is now identified in Chinese as well as English.

**11** KHAL ADATH JERUSHUN
SYNAGOGUE

**12** JARMULOWSKY BANK

**13** GARDEN CAFETERIA

**14** FORWARD BLDG.

**15** SEWARD PARK

**16** BETH HAMEDRASH
HAGODOL SYNAGOGUE

**17** BANCA STABILE

**18** 240 CENTRE STREET

**20** OLD ST. PATRICK'S
CATHEDRAL

**Four hours**

people the "Bloody old Sixth". This was the worst slum area
in the history of New York. Until the mid-19th century, it was
predominantly Irish; then Italians flocked here in search of
cheap accommodation, cramming themselves into tiny
apartments and living on top of each other, sometimes twelve
or more to a room. In 1892 the slums of Five Points were
demolished and replaced by Columbus Park. Almost as soon
as it was built the park became a favorite site for open-air
concerts and patriotic ceremonies. On Columbus Day and
other public holidays, local musicians would gather in the
park to play Italian melodies; street peddlers sold
refreshments and the festive mood was heightened by
fireworks displays.

**CHURCH OF THE TRANSFIGURATION.** 25 MOTT ST. This
Georgian-style church, built in 1801 by the community of the
First Episcopal Church of Zion, has seen some extraordinary

**CHINATOWN HISTORY
MUSEUM**
The Chinatown
History Museum
occupies one floor of
the public school on
the corner of Bayard
and Mulberry sts. It
contains a collection
of documents and
personal letters
written by the local
inhabitants.

191

changes. In 1853, the Catholic Church bought the building for its thriving Italian and Irish communities. Then, in the 1950's, an increasing number of Chinese joined the parish, which is now almost exclusively Chinese. Under the times of services posted at the entrance to the church, there is a notice explaining that Mass is celebrated in Mandarin, Cantonese and English.

**QUONG YEUN SHING & CO.** 32 MOTT ST. This store is opposite the Church of the Transfiguration. It was founded in 1877 by the Lee family three generations ago and is the oldest store in Chinatown. This establishment started life as a grocery store, which doubled variously as a post office, a social center, a message service and a bank. It still has its original interior and façade and is a remnant of old Chinatown.

**KAOSHEN CLUB.** 12 MOTT ST. The headquarters of a secret political organization used to be based in this building (Kaoshen means "high mountain"). In 1895, Doctor Sun Yat-sen (founder and first president of the Republic of China) set

## GREETINGS FROM

up the New York branch of the secret revolutionary party Hsing Chung Hui in this building. This party brought about the demise of the Ch'ing imperial dynasty and established a republican government in China.

**SUN WEI ASSOCIATION.** 24 PELL ST. The exterior of this building offers an interesting example of Chinese symbolism. It is topped with an intricately carved wood pagoda, decorated with two carved fish representing financial profit. The association's colors are red, gold and green. Red symbolizes luck, gold symbolizes wealth and green symbolizes success in business.

**HIP SING TONG.** 16 PELL ST. This was one of the fraternal Chinese organizations, whose name, "tong", originally meant "hall" or "meeting place". Membership of these societies is shrouded in mystery and their money-making "activities" are

**THE STREETS OF CHINATOWN**
In the 19th century Doyers St. and Pell St. (above, in 1927) were dotted with Irish bars. A Chinese restaurant, Pell's Dinty (at 25 Pell St.) retains the name of the previous establishment. The Chinatown post office now occupies the site where one of the most popular bars of the time, Callahan's, used to stand. These bars used to employ scantily dressed waitresses and singers to draw in customers. Al Jolson and Irving Berlin were two very popular Jewish performers who used to work in Callahan's.

frequently the subject of controversy. The tongs were secret fraternal societies created in China several hundred years ago and known then as "Triads". They were established in New York at the end of the 1870's to protect their members' interests. Over the years some tongs became involved in criminal activities including drug trafficking, embezzlement, prostitution, gambling and usury. However, today most tongs remain social organizations, helping new immigrants to find accommodation and employment

**CHATHAM SQUARE.** CORNER PARK ROW, BOWERY and EAST BROADWAY. This part of the city, which has been a prosperous center for trade since 1800, owes its name to the first Earl of Chatham, William Pitt the Elder. Lord & Taylor and Brooks Brothers opened their first clothing stores here. The arch in the center of the square was erected in 1962 as a memorial to Benjamin Ralph Kim Lau, a resident of Chinatown who died during World War Two, and to all the other Chinese soldiers who served under the American flag during the war. It is also sometimes called Kim Lau Square.

**FIRST SHEARITH ISRAEL GRAVEYARD.** 55 ST. JAMES PLACE. Half a block from Chatham Square, the first graveyard of the Spanish and Portuguese synagogue Shearith Israel, runs the length of St. James Place. This site, designated a "National Historic Landmark" and a "New York City Landmark" dates back to 1682. It is the oldest Jewish cemetery in the United States and one of the oldest cemeteries in New York.

**ST. JAMES CHURCH.** 132 JAMES ST. (1837). Although the parish was created in 1827 by Irish immigrants, St. James Church, now designated a "New York City Landmark", was not built until 1837. As can be seen from the plaque to the right of the entrance, its first pastor was Father Felix Valera (1788–1853), who was born in Cuba. To the left of the entrance, another plaque commemorates the formation, in 1836, of the Ancient Order of Hibernians, Hibernia being the Latin name for Ireland. The A.O.H. helped Irish immigrants to find work and gave them legal and occasional financial aid, as required.

**MARINERS' TEMPLE.** 12 OLIVER ST. (1842, arch. Minard Lafever). This Ionic-order, Greek Revival church was built by a Baptist congregation to serve the spiritual needs

**DOYERS STREET**
At the end of the 18th century this street served as a cart lane for a distiller, Anthony H. Doyer. A hundred years later, the bend half way down Doyers St. was nicknamed "Bloody Angle" during a "tong war" which raged in Chinatown at the time. The Hip Sing and the On Leong used to battle here for control of local criminal activities.

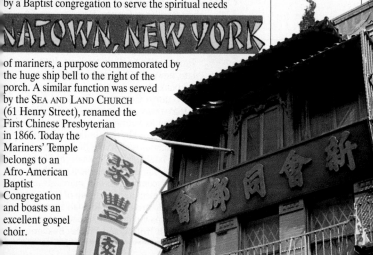

NATOWN, NEW YORK

of mariners, a purpose commemorated by the huge ship bell to the right of the porch. A similar function was served by the SEA AND LAND CHURCH (61 Henry Street), renamed the First Chinese Presbyterian in 1866. Today the Mariners' Temple belongs to an Afro-American Baptist Congregation and boasts an excellent gospel choir.

**BROAD AVENUES**
At the end of the 19th century, the Bowery (right), which in the 17th century led to Dutch farmland, was populated by the homeless, and the neighborhood also had a high concentration of bars dealing in all kinds of illegal activities. In 1884, 27 percent of arrests in New York were made in the Bowery. That year, the neighborhood numbered 82 bars, an average of six per block.

**THE EDUCATIONAL ALLIANCE**
The Educational Alliance, on the southeast corner of East Broadway and Jefferson St., was founded in 1891 by German Jews from Uptown to help Eastern European immigrants adjust to the American way of life. It offered lessons in English, civics and health education.

## THE JEWISH NEIGHBORHOOD

**KHAL ADATH JERUSHUN AND ANSHEI LUBZ SYNAGOGUE.** 12–16 ELDRIDGE ST. (1886, arch. Herter Brothers) This Moorish-style building was built by Russian-Polish Jews. The building's religious identity is not that clear from its façade, which sports a rose window similar to those found on some churches, but the interior is that of a fine Orthodox synagogue, with women's galleries and an ark for holding the Torah scrolls. The building is currently being restored under the auspices of the Eldridge Street Synagogue Project. It is open to the public on Sundays and on request.

**JARMULOWSKY BANK.** Southwest corner of CANAL and ORCHARD STS. (1912). This eleven-story building was built by Sender Jarmulowsky, a Polish Jew who arrived in America in 1856 and opened his bank in 1873. His customers were mainly immigrant Jews who were sending money back to the Old World to help their families to cross the Atlantic. By 1913 the bank was doing well, a state of affairs that continued until the outbreak of World War One, when a large number of the bank's Jewish customers withdrew their money to send it immediately to their families in Europe. Because they did not trust paper money, they demanded gold and silver coins. There was such a rush on the counters that the federal controller shut the Jarmulowsky bank on August 4, 1914 – too late, however, to save its founder from bankruptcy.

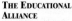

**GARDEN CAFETERIA.** Corner of EAST BROADWAY and RUTGERS ST. The Wing Shoon Restaurant stands on the site once occupied by the Garden Cafeteria, a famous rendezvous of the local intelligentsia. Some of the United States' most eminent socialists, communists and anarchists used to meet here for a cup of tea. Among them were the Russian anarchists Emma Goldman, Alexander Berkman, Leon Trotsky, and Nikolay Bukharin.

> "NOT TO HAVE SEEN THOSE HUCKSTERS AND THEIR CARTS, AND THEIR MERCHANDISE, AND THEIR EXTRAORDINARY ZEST FOR BARGAINING IS TO HAVE MISSED A SIGHT THAT ONCE SEEN DECLINES TO BE FORGOTTEN."
>
> *HARPER'S WEEKLY*

**GUSS'S PICKLES**
Essex St. is the heart of the old Jewish business district. The famous Guss's Pickles can be found at no. 35. On Sundays New Yorkers come to buy his famous gherkins at 25 cents apiece, a good deal more than the 5 cents they once used to cost.

Isaac Bashevis Singer is said to have written many of his books at the Garden Cafeteria.

**FORWARD BUILDING.** 175 EAST BROADWAY (1912, arch. George A. Boehm). The former Forward Building stands southeast of Nathan Straus Square. The Jewish community still regards this apartment building, with its huge clock and the Yiddish word "Forvets" carved into the stone at the top, as a symbol of the power of socialism and the workers. Until 1975 it was the headquarters of the Jewish *Daily Forward*, once one of the major socialist Yiddish publications in the world. The building now houses a church and a Bible-making works, the New York Ling Liang Church. On the west façade of the building a Mandarin slogan that translates, "Through Christ you will find salvation" points up the changes that have taken place in the neighborhood's ethnic make-up.

**SEWARD PARK.** Corner of EAST BROADWAY and ESSEX ST. This park, which dates from 1901, was designed to provide an open space in New York's most densely populated neighborhood. One of the memorable moments in the history of Seward Park occurred during the Cloakmakers' Strike in 1910. About sixty thousand striking workers from many different trades thronged the corner of East Broadway and Essex, opposite the Forward Building. This was also where immigrant workers used to congregate with their signs in Yiddish, Italian and English, calling for better pay and work conditions.

**BETH HAMEDRASH HAGODOL SYNAGOGUE.** 60 NORFOLK ST. This is the synagogue of the oldest Orthodox Ashkenazic community in the United States. It was founded in 1852 and used to be situated on Allen Street. The Ashkenazic community bought the building, originally the Norfolk Baptist Church, in 1885. The synagogue, open to the public during daily prayers, has retained the fine Gothic interior of the original Baptist church.

**AT THE MARKET**
Around 1910 hundreds of thousands of Jews lived in this neighborhood, many working as street vendors. Hester St. was the busiest, liveliest part of the Lower East Side, especially on Thursday evenings, when women came to buy provisions for the Sabbath.

195

Washday on Monday, c. 1900, in the tenements of Little Italy.

## LITTLE ITALY

**BANCA STABILE.** 189 GRAND ST. Corner of S.W. MULBERRY and GRAND STS. (1885). This building used to house an Italian bank, a family business founded in 1865 to help immigrant Italians. The Stabile offered various other services in addition to banking, including translation and steamship reservations. This can be seen from the gilt lettering above one of the counters, where tickets for transatlantic crossings could be bought. Note the tin ceilings, the terrazzo floor, the huge vault and the original brass grilles.

**240 CENTRE STREET.** (1909, arch. Hoppin, Koen & Huntington) This huge stone building in French-Baroque style was originally built for the New York police headquarters. At the time, this neighborhood was a hive of criminal activity. The headquarters were deliberately situated near the city's main prison, called "The Tombs" ▲ *183*, itself not far from the insalubrious "Five Points" area ▲ *191*. The building was converted into condominiums in the late 1980's.

**MOST HOLY CRUCIFIX CHURCH.** 378 BROOME ST. This Neapolitan Catholic church was consecrated in 1926. At that time, so the story goes, a group of Neapolitans had established a community in the neighborhood. When they wrote home, they told their families that they worshipped together, so their wives decided to dispatch a priest to New York from the village of their birth. The only land they could build on within a radius of three blocks was this plot, between Mott and Mulberry streets. The church was built extremely swiftly, so that when he arrived the priest would find a parish in which he could preach and hold services.

**OLD SAINT PATRICK'S CATHEDRAL.** MULBERRY ST. at PRINCE ST. (1809–15, arch. Joseph Mangin). This building was New York's first Catholic cathedral before the construction, Uptown, of the present St. Patrick's on 5th Avenue. A fire in 1868 destroyed much of it, and restoration costs proved so prohibitive that its rose window was walled over and the damaged Gothic decorative elements were covered.

### SICILIANS, MILANESE, NEAPOLITANS

The Italian stretch of Mulberry St. (also known as Via San Gennaro) is still lined with shops selling fresh pasta, freshly baked bread and cheese made on the premises (above, at the turn of the century). The Caffè Roma is on this street. In the 1930's it was a haunt of Italian actors. Migliaccio, a popular performer of Neapolitan folk songs who appeared in theaters in the Bowery under the name of Farfariello (meaning "little butterfly"), lived nearby. His act consisted of making good-humored fun of the people living in the neighborhood.

# AROUND
# WASHINGTON
# SQUARE

# ▲ WASHINGTON SQUARE TO SOHO-TRIBECA

1 WASHINGTON SQUARE  2 N.Y. UNIVERSITY  3 ASCH BLDG.  4 E. HOLMES BOBST LIBRARY  5 JUDSON MEMORIAL CHURCH  6 MILLS HOUSE NO.1  7 MACDOUGAL-SULLIVAN GARDENS  8 MUSEUM FOR AFRICAN ART  9 NEW MUSEUM OF CONTEMPORARY ART  10 GUGGENHEIM MUSEUM  11 LITTLE SINGER BLDG.  12 HAUGHWOUT BLDG.  13 ROOSEVELT BLDG.

✗ Seven hours

## WASHINGTON SQUARE ★

This square has been the artistic and intellectual hub of Greenwich Village ▲ *210* since the turn of the century. Until the end of the 18th century, it was simply a vast tract of marshland with a stream, the MINETTA BROOK ▲ *202*, running through it. It was then converted into a potter's field, for the interment of victims of the great cholera and yellow fever epidemics. In the early 1800's it also served as the site of public hangings – events commemorated by the great elm that stands at the

northwest corner of the park, which was used as a gallows. During his trip to New York in 1824, Lafayette was invited to watch the hanging of twenty highwaymen. In 1826, when the streets were being laid and the surrounding lands were developed for sale as building lots, the municipal government drained the swamp and built the WASHINGTON MILITARY PARADE GROUNDS, which were inaugurated on July 4, 1828. The area around Washington Square soon became popular with wealthy New Yorkers, who built imposing residences around the park. Henry James, who was born in 1843 at 27 Washington Place, not far from the Square, immortalized this neighborhood in his novel *Washington Square*. The WASHINGTON ARCH, which has stood at the north of the park since 1895, perfectly encapsulates the main cultural trend of the time, which has

**A FORMER MILITARY PARADE GROUND**
Washington Square sits on former marshland which was drained and converted into a military parade ground in 1826 (above, in 1851). When it was not an arena for military parades, it was used as a park where various entertainments were staged. This park, which was dearly loved by New Yorkers, gave the neighborhood a new lease on life. When the park was redesigned in 1971, the central island, which sports a fountain and was once used by buses for turning round, was closed to traffic by the municipal government.

Washington Square (right) in the early 1900's.

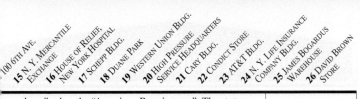

**100 6TH AVE.** **15 N.Y. MERCANTILE EXCHANGE** **16 HOUSE OF RELIEF, NEW YORK HOSPITAL** **17 SCHEPP BLDG.** **18 DUANE PARK** **19 WESTERN UNION BLDG.** **20 HIGH PRESSURE SERVICE HEADQUARTERS** **21 CARY BLDG.** **22 CONDICT STORE** **23 AT&T BLDG.** **24 N.Y. LIFE INSURANCE COMPANY BLDG.** **25 JAMES BOGARDUS WAREHOUSE** **26 DAVID BROWN STORE**

been described as the "American Renaissance". The statues that grace its piers were added later; these are "Washington in War", by Hermon A. MacNeil (1916) and "Washington in Peace", by A. Stirling Calder (1918). The second half of the 19th century brought a fresh influx of European immigrants into Greenwich Village, a neighborhood lying west and south of Washington Square, which became a French and Italian enclave. At that time most of the houses were converted into apartments or replaced by tenements. Many artists chose to live in this part of the city, lured by its beauty and sense of history, while the gentry, who lived north of the square, gradually moved Uptown, deserting the district.

SoHo

GRAND ST.

TriBeCa

VARICK ST.

LEONARD ST.

THOMAS ST.

DUANE ST.

HUDSON ST.

HARRISON ST.

WEST BROADWAY

From the beginning of the 20th century this neighborhood was largely bohemian in atmosphere, attracting those who wanted to mix with avant-garde artists. The writers Eugene O'Neill, Edna St. Vincent Millay and Theodore Dreiser followed in the footsteps of their famous forebears, Edgar Allan Poe, Herman Melville, Mark Twain and Henry James. Painters, including the members of the Ashcan school ▲ 217, set up their studios in some of the old houses. You have only to look upward when crossing certain streets to see the large skylights that crown these buildings. The former speakeasies, theaters, cafés and jazz clubs are still haunted by the memory of the celebrities who used to frequent them.

**WASHINGTON ARCH**
To commemorate the centenary of George Washington's inauguration ● 27, on April 30, 1889, the architect Stanford White was commissioned to create a temporary wooden triumphal arch. It stood at the north of the park at the bottom of 5th Ave. and was garlanded with strings of lights. The arch was such a resounding success that the city arts council asked White to build another, this time in marble, modeled on those in Rome and Paris.

199

**SAMUEL F.B. MORSE (1791–1872)**
Although he is primarily known as the inventor of the electric telegraph and the alphabet of audible signals that bears his name, Morse was also a highly esteemed painter. He was a founder and first president of the

*National Academy of Design*, opened in 1826. Nine years later he became a lecturer in art at N.Y.U., where he also set up a laboratory in its Main Building for his scientific experiments. He patented his telegraph system in 1837.

**JUDSON MEMORIAL CHURCH**
This church, which is dominated by the Romanesque-style campanile, is decorated with Italian Renaissance motifs adorned with terracotta moldings.

## SOUTH VILLAGE

**NEW YORK UNIVERSITY, MAIN BUILDING.** 100 WASHINGTON SQUARE EAST (1894–5, arch. Alfred Zucker). New York University (N.Y.U.), founded in 1831 by ALBERT GALLATIN, a member of Thomas Jefferson's cabinet, is the largest private university in the United States. The MAIN BUILDING, at the center of a campus which is spread throughout the Village, occupies the site of the first university building, completed in 1833. This created a furore, as the administrators, eager to cut costs, had employed convicts from Sing Sing prison – a virtually cost-free work force – on the building. Local construction workers staged a union demonstration, one of the first of its kind organized in New York. When it degenerated into violence, the "Stone Cutter's Guild Riot", as it became known, had to be quelled by the

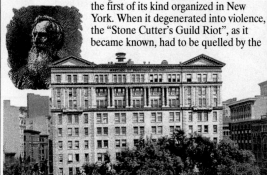

National Guard. This building is also famous for occupants such as SAMUEL F. B. MORSE, the inventor of the telegraph, and SAMUEL COLT, the designer of the famous revolver. All that remains of this building, destroyed in 1894, is a turret on Washington Square East.

**THE BROWN BUILDING, FORMERLY THE ASCH BUILDING.** 29 WASHINGTON PLACE. In 1911 this manufacturing loft, later converted into lecture halls for N.Y.U., was devastated by a fire that claimed 146 victims, all of them young women employed by the TRIANGLE SHIRTWAIST CO., one of the "sweatshops" in the clothing industry ● 38. At the request of the *International Ladies' Garment Workers' Union*, founded in 1900, a plaque was fixed to the building to commemorate this tragedy.

**ELMER HOLMES BOBST LIBRARY.** 70 WASHINGTON SQUARE SOUTH (1972, arch. Philip Johnson and Richard Foster). This library, built for New York University, owes its nickname of "Redskin" to its red sandstone façade. The interior boasts a fine atrium and a checkerboard floor of gray, white and black marble based on one in the church of San Giorgio Maggiore in Venice.

**JUDSON MEMORIAL CHURCH.** 55 WASHINGTON SQUARE SOUTH (1888–93, arch. McKim, Mead & White) ● 90. This church was built in homage to Adinoram Judson, the first American Baptist missionary in Burma, and financed partly by JOHN D. ROCKEFELLER ▲ 276, who devoted some of his fortune to the city's Baptist congregations.

Program cover for an Off-Broadway show in Greenwich Village.

So this is Gay Paree...
Come on along with me
we're stepping out to see
the LATIN QUARTER

**THE "LATIN QUARTER".** In the 1850's, "Frenchtown" was the nickname given to the area south of Washington Square inhabited by a community of French immigrants. However, most of the French families moved out of the neighborhood by 1875 because the many brothels and sleazy dance halls had lowered the tone of the area. Toward the end of the 19th century, a new wave of Italian immigrants settled in the neighborhood. They opened cafés and restaurants next door to the French stores that were still in business and the sector was named the "Latin Quarter". The neighborhood, which was very popular with intellectuals at the beginning of this century, became a magnet for jazz musicians and, later, in the 1950's, for "beat generation poets". In the 1960's Bob Dylan and other folk singers transformed it into a center for folk music. It is still the place to go if you want to catch the up-and-coming stars or linger over an espresso on a Sunday afternoon. Bleecker Street is lined with numerous picturesque bars: the Bitter End, the Peculiar Club, Kenny's Castaways, the Back Fence; as well as the famous Village Gate and the Circle in the Square, one of the best Off-Broadway theaters. On MACDOUGAL STREET you will find the Caffè Dante, the Caffè Reggio, opened in 1927, the Café Borgia and Le Figaro Café.

**PROVINCETOWN PLAYHOUSE.** 133 MACDOUGAL ST. The Provincetown Players, an improvisational theater company, made their debut in New York at no. 139 MacDougal Street before moving into this former stable (below). They were responsible for launching the young playwright Eugene O'Neill, by giving the first performance of his play *Bound East for Cardiff*, in 1916. The writer later received the Pulitzer Prize and became one of America's most celebrated playwrights. The company disbanded in 1930 but the theater was rebuilt around 1940 and is still in use today, keeping the spirit of the legendary company alive.

**SAMUEL COLT (1814–1862)**
In 1831, Colt invented the "six-shooter", a revolver whose main innovation was the revolving breech containing six chambers for cartridges, which allowed the weapon to be automatically recharged after every shot was fired. This technique gave the revolver its name. The colt soon became a favorite with cowboys, and this legendary weapon played its part in winning the West. Colt, who began his career as a wandering comic actor, finished life in the lap of luxury due to this invention, which made him an international celebrity.

**PROVINCETOWN PLAYERS**
This theater company derived its name from Provincetown, in Cape Cod, where the troupe was formed by a group of Villagers on their summer holidays. It was the journalist, John Reed, who persuaded the group to continue to perform on their return to New York.

At the end of the 1850's the engineers James Bogardus and Daniel Badger produced the first sales catalogue of cast-iron architectural decorative pieces ● *84*. The catalogue contained details of ready-made models, with understated ornamentation in the latest styles. It was

possible to buy a façade by the foot.

The clothes market on Spring St. (opposite).

**RICHMOND HILL HOUSE**
In 1831, the manor house on the Richmond Hill estate was converted into a theater (below in 1832). In 1849 it was destroyed to build offices and workshops to meet the needs of

a neighborhood going through a period of intense commercial growth.

**MINETTA STREET.** This street follows the erstwhile course of Minetta Brook, filled in around 1820, and was home to a large population of Blacks in the 18th century, hence its former nickname of "Little Africa". In the mid-19th century, the neighborhood deteriorated, becoming squalid and dangerous because of the brawls that regularly broke out there, especially at the time of the Draft Riots ● *28*. The following decades saw the street gradually fill up with Italian, French and then German immigrants ● *44*. Nearby, at 113 MacDougal Street, is the MINETTA TAVERN, a real "drinkers' museum", its walls covered with caricatures of Village personalities.

**THE ATRIUM, ORIGINALLY MILLS HOUSE No. 1.** 160 BLEECKER ST. (1896, arch. Ernest Flagg). At the end of the 19th century, many tenements were built south of Washington Square. The architect Ernest Flagg, who was interested in this type of housing, designed this Renaissance-style building. It was composed of 1,500 units, arranged around a grassy court. These rooms were mostly for newly arrived immigrants who could spend the night there for the modest sum of 20 cents. Subsequently, the courtyard was paved over, then covered, and the building became a shabby hotel, the Greenwich, before being converted into a private residence complete with ATRIUM in 1976.

**MACDOUGAL-SULLIVAN GARDENS ★.** Designated a "Historic District", this neighborhood consists of twenty-four Greek Revival ● *84* houses built back-to-back on two streets. Its layout served as a model for similar housing plans in New

York in the 1920's. By 1923 the houses were badly run-down. They were bought and renovated by property developer, William Sloane Coffin. He removed the entrance steps, standardized the façades, using a style influenced by colonial architecture, and linked the backyards together to create a private common garden.

**CHARLTON-KING-VANDAM HISTORIC DISTRICT.** Between 6TH AVE. and VARICK ST. This historic enclave, which abuts on an industrial area, is a fine example of New York residential town planning in the last century. It boasts the longest unbroken row of Federal-style ● *82* townhouses in the city, dating from the 1820's, and a number of Greek Revival houses built between 1830 and 1850, the most eye-catching examples of which are nos. 37 and 39 Charlton Street and no. 203 Spring Street. This district occupies the former site of Richmond Hill, an estate of some 25 acres, whose Georgian manor house served as George Washington's headquarters in 1776 ● *27*. The lands were subsequently bought by Aaron

Burr, who laid out the present network of roads in 1797 in order to divide up the estate into building lots. He unfortunately had to sell the estate to JOHN JACOB ASTOR, who completed the task of parceling it out.

## SoHo Cast-Iron Historic District ★

Around 1850, the area now called SoHo (a contraction of "South of Houston Street") was the major industrial and commercial center of New York. This historic district contains the highest concentration of cast-iron structures ● *94* in the United States, presenting an amazingly homogeneous urban landscape. These palaces of commerce were built for grocers, textile merchants and furniture store owners who, above all, needed vast interior spaces and attractive shop fronts. Initially, architects tried to give the cast iron the appearance of stone, by covering it with paint mixed with sand (the HAUGHWOUT BUILDING, of 1857 ▲ *204* is a typical example). Then, in the light of its success, they began to exploit the properties of cast iron, creating new motifs, including the slender colonnettes called "Sperm candles". This craze for the new material brought about a volte-face, and stone began to imitate the appearance of cast iron, as at 502 Broadway. (A foolproof way of telling the difference is to use a magnet.) By the beginning of the 1960's, SoHo had lost its commercial importance and many former warehouses and industrial premises stood empty. Consequently, artists looking for large, bright reasonably priced studios began to move in. A special artists' statute, responding to tenants' requirements, authorized the conversion of these buildings into studios and apartments. SoHo is now a lively neighborhood with many avant-garde galleries, fascinating shops and charming restaurants. Moreover, the presence of three new museums – the Museum for African Art, the New Museum of Contemporary Art and the Guggenheim Museum of SoHo – grouped together along Broadway and called MUSEUM ROW – has enhanced the area's status as a cultural enclave.

**MUSEUM FOR AFRICAN ART.** 593 BROADWAY (1993, interior design Maya Lin). This museum, which moved here in 1993, is one of only three in the United States to

Joe Gould, a resident of MacDougal St. (above, in the 1950's) and of Minetta Tavern claimed to be writing an "oral history of the world" in order to earn money at meal times from the restaurant clientele. After his death in 1957 no manuscript was found, only a series of disconnected conversations.

**CAST IRON**
The bolting process can be seen in the old and new façade of this factory in TriBeCa.

*Bemba Figure*, below, a sculpture exhibited at the Museum for African Art.

**Richard Morris Hunt**
Richard Morris Hunt was the first American architect trained at the École des Beaux Arts and a founder of the American Institute of Architects. He represented a whole generation of architects inspired by the Old World. His work includes the Roosevelt Building (below) as well as mansions for the élite.

specialize in ancient and modern African art, the others being the Maryland Museum of African Art and the Smithsonian's National Museum of African Art in Washington, D.C.

**New Museum of Contemporary Art.** 583 Broadway (1896–7, arch. Cleverdon & Putzel). This museum, which has been at this address since 1983, represents a complete break with tradition, as it exhibits only works less than ten years old, placing the emphasis on artists who have not yet acquired a wide following.

**Guggenheim Museum of SoHo.** 575 Broadway (1881–2, arch. Thomas Stent). This companion to the museum on 5th Avenue ▲ *338* was opened at the end

of 1992 and symbolizes the neighborhood's renaissance. The warehouse, with its red-brick façades and cast-iron window frames was given a completely new image by the architect Arata Isozaki, who created an interior exhibition area of nearly 3,600 square yards, large enough to exhibit part of the collections from the Uptown Guggenheim. The metal signs gracing the museum's façades are replicas of the ones that used to appear on all workshops and warehouses at the height of the district's commercial success.

**Former Little Singer Building ★.** 561–563 Broadway (1904, arch. Ernest Flagg). This L-shaped Art Nouveau building was designed for the famous sewing machine manufacturer. When Flagg designed a larger Singer Tower ▲ *152* in 1908, he called this one the "Little Singer". Flagg's aesthetic sense, developed at the École des Beaux Arts in Paris, can be seen in the building's prefabricated metal frame and interlaced floral motifs.

**Haughwout Building.** 488–492 Broadway at Broome St. (1856–7, arch. John P. Gaynor) ● *94*. When Eder V. Haughwout, a specialist in tableware, commissioned this building, he got one of the very first cast-iron masterpieces, complete with open-cage elevator, installed by Elisha Otis.

**Roosevelt Building.** 478–482 Broadway (1873–4, arch. Richard M. Hunt). This building shows how much could be achieved with cast iron. Three wide bays with colonnettes give the structure a sense of grace and lightness. When it was first built the building boasted superb brightly colored ornamental motifs. The ground floor and the basement, like several of the other buildings in the neighborhood, are occupied by stores – in this case, a fabric store (left).

**GREENE STREET ★.** This street has the most remarkable assortment of cast-iron buildings and its cobblestone paving, recently repaired, is an unusual sight in New York. Between nos. 8 and 34, a collection of cast-iron façades sets up a subtle, regular rhythm of alternating solid and hollow forms, light and shadow, as a counterpoint to the fire escapes. Built between 1872 and 1896, these buildings are the work of Warner, Wright, Duckworth and Snook.

**N.Y. CITY FIRE MUSEUM.** 278 SPRING ST. (1904, arch. Edward P. Casey). This small, fascinating and little-known museum is housed in a neo-classical fire station built just after the turn of the century. It retraces the history of fire fighting in the city, and boasts a superb collection of exhibits, including wooden firemarks dating from the 17th century and old fire engines.

**THE EAR INN, FORMERLY THE JAMES BROWN RESIDENCE.** 326 SPRING ST. (1817). This Federal-style house originally stood on the edge of the Hudson. As port traffic became heavier, the river was filled in as far as West Street, so that more docks could be constructed. The house was then converted into a distillery, then, during Prohibition, a brothel with a speakeasy upstairs. It is now a slightly timeworn, but lively, bar.

**ISAAC MERRITT SINGER**
The American Dream came true for this inventor, who began his career as a humble laborer. While repairing one of the early sewing machines, Singer was struck by the idea for his revolutionary, simplified model. He designed the machine in barely twelve hours, but he then had to borrow $40 to complete his prototype and apply for a patent (1851). He went into partnership with Edward Clark, founded the Singer Manufacturing Company and built up an enormous industrial empire.

**"DAYLIGHT FACTORIES"**
The façade of this Art Deco industrial building (1928) is decorated with bas-reliefs depicting laborers and craftsmen. This is a typical example of what was called a "daylight factory", several of which were built during the 1930's near the Holland Tunnel.

**HOLLAND TUNNEL**
The mouth of the tunnel, which was built in 1927 to link Manhattan with New Jersey, is adjacent to the site of a former railroad depot. Until 1850, this was a stylish residential area around St. John's Park. In 1869 Cornelius Vanderbilt bought the park and built the depot there. The freight trains had to run alongside the Hudson on West St. to reach St. John's Park. The depot was demolished in 1936, two years after a new terminal had been constructed a few blocks south.

The former headquarters of the New York Life Insurance Company boasts one of the last mechanical clocks in New York. It is worth a visit to admire the machinery.

## TRIBECA WEST HISTORIC DISTRICT

TriBeCa – a recent coinage derived from "TRIangle BElow CAnal" – is bounded by CANAL STREET to the north, BROADWAY to the east and the HUDSON RIVER to the west. It falls into two distinct areas; the eastern part, which sports Italianate palaces of commerce with their marble façades, and the western part, with its Romanesque Revival warehouses and factories ● *90*, as well as two influential skyscrapers of the 1920's – the Western Union Building and the New York Telephone Company Building.

**THE HISTORY OF THE NEIGHBORHOOD.** During the English colonial period, the land belonged to Anthony Lispenard and the parish of Trinity Church ▲ *154*, which had been given this grant of land by Queen Anne in 1705. When the lands were later mapped for development and sold off, the streets were given the names of these landowners – Lispenard and his children Leonard, Thomas and Anthony (today Worth Street) – or of key figures in the parish such as Chambers, Murray, Duane, Reade and Watts. Between

850 and 1920 the western part of the present TriBeCa was
he trading center for wholesale fruit and vegetables and dairy
products and supplied Washington Market, which covered
part of the site now occupied by the World Trade Center.
**INDUSTRIAL ARCHITECTURE.** The sector's trading activities
vere given a boost by the new piers and warehouses and by
he extension of rail facilities thanks to the NEW YORK
CENTRAL & HUDSON RIVER RAILROAD
FREIGHT DEPOT, built in 1869 for
Cornelius Vanderbilt ▲ *260*. This
huge freight depot stood on the
site of ST. JOHN'S PARK (a
residential public square with
landscaped garden) and was
demolished in 1936 when the
HOLLAND TUNNEL, linking
Manhattan and New Jersey, was
built. TriBeCa is mainly a
neighborhood for warehouses
● *85*, whose utilitarian function
is still apparent from their
loading ramps, metal canopies
and security gates. The district
boasts a whole range of styles,
from the starkest lines,
represented by the minimalism
of the WAREHOUSE AT 135
HUDSON STREET (1886–7, arch.
Kimball & Ihnen, right), to the
most elaborate, such as the
FLEMING SMITH WAREHOUSE
1891–2, arch. Stephen Decatur
Hatch) in Flemish style, at nos.
451–453 Washington Street. There are still some wholesale
stores around the small triangle of DUANE PARK but the rest
of TriBeCa has become a residential area. Buildings are being
restored and businesses are constantly springing up.
**FORMER NEW YORK MERCANTILE EXCHANGE.** 6 HARRISON ST.
1886, arch. Thomas R. Jackson). In 1872 the dairy farmers
founded the BUTTER AND CHEESE EXCHANGE on Greenwich
Street. Some ten years later, this Queen Anne-style building
was built, and business carried out in the huge hall paved with
polychromatic flags. After the Mercantile Exchange moved to
the World Trade Center in 1977, this building was converted
into apartments; one of New York's finest restaurants, the
Chanterelle, now occupies the ground floor.
**HARRISON STREET ROW.** 25–41 HARRISON ST. (1796–1828).
Most of the houses in this residential neighborhood were
demolished during the second half of the 19th century to
allow Washington Market to expand and to make way for the
development of the docks. In 1975 it was decided to save the
few remaining houses that now form this row. Two of them
(nos. 31 and 33) stood here originally, while the others came
from adjacent Washington Street. At the end of the street,

The New York
Central & Hudson
River Railroad
Freight Depot in
1869.

**WASHINGTON
MARKET**
After the Civil
War and the
development of
steamship traffic, the
narrow straits of the
East River were
abandoned for the
wider stretches of the
Hudson. Docks
gradually sprang up
all along the bank,
and as a result, the
part of southwest
Manhattan now
called TriBeCa
underwent a period
of intense commercial
growth. Products
were unloaded and
taken to Washington
Market (above, in
1888).

The Hudson River alongside West St. in 1921.

Manhattan COMMUNITY COLLEGE's walkway over Harrison Street affords a fine view of the World Trade and World Financial Centers ▲ *138*.

**ORIGINALLY HOUSE OF RELIEF, NEW YORK HOSPITAL.** 67 HUDSON ST. (1893, arch. Cady, Berg & See). This square Renaissance-Revival structure was an annex of New York Hospital, the oldest medical institution in the city, its charter granted by George III in 1771. The old ambulance garage can be reached by a covered walkway that bestrides Staple Street.

**165 DUANE STREET.** (1881, arch. Stephen D. Hatch). This imposing, ten-story Romanesque Revival ● *90* factory used to house the headquarters of Leonard Schepp's company, which imported fine foods and spices. Schepp was responsible for introducing exotic products such as shredded coconut to the United States. The building is now residential; there is a restaurant, Le Bouley, on the ground floor.

The Franklin St. elevated railroad, opened in 1870 (here, in 1878), linked southwest Manhattan to Broadway.

**DUANE PARK.** This triangular park, dating from 1795, is bordered by dairy product wholesalers, who are continuing a neighborhood tradition. Notice the small building whose original cast-iron ▲ *203* structure can be seen in front of the new façade.

**WESTERN UNION BUILDING.** 60 HUDSON ST. (1928–30, arch. Voorhees, Gmelin & Walker). This sheer mountain of brick occupies a whole block. Once the headquarters of the Western Union telegraph company, the building is notable for its bold masses interrupted by recesses and for the complexity of its brick motifs. It shows how strongly American architecture was influenced by Dutch and German Expressionism. The lobby's dramatically illuminated orange brick walls set off a basket arch ceiling faced with "Guastavino" glazed tiles, named after their manufacturer.

**HIGH PRESSURE SERVICE HEADQUARTERS OF THE N.Y. CITY FIRE DEPARTMENT.** 226 WEST BROADWAY (c. 1905, arch. August D. Shepard, Jr). The most striking characteristic of this municipal building, with its neo-classical façade covered in cream glazed terracotta, is the use of utilitarian symbols – fire hydrants, valves and hosepipes – as ornaments.

**2 WHITE STREET HOUSE.** (1808–9). This old wooden house with brick façade, sloping roof and dormer windows is one of the last vestiges of the period when TriBeCa was a residential neighborhood. It was built before wooden structures were banned

El International
Restaurant.

**FORMER CARY
BUILDING**
This building, at
105–107 Chambers
St. (left), built in 1857
by the architects King
& Kellum ● 88, is a
perfect example of a
"first generation"
cast-iron building,
with its two Italianate
façades (which
imitate stone). It was
built for the grocery
store Cary, Howard &
Sanger and remains a
monument to the
commercial
prosperity around
City Hall in the mid-
19th century.

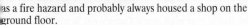

as a fire hazard and probably always housed a shop on the
ground floor.

**AT&T (AMERICAN TELEPHONE & TELEGRAPH COMPANY).**
32 6TH AVE. (1930–2, arch. Ralph Walker). This Art Deco
building originally housed the technical offices for transatlantic communications. In 1984, after the new headquarters
building at 550 Madison Avenue was sold to Sony, the
company moved its head offices into the 6th Avenue building.
The linear quality of the façades and their ornamentation, the
vast tiled map of the world on the wall of the lobby, as well as
the mosaic allegories on the ceiling, endow the building with
an industrial aesthetic in keeping with its function.
**NEW YORK LIFE INSURANCE COMPANY BUILDING "THE
CLOCKTOWER"** ★. 346 BROADWAY (1894–9, arch. Stephen D.
Hatch and McKim, Mead & White). This neo-Renaissance
building now serves as offices for the City of New York. Visit
the CLOCKTOWER which houses an art gallery and stages free
shows under the auspices of the Institute for Art and Urban
Resources. You can enjoy a superb view of the Woolworth
Building ▲ 180, and Foley Square ▲ 182 from its terrace.
**JAMES BOGARDUS WAREHOUSE.** 85 LEONARD ST. (1861). This
cast-iron building was built to house the grocery store
KITCHEN, MONTROSS & WILCOX. It is one of the few
remaining structures designed by the architect James
Bogardus, who did pioneering work with this material.
**DAVID BROWN STORE.** 8 THOMAS ST. (1875–6, arch. J. Morgan
Slade). This building, commissioned by a soap and eau de
toilette manufacturer, is an exceptional example of High
Victorian Gothic as applied to a commercial building ● 86.

This building, at 55
White St., built by
John Kellum & Son
in 1861, sports a cast-
iron version of the
stone "Sperm candle"
façade built by the
same architect for 502
Broadway.

1 JEFFERSON MARKET COURTHOUSE LIBRARY  2 WASHINGTON COURT  3 NORTHERN DISPENSARY  4 CHRISTOPHER PARK  5 SHERIDAN SQUARE  6 GREENWICH HOUSE  7 175–179 W. 4TH ST.

GANSEVOORT MEAT MARKET

GREENWICH VILLAGE

WEST VILLAGE

Five hours

"Céline said New York was a 'standing city'. True; but it seemed to me from the very first a *lengthwise* city. All priorities are given to length. Traffic stands still in the side streets but rolls tirelessly on the avenues. How often do cab drivers, who willingly take passengers north and south, refuse flatly to drive them east and west! The side streets are hardly more than the outlines of the buildings between the avenues. The avenues pierce them, tear them apart, and speed toward the north."

Jean-Paul Sartre,
*Manhattan: the Great American Desert*

## GREENWICH VILLAGE

A "VILLAGE" WITHIN A CITY. With its low buildings and crooked streets, this neighborhood has, visually, something of the character of a small provincial town, deliberately rejecting the grid system typical of most of Manhattan. Nevertheless, its heterogeneous population perfectly accords with New York's cosmopolitan character. Earlier inhabitants of Manhattan, the CANARSIE INDIANS, called this swampy, wooded area *Sapohanikan*. They set up a trading post – dealing in goods between Hoboken and Manhattan – on the shore, near what is now Gansevoort Street. Tobacco farming was very important during the Dutch period (1613–64) and Governor Wouter Van Twiller appropriated 222 acres of "Northwyck" (as the Dutch called this area) for a private plantation. In 1696, Van Twiller's *Bossen Bouwerie* "wooded farm", was renamed Greenwich Village by the English. Over the next century or so, houses in various styles – Georgian, Federal and Greek Revival ● *82, 84* – were built bordering the huge estates. Greenwich became a thriving, prosperous village, whose activity was centered around the shipping industry. In the 1820's, as a result of an influx of New Yorkers from lower Manhattan, fleeing the cholera and yellow fever epidemics, Greenwich experienced rapid urbanization. In 1829 the male population of Newgate Prison, in the heart of the Village, was transferred to Ossining, along the Hudson River. Today Greenwich Village is a multifarious neighborhood offering an overview of three centuries of architecture.

**"BOHEMIA".** In the early 20th century, various social reformers interested in art joined the "Bohemians" living in the Village. These included the anarchist Emma Goldman and the "vagabond poet", Harry Kemp, who, around 1910, used to publish his writings in *The Masses*, a daily newspaper edited by Max Eastman, and in *Seven Arts*, a magazine that published such

**JEFFERSON MARKET**
View of Jefferson Market with its Fire Tower, in 1830.

JEFFERSON ASSEMBLY ROOMS

## JEFFERSON MARKET COURTHOUSE

In 1906 this court (below in 1881) tried the millionaire Harry K. Thaw for the murder of the architect Stanford White. In 1931 the jail which used to abut on the courthouse was replaced by an Art Deco-style Women's House of Detention. This, in turn, was destroyed in 1974 and replaced by a park. The court had not been used since 1945, and the fate of its building, which was threatened with demolition, became a key issue in the early years of the architectural preservation movement. The local residents financed the restoration of the tower and hounded the municipal government until it granted the requisite funds for the building's conversion into a branch of the New York Public Library. It was restored by Giorgio Cavaglieri in 1967.

writers as D. H. Lawrence and the Marxist journalist John Reed. Although the golden age of the Village came to an end at the beginning of the 1930's when many of the "bohemians" settled down or left the neighborhood, the influence of this period can still be felt.

**JEFFERSON MARKET COURTHOUSE LIBRARY ★.** 425 6TH AVE., at 10TH ST. (1874–7, arch. Withers & Vaux). This Victorian-Gothic building combines intricately carved, brightly colored materials with naturalistic ornaments. Built on the site of the old Jefferson Market ● 86, the courthouse was converted into a public library in 1967.

Detail of the façade
of Bigelow's Pharmacy

**BREVOORT HOUSE**
The hotel which has now been torn down made the news when its Basque owner, Raymond Orteig, promised a reward of $25,000 to a pilot who would fly non-stop from New York to Paris. Charles Lindbergh, who landed his monoplane *Spirit of Saint Louis* in Paris in May 1927, was the first pilot to achieve this. On his return, Lindbergh was carried in triumph to the hotel, on 5th Ave. (below), where Orteig gave him the prize.

**WASHINGTON COURT.** 6TH AVE., between WAVERLY and WASHINGTON PLACES (1986, arch. James Stewart Polshek & Partners) ● *102*. This group of Postmodern-style apartments blends in well with the profile of the Village.

**BIGELOW CO. PHARMACY.** 414 6TH AVE., at 9TH ST. (1902, arch. John E. Nitchie). This pharmacy, founded in 1838, is a fine example of commercial architecture at the turn of the century, with its three striking Beaux Arts-style double bays. The interior, recently restored, still boasts its apothecary jars and all the prescriptions made up since the pharmacy opened, including one they had prepared for Mark Twain, who lived nearby.

**PATCHIN PLACE** (W. 10TH ST.) **AND MILLIGAN PLACE** (6TH AVE.) (1848–52). These two cul-de-sacs, enclosed by iron gates, are lined with redbrick houses which once served as accommodation for staff at the nearby Brevoort House. Among the most famous residents of Patchin Place are the poet e. e. cummings and John Reed, the committed left-wing journalist who covered the Russian Revolution and wrote *Ten Days that Shook the World* (1919).

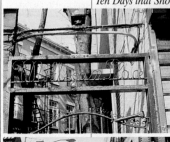

**GAY STREET.** This narrow lane, which epitomizes the neighborhood's charm, served as a mews in colonial times. The stables were later replaced by a harmonious group of late Federal-style houses (1827–31) and later by some Greek Revival houses (1844–60). Note the graceful columns flanking the doors, the brick masonry and the wide dormer windows of nos. 12 and 14 (1827–8).

**NORTHERN DISPENSARY.** 165 WAVERLY PLACE (1831). The Northern Dispensary was established by a group of citizens to care for the poor and is one of New York's oldest public hospitals. The triangular Greek Revival building was completed in 1831 and an extra story was added in 1854. The writer Edgar Allan Poe, one of the hospital's benefactors, was treated here for a head cold in 1837.

**"GAY LIBERATION"**
In 1992, in Christopher Park, two statues by George Segal – two couples, one male, one female – were erected in honor of the gay rights movement. Since the 1969 riot, every year, in June, the "Gay Pride March" is organized. It departs from the site of the Stonewall Inn, now demolished.

**CHRISTOPHER PARK AND SHERIDAN SQUARE.** These two squares stand side by side. The larger of the two is Christopher Park, in which a statue of the Union general Philip Sheridan, by Joseph Pollia, was erected in 1936. Sheridan Square is a small garden at the southeast end of Christopher Park. In July, at the height of the Civil War, Christopher Park was the site of the draft riots. Poverty-stricken Irishmen, who feared that if they had to go to war their jobs would be taken by Blacks, went on the rampage. Despite the forceful intervention of the National Guard, eighteen Blacks were lynched by the Irish. A century later, Christopher Park was also the site of the Stonewall Inn Riot; on the night of June 28 1969, the police raided the Stonewall Inn, a gay bar at 51 Christopher Street. The raid ended in a riot, which marked the start of the Gay Rights Movement ● *53*. At 1 Sheridan Square, the Charles Ludlam Theater puts on brilliant and farcical plays in drag.

**ROBERT FRYER** presents

# Rosalind Russell
~ THE NEW MUSICAL COMEDY

# Wonderful Town

**175–179 W. 4TH STREET** (1833–4). These houses feature the original door frames as well as Flemish bonding, overhanging roofs pierced by dormers at nos. 177 and 179 and the dimensions characteristic of the Federal style.

**26–30 JONES STREET** (c. 1830). The distinctive features of these three Greek Revival houses are their dentiled cornices, their wrought-iron stoop railings (nos. 28 and 30), their lantern-embellished doors (nos. 26 and 28) and their small-paned windows.

**GREENWICH HOUSE.** 29 BARROW ST. (1917, arch. Delano & Aldrich). This neo-Georgian building, built to serve as a social center for immigrants, is still used for socio-cultural activities.

## AROUND ST. LUKE'S IN THE FIELD

With its array of well-preserved brick- and brownstone-Italianate houses built 1852–3 (nos. 5–16), St. Luke's Place is one of the most attractive streets in Greenwich Village.

**39 AND 41 COMMERCE STREET** (1831–2). Contrary to popular

Ruth McKenney, who lived at 14 Gay St. in the 1920's, published a group of stories in *The New Yorker* set against the bohemian backdrop of the Village. It described the ups and downs of life there with her younger sister, an actress finding it difficult to break into the big time. The stories were

# "My Sister Eileen"

legend, these two houses, nicknamed the "Twin Sisters", were not built by a naval officer for his two daughters, but by a milkman, Peter Huyler. They have a somewhat old-fashioned air, with their leafy courtyard and their mansard roofs, which were added after 1870, and give the Greek Revival architecture a top-heavy appearance.

**CHUMLEY'S.** 86 BEDFORD ST. (1831). During Prohibition, this innocuous-looking building housed one of the best-known speakeasies in New York. Its clientele included Edna St. Vincent Millay, Upton Sinclair, John Dos Passos and Theodore Dreiser. The owner disguised the façade with a garage front in order to put the police off the scent and his

used as material for a Broadway hit musical called *Wonderful Town*.

**ST. LUKE'S PLACE**
In 1922 the writer Theodore Dreiser moved into 16 St. Luke's Place and began work on his novel *An American Tragedy*. The gas lamps that stand in front of No. 6 mark the residence of Mayor James J. Walker, who was notorious in the 1920's for his dissolute lifestyle. The playground on the other side of the road is a former graveyard in which Edgar Allan Poe once liked to stroll.

**GANSEVOORT MEAT MARKET**
General Gansevoort was the grandfather of Herman Melville. After years of adventure on the high seas and disillusioned by a career that did not pay him enough, the writer returned, in 1863, to his native neighborhood, where he became a district inspector of customs.

customers used to enter discreetly through the old stables at the back, at 58 Barrow Street. Two traditions that persist to this day are the absence of an inn sign and a display of the dust jackets from books by regulars. Take a look at 95 BEDFORD STREET, where another old stable, built in 1894, was converted into apartments in 1927. The brick and stone façade is embellished with a fancy ornamental cornice and the building still has its wide original doors.

**17 GROVE STREET** (1822). This frame house is one of the few vestiges of the period before laws were passed banning this type of structure in Manhattan for reasons of safety. The beautiful Greek Revival entrance is original, whereas the cornice and decorative wooden panels date from 1870, when another story was added.

Grove St. at the corner of Bedford St. (above).

❝Rich, hemm'd thick all around with sailships and steamships, an island sixteen miles long, solid-founded, Numberless crowded streets, high growths of iron, slender, strong, light, splendidly uprising toward clear skies.❞
Sinclair Lewis, *The Empire City*

U.S. Appraisers' Stores.

**TWIN PEAKS.** 102 BEDFORD ST. (c. 1830). This "neo-Alpine style" half-timbered building was created by the artist Clifford Reed Daily. He converted this residence in 1925, aiming for a startling effect in defiance of the homogeneous Federal style of the other houses on this peaceful street. He even managed to persuade Otto Kahn, his wealthy patron, to finance the project.

**LUCILLE LORTEL THEATER.** 121 CHRISTOPHER ST. In the 1950's the former Hudson Cinema was converted into a theater specializing in experimental productions ▲ *258*.

**GROVE COURT ★.** Through the gate between 10–12 GROVE ST. (1853–4). This address marks the entrance to six small houses, built by Samuel Cocks, a local grocer, to rent to workers. The courtyard once bore the name "Mixed Ale Alley", probably because of the inhabitants' propensity to drink. The houses were restored around 1920 and given their current name.

**CHURCH OF ST. LUKE IN THE FIELDS.** 485 HUDSON ST. (1822, arch. James N. Wells). Built by local residents with funds supplied by Trinity Parish, this was originally a village church adjoining several farms along the riverbank. Some parishioners used to come to church by boat – easier than traveling by road at that time. The brick exterior, whose simplicity verges on the severe, gives the church a distinctively rural look even today. The row of Federal-style houses bordering the old churchyard – especially the numbers 473 to 477 and 487 to 491 Hudson Street – creates an attractive setting for the church and its garden. The writer Bret Harte spent his boyhood at no. 487.

**FORMER UNITED STATES APPRAISERS' STORES.** 666–668 GREENWICH ST. (1892–9, arch. Willoughby J. Edbrooke). This massive Romanesque Revival structure, with its sturdy brick arcading, was used as a bonded warehouse when port activity was at its peak. The building was later used to house archives before being converted, in 1988, into apartments. Only the name of the MELVILLE BAR, on the corner of Barrow and Washington streets, evokes the ghost of the writer Herman Melville, who once worked as a customs inspector.

# WEST VILLAGE

**FORMERLY BELL LABORATORIES.** 463 WEST ST. and 155 BANK ST. (1880–1900, arch. Cyrus W. Eidlitz). The first transcontinental telephone call was made from here on January 25, 1915, when Alexander Graham Bell spoke to Thomas Watson in San Francisco; the first experimental radio set, the 2XS, was invented here, as was the sound projector, in 1925, which paved the way for the talkies. It was also here, on April 7, 1927, that journalists attended the first television broadcast, during which the Secretary of Commerce and future President, Herbert Hoover, made a speech from the Capitol, Washington, D.C. ● *54*. The building now forms part of a complex of lofts and studios for artists.

**THE HAMPTON.** 80–82 PERRY ST. (1887, arch. Thom & Wilson). The distinctive features of this apartment building, which blends in well with its surroundings, are its Moorish arches, its intricate brick decoration and its brownstone reliefs.

**PIERRE DEUX.** 369 BLEECKER ST. (1867). This attractive home decoration store, owned by two antique dealers both answering to the name of Pierre, occupies a complex designed to be divided into apartments, with commercial space on the ground floor. It was one of the first apartment buildings in New York.

**301–319 W. 4TH STREET** (1836–7). Out of these ten Greek Revival houses, nos. 311 and 313 still have their original proportions, while the others have been heightened with Italianate cornices ● *88*. The original wrought-iron railings still adorn the front steps.

**YE WAVERLY INN.** 16 BANK ST. (1844–5). This inn is part of a group of buildings that combine elements of late Greek Revival style with typical Gothic Revival decoration, such as the motifs on the carved lintels. The inn has low beamed ceilings and wooden alcoves.

**GANSEVOORT MEAT MARKET.** This covered wholesale meat market can be found east of 9th Avenue, between Gansevoort and 14th streets. Visit the market at dawn, when the auctioneering begins, or in the evening when the Florent restaurant is open.

**"INSPECTOR 75"**
Gansevoort Meat Market (above, in 1885) was a regular haunt of Herman Melville's for 19 years. During this time, he wrote *Billy Budd*, a novel that was discovered after his death in 1891. A scrap of paper was found on his desk, bearing the message "Keep true to the dreams of thy youth . . ."

**WHITE HORSE TAVERN**
This establishment, at 567 Hudson St., is a shrine to the Welsh poet and playwright Dylan Thomas. It was his usual "watering hole" during his stay in New York until he died of alcohol poisoning in 1953. In the tavern's Dylan Thomas Room a plaque has been placed above "his" table.

Gansevoort Meat Market, in 1885.

🏃 Four hours

**CONSTRAINTS ON PROPERTY DEVELOPERS**
Rows of identical townhouses were built in response to the conditions laid down by landowners in their tenants' leases. How the land was used, the size of the residences (in case of construction), materials, even their decoration, were all strictly regulated. These constraints meant that homeowners often had to build their stables at some distance from their dwellings.

## FROM WASHINGTON SQUARE TO 14TH STREET

**THE ROW.** 1–13 WASHINGTON SQUARE NORTH (1832–3). Some elegant residences were built around the square after the parade ground was constructed. This group is the most important row of early 19th-century houses in the city, and in their time they served as a model for adapting the Greek Revival style to private accommodation in New York. They are handsome redbrick residences, with porches, stairs and balustrades of white marble and railings embellished with acanthus finials and other classical motifs.
No. 3 was occupied, among others, by certain members of the Eight ● *109* and, later, by the painter Edward Hopper ● *111*. The houses at nos. 19–26 (1828–39) are in the same style but offer greater diversity, with their balconies and French doors, their varying shades of brick and their rich decoration.
**WASHINGTON MEWS ★.** Between UNIVERSITY PLACE and 5TH AVE. This charming cobblestone alley behind The

Row is lined on the north side by its former stables, now converted into houses. The south side was built in 1939.
**ONE 5TH AVENUE.** (1929, arch. Helmle, Corbett & Harrison; Sugarman & Berger).

**MADISON SQUARE**

**5TH AVE.**

**FLAT IRON BLDG**

**70TH ST.**

**10TH ST.**

**UNION SQUARE**

**14 TH ST.**

**13TH ST.**

**12TH ST.**

**11TH ST.**

**10TH ST.**

**9TH ST.**

**8TH ST.**

**UNIVERSITY PLACE**

**AVE. OF THE AMERICAS**

**WASHINGTON SQUARE NORTH**

This Art Deco monument looms above a landscape of smaller houses. Having been rather insensitively restored, it has lost the subtle original shading of its brick cladding.

**MACDOUGAL ALLEY.** MACDOUGAL ST., BETWEEN 8TH ST. AND WASHINGTON SQUARE NORTH (1833–8). The former stables of this cul-de-sac were renovated at the turn of the century and rented out cheaply, attracting artists who converted them into studios.

**NEW YORK STUDIO SCHOOL.** 8 W. 8TH ST. (1838, altered in 1931 and 1936 by Auguste L. Noel). In 1907 the sculptor Gertrude Vanderbilt Whitney opened the Studio Club in MacDougal Alley. She championed the American avant-garde and collected neglected works by her friends in the Eight. In 1931, she converted these three houses on 8th Street into a private gallery and residence. In 1936 they became the first home of the WHITNEY MUSEUM OF AMERICAN ART ▲ *326*. An Art Deco stucco was added at a later date.

**LOCKWOOD DE FOREST RESIDENCE.** 7 E. 10TH ST. (1887, arch. Van Campen Taylor). This house boasts an extravaganza of carved

**"ASHCAN SCHOOL"** Gertrude Vanderbilt Whitney, granddaughter of Cornelius Vanderbilt and wife of the financier Harry Payne Whitney, was the patron of the group of the Eight. These artists were also known as the "Ashcan school", because they flew in the face of academic tradition and concentrated on realistically portraying city life in all its ugliness as well as its beauty. The Whitney Collection moved Uptown in 1954 and the 8th St. museum became the New York Studio School of Drawing, Painting, and Sculpture.

217

**CHURCH OF THE ASCENSION**
This Episcopal church, on 5th Ave. at 10th St., was built in 1841 by Richard Upjohn. The interior was remodeled 1885–9.

**MARCEL DUCHAMP** (1887–1968). When he settled in New York in 1915, Duchamp abandoned painting to concentrate on his "ready-mades", everyday objects that he presented as works of art. Around 1935 the artist turned from the world of art to the art of chess. His anti-art stance had a great impact on all the major artistic trends of the day.

teakwood. It was built for De Forest, who had worked in the Middle East and India, where he founded studios to encourage a revival in the art of woodcarving.

**THE CLUBS.** Artists' clubs once abounded in the Village, and those that survive are open to the public. They were formed when friends with the same taste in art and conversation began to meet regularly. Among them are the TILE CLUB (58 West 10th Street) founded in 1877, and the SALMAGUNDI CLUB ● 88, formed in 1870 and located at 47 5th Avenue since 1917. This club owes its name to the journal run by Washington Irving, *Salmagundi*, an essentially mysterious name possibly from the French for a kind of "mixed salad". Women painters, who were barred from these clubs, founded the PEN & BRUSH (16 East 10th Street) in 1893; its beautifully appointed Victorian rooms are regularly used for exhibitions, concerts and receptions. The MARSHALL CHESS CLUB, at 23 West 10th Street, was founded in 1915 by Frank J. Marshall, United States champion between 1909 and 1936. Businessmen such as Edward Cornell and Gilbert Colgate rubbed shoulders here with the likes of Sinclair Lewis and Marcel Duchamp. Bobby Fischer, world chess champion in 1972, played his first competitive matches here. It is not unusual to see people playing it in Washington and Abingdon squares.

**18 WEST 11TH STREET.** (1845). This house was originally part of a group of rowhouses, but in March 1970 the façade was blasted away by a bomb being made by the daughter of the owner of the house and her cohorts, a terrorist organization called the *Weathermen*. For years, the maimed house proffered its gaping holes to passersby until a controversial modern design with a projecting rough brick façade was implemented.

**SECOND SHEARITH ISRAEL CEMETERY.** 72–76 W. 11TH ST. (1805–25). This tiny enclave is all that remains of the second graveyard of the oldest American Jewish community, most of whose tombs have been moved to another graveyard on 21st Street.

**FORBES BUILDING ★.** 60–62 5TH AVE. N. W. CORNER 12TH ST. (1925, arch. Carrère & Hastings and Shreve & Lamb). This neo-classical building was the headquarters of the MACMILLAN publishing house (which published *Gone with the Wind* in 1936), then the *Forbes* magazine headquarters.

**NEW SCHOOL FOR SOCIAL RESEARCH.** 66 W. 12TH ST. (1930, arch. Joseph Urban). This innovative institution, founded in 1919 by two lecturers from Columbia University, moved, in 1930, into this Bauhaus-inspired building ● 98. Three years later the New School developed a curriculum for scholars and academics fleeing Nazi Germany; it became a veritable "university in exile" for the social sciences.

**VILLAGE COMMUNITY CHURCH.** 143 W. 13TH ST. (1847, attrib. Samuel Thompson) ● 84. This former Presbyterian church, inspired by the Theseum in Athens, is one of the finest examples of Greek Revival style. It was converted into apartments in 1982.

## CHELSEA

This neighborhood, which lies between 14th and 34th streets from 6th Avenue to the Hudson River, is named after Captain Thomas Clarke, a retired English naval officer who, in 1750, bought a large plot of land along the river here for a country estate. He named it Chelsea in honor of the Chelsea Royal Hospital in London. His grandson, the scholar Clement Clarke Moore (author of "A Visit from St. Nicholas"), parceled out the estate with the aim of creating a middle-class neighborhood. Although Chelsea was never to become the residential haven that Clarke had imagined, this area and the neighboring blocks did attract wealthy families. However, by the end of the 19th century, Chelsea had lost some of its residential character due to the arrival of the department stores that

Coats of arms of the American nations hang above 6th Ave., renamed the Avenue of the Americas in honor of the founding of the Organization of American States, 1948.

**NEW SCHOOL FOR SOCIAL RESEARCH**
This school's famous lecturers have included the photographer Berenice Abbott, the composer John Cage, the anthropologist Claude Lévi-Strauss and the writers William Styron and Tom Wolfe.

**FORBES GALLERIES**
The ground floor of the Forbes Bldg. houses an exhibition of Malcolm Forbes' superb collections: 12 Fabergé eggs and more than 500 scale models of boats, made between 1870 and 1950.

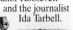

**TILE CLUB**
This club was founded in 1877 by twelve artists who painted on glazed tiles. They were later joined by members active in different creative professions such as Pearl Buck, Stanford White, Eleanor Roosevelt and the journalist Ida Tarbell.

Siegel Building.

drove away the wealthy residents. Warehouses and piers sprang up in the west of the neighborhood, attracting poor immigrants in search of work, and tenements were built to house them. The neighborhood is now in two distinct parts: west of 7th Avenue, where attractively restored rowhouses abound, and the more commercial area along 6th Avenue toward Broadway.

**FORMER SIEGEL-COOPER DRY GOODS STORE ★.** 616–632 6TH AVE., between 18TH and 19TH STS. (1895–7, arch. DeLemos & Cordes). On September 12, 1896, 150,000 spectators jostled at the inauguration of this department store (above), which the advertising campaign boasted was "a city in itself". The man behind the idea, Henry Siegel, revolutionized commerce by using every form of advertising available and by handing out samples to customers. This building was also famous for the fountain in its entrance hall, which boasted a statue by Daniel Chester French.

**FORMER B. ALTMAN DRY GOODS STORE.** 621 6TH AVE., between 18TH and 19TH STS. (1877, arch. D. & J. Jardine). The oldest cast-iron department store on 6th Avenue and famous for its sophisticated clothing, its silks, velvets and satins. In 1913, ALTMAN gave his collection of Italian Renaissance and Baroque paintings to the Metropolitan Museum of Art.

❝The most famous apartment house [located at 222 W. 23rd St.] inaugurated in 1884, still exists. The Chelsea Hotel, whose semi-Victorian, semi-

# Hippest Digs in N.Y.: Still a Chelsea Morning

## From Dylan Thomas to Sid Vicious

Gothic architecture still stirs passersby. These early buildings were striking because of their extremely flexible approach to composition.❞
Anka Muhlstein, *Manhattan*

**THE DINERS**
Long before the arrival of fast food chains, the American "diner" – originally shaped like a railroad dining car – served inexpensive food at all hours of the day and night. The Empire Diner (below), founded in 1943, is located at 210 10th Ave.

**FORMER HUGH O'NEILL'S STORE.** 655–671 6TH AVE. between 20TH AND 21ST STS. (1875, arch. Mortimer C. Merritt, additions 1890–5). Hugh O'Neill's low prices were aimed at the working classes rather than a wealthy clientele. In 1902, at O'Neill's death, no one wanted to take over from the "Fighting Irishman of 6th Avenue". The establishment closed in 1915. The cast-iron building was later made into offices and the two cupolas that used to crown the building's corners disappeared.

**CHURCH OF THE HOLY COMMUNION ★.** 49 W. 20TH ST. (1846, arch. Richard Upjohn) ● 86. This was the first asymmetrical Gothic Revival church in the United States. Despite its conversion into a discothèque, The Limelight, it still retains most of its interior decorations. (You can enjoy an excellent view of the Empire State Building from the corner of 6th Avenue and 23rd Street.)

**CUSHMAN ROW.** 406–418 W. 20TH ST. (1839) ● 84. These Greek Revival rowhouses, built by Don Alonzo Cushman, are in mint condition.

**GENERAL THEOLOGICAL SEMINARY ★.** (mainly 1883–1902, arch. Charles C. Haight). Clement Clarke Moore gave the land in 1818 for the seminary. An exhibition on the history of Chelsea is now housed in the building.

**DIA CENTER FOR THE ARTS.** 548 W. 22ND ST. This modern art center is housed in a former warehouse. The terrace affords a view over the "sea of warehouses" lining the Hudson.

# Around
# Union Square

# ▲ FROM UNION SQUARE TO THE EAST VILLAGE

✻ Five hours

On April 10, 1927, *The New York Times* led with the story of Sacco and Vanzetti's death sentence. The

L ocated at the intersection of BROADWAY and 4th Avenue (which in colonial times led to Albany and Boston), Union Square was laid out in 1831 and opened in 1839. In the 1840's this was a wealthy residential area; after the Civil War, it became New York's theater district, with the presence of the ACADEMY OF MUSIC on 14th Street (the site now occupied by the Con Edison building), and several other theaters. In the 1880's, with the development of the Ladies' Mile, commercial establishments moved to the neighborhood and a few early examples of skyscrapers were erected to the west of Union Square. After 1910, as commercial and artistic establishments moved uptown, it became a favorite site for labor-union gatherings

## The New York Times.

**SACCO AND VANZETTI GUILTY, SAYS FULLER, AND MUST DIE; BAY STATE GOVERNOR UPHOLDS JURY, CALLS TRIAL FAIR; HIS BOARD UNANIMOUS, EXECUTION OF PAIR SET FOR AUG. 10**

execution was deferred until August 23. A strike was called and on the 22nd some 5,000 workers converged on Union Square, where they kept vigil until the time of the execution.

and political demonstrations, particularly during the inter-war years. These have included such unforgettable gatherings as the demonstration on August 22, 1927 against the execution of Sacco and Vanzetti,

and the protest march of 35,000 unemployed workers in March 1930, during the Great Depression. A fruit and vegetable market now occupies Union Square four days a week. The best day to go is Saturday, especially at the end of summer and in the fall, at harvest time.

## AROUND UNION SQUARE

The few remaining commercial buildings around the square are fine examples of early skyscrapers ● *94*. At 1 Union Square West, there is the Romanesque Revival LINCOLN BUILDING (1889–90, arch. R. H. Robertson); farther north, at no. 31, stands the FORMER BANK OF THE METROPOLIS BUILDING (1902–3, arch. Bruce Price), an interesting

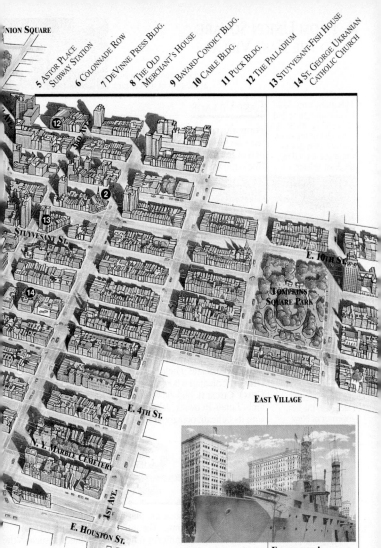

UNION SQUARE

**5** ASTOR PLACE SUBWAY STATION  **6** COLONNADE ROW  **7** DEVINNE PRESS BLDG.  **8** THE OLD MERCHANT'S HOUSE  **9** BAYARD-CONDICT BLDG.  **10** CABLE BLDG.  **11** PUCK BLDG.  **12** THE PALLADIUM  **13** STUYVESANT-FISH HOUSE  **14** ST. GEORGE UKRANIAN CATHOLIC CHURCH

STUYVESANT ST.

E. 10TH ST.

TOMPKINS SQUARE PARK

EAST VILLAGE

E. 4TH ST.

N. Y. MARBLE CEMETERY

E. HOUSTON ST.

**ENLIST NOW!**
In May 1917, two months after the U.S. entered World War One, John Mitchell, Mayor of New York, had a model of a warship *The Recruit* constructed in Union Square. In this building naval officers recruited marines to fight in the war.

example of neo-Renaissance tripartite architecture as applied to the skyscraper; and, close by, at no. 33, the Moorish-style DECKER BUILDING ★ (1892–3, arch. John Edelman), which for a time housed the Decker Piano Company. The finest building on Union Square is arguably the CENTURY (1880–1, arch. William Schickel) ★, at 33 East 17th Street, in Queen Anne style, with its abundance of highly fanciful ornaments. It was once the headquarters of the Century Publishing Company, which in the late 1800's, published various magazines including the *Century* and, for children, *St. Nicholas*. On the east side of the square, at no. 20, stands the former UNION SQUARE SAVINGS BANK.

This severely neo-classical granite building (1924, arch. Henry Bacon) was designed by the architect of the Lincoln Memorial in Washington, D. C.

A demonstration in Union Square (opposite) in the 1880's.

Cooper Square (opposite)
at the turn of the century.

This mural outside a Ukrainian café at 2nd Ave. and E. 9th St. is a reminder of the many Eastern Europeans who have settled in the East Village.

The entrance of the CBGB (below right), on the Bowery.

**PETER STUYVESANT (1592–1672)**
This stern, rigidly moralistic man, always dressed in black, was the last governor of New Amsterdam (1647–64). He established a bouwerie (farm) on Indian territory, between Broadway and the East River and what are now 3rd and 23rd streets, from which the present-day Bowery takes its name. The Federal-style house at 21 Stuyvesant St. was given by his great-

grandson to his daughter as a wedding present in 1804. Since 1861 the site has been occupied by a group of Italianate brick and brownstone houses, known as the Renwick Triangle.

## EAST VILLAGE

Formerly part of the Lower East Side ▲ 189, the East Village lies east of the Bowery and north of Houston Street. At the end of the last century, many immigrants – mainly Germans at first – moved into the neighborhood, where they settled in the many tenements, especially around Tompkins Square. A couple of wealthy German benefactors, Oswald and Anna Ottendorfer, founded the GERMAN POLIKLINIK (Dispensary) and the FREIE BIBLIOTHEK UND LESEHALLE on 2nd Avenue to help the poorest inhabitants.
**THE NEW BOHEMIA.** After World War Two a new generation of artists moved into this neighborhood, where rents were lower than in Greenwich Village ▲ 210. They created a new Bohemia and gave the area its present name. The 1950's saw the arrival of the founders of the beat generation: the writers Allen Ginsberg, Jack Kerouac, William Burroughs and poet Gregory Corso; also the novelist Norman Mailer, the painter Andy Warhol, the jazz musicians Thelonius Monk, Charles Mingus and Ornette Coleman who created the underground movement.
**GRACE CHURCH.** 800–804 BROADWAY AT E. 10TH ST. (1845–6, arch. James Renwick, Jr) ● 86. This Gothic Revival church with its delicate octagonal spire, was built where Broadway

veers to the west, a location that makes it visible, even today, many miles to the south. The interior boasts a fine mosaic floor and some magnificent stained glass windows, such as the "Te Deum" in the choir (1879).

## ST. MARK'S HISTORIC DISTRICT

The neighborhood to the northeast of Stuyvesant Street belonged to Peter Stuyvesant's bouwerie, in the 17th century, and the street that now bears his name was once a private alley between Bowery Road and his mansion. His great-grandson, Petrus, divided up the estate for development at the end of the 18th century. The church of St. Mark's-in-the-Bowery, the Stuyvesant-Fish House and the Nicholas William Stuyvesant House date from this period. Today, St. Mark's Place, which runs between 3rd Avenue and Tompkins Square, is a lively street lined with bars and restaurants.
**ST. MARK'S-IN-THE-BOWERY** ★ 2ND AVE. AT E. 10TH ST. (1799). The land on which the private chapel of Stuyvesant's

bouwerie is believed to have stood was sold to the Episcopal Church in the late 18th century for a token dollar. The small Georgian-style church built in 1799 was enhanced by a Greek Revival steeple in 1828 and an Italianate cast-iron porch in 1854.

## LAFAYETTE STREET HISTORIC DISTRICT

In its heyday, the second quarter of the 19th century, this area, lying east of Broadway and running the length of Lafayette and Bond streets, was an elegant residential neighborhood, rivaling Washington Square as a Manhattan's smartest address. Two of the most influential businessmen of the 19th century, Peter Cooper and John Jacob Astor, contributed to its growth by building the Cooper Union and the Astor Library. After the Civil War, as the city continued to spread northward, this neighborhood became a commercial district.

**COOPER UNION BUILDING.** COOPER SQUARE (1859, arch. Frederick A. Peterson). This Italianate brownstone building ● *88*, was built to house the college founded by Peter Cooper in 1859. It incorporated various structural innovations such as an iron-frame elevator. The top-floor studios added in the 1890's, were lit by glass roofs and contained an exhibition of decorative arts which became

**COOPER UNION**
This school of art and engineering was founded in 1859 by Peter Cooper (1791–1883), an industrialist, philanthropist and inventor who wanted to provide free education in the arts and sciences for working-class people. The owner of an ironworks and glue factory, Cooper designed the first American steam locomotive, called "Tom Thumb", produced the first steel train rails and started his own telegraph company.

The first Wanamaker's department store (below).

**ASTOR PLACE RIOT**
When the curtain of the Astor Place Opera House rose on the English actor William Macready in the title role of *Macbeth* on May 10, 1849, the audience, giving vent to anti-British feelings, booed and hissed. Meanwhile, a crowd numbering ten to twenty thousand gathered in the square and threw stones at the theater's entrance. The 7th Regiment of the Tompkins Market Armory quelled the riot by firing into the crowd, killing thirty-one people and wounding one hundred fifty others. The former Mercantile Library at 13 Astor Place now stands on the site of the opera house.

Astor Place Subway Station (right).

the nucleus of the future Cooper-Hewitt Museum ▲ *320* and which were used by the students as models. The building's Great Hall became a forum for lectures by such celebrities as Mark Twain, Andrew Carnegie, Fiorello La Guardia and Orson Welles. Above all, the hall is famous as the scene of Abraham Lincoln's first speech on slavery, "Right Makes Might", in 1860, which was a decisive factor in his election as President of the United States.

**PUBLIC THEATER, FORMERLY ASTOR LIBRARY.** 425 LAFAYETTE ST. (south wing 1849–53, arch. Alexander Saeltzer; center wing 1856–9, arch. Griffith Thomas; north wing 1879–81, arch. Thomas Stent). JOHN JACOB ASTOR founded the first public library in New York. Constructed in three stages, the building reflects the German influence on commercial architecture in mid-19th-century New York. In 1965, the theatrical director and producer JOSEPH PAPP persuaded the city to buy the building which, one year later, became the home of the SHAKESPEARE FESTIVAL.

**ASTOR PLACE SUBWAY STATION** (1904, arch. Heins & La Farge). This is one of the few subway stations that still have their original decoration. Among them are plaques

The logo of one of Theodore De Vinne's publications.

representing a beaver, symbol of the Astor fortune, which originated in the fur trade.
A black steel cube, entitled "Alamo" (1966), by Bernard T. Rosenthal, stands in the center of this square.

**COLONNADE ROW.** 428–34 LAFAYETTE ST. (1832–3, attributed to Seth Geer) ● *84*. These Greek Revival houses, with their marble façades, once ranked among the most magnificent residences in New York – home to such families as the Vanderbilts and the Astors. The series of Corinthian columns imposes a stylistic unity on the houses, which have suffered from lack of maintenance and infelicitous alteration. Only four of the nine original houses – formerly called LaGrange Terrace after Lafayette's estate in France – are still standing.

**DE VINNE PRESS BUILDING.** 393–9 LAFAYETTE ST. AT E. 4TH ST. (1885–6, arch. Babb, Cook & Willard) ● *91*. This printing works was one of several press buildings on Lafayette Street. The printer Theodore De Vinne (1828–1914) published books and magazines such as *Century*.

**THE OLD MERCHANT'S HOUSE ★.** 29 E. 4TH ST. (1831–2, attributed to Minard Lafever) ● *82*. This building (left), originally one of a group of six, was built by the property developer JOSEPH BREWSTER, and sold in 1835 to a wealthy hardware dealer, SEABURY TREDWELL. In 1936 it was converted into a museum evoking the life of a prosperous New York family in the 19th century.

**BAYARD-CONDICT BUILDING ★.** 65–69 BLEECKER ST. (1897–9, arch. Louis Sullivan and Lyndon P. Smith) ● *94*. This is the only work in New York by LOUIS SULLIVAN, one of the foremost architects of the Chicago school of architecture and Frank Lloyd Wright's revered "Master".

**CABLE BUILDING.** 621 BROADWAY (1894, arch. McKim, Mead & White). This building was once the head offices and power station for Manhattan's streetcars. Its arcaded bays, classically inspired stone carvings and prominent cornice, with its acanthus-motif ridgepole, make it one of the finest commercial buildings by the firm of McKim, Mead & White.

**PUCK BUILDING.** 295–309 LAFAYETTE ST. (1885–6 and 1892–3, arch. Albert Wagner, John Wagner). The originality of this 19th-century Romanesque Revival building lies in its wide arched windows and highly elaborate brickwork. It was built to house the satirical magazine *Puck*. The building was constructed in three stages, the last of which was when Lafayette Street was widened.

A statue of Puck, a character from Shakespeare's *A Midsummer's Night's Dream*, with the legend "What fools these mortals be", keeps watch over both entrances to the Puck Building. The statue at the former main entrance on Houston St. is the work of Caspar Buberl; the one on Lafayette St. is by Henry Baerer.

The cover of *Puck* Magazine of September 13, 1899 (above), attacking corruption.

227

Tammany Hall decorated for the national convention of July 4, 1868. During this period, the Democrats were based on 14th St., next to the Academy of Music, on the site of the future Con Edison Building.

During the 1840's, the district between Union Square and Gramercy Park became New York's newest and most glamorous residential area. Large private mansions sprang up along parks and avenues, cheek by jowl with the humblest row houses in adjacent streets. In the following decades, while the area west of 4th Avenue (now Park Avenue South) developed commercially around the "LADIES' MILE" of shops and stores, the area to the east remained staunchly residential. Around the turn of the 20th century, Gramercy Park became the chosen neighborhood of wealthy New Yorkers who preferred its artistic, liberal flavor to the more staid luxury of Uptown.

## AROUND IRVING PLACE

**TAMMANY HALL.** E. 17TH ST N. E. CORNER OF UNION SQUARE E. (1928, arch. Thompson, Holmes & Converse). The Tammany Society – whose name was derived from TAMMANEND, a Delaware chief famed for his wisdom – was initially a patriotic organization, founded in 1789 as a response to the aristocratic Federalist party. Ten years after it was formed, the society began to take an interest in politics. Eventually it became the powerful New York Democratic Party machine, notorious for its corruption – especially under "Boss" Tweed ● 40. Between 1866 and 1871 the Tweed Ring, which controlled key posts in the city government, pocketed several million dollars ▲ 185 of city funds. In 1928 the Tammany Society which, even after the death of "Boss" Tweed, still had a stranglehold on local politics, commissioned this Colonial-style building, inspired by Federal Hall (on Wall Street). In 1943 the International Ladies Garment Workers Union bought the building and turned it into their union headquarters. It now houses the UNION THEATER.

**SO-CALLED WASHINGTON IRVING HOUSE.** S. W. CORNER OF IRVING PL. AND 17TH ST. This house was designed in 1845 and

**BOSS TWEED**
Caricature of "Boss" Tweed, the notorious leader of the ring of the same name, who embezzled a huge amount of money from the city between 1866 and 1871.

Advertisements (below) that appeared in the press promoting restaurants and shops established around Gramercy Park early in this century.

its cast-iron verandah, wrought-iron balconies and wooden hood molding set it apart from the other 19th-century townhouses on the street. Elsie de Wolfe, the first professional interior designer in the United States, lived here with her companion, the playwright Elisabeth Marbury, from 1894 to 1911.

**WASHINGTON IRVING HIGH SCHOOL.** 40 IRVING PLACE (1908–13, arch. C. B. J. Snyder). This school, which was originally a women's college until 1986, takes its name from the writer WASHINGTON IRVING, author of *A History of New York from the Beginning of the World to the End of the Dutch Dynasty* (1809), a comic version of

the city's history written under the name of Dietrich Knickerbocker. The neo-Gothic entrance hall is decorated with very fine murals by BARRY FAULKNER depicting scenes from Irving's work.

**CON EDISON BUILDING.** CORNER OF 14TH ST. AND IRVING PLACE (1915–29, arch. Henry Hardenbergh). This is the headquarters of the Consolidated Edison Company, which provides New York's gas and electricity supply. Its tower (1926–9, arch. Warren & Wetmore) which is brightly illuminated at night and called the "Tower of Light", was erected in memory of company employees who died in World War One. The building stands partially on the site of the Academy of Music, a huge concert hall, opened in 1854, which hosted performers such as Jenny Lind, Adelina Patti and Edwin Booth until it was superseded in 1883 by the Metropolitan Opera House, on Broadway. The CON EDISON ENERGY MUSEUM, at 145 East 14th Street, is devoted to the engineer Thomas Alva Edison (1847–1931) and his inventions (quadruplex telegraph system, phonograph, incandescent lamp, kinetoscopic camera – one of the forebears of the projector). It also has a model of the first power plant, built on Pearl Street.

**PETE'S TAVERN.** 129 E. 18TH ST. This bar, opened in 1864, remained open even during Prohibition ● *40*. In its years as a speakeasy, customers entered through the door of the cold room in a florist's shop next door. The walls are lined with photographs and press clippings which recall the bar's history and the notables who used to drink here, including politicians from Tammany Hall and the short-story writer O. HENRY, who wrote "The Gift of the Magi" here.

The HEARTHSTONE
102 East 22nd St. ● GR 5-1889
A GRAMERCY LANDMARK
Lunch 95-1.75        Dinner 1:50-2.25
Holiday Candlelight Dinner
Dec. 22 — $2.50
Order for HOME Dining
Our Popular T.V. Dinners
Closed Sundays and Christmas Day

Serving Fine
Food and Liquor
LUNCH • DINNER
COCKTAILS

weathervane inn

Dining Room Open 11 a.m. to 9:30 p.m. Mon. thru Sat.
30 East 29th St. (Bet. Madison and 4th)
Phone: LExington 2-8125

Gramercy Pastry Shop
Est. 1932
272 Third Ave. (bet. 21st & 22nd Sts.)
FRENCH PASTRIES        BUTTER COOKIES
HORS D'OEUVRES
BIRTHDAY AND WEDDING CAKES
GR 3-6734

**THE "BLOCK BEAUTIFUL"**
The townhouses on 19th St. were remodeled in the 1920's and many were given stucco façades adorned with painted, glazed tiles, wrought iron and sculptures, such as these jockeys (left). The faces of these characters were originally black but were later repainted, as they were regarded as racist stereotypes.

The Con Edison Building.

**SAMUEL B. RUGGLES**
Born in 1800 in New Milford, Connecticut,

Samuel Ruggles attended Yale University, then studied law under his father, an influential lawyer twice elected to the Connecticut legislature. In 1820 Ruggles moved with his wife, Mary R. Rathbone, to New York, where he established his own practice.

Behind the railings of Gramercy Park stands the statue of Edwin Booth, a bronze commissioned by the Players Club from Edmond T. Quinn,

who has captured the actor in the role of Hamlet. It was erected in 1918.

Carved faces of Franklin, Milton, Goethe and Dante adorn the façade of the National Arts Club in true Italianate style, as was the fashion at the time of the building's restoration. The façade has been listed as a landmark since 1966. Woody Allen used this building for one of the scenes in his film *Manhattan Murder Mystery*.

## GRAMERCY PARK ★

The name "Gramercy" is an anglicization of the Dutch names *Krom Moerasje*, "crooked little swamp", which described a meandering brook that used to run through here. In the early 1830's, Samuel B. Ruggles, who owned the land and who advocated planning towns around green spaces, designed the park and sold sixty-six building lots around it, stipulating that their owners would maintain the park and have exclusive access to it. To this day, Gramercy Park remains the only private square in New York.

**EARLY HOUSES.** Of the houses and other buildings designed in Ruggles' time, a few remain along the west and south sides of the park – among them nos. 3 and 4 GRAMERCY PARK WEST and the Friends' Meeting House, at 28 Gramercy Park South. Designed by King & Kellum for the Quakers between 1857 and 1859, this Italianate building was renovated in 1975 and sold to its current owners, the BROTHERHOOD SYNAGOGUE. At 34 Gramercy Park East, the GRAMERCY, built in 1883 by the architect George da Cunha, was one of Manhattan's first cooperative apartment buildings. It is also a fine example of New York Queen Anne style ● *90*, with its use of contrasting materials: brick, terracotta, wrought iron and stone. The sumptuous lobby boasts a mosaic floor and stained glass ceiling. Close by, at 36 GRAMERCY PARK EAST, stands the residence built between 1908 and 1910 by the architect James Riley Gordon. This building is almost entirely clad in terracotta with motifs of medieval inspiration.

**THE PLAYERS.** 16 GRAMERCY PARK SOUTH (1845; remodeled 1888–9, arch. Stanford White). In 1888, in founding The Players Club, the actor Edwin Booth realized a long-cherished dream – expressed in these words from 1886: "An actors club has been a dream of mine for many years. Having quite a number of theatrical books, pictures, etc., etc., I have dreamed of furnishing such an establishment with them someday. When I step aside and before I go, I hope to accomplish something of this kind." The only condition stipulated by Booth was that he should have an apartment at the club. The chosen premises, a townhouse in Gothic Revival style, were remodeled by Stanford White (free of charge) who added the porch, the impressive iron railings and the cornice graced with theatrical masks. The Players soon became the haunt of actors and their friends, including Stanford White and Mark Twain.

**NATIONAL ARTS CLUB.** 15 GRAMERCY PARK SOUTH (1845). The two original townhouses here were combined and remodeled between 1881 and 1884 by Calvert Vaux for the lawyer SAMUEL J. TILDEN, who had been governor of New York between 1874 and 1876. The elegant Victorian Gothic façade, with brick cladding in contrasting shades, is in typical

The stained glass roof (above) of the National Arts Club, executed by MacDonald.

### 3 AND 4 GRAMERCY PARK WEST

These two residences boast the finest cast-iron porches in New York. The two lamps that stand in front of no. 4 are a reminder that the house was the home of James Harper, Mayor of New York between 1844 and 1845 (and one of the founders of the publishers J. & J. Harper). Following a tradition dating back to Dutch times, the entrance to the mayor's house was flanked by two lamps which were lit when he was at home.

Ruskinian style; note the carved medallions of birds and plants over the windows and the busts on the first floor. The panels to the right of the porch are engraved with plants, animals and insects indigenous to New York. Three rooms were knocked together to house Tilden's library. This became the property of the New York Public Library in 1886 after the politician's death. In 1906 the residence was bought by the National Arts Club. This club, founded in 1898, was one of the first in New York to welcome a mixed membership. The residence was refurbished for its new owners, but the original decoration was preserved. A temporary exhibition hall provides a taste of the sumptuous interiors.

▲ FROM UNION SQUARE
TO MADISON SQUARE

1 TAMMANY HALL
2 49 IRVING PLACE
3 W. IRVING HIGH SCHOOL
4 CON EDISON BLDG.
5 PETE'S TAVERN
6 GRAMERCY PARK
7 THE PLAYERS AND
NATIONAL ARTS CLUB

B etween the 1860's and 1910, "Ladies' Mile", the stretch of Broadway and 5th and 6th avenues (left) running from 8th to 23rd Street, was the most fashionable area in New York. The most elegant shops and department stores of the "Ladies' Mile" were clustered along Broadway between Union Square and Madison Square. There was a constant stream of fashionable ladies in pursuit of luxury goods. Most of the shops that catered for this trade have long since closed down or moved Uptown.

## VESTIGES OF THE COMMERCIAL ERA

**FOR MEN OF BRAINS Cortez CIGARS** —MADE AT KEY WEST—

**TEDDY BEAR**
A Brooklyn manufacturer decided to make a plush bear after he learned that president Theodore Roosevelt (shown below as a child) had spared a small bear while hunting. The president agreed to let it be called Teddy's Bear, in memory of his generous gesture.

**FORMER ARNOLD CONSTABLE & Co.** 881–7 BROADWAY, S. W. CORNER OF 19TH ST. (1868–9, arch. Griffith Thomas). In 1825 Aaron Arnold, an English immigrant from the Isle of Wight, opened a little dry-goods store on Pine Street, in Lower Manhattan. Business thrived, and in 1853 his son-in-law, James Constable, became his partner. Subsequently, the store moved farther north several times, before opening on the "Ladies' Mile" in 1869. The new store was such a success that it had to be extended on 19th Street up to 5th Avenue. The extension is a cast-iron building with a mansard roof, the most striking in New York.

**FORMER W. & J. SLOANE.** 884 BROADWAY, S. E. CORNER OF 19TH ST. (1881–2, arch. W. Wheeler Smith). For more than a century, Sloane's has been a renowned dealer of luxury furniture and carpets (the store supplied furnishings for the coronation of Tsar Nicholas II). The superb cast-iron store fronts can still be seen. Note also the plants carved around the columns inside.

**FORMER GORHAM MANUFACTURING COMPANY.** 889–91 BROADWAY, N. W. CORNER OF 19TH ST. (1883–4, arch. Edward Kendall). This impressive Queen Anne-style ● 90 building housed the main New York outlet of the GORHAM SILVER COMPANY.

**FORMER LORD & TAYLOR DRY GOODS STORE.** 901 BROADWAY, S. W. CORNER OF 20TH ST. (1867, arch. James H. Giles). This cast-iron building has a corner turret which was designed to attract customers. The store, founded around 1830 by two Englishmen, Samuel Lord and George W. Taylor, was originally a small shop in Lower

UNION SQUARE

13
11
10
8
9

232

🚶 Four hours

The Broadway Central Hotel c. 1900

**LADIES' MILE**
"Looking out from Union Square, as this oasis in the desert of buildings is called, we get an idea of how interminable a Broadway crowd is. About a quarter of a mile farther north, Madison Square relieves the confinement of the street with fountains, grass, shrubs and trees, and between the two such a parade may be seen on fine afternoons, especially Saturdays, as no other city in America and few other cities in the world, can show. The great retail houses of the Stewarts, the Tiffanys, the Arnold Constables, and the Lords and Taylors, are concentrated within these limits . . . and women in their most elegant attire appear in quest of new addition to their already voluminous apparel."

*Harper's New Monthly Magazine, 1878.*

Manhattan. Later it became one of the big names in retailing, offering a wide range of ready-to-wear clothing – as it still does on 5th Avenue at 38th Street.

**THEODORE ROOSEVELT'S BIRTHPLACE.** 28 E. 20TH ST. President Theodore Roosevelt was born here in 1858. The present building is a reconstruction dating from 1923, undertaken by his sisters, who engaged one of the first women architects, Theodate Pope Ridde, for the work. Inside, High Victorian Gothic rooms contain a MUSEUM devoted to Roosevelt's achievements as explorer, naturalist and politician.

**FLATIRON BUILDING ★.** BROADWAY AND 5TH AVE. AT 23RD ST. (1902, arch. D. H. Burnham & Co.) ● 96. This slender building, originally called the FULLER BUILDING after its developer, soon acquired its present name by virtue of its triangular shape – dictated by the awkward site. Its dramatic silhouette made it a familiar symbol of New York as well as a favorite subject for photographers and artists at the beginning of the 20th century ● 109. This corner of 23rd Street and 5th Avenue was a popular haunt for "voyeurs", who took advantage of the air currents that swirled around the building, lifting women's skirts, to catch a glimpse of their ankles.

## MADISON SQUARE

**MADISON SQUARE GARDEN NEW YORK. THE WORLD FAMOUS METROPOLITAN HOME OF THESE COMBINED STUPENDOUS SHOWS.** Madison Square Garden in 1910. It was on the roof of Madison Square Garden (above, 1910) on June 25, 1906, that Stanford White was killed by the husband of a former mistress.

**FLATIRON BUILDING** Much later, this name was given to other buildings on triangular sites, which occurred because of Broadway's irregular shape within the checkerboard town plan.

This square, which was named in memory of JAMES MADISON (1751–1836), president of the United States from 1809 to 1817, was established as a park on this site in 1811. The commemorative statues in the square include one of ADMIRAL DAVID FARRAGUT, who was a hero of the Mobile Bay naval battle, during the Civil War. This is the work of Augustus Saint-Gaudens (1880): the base, in the form of a bench, was designed by Stanford White.

**METROPOLITAN LIFE TOWER ★.** 1 MADISON AVE. (1893, 1909, arch. Napoleon LeBrun & Sons) ● 96. The tower at the corner of 24th Street (modeled on Saint Mark's Campanile in Venice) is the company's symbol and was erected in order to make the building the tallest in the world (it was deposed by the Woolworth Building ▲ 180 in 1913). In 1932 Met Life enlarged its premises with another building on the opposite side of 24th Street, whose Italian marble lobby is particularly worth a visit. The existing building is a partial version of the project (above) which provided for a tower nearly 100 stories high; it was left incomplete because of the Depression.

**APPELLATE DIVISION COURTHOUSE ★.** 35 E. 25TH ST. (1900, arch. James Brown Lord) ● 92. This small building, a Beaux Arts masterpiece, houses the Appellate Division of the New York State Supreme Court. The classical façade is adorned with sculptures depicting key figures from the history of law and various allegories evoking different aspects of Law and Justice. The lobby and the courtroom, which are richly decorated with murals and magnificent stained glass windows, are open to the public.

**NEW YORK LIFE INSURANCE COMPANY.** 51 MADISON AVE. (1928, arch. Cass Gilbert). This neo-Gothic skyscraper stands on the site of the first two Madison Square Gardens.

**GILSEY HOUSE.** 1200 BROADWAY (1869–71, arch. Stephen D. Hatch) ● 89. This building, with its enormous mansard roof, now a private residence, was originally one of the city's most luxurious hotels.

# AROUND
# GRAND CENTRAL
# TERMINAL

▲ GRAND CENTRAL TERMINAL TO MADISON SQUARE GARDEN

1 GRAND CENTRAL TERMINAL
2 PHILIP MORRIS INC. BLDG.
3 POLISH CONSULATE
4 UNION LEAGUE CLUB
5 PIERPONT MORGAN LIBRARY

❝Five dollars. Grand Central. Three fifty. Penn Station. [He] got into the gleaming taxi. Horns were hooting everywhere . . .❞
J. P. Donleavy

"Grand" is certainly the word for the large and imposing Grand Central Terminal – considered one of the finest public buildings in the United States. It is the focal point of an area that embraces an interesting mixture of urban functions and includes three more of New York's most distinguished landmarks: the Chrysler Building ▲ *266*, the Empire State Building ▲ *242* and the New York Public Library ▲ *254*. The presence of the United Nations headquarters ▲ *264*, at the easternmost end of 42nd Street, as well as the many consulates and diplomatic residences, gives the eastern end of this area an international flavor. Just to the south of Grand Central Terminal lies Murray Hill, one of the most sought-after residential addresses in New York. To the west, along 5th Avenue, are some of the city's most elegant stores; farther west, Times Square

�за Five hours

**GRAND CENTRAL DEPOT**
Grand Central Depot (below), the predecessor of the present terminal, was the first station opened in 1871 by the "Commodore".

and the theater district. it is often said that New York is "the city that never sleeps"; and this is particularly true of the glamourous, glitzy – and, in places, sleazy – Times Square area.

## GRAND CENTRAL TERMINAL

**AUSPICIOUS BEGINNINGS.** The original terminal (commonly called Grand Central Station) was built in 1871 by "Commodore" Cornelius Vanderbilt. The present building dates from the time of his grandson, William K. Vanderbilt, chairman of the New York Central Railroad, which included three major rail networks operating out of Manhattan. In 1903 a closed competition was launched for the reconstruction of the station. The winning firm, Reed & Stem, planned the layout of the station; later, Warren & Wetmore were asked to aid in the revision of the original design. The new station was opened in 1913. It was the proverbial tip of the iceberg, with tracks running on two levels under Park Avenue. The terminal was central to an ambitious town-planning project devised by William Wilgus, the chief engineer of the New York Central Corporation. This program included electrifying the network and laying down and organizing the underground tracks. Concerned with obtaining a good return for its investment, the railroad company rented out the building rights of the land above the tracks. Hotels, offices and luxury apartments were built along Park Avenue, which became one of the most prestigious addresses in Manhattan. The view down the avenue toward the station, crowned by the New York Central Building (now the Helmsley Building) was one of New York's finest. When, in the early 1960's, the huge Pan Am (now MetLife) Building

> "I must admit, however, that I am starting to become reconciled with the Pan Am Building, which juts out of Grand Central Station like the shoulder piece of a bayonet sticking out of a fine animal that has been stabbed in the back."
> Donald Westlake,
> *Strange Brothers*

# GRAND CENTRAL TERMINAL TO MADISON SQUARE GARDEN

**PEDIMENT OF GRAND CENTRAL TERMINAL**
The central sculptural group on the station's pediment represents, Mercury (shown right), flanked by Hercules and Minerva. According to Warren, they embody, respectively "the glory of commerce", "moral energy" and "mental energy". The work was commissioned from Jules Coutan.

The Main Concourse of Grand Central Terminal.

was imposed on the station, thus spoiling this view, it raised a storm of public protest.

**A CLASSICAL FAÇADE.** The 42nd-Street façade, by the Beaux Arts-trained Whitney Warren, who was responsible for the station's exterior decoration, is a piece of architectural bravura. The architect saw the terminal as a triumphal gateway to the city and the façade, a stone facing on a metal frame, is remarkable for its use of a limited number of unusually large, boldly defined elements.

**THE INTERIOR.** The layout of Grand Central Terminal was revolutionary for its time. A system of ramps, which can be reached via the subway or from outside the station, helps prevent disorderly crowds, a common problem in other stations. The MAIN CONCOURSE was originally used exclusively for long-distance trains. Its VAULTED CEILING is decorated with the constellations: electric bulbs representing 2,500 stars joined by a gilt border "to form the celestial figures". The ARRIVAL HALL which is much smaller, formed part of the former Biltmore Hotel, now replaced by an office building. The original hall for suburban trains is on the lower level, along with the Oyster Bar, a restaurant known for its décor and seafood specialties.

GRAND CENTRAL TRM
Sectional View from Biltmore Hotel Looking East Towrd Lexin
SHOWING PASSAGEWAYS TO HOTELS, OFFICE BL

① Hotel Commodore
② Biltmore Hotel
③ Hotel Roosevelt
④ New York Central Bldg. 230 Park Ave.
⑤ Graybar Building
⑥ Grand Central Terminal Office Building

Ⓐ Cab Baggage Service
Ⓑ Travel Information Bureau
Ⓒ Newsreel Theatre
Ⓓ Lower Level
Ⓔ Stairways from Vanderbilt Ave. to Upper & Lower Levels
Ⓕ Ticket Offices

EXPRESS TRAINS

SUBURBAN TRAINS

TO INCOMING TRAINS

Cross section of Grand Central Terminal.

**THE "PALACE OF DEPARTURE".** This is how the French writer and diplomat Paul Morand labelled the terminal, whose monumentality, comfort and cleanliness are a source of admiration for European visitors. Movie-makers have filmed some unforgettable farewell scenes and chases here. For example, Alfred Hitchcock used it for some sequences for *North by Northwest*, starring Cary Grant. Grand Central Terminal's passenger figures reached a peak, in 1947, of 65 million – in other words more than 40 percent of the U.S. population at that time. Now that the era of transcontinental trips in Pullman cars is over, the concourse has lost some of its air of excitement, though its serenity is periodically shattered by hordes of scurrying commuters. In recent years the terminal almost suffered the fate of Pennsylvania Station ▲ *249*, which was demolished in 1963 to make way for the new Madison Square Garden ▲ *249*. In 1968, the Penn Central Corporation, the railroad's new owners, planned to demolish Grand Central's 42nd-Street façade and the waiting rooms to construct a 55-story tower designed by Marcel Breuer. The terminal was saved by a high-profile campaign led by Jacqueline Kennedy Onassis and the architect Philip Johnson, and the station was listed on the National Register of Historic Places in 1983. A vast rehabilitation program also includes the renovation of the entire station.

The building site in 1911.

"The evening she arrived at Grand Central Station was the turning point of her life. Disoriented, scared, she had crossed the huge concourse of the station, carrying her one and only suitcase; she had looked up and had stopped dead. She was probably one of the few people to have immediately realized that the heaven of the great vaulted ceiling had been painted back to front. The Eastern stars were in the West."
Marry Higgins Clark,
*The Night of the Fox*

**A PATRIOTIC WOMAN**
According to a Revolutionary War legend, Mrs Murray (whose family name survives in Murray Hill (right, during the 1860's) played a trick on the British. By inviting General Howe and his officers – who had just landed with their troops – to tea, she enabled George Washington and his men to retreat to northwest Manhattan.

Façade, 149 E. 38th St.

**POLISH CONSULATE**
233 Madison Ave. This mansion, built in Second Empire style by C. P. H. Gilbert, was formerly the headquarters of the National Democratic Club. Its interior (below) is as opulent as its exterior.

## MURRAY HILL

This neighborhood, lying between 34th and 42nd streets and between 5th and 3rd avenues, takes its name from Robert Murray, who, during the British colonial period, owned a country house in the center of this area. At the end of the 19th century, Murray Hill consisted of a collection of stables and outbuildings belonging to the private mansions on 5th Avenue owned by the "Upper Four Hundred". This expression referred to the four hundred people from the top families in New York, who were invited to Mrs Astor's annual ball (her ballroom being able to accommodate that number). When the mansions on 5th Avenue were demolished at the beginning of the 20th century to make way for department stores, a number of these outbuildings were refurbished. They now rank among the most sought-after addresses in the city.

**PHILIP MORRIS INC. BUILDING.** 120 PARK AVE. (1982, arch. Ulrich Franzen and Associates) ● *103*. The ground floor of the New York headquarters of this well-known cigarette manufacturer (open to the public) houses an enclosed garden, a café and an annex of the Whitney Museum of Modern Art ▲ *326*, which mounts temporary exhibitions.

**38TH STREET.** With its varied styles of houses, the part of 38th Street between Park and 3rd avenues epitomizes the charm of the neighborhood. At no. 108, a small Art Deco building, built in 1930, proffers a "Cubist" façade, its redbrick bonding enhanced with polychromatic stringcourses made of glazed terracotta. At the corner of Lexington Avenue two PRIVATE MANSIONS stand opposite each other: no. 136, in Victorian style with little windowpanes made of blown glass, and no. 125, a well-preserved example of Old Charleston style. Farther east, at no. 149, is a Flemish Renaissance-style carriage house (above, left) decorated with the heads of bulldogs and horses. At no. 150–152, there is a Federal-style residence from 1858 (remodeled in 1935), dating from the time when Murray Hill was still a suburb of New York. This was the home of a member of the family of Martin Van Buren, the eighth President of the United States (1837–41).

"WHEN I WALKED DOWN MADISON AVENUE, PARK AVENUE, I KNEW I WAS WALKING THROUGH THE VIOLENT CORRIDORS OF A MUSEUM IN WHICH THE WOMEN WERE INTOXICATING FIGURES, THAT THE WHOLE OF NEW YORK WAS A BOOK OF THE NEW ART."

P. BOURGEADE

**MORGAN, FATHER AND SON**
John Pierpont Morgan, Sr (1837–1913) and his son, John Pierpont, Jr (1867–1943), built up the most influential financial trust in America before the 1929 crash. Their bank served the most important families in New York, such as the Astors, Vanderbilts and Guggenheims, and it saved the city from bankruptcy on three occasions. Until 1933 a letter of credit from the Morgan bank was regarded as an impeccable testimonial. J. Pierpont Morgan, Sr (above) was not only the greatest financier of his time but also an unrivaled collector of rare books and manuscripts, for which he built his private library (left). It was opened to the public in 1924, in accordance with his wishes.

**SNIFFEN COURT HISTORIC DISTRICT ★.** 150–158 E. 36TH ST. (1850–60). Grouped around a small court, these ten Romanesque Revival brick houses once served as stables for some wealthy 5th Avenue residents. In the 1920's they were converted into homes, studios and offices.

**UNION LEAGUE CLUB.** S. W. CORNER OF PARK AVE. AND E. 37TH ST. (1931, arch. Morris and O'Connor). This imposing building in neo-Georgian style is the headquarters of a club founded in 1863 by some Republican former members of the Union Club. A conflict had arisen between them and some other members over the Club's admission of some Confederate sympathizers. To express their staunch support for the Northern cause and President Lincoln, these Republicans formed their own club, which they called the Union League.

**PIERPONT MORGAN LIBRARY ● 93 ★.** 29 AND 33 E. 36TH ST. AND 231 MADISON AVE. The Pierpont Morgan Library comprises three buildings. At 29 East 36th Street, the former library of J. P. Morgan, Sr ● 93 (designed by Benjamin W. Morris) contains his collection of works of art and antique manuscripts and books, including a Gutenberg Bible. The main entrance to the library is through the annex at 29 East 36th Street, a museum that mounts temporary exhibitions. A pleasant covered garden leads to 231 Madison Avenue, a brownstone ● 88 that was once the home of J. P. Morgan, Jr. It was bought in 1990 by the museum to house a bookshop and a conference hall.

The plans for the Empire State Building, located on the corner of 5th Avenue between 33rd and 34th streets, were unveiled to the press on August 29, 1929. John J. Raskob, the prime mover behind this project and vice-president of General Motors, decided to go one better than his rival, Chrysler: the building was to reach a height of 1,250 feet, taller than the Chrysler Building by 202 feet, to become the highest building in the world until the construction of the World Trade Center and the Sears Roebuck Tower in Chicago in the early 1970's. The Empire State Building also set a new record for the speed of construction – more than four floors per week – and because of the Depression it cost less than the estimate ($41 million instead of 60).

Below, work begins on the Empire State Building.

**TEAMWORK**
The army of laborers employed to build the Empire State Building figured in a report by the photographer Lewis Hine (right and opposite).

The Waldorf-Astoria (left), demolished in 1929 and replaced by the Empire State Building.

### AN ENORMOUS PROJECT
The photomontage on the right shows an early design for the Empire State Building superimposed onto the background of the city. This design was not finally used.

### "THE HAPPY WARRIOR"
Alfred E. Smith (right), a former governor of the State of New York and president of the corporation that managed the building, announced the project in 1929.

### A FAILURE
When it was opened on May 1, 1931, the "Empty State Building" had rented out only 46 percent of its office space, despite an extensive publicity campaign.

**IN THE FOREFRONT OF PROGRESS**
Raskob, examining the first model of the flat roof designed by the architect, William Lamb, is supposed to have exclaimed: "This building needs a hat!".

**AN AIR TERMINAL!**
A mooring mast, able to withstand crosswinds of up to 50 tons, was designed for airships, thought then to be the transport of the future: the Graf Zeppelin had just crossed the Atlantic and regular lines were being scheduled. Everything appeared to have a functional use: the balloon was to be attached to the cone at the top and the mooring apparatus, contained in a cylinder 26 feet tall, was connected to a winch and a control mechanism on the 87th floor. Forty passengers could alight at the 102nd floor, onto the 4 foot wide platform from where a stairway led to the circular observation chamber where they could take a lift down to the mini-airport on the 85th floor – comprising a waiting room, cloakroom and customs office.

**A PRECARIOUS DESCENT**
After several landings, with these monsters swaying precariously in the middle of Manhattan, the venture was deemed too hazardous.

The top illuminated to celebrate St. Patrick's Day, Independence Day, Easter Week, Halloween, Memorial Day, Christmas and New Year, Gay's Day.

**5,000 VISITORS PER DAY**
he observatory on the 86th floor
an invaluable source of income
r the Empire State Building.

MOST FAMOUS

FAMOUS

SOUVENIR OF VISIT TO THE

BUILDING IN THE WORLD

EMPIRE STATE OBSERVATORIES

MPIRE S
BSERVAT

3155175

3155175

**WO SIGNS OF THE FUTURE**
he dream of utopian architects and
ience-fiction authors was a union
kyscrapers and air transport.

**HIGH WAVES**
The mooring mast, having become obsolete, was topped with a telecom- munications antenna, like the Eiffel Tower.

**TARS**
he terrace has
elcomed heads of
ate and government
Mussolini, Churchill,
astro, Khrushchev),
owned heads and a
rong of celebrities.
n the west side of the
ass observatory, there
e comfortable rattan
hairs where you can sit
nd admire the sunset.

## REAL CATASTROPHES

The Empire State Building has been the scene of many spectacular disasters, at least as dramatic as the one in the legendary film, *King Kong*.

### THE BIG JUMP

Sixteen people have committed suicide by jumping off the top of the platform on the 86th floor. A railing was erected to stop suicide attempts, but has done nothing to discourage the truly desperate. This figure is actually fairly low given that 70 million visitors have come up to admire the view; the Eiffel Tower has recorded 400 suicides.

### FACT IS STRANGER THAN FICTION

On July 28, 1945, a B-25 bomber, piloted by William Smith, flew over Manhattan at more than 186 mph and at an altitude of 1148 feet, less than half the minimum authorized altitude. It is not known why he was weaving between the skyscrapers of Midtown but at 9.52am, having just missed the Helmsley Building, he crashed into the Empire State Building, devastating the north façade of the 79th floor. One of the engines went straight through the tower and crashed down on the other side of 33rd St. The outcome of this catastrophe was fourteen dead and twenty-six wounded. Luckily, as it was a Saturday, the offices were all virtually deserted.

# MIRACLE ON 3⁴

## Gust of wind saves woman who leaped from 86th floor of Empire State Building

Left, lightning striking the spire.

## THE "POPE" OF POP ART

Andy Warhol (1928–87) came to New York in the summer of 1949 as a commercial illustrator. For his paintings he drew inspiration from comic-strip imagery, news, and advertising. His use of silk screen techniques in his "Factory" (right), with entrances at 19 E. 32nd St. and 22 E. 33rd, enabled him to accentuate and multiply the serial aspect of his works (repetition of the same subject with changes of color against a constant background). Warhol's use of imagery is not far removed from cinema techniques, with which he experimented from 1963. An artist much in the public eye, a Pop Art star, he called himself "the great prostitute of the art world", a world that he invariably held up to derision in paintings that depicted American society in the most harshly realistic and provocative terms.

## AROUND THE EMPIRE STATE BUILDING

**FORMER B. ALTMAN BUILDING ▲** *361.* 5TH AVE. BETWEEN 34TH AND 35TH STS. (1906, arch. Trowbridge & Livingston). Benjamin Altman was the first to open a department store in this previously residential neighborhood. He built it in the style of a grand Italianate palace to blend in with the surrounding mansions. The store closed in 1990, but the building is being redesigned to house the New York Public Library's Science and Industry collection.

**HERALD AND GREELEY SQUARES.** INTERSECTION OF 6TH AVE., BROADWAY AND 34TH ST. These two triangular squares face each other. Herald Square commemorates the New York Herald Building (founded in 1835 by James Gordon Bennett) whose headquarters, built in 1893, stood just north of here. The clock that used to crown the building, which was demolished in 1921, now lords it over the square. Two bronze figures, nicknamed Stuff and Guff, chime the hours. The statue of Horace Greeley, founder of the *New York Tribune* (1841) and a crusading journalist, particularly in the cause of the abolition of slavery, seems to watch them from Greeley Square, just to the south. The statue was erected in 1890.

## A DETOUR TOWARD THE JACOB JAVITS CONVENTION CENTER

Between 11th and 12th aves., 34th and 37th sts., this exhibition center was inaugurated in 1986 and has the facilities to accommodate nearly 86,000 visitors daily. Its architect, I. M. Pei, designed a glass structure that is opaque by day and reflects the skyline of Midtown but becomes transparent when illuminated at night.

Pennsylvania Station before its demolition in 1963.

**MACY'S.** BROADWAY AND 7TH AVE., BETWEEN 34TH AND 35TH STS. (1901, arch. De Lemos & Cordes, additions 1924–31, arch. Robert D. Kohn). R. H. Macy, the former captain of a whaler, founded what was to become "the world's largest store" (as trumpeted by the huge billboard on the Broadway façade) in 1858. After occupying premises in the vicinity of 14th Street, Macy's moved to Broadway and 34th Street in 1902. Over the years the store was extended successively farther west to 7th Avenue. The 34th Street entrance still possesses its superb original decorations: four caryatids hold the emblems of commerce and abundance in their hands.

**MADISON SQUARE GARDEN CENTER.** BETWEEN 31ST AND 33RD STS., 7TH AND 8TH AVES. (1968, arch. Charles Luckman Assocs.). A masterpiece, Penn Station was destroyed in 1963 to make way for this vast leisure and office complex. By the 1960's Pennsylvania Station was one of the few "grand horizontals" left in an increasingly "vertical" New York. Built in 1910 and only four stories high, it covered 12 acres of land. Its architects, McKim, Mead & White, drew their inspiration directly from the great buildings of the Roman Empire. The general waiting room, which was modeled on the Baths of Caracalla, and the steel and glass roof over the train concourse, were particularly fine features. The demolition of the station gave rise to the first major public outcry in support of preserving landmarks. By contrast, the present Penn Station is unobtrusively hidden underground, below Madison Square Garden. This massive complex, which offers cultural and sporting events all year round, is the third with this name; the first was located at Madison Square and the second on 9th Avenue at 49th Street. All of them fell victim to fire.

**AN INSTITUTION**
Every year Macy's organizes the Thanksgiving Day Parade ● *53*. Early in the morning, the parade leaves the Museum of Natural History, on Central Park West, and heads for the store.

Macy's logo, a red star, was once the emblem of Macy the whaler captain.

**GENERAL POST OFFICE OF NEW YORK**
Between 8th and 9th aves., 31st and 33rd sts. Impressed by McKim, Mead & White's Penn Station, the government commissioned this firm to design the General Post Office, which was completed in 1913. Forty percent of its mail used to come via the station, which it faced across 8th Ave. It is, however, merely a pale reflection, aesthetically, of its former neighbor. The width of the façade bears a quotation, loosely adapted from Herodotus: "Neither snow nor rain nor heat nor gloom of night stays these couriers from the swift completion of their appointed rounds."

# ▲ GRAND CENTRAL TERMINAL TO THE THEATER DISTRICT

**1** GRAND CENTRAL TERMINAL  **2** LINCOLN BLDG.  **3** GEN. SOCIETY OF MECHANICS AND TRADESMEN  **4** CENTURY ASSOCIATION  **5** N. Y. PUBLIC LIBRARY  **6** BRYANT PARK  **7** N. Y. YACHT CLUB  **8** ROYALTON HOTEL  **9** ALGONQUIN HOTEL

## TOWARD THE NEW YORK PUBLIC LIBRARY

**LINCOLN BUILDING.** 60 E. 42ND ST. (1929–30, arch. J. E. R. Carpenter). This neo-Gothic tower, designed at the end of the 1920's when skyscraper architecture was booming, rigorously applied the regulations laid

W. 48TH ST.

W. 47TH ST.

W. 46TH ST.

W. 45TH ST.

W. 44TH ST.

W. 43RD ST.

W. 42ND ST.

W. 41ST ST.

9TH AVE.

8TH AVE.

7TH AVE.

THEATER DISTRICT

🥾 Six hours

Harvard Club.

down by the Zoning Resolution ● 97. When it was opened, the developers claimed that never before had an office structure benefited from so much fresh air, or so much bright light. The lobby contains Daniel Chester French's bronze model of Abraham Lincoln for the Lincoln memorial in Washington, D.C. There are quotations from Lincoln's speeches on the walls in the entrance hall.

**GENERAL SOCIETY OF MECHANICS AND TRADESMEN.** 20 W. 44TH ST. (1891, arch. Lamb & Rich). This society, founded in 1785 and modeled on European trade guilds, used to offer evening classes. The impressive library, formed in 1820 for the use of apprentices, contains some extensive collections documenting the cottage industries and the decorative arts in New York. The society's museum includes a collection of locks.

250

BUSH TOWER
**11** EX-KNICKERBOCKER HOTEL
**12** TIMES SQUARE
**13** EX-PARAMOUNT BLDG.
AND THEATER
**14** EX-MCGRAW-HILL BLDG.
**15** FILM CENTER
**16** LANDMARK TAVERN
**17** INTREPID SEA-AIR-
SPACE MUSEUM
**18** MARRIOTT MARQUIS HOTEL
**19** FATHER DUFFY SQUARE
**20** MCGRAW-HILL BLDG.
**21** ROCKEFELLER CENTER
**22** HELMSLEY BLDG.
**23** METLIFE BLDG.
**24** GRACE BLDG.
**25** THE N.Y.
TIMES BLDG.

**THE CLUBS.** This neighborhood is the home of some of the city's most venerable clubs. Leading universities such as Yale, Princeton and Harvard have established their clubs here, and admission is reserved exclusively for former students. The lobby of the Yale Club, at the corner of Vanderbilt Avenue and 44th Street, contains a commemorative plaque for one of the university's former students, Captain Nathan Hale, ▲ *168*, a hero of the American Revolution.

**CENTURY ASSOCIATION**
7 W. 43rd St. This Italianate-style club, founded in 1891 to provide a forum for artists and intellectuals, takes its name from its original number of members – one hundred.

**NEW YORK YACHT CLUB** ★. 37 W. 44TH ST. ● *93* (1901, arch. Warren & Wetmore). The extraordinary windows which suggest the stern of an 18th-century ship and the waves, shells, and seaweed which are carved into the façade ● *93*, indicate this club's sphere of activity. Founded in 1844, the New York Yacht Club is the patriarch of American yacht clubs. Until 1983 it organized the celebrated America's Cup ● *65*, which has taken place every four years since 1851.

**THE AMERICA'S CUP**
In 1851, when Queen Victoria asked who had come second in the race, she received the answer "But, Ma'am, there is no second place".

251

The lobby (right) of the Royalton Hotel.

**ALGONQUIN HOTEL**
Harold Ross, who founded the witty, intellectual magazine *The New Yorker*, regularly attended meetings of the Algonquin's Round Table, whose sparkling conversation enlivened lunchtime in the hotel's Oak Room. One of its members, the cartoonist James Thurber, became a contributor to the magazine.

**N.Y. PUBLIC LIBRARY**
The main façade, which is set back from 5th Ave., is dominated by a triumphal arch crowned by allegorical figures by Paul Wayland Bartlett, representing, from left to right, History, Drama, Poetry, Religion, Romance, and Philosophy. The statues above the fountains on the terrace are the work of Frederick MacMonnies, while the two white marble lions guarding the steps (dubbed Patience and Fortitude) are by Edward Clark Potter. In fine weather the terrace is an ideal spot from which to watch the world go by – perhaps while having a drink in one of its two cafés.

**ROYALTON HOTEL.** 44 W. 44TH ST. The ultra-modern lobby of this hotel, designed by Philip Starck, is worth a visit. The writer William Saroyan used to stay here for long periods of time; this is where he was living when he was awarded the Pulitzer Prize for his play *The Time of Your Life* in 1940.

**ALGONQUIN HOTEL.** 59 W. 44TH ST. (1902, arch. Goldwyn Starrett). In the 1920's, this hotel served as a meeting place for leading figures in theatrical and literary circles. Its oak-paneled dining room has been immortalized for the lovely lunches held here by the Round Table, a group of wits, mainly from *The New Yorker*, including Robert Benchley, Edna Ferber, Ring Lardner, George S. Kaufman and Dorothy Parker. The place to be seen in now is the Blue Bar in the lobby.

**FRED F. FRENCH BUILDING ★.** 551 5TH AVE. AT N. E. CORNER OF 45TH ST. (1927, arch. H. Douglas Ives and Sloan & Robertson). The faience mosaics decorating the upper setbacks of this building were sharply criticized when it was completed. They are now praised for their originality. The lobby is typical of those found in skyscrapers of this period.

## NEW YORK PUBLIC LIBRARY

**HISTORY.** With its valuable collections and majestic, lavishly decorated architecture, the Main Branch of the New York Public Library ranks among the great libraries of the world.

Its research collection was founded on May 23, 1895, with a bequest from Samuel J. Tilden which enabled the collections of the Astor and Lenox libraries to be consolidated. New York's municipal government agreed to contribute a plot of land on the condition that the library be open to the public in the evenings and on Sundays and public holidays. The library site, on 5th Avenue between 40th and 42nd streets, had formerly been occupied by the Croton Reservoir, which was erected in 1842 to supply the city with drinking water. The new library, designed by the Beaux Arts architects John M. Carrère and Thomas Hastings, was opened in 1911. Built of white marble, it sits grandly back from the street on a terrace, approached by wide steps flanked by two haughty-looking stone lions.

**THE INTERIOR.** On the first floor, the Gottesman Exhibition Hall mounts some extremely interesting temporary exhibitions. Since 1983 the murals by Richard Haas, depicting the headquarters of New York's leading newspapers and publishing houses, have graced the De Witt Wallace Periodical Room. This room owes its name to the founder of the *Reader's Digest*, who recopied the first texts he was to publish here. The main Reading Room, on the top floor, which is divided by the delivery desk, runs the length of the building and can accommodate seven hundred readers. There is a guided tour which includes all the rooms.

**THE COLLECTIONS.** The library holds about 36 million objects, including 11.3 million books. Its specialist departments include the Jewish, Slavic and Oriental divisions; the History and Genealogy department, which boasts a collection of 100,000 views of New York; the Scientific department, in which Edwin Land, inventor of the Polaroid camera and Chester Carlson, inventor of xerography, did research; and the Economics department, which houses 1.5 million books and 11,000 periodicals. The library is also the proud owner of some rarities such as a Gutenberg Bible and a globe dating from 1519, the first one to show America.

The third floor landing hall, above the lobby is sumptuously decorated with carved wood, stucco and murals by Edward Laning.

**TRAFFIC JAMS**
Traffic along 5th Ave. had already become snarled by the 1920's. Before automatic traffic lights were installed in 1930, the architect Joseph H. Freedlander designed some control towers, one of which was situated at the intersection of 42nd St. and 5th Ave. From the cabin of this bronze and glass tower, 23 feet high, a policeman could monitor and direct the flow of traffic. The three traffic lights sat on top of the tower.

In 1970 the small shops lining the Avenue of the Americas, or 6th Ave. (above) between 43rd and 44th sts. were knocked down and 1133 (below) was built in their place, continuing the transformation of the avenue.

## AMERICAN STANDARD BUILDING

The carved allegories on the façade of this building, first owned by the American Radiator Company, symbolize the transformation of matter into energy. This figure (right) embodies hydraulic energy.

1133 Ave. of the Americas.

# FROM THE NEW YORK PUBLIC LIBRARY TO TIMES SQUARE

**REPUBLIC NATIONAL BANK TOWER, FORMER KNOX HAT BUILDING.** 452 5TH AVE., S. W. CORNER 5TH AVE. AND 40TH ST. (1902, arch. John H. Duncan). This Beaux Arts-style building originally housed an enormous hat store owned by Colonel Edward M. Knox, the "hatter of presidents".

**BRYANT PARK.** The site of Bryant Park – and of the New York Public Library ▲ *252* – was a potter's field in 1823. In 1853 the Crystal Palace ● *39* (a replica of the one in London) was built on this site to host the first American world's fair; it was destroyed by fire five years later. The park was named after the poet and journalist William Cullen Bryant in 1894 and redesigned in its present form in 1934. During lunch hour people working in the neighborhood come to unwind in this green oasis, the only one in Midtown. It affords a splendid view of the surrounding buildings.

**AMERICAN STANDARD BUILDING, FORMER AMERICAN RADIATOR BUILDING ★.** 40 W. 40TH ST. (1924, arch. Hood & Fouilhoux). This was the first Art Deco building constructed in New York by Hood, who subsequently designed the *Daily News* Building and much of Rockefeller Center ▲ *274*. The characteristic features of this building are the top's black brickwork with gold terracotta trimmings (designed by Hood) and the bronze and black granite façade of the ground floor. Its black marble lobby gleams with mirrors.

**BUSH TOWER.** 132 W. 42ND ST. (arch. Helmle & Corbett). "We wanted to make the structure a model for the tall, narrow building in the center of a city block", the architects remarked about this slender skyscraper, regarded as a prototype for the next ten years. It was built to house the headquarters of the Bush Terminal Company, a shipping firm. Note the allegories carved above the façade and the trompe l'oeil brickwork on the side walls which enhance the effect of verticality.

**FORMER KNICKERBOCKER HOTEL.** 1466 BROADWAY, AT S. E. CORNER OF 42ND ST. (1902, arch. Marvin & Vavis). This hotel was built by Colonel John Jacob Astor IV. One of its famous residents, Enrico Caruso, lived here in a fourteen-room apartment between 1908 and 1920. Mary Pickford, the silent movie star, also stayed here.

## TIMES SQUARE

Times Square owes its name to *The New York Times*, which in 1904 moved into the Times Tower, at the south end of the square. This intersection of Broadway and 7th Avenue was, from the turn of the century until the 1960's, the center of the performing arts in New York.

Times Square has lost most of its glamour in recent years and looks distinctly seedy. However, one popular tradition from its heyday persists: people still come in their thousands to welcome in the New Year. The illuminated ball that used to descend along the façade at the stroke of midnight has been replaced by a big apple.

**1 TIMES SQUARE, FORMER TIMES TOWER.** (1904, arch. Eidlitz & MacKenzie). *The New York Times* occupied Times Tower for only about ten years before moving most of its operations into its present premises at 229 West 43rd Street. In 1966 the tower was converted (and renamed the Allied Chemical

**"**The age of the huge advertising billboards dawned in 1916. The whole district was electrified. Times Square . . . was a new wonderland, an electric city, the Great White Way of Broadway.**"**

Jerome Charyn,
*Metropolis*

Tower) and its original granite and terracotta facing was replaced by a marble one. Today the moving electric sign that wraps around the tower is operational again after several years of darkness. When first switched on in 1928, it announced the result of the presidential elections with Herbert Hoover's victory.

**FORMER PARAMOUNT BUILDING.** 1501 BROADWAY (1927, arch. Rapp & Rapp). The most eye-catching building on Times Square used to house the offices for Paramount Pictures, as well as the Paramount Theater which no longer exists. The day after its opening, in 1926, the *New York Times* ran this advertisement: "30,222 spectators in two days! Into the paradise of luxury, color and enchantment they came." The grandiose "movie palace" seating 3,664 people, had a huge lobby, the Grand Hall, larger than that of the Paris Opera House, as well as various lounges and promenades. The movie theater had to close in 1965, as it was not making a profit, and the building was converted into offices. Dolly Down, a singer who once performed there, said of its new occupants: "These kids have no idea what it was and they'll never know because there will not be anything like those theaters again." This building has fourteen symmetrical setbacks, rising to a sphere, formerly illuminated, at the top.

**PARAMOUNT THEATER**
Before the 1929 crash, an evening's program here comprised sketches, a play and a movie from Paramount Pictures.

The Paramount subsequently billed big bands and singers. Frank Sinatra gave some of his most famous performances here, singing with the Tommy Dorsey Orchestra.

## LOBBY OF THE FILM CENTER BUILDING

Although the exterior of the Film Center Building is ordinary, its lobby is stunning. The architect, Albert Kahn, was influenced by the Decorative Arts exhibition in Paris (1925) and this building marked the start of his polychromatic phase. For the floor he created a composition combining pinkish marble circles with white and black marble strips; for the walls (above right) a mosaic of blue and orange tiles.

Façade of the Actors Studio.

## MURAL PAINTING

The façade of this bicycle store at the corner of 9th Ave. and 47th St. is decorated with a reproduction of a drawing by Sempé, whose *New Yorker* illustrations had caught the eye of the store's owner.

## DETOUR TO THE HUDSON RIVER

Rather than continuing toward the Theater District, leave Broadway and head for the Hudson River.

**FORMER McGRAW-HILL BUILDING.** 330 W. 42ND ST. (1931, arch. Hood, Godley & Fouilhoux). This New York landmark ● *99*, a fusion of Art Deco and International Style, has a beautifully decorated lobby, whose opaque Carrera glass and stainless steel benefit from a sophisticated lighting system.

**FILM CENTER BUILDING ★.** 630 9TH AVE. (1929, arch. Ely Jacques). This building is a typical example of 1920's Art Deco ● *99* architecture. Its extraordinary polychromatic lobby is well worth the walk from Broadway.

**ACTORS STUDIO.** 432 W. 44TH ST. (1858). The famous drama school, founded by Elia Kazan in 1947, moved into this former Presbyterian church in 1955. The Actors Studio became internationally famous through the work of its director, Lee Strasberg, and radically influenced the New York theater scene. The "Strasberg Method", inspired by Stanislavsky and his Art Theater in Moscow, advocated an intensive course of mental exercises to improve actors' self-awareness and their empathy with the character. Marlon Brando attended classes here.

**"HELL'S KITCHEN".** The area lying to the west of 6th Avenue, between 30th and 57th streets was long known as "Hell's Kitchen". This nickname allegedly emerged from a conversation between two policemen who had been called out to deal with a street brawl at the height of summer. One of them apparently exclaimed, "It's as hot as Hell here." The other corrected him, saying "It's cool in Hell. This is Hell's kitchen." Until 1945 the nickname was fairly apt, for the area was then controlled by the underworld. Over the past few decades, however, the inhabitants and real estate developers have done their utmost to revamp its image, including renaming it Clinton, after the current President.

**LANDMARK TAVERN.** S. E. CORNER 11TH AVE. AND 46TH ST. (1868). This establishment has remained more or less unchanged for years. Inside, the dark wood paneling, the old mirrors, the paved floor and the wood-burning stoves give visitors the impression of having stepped back in time.

**INTREPID SEA-AIR-SPACE MUSEUM.** PIER 86, W. 46TH ST. The *Intrepid* is an aircraft carrier from World War Two which has been converted into a floating museum. Two blocks farther north is the N.Y.C. Passenger Ship Terminal, which belongs to the Port Authority of New York and New Jersey. This was built by the city in 1974 to accommodate the huge luxury cruisers, but with the exception of the *Queen Elizabeth II*, few liners have actually opted to use it.

**INTREPID SEA-AIR-SPACE MUSEUM**
This museum comprises four units: the *Intrepid* itself, a submarine, a destroyer and a lightship. The aircraft carrier holds an exhibition including model ships, satellites

## TOWARD THE THEATER DISTRICT

**MARRIOTT MARQUIS HOTEL.** 1531–49 BROADWAY (1985, arch. John C. Portman & Assocs.). Three theaters were demolished to make way for the Marriott, one of Manhattan's largest hotels. Like many hotels of this period, it is built around a spectacular atrium. Take a dizzying ride in one of the hotel's transparent elevators.

**I. MILLER BUILDING.** N. E. CORNER OF 46TH ST. AND 7TH AVE.

The south façade here is decorated with an impresssive array of sculptures by A. Stirling Calder (1929), depicting actresses and singers in their most famous roles: Mary Pickford as Little Lord Fauntleroy, Ethel Barrymore as Ophelia, Rosa Ponselle as Norma and Marilyn Miller as Sunny.

**FATHER DUFFY SQUARE.** The north triangle of Times Square was named after Father Duffy, the "Fighting Chaplain of the 69th regiment". This New York unit served in France during World War One. Later, in his parish church, Holy Cross Roman Catholic Church (42nd Street), Father Duffy became friendly with many actors and comedians. His statue (1937, Charles Keck) is decorated with a Celtic cross. Father Duffy Square is also the site of the TKTS booth, where one can buy half-price tickets for Broadway shows.

**1580 BROADWAY.** BETWEEN 47TH AND 48TH STS. (1989, arch. Mayers & Schiff). This building's enormous advertising billboards are reminiscent of Times Square during the 1940's, when it used to sparkle with a constellation of lights. This building boasts a bold glass spire and, along with 750 7th Avenue (1989, arch. Roche, Dinkeloo & Assocs.), is one of the new office towers that, during the 1980's transformed the skyline north of Times Square.

and an Apollo space capsule. There is a film archive relating to submarines as well as World War Two and the Vietnam War. In the submarine, which, like the *Intrepid*, is a veteran of World War Two, visitors can take part in simulated submersions.

**GEORGE M. COHAN**
This actor-director and author-composer, immortalized in 1959 by Georg John Lober, "gives his regards to Broadway" forever in Father Duffy Square;

"Give My Regards to Broadway" is his best-known song.

For over a century, Broadway has been almost synonymous with American theater. There is no better yardstick of talent than acting or directing on Broadway. Originally New York's theater district was centered around City Hall ▲ *168*, but by the end of the 19th century it had moved to Broadway, around 42nd Street, and it has stayed there ever since. In the 1920's, the movie companies moved here and built huge movie palaces in the vicinity of Times Square. The recession in the movie industry during the 1950's and 1960's led to the closing of several movie theaters. Today the Theater District includes some forty legitimate theaters located between 40th and 57th streets, 6th and 8th avenues. A subtle hierarchy distinguishes between "Broadway" shows (large-scale productions staged in the Theater District), "Off Broadway" shows (more modest-sized productions) and "Off-off Broadway" productions (avant-garde and fringe theater).

**WINTER GARDEN THEATER,** 1634 Broadway at 50th St. (1911). This theater's opening starred Al Jolson. Below, Chanin's Theater and Biltmore Theater (above right), built by the Chanin brothers.

**"SIN STREET".** At the beginning of the century, the first theaters in the district, some twelve in all, were clustered along a small stretch of 42nd Street, between Broadway and 8th Avenue. Most of them are now sex shops and cinemas showing "adult" movies, hence the name "Sin Street". The NEW AMSTERDAM THEATER (1903), at 214 West 42nd Street, closed since 1983 and currently being restored, is the most interesting of the theaters on 42nd Street. The producer Florenz Ziegfeld was a partial owner and he converted the roof into another theater, AERIAL GARDENS. Ziegfeld's famous revue – the annual Ziegfeld Follies, was performed at the New Amsterdam from 1913 until 1927, when he had his own

**BOOTH THEATER** 222 W. 45th St. (1913) The theater (below, center) owes its name to the actor Edwin Booth ▲ *230*. Flanking it are the Shubert and Majestic Theaters.

theater built on the corner of 54th Street and 6th Avenue. THE LYRIC (1903), at 213 West 42nd Street, was the New Amsterdam's main rival and engaged prestigious stars such as Douglas Fairbanks and Fred Astaire and his sister Adele; the Astaires were wooed by both theaters. In 1925 the Lyric staged the first performance by the Marx Brothers of George S. Kaufman's play *The Cocoanuts*, with music by Irving Berlin.

## THE "GREAT WHITE WAY".

The stretch of 44th Street between 7th and 8th avenues includes five Broadway theaters. The MAJESTIC (1927) at no. 245, the HELEN HAYES (1912) at no. 238 and the BROADHURST (1917) at no. 235 were all the work of Herbert J. Krapp. Krapp was a prolific and talented architect who designed some twenty theaters; all are highly regarded for the quality of their acoustics, their unimpeded sightlines and their decoration. The SHUBERT THEATER (1913) at 225 West 44th Street, was built at the same time as the Booth Theater for

Rodger's Theater, 1924, the former Chanin's Theater.

### BARRYMORE THEATER
243 W. 47th St. (1928). This theater was built in honor of the actress Ethel Barrymore. Fred Astaire appeared in Cole Porter's *The Gay Divorce* (1932). In 1947, Marlon Brando made his debut, alongside Jessica Tandy, in *A Streetcar Named Desire*.

the Shubert brothers. It runs along the east side of Shubert Alley, a famous passageway formerly frequented by actors who would meet outside the offices of Sam J. J. and Lee Shubert when new productions were being cast. The LAMB'S THEATER (1904) situated at 130 West 44th Street, shares the former premises of the Lambs Club with the Manhattan Church of the Nazarene. Many personalities , such as Al Jolson, W. C. Fields, Spencer Tracy and John Barrymore used to meet and stay at the Lambs Club. One block away, at 149 West 45th Street, is the LYCEUM THEATER, the first of the Times Square theaters to be built north of 42nd Street. Completed in 1903, it was considered the height of modernity, for its auditorium had no balcony and there were gift shops inside. The most famous venue for musicals is the IMPERIAL THEATER (1923), 249 West 45th Street; shows by such greats as George and Ira Gershwin, Cole Porter, Irving Berlin and Leonard Bernstein have been staged here. The LONGACRE THEATER (1913), at 220 West 48th Street, had its heyday in the 1930's when the Group Theater staged plays directed by Lee Strasberg.

### LYCEUM THEATER
A window in the apartment of producer Daniel Frohman, for whom this theater was built (1903), looked out over the stage, apparently so he could watch his wife Margaret Illington in plays.

From left to right, the Longacre, Simon and Imperial theaters.

**CORNELIUS VANDERBILT** (1794–1877) Vanderbilt's statue used to grace the pediment of his Hudson River Railroad Freight Depot, built in 1869. When the depot became obsolete in 1927, the statue was moved to Grand Central Terminal.

The building site of Grand Central Terminal ▲ 239, in 1910, seen from the north.

**THE HELMSLEY EMPIRE**
Harry and Leona Helmsley have taken their place among New York's legendary entrepreneurs. He possesses a huge property empire and a fortune estimated at $5 billion. Among the jewels in their crown are the Helmsley Building (right), the Empire State Building and the Helmsley Palace Hotel ▲ 284.

## PARK AVENUE TO SUTTON PLACE

**PARK AVENUE.** In 1888 the city of New York re-named the section of 4th Avenue between 43rd and 96th streets. Although enjoying the new name of Park Avenue, it remained a mass of railroad tracks until the rails were electrified in 1904 and then completely covered. This incentive was part of an overall planning program which included the reconstruction of Grand Central Terminal (1903–13) ▲ 236, as well as the construction of office buildings, hotels and luxury apartments along Park Avenue.

**HELMSLEY BUILDING, FORMERLY NEW YORK CENTRAL BUILDING.** 230 PARK AVE., BETWEEN 45TH AND 46TH STS. (1929, arch. Warren & Wetmore). This was built to house the headquarters of the railroad company founded by Cornelius Vanderbilt. "Commodore" Vanderbilt was, by the time he died in 1877, the most famous millionaire in the United States. By 1810, at the age of sixteen, he had bought a sailing ship and started a ferryboat service between Staten Island and Manhattan. He then assembled a fleet of transatlantic liners and coasting vessels. At the age of seventy he embarked on a career as railroad magnate, eventually creating the New York Central Railroad Company. The former New York Central Building, which is now part of the Helmsley real estate empire, has the disctinction of being the only building in New York to straddle an avenue. Two giant portals provide vehicles with access, in the south, to the Pershing Viaduct, built in 1919, and to Park Avenue South. The building's elegant white marble lobby is well worth a visit.

**METLIFE BUILDING, FORMERLY PAN AM BUILDING.** 200 PARK AVE. (1963, arch. Emery Roth & Sons, Pietro Belluschi and Walter Gropius). Built for Pan Am and bought in 1981 by the Metropolitan Life Insurance Company, this fifty-eight-story skyscraper is disliked by almost all New Yorkers. It looms over the Helmsley Building and Grand Central Terminal ▲ 236, spoiling the view down Park Avenue. In 1977 its roof was the scene of a helicopter crash. Trying to land

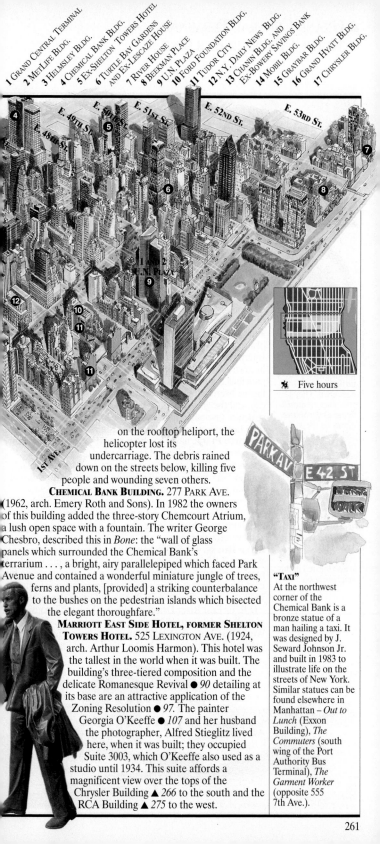

**%** Five hours

on the rooftop heliport, the helicopter lost its undercarriage. The debris rained down on the streets below, killing five people and wounding others.

**CHEMICAL BANK BUILDING.** 277 PARK AVE. (1962, arch. Emery Roth and Sons). In 1982 the owners of this building added the three-story Chemcourt Atrium, a lush open space with a fountain. The writer George Chesbro, described this in *Bone*: the "wall of glass panels which surrounded the Chemical Bank's terrarium . . . , a bright, airy parallelepiped which faced Park Avenue and contained a wonderful miniature jungle of trees, ferns and plants, [provided] a striking counterbalance to the bushes on the pedestrian islands which bisected the elegant thoroughfare."

**MARRIOTT EAST SIDE HOTEL, FORMER SHELTON TOWERS HOTEL.** 525 LEXINGTON AVE. (1924, arch. Arthur Loomis Harmon). This hotel was the tallest in the world when it was built. The building's three-tiered composition and the delicate Romanesque Revival ● *90* detailing at its base are an attractive application of the Zoning Resolution ● *97*. The painter Georgia O'Keeffe ● *107* and her husband the photographer, Alfred Stieglitz lived here, when it was built; they occupied Suite 3003, which O'Keeffe also used as a studio until 1934. This suite affords a magnificent view over the tops of the Chrysler Building ▲ *266* to the south and the RCA Building ▲ *275* to the west.

**"TAXI"**
At the northwest corner of the Chemical Bank is a bronze statue of a man hailing a taxi. It was designed by J. Seward Johnson Jr. and built in 1983 to illustrate life on the streets of New York. Similar statues can be found elsewhere in Manhattan – *Out to Lunch* (Exxon Building), *The Commuters* (south wing of the Port Authority Bus Terminal), *The Garment Worker* (opposite 555 7th Ave.).

**TURTLE BAY**
The name of this neighborhood refers to a marshy cove in the East River where turtles once abounded. They – and other creatures – figure as decorative motifs on the walls and the newel posts of the railings of some of the houses in the Turtle Bay Historic District. The area's distinguished residents have included E. B. White, Leopold Stokowski, Tyrone Power and Katharine Hepburn. The U.N. Headquarters ▲ 264 is also located in this neighborhood.

**TURTLE BAY GARDENS HISTORIC DISTRICT.** 227–247 E. 48TH AND 226–246 E. 49TH STS. (1820, restored in 1920, arch. Dean and Bottomley). In the mid-19th century, Turtle Bay, the site on which the Dutch governor William Kieft had built his farm in 1639, was overrun by factories and slaughterhouses. However, some attractive Italianate rowhouses were also built in this period, and in 1920 an enlightened developer bought a group of them and combined all their back gardens into one common garden. The houses were remodeled so that the living rooms face the garden, thus turning their backs on the surrounding commercial activity.

**FORMER LESCAZE HOUSE.** 211 E. 48TH ST. (1934, arch. William Lescaze). The style and size of this white house form a contrast with the brownstones of Turtle Bay Gardens. Lescaze designed this International Style ● 100 residence-cum-studio to advertise his own firm. The influence of Le Corbusier is apparent in the judicious use of materials: the glass block panels used in the façade overlooking the street create a bulwark against the city, and the glazed bays at the rear overlook a terrace. This structure fascinated neighbors to such an extent that for a time Lescaze opened his home to visitors.

**BEEKMAN PLACE.** BETWEEN 49TH AND 51ST STS. This pleasant site overlooking the East River is named after a local resident, James Beekman, whose mansion, Mount Pleasant, built in 1765, was used by the British as headquarters during the War of Independence ● 27. Nathan Hale ▲ 168 was sentenced to death here for spying and hanged on September 22, 1776. The house was destroyed in 1874 when, due to the proliferation of harbor industries, the area became rundown and overcrowded.

**RIVER HOUSE.** 435 E. 52ND ST. (1931, arch. Bottomley, Wagner & White). Originally, yacht-owning tenants could reach this luxury apartment block from a landing stage on the East River. The residence was cut off from the river in the 1940's when the Franklin D. Roosevelt Drive (also called F.D.R. or East River Drive) was built. The landfill consisted partially of debris from bombing raids on London during World War Two, which had been used as ballast for ships carrying American troops back to the United States.

Turtle Bay in 1852.

## A DETOUR NORTH: SUTTON PLACE.

BETWEEN 57TH AND 58TH STS. This little enclave, lined with townhouses, owes its name to Effingham B. Sutton, who made his fortune during the California Gold Rush of 1849 and launched the first shipping line operating between New York and San Francisco. He invested some of his profits to develop this neighborhood, but it did not become fashionable until the 1920's. Nearby Riverview Terrace consists of five townhouses, with terrace gardens, overlooking the East River, Queensboro Bridge and Roosevelt Island.

## THE UNITED NATIONS

Located along the bank of the East River, between 42nd and 48th streets, the headquarters of the U.N.O. (United Nations Organization) covers more than 15 acres .

**THE WORLD'S PARLIAMENT.** The U.N.O., created in the aftermath of World War Two, succeeded the League of Nations, its fundamental task being to "save succeeding generations from the scourge of war". The General Assembly, which is a true international parliament, is presently made up of delegations from 180 states. It meets every year from September to December, dealing with some 150 cases relating to issues as diverse as disarmament, economic aid and women's rights.

**THE ROLE OF NELSON A. ROCKEFELLER.** The fifty founding states of the U.N.O. agreed, at the first General Assembly in London, in 1946, that the headquarters should be located in the United States. Several sites were considered: New York, Connecticut, Boston, Philadelphia and San Francisco. Once New York had been chosen, a committee of prominent figures, including Nelson Rockefeller, tried to promote Flushing Meadow, the site of the Universal Exhibition of 1939, as a suitable base. The U.N.O. rejected this proposal (although the General Assembly did meet there between 1946 and 1949).

Construction of F.D.R. Drive along the East River, viewed from the Queensboro Bridge.

**U.N. SECRETARIAT BUILDING**
Along 1st Ave., the multicolored flags of the member nations mark the boundary between the territory of New York and the international enclave of the United Nations. The grayish-blue glass skin of this skyscraper's east and west façades was chosen to minimize the effects of the sun; its north and south façades are clad in Vermont marble. The thirty-eighth floor houses the Secretary General's offices.

**AN ARCHITECTURAL COMPLEX**
A team of ten architects, including Le Corbusier and Oscar Niemeyer, began work on the U.N. headquarters in January 1947. They opted for three self-contained buildings: the Secretariat, the General Assembly and the Conference Building. The first cornerstone was laid on October 24, 1949 (above) and at the end of August 1950 the first civil servants moved into their offices. The library – south of the General Assembly – was added in 1963.

U.N. coat of arms.

**THE CONFERENCE BUILDING**
This building houses the Security Council Chamber, the Trusteeship Council Chamber, the Economic and Social Council Chamber and a number of smaller rooms. There are daily tours around the U.N. and it is possible to attend public meetings of the General Assembly and the Security Council, here shown (right) in a meeting on January 31, 1992.

As the United Nations was on the point of opting for a head-quarters in Philadelphia, Nelson Rockefeller persuaded his father, John D. Rockefeller, Jr, to donate the $8.5 million needed to buy some land along the East River.

## TUDOR CITY

**SHCHARANSKY STEPS.** These steps leading to Tudor City were named in homage to the Soviet Jewish dissident Anatoly Shcharansky. The best view of the United Nations headquarters can be obtained from the top of these steps.

## GENERAL ASSEMBLY BUILDING

The curved roof of this building is crowned with a dome, which is considered a symbol of governmental authority.

**A "SELF-CONTAINED CITY".** (1925–8, arch. Fred F. French Co.). Tudor City occupies the entire area between E. 40th and E. 43rd streets, 1st and 2nd avenues. Exclusively financed by private funds, and built in a quasi-Tudor style which inspired its name, it was a bold attempt at urban renewal. The aim was to create "a self-contained city" in a then insalubrious neighborhood. There are twelve apartment buildings containing three thousand apartments, a hotel with six hundred

## FORD FOUNDATION BUILDING

This elegant example ● *101* of the International Style, whose main entrance is at 321 E. 42nd St., houses the Ford Foundation, patrons of the arts, humanities and science. Constructed of warm-toned brick, rust-colored Cor-Ten Steel and glass, it has an interior garden (above) which is open to the public. An ornamental pond, replenished by condensation, acts as a self-sustaining irrigation system.

rooms, a post office, various stores and private parks. Around the turn of the century this area was frequented by criminals and gangsters. At one time, it was dubbed "Corcoran's Roost", after the notorious band it Paddy Corcoran and his "Rag Gang". The neighborhood was also heavily industrialized, filled with factories, breweries and slaughterhouses. Consequently the architects designed its buildings so they faced inward, placing very few windows in the walls bordering the surrounding squalor. Today its residents regret being deprived of some stunning views.

1 VISITORS' ENTRANCE
2 LOBBY
3 GENERAL ASSEMBLY HALL
4 DELEGATES' LOUNGE
5 SECRETARIAT BUILDING
6 CONFERENCE BUILDING
7 SECURITY COUNCIL
8 TRUSTEESHIP COUNCIL
9 ECONOMIC AND SOCIAL COUNCIL

Walter Percy Chrysler (1875–1940) began his career as an apprentice in a railroad machine shop; by 1925, he was president of the Chrysler automobile company. In 1928 he resuscitated a project initially conceived by the property developer William H. Reynolds for a skyscraper at the corner of Lexington Avenue and 42nd Street. His architect, William Van Alen, persuaded him to aim at setting a new record for the world's tallest building: in 1930, a stainless steel spire enabled him to achieve his goal, but it was soon surpassed by the Empire State Building.

## The "Vertex"
The spire, which measures 197 feet in height and weighs about 30 tons, was designed in secret by Van Alen and hoisted in one piece to the top of the tower, an operation that took only an hour and a half.

## The sky's the limit
Chrysler had two goals: to top the Woolworth Building and to snatch the title of the tallest structure in the world from the Eiffel Tower. He was not the only one: the Empire State Building ▲ 242 and the Bank of Manhattan ▲ 161 were also competing in this vertical race.

## A contest to settle accounts
What started as simple rivalry turned into an attempt to settle old scores between Van Alen and his former partner and now sworn enemy, H. Craig Severance, the architect of the Bank of Manhattan. Chrysler and Van Alen produced their trump card only after they had led Severance to believe that his building would be the victor. Their "joker" was a spire which Van Alen called "the Vertex". When the building was nearly completed, workers hoisted huge sheets of steel to the 65th story and, with the help of a derrick, raised the spire to the top of the tower.

Once the Vertex was in place, it brought the height of the Chrysler Building to 1,048 feet, higher than the 71-story Bank of Manhattan Company.

**THE "HIGHEST MAN IN THE WORLD"**
A luxurious duplex apartment (left) was built for Walter Chrysler in the building's spire. The triangular windows of the apartment looked out over the vast panorama of Manhattan. The Cloud Club (bottom) was a meeting room for American industrial magnates and is also decorated in the purest Art Deco style. The view is complemented by a painted mural of the city.

**"WALKING BUILDING"**
The anthropomorphic character of the Chrysler Building is due to the spire, which has been compared to a wildly exaggerated hairstyle. Van Alen himself wore a replica of it to the Beaux Arts Ball.

Van Alen, who had been an outstanding student at the École des Beaux Arts, was nicknamed "the Ziegfeld of his profession" by one of his colleagues in *The American Architect*.

This architect, with his wearing of the replica of the Chrysler building spire, created rathe spectacle worthy of the best shows of Busby Berkeley.

On the sixteenth story, you can see classical urns reworked to reflect an Art Deco vision.

## IN HONOR OF THE AUTOMOBILE

The corners of the main setbacks, designed in compliance with the 1916 Zoning Resolution, are set off by ornamental sculptures made of reflective sheets of steel. The skyscraper's "neck" is adorned by eight stylized eagle heads, modern style gargoyles (below). The thirtieth story, which houses the mechanical equipment and is therefore blind, sports a frieze of two-colored brick representing car wheels with their metal hubcaps and fenders. The corne are decorated with giant Chrysler radiator caps, inspired by Mercur winged helmet (above).

## A BEACON ON THE NEW YORK SKYLINE

The building's visual impact is due partly to the richness of form and partly to the clever use of materials, in particular the plates of stainless steel – evocative of car ornaments – which glitter in the sunshine.

## AN EXPRESSIONIST SPIRE

The spire, with its dovetailed arches fitting inside each other like Russian dolls (right), differs markedly from other skyscraper tops of the period, which were inspired mainly by the 1925 Exhibition of Decorative Arts in Paris. The Chrysle Building's spire ha more in common w German Expressionism, the utopian drawings o Bruno Taut and movie sets, such as those in Robert Wiene's *The Cabin of Dr Caligari* (191

## A SUBTLE BALANCE

Adding the spire of the building – which has been compared to Nijinsky's headdress in a ballet produced by Sergei Diaghilev, or a Balinese dancer's headdress or the crown worn by some exotic monarch – to the main part of the building entailed a subtle arrangement of façades, in which the curved, vertically thrusting shapes rhythmically echo the outline of the three central bays, in turn stabilized by horizontal bands of decoration. The result is as exuberant as New York itself. The complete elevation ▲ 266, clearly illustrates the use of different motifs.

A door (right) in the main entrance.

'We certainly do lead the world in architecture,' said Professor Timson. 'Architecture, I take it, is the natural artistic expression of a young nation. Youth wants to build, and Manhattan Island kind of looks as though we've done what we wanted.'...

Erik Linklater
*Juan in America*

**THE LOBBY**
The Chrysler Building's décor is eye-catching from top to bottom. The truncated shape of the deeply recessed entrance, which some critics have compared to that of a coffin, and which rises over three stories, sets the tone for the angular interior polished design. For example, metal triangles are superimposed on the notched strip dividing the doors of a huge stained-glass window. The extraordinary triangular lobby narrows as it rises. Glowing red in the semi-darkness, it is probably the most spectacular interior to be found in any office building built during the inter-war years. Red Moroccan marble walls, sienna-colored floor, moldings made of amber-colored onyx and bluish marble are orchestrated in a vivid symphony which builds to a climax: the ceiling, painted by Edward Trumbull, symbolizing Energy, Result, Workmanship and Transportation. . . .

UNITED S...

**ZIGZAG MOTIFS**
The lavishness of the décor – even the veins in the huge marble slabs of the walls form zigzag motifs – is breathtaking. The fountain motifs (top left), the palm leaves and the vividly portrayed eagles on the mailboxes (left) add to the profusion of images. Taken as a whole, the decoration of the Chrysler Building represents an ape... Art Deco design, style which, thoug created in Europe became immensel popular in the Un States.

## GEOMETRIC FRIEZES IN ART DECO STYLE

Art Deco style is characterized by the systematic use of simple geometric shapes in dynamic compositions. It marks a break with the Art Nouveau style popular at the beginning of the century, which was inspired by the sinuous contours of plants.

## PORTRAIT OF BUILDING

The paintings on the lobby ceiling celebrate the innovation of air mail and the skyscraper itself, depicting its façade and scenes from its construction. This sort of "narcissistic self-portraiture" was one of the most fashionable themes used by interior designers in skyscrapers of his period. It also enabled visitors to take in the whole building and its gigantic dimensions, something that was impossible to do from the boxed-in streets.

A digital clock used to hang over an information desk, opposite the main entrance, a focal point like the altar in a modern-day cathedral, consecrated to the worship of information.

## MARBLE AND FINE WOODS

The elevators, divided from the lobby by sections of cathode ray tubing, creating the effect of a theater curtain in the process of opening, comprise four banks of eight cars, each decorated differently with superb inlays. It took eight varieties of wood – from such places as Japan, England and Cuba – to create the fine marquetry of the doors (right). These elevators, whose splendor and speed are unsurpassed, served as models for the elevators of recent Postmodern skyscrapers, such as the AT&T (now Sony) Building.

Details of the elaborate
radiator grills from the
Chanin Building, designed
by René Chambellan.

**LOBBY OF THE
CHANIN BUILDING**
This was designed by
Jacques Delamarre to
celebrate the success
of Irwin Chanin in
New York and to
illustrate "the story of
a city in which it is
possible for a man to
rise from a humble
place to wealth and
influence by the sheer
power of his mind
and hands".
New York, 1930

**THE NEWS BUILDING.** 220 E. 42ND ST. (1930, arch. Howells &
Hood). This is the headquarters of one of New York's few
remaining daily newspapers, which still boasts a wide
circulation. It was founded in 1919 as the *Illustrated Daily
News* by two army officers, Captain Patterson and Colonel
("Bertie") McCormick. The first issue, on June 26, 1919,
proclaimed: "See New York's most beautiful girls every
morning in the *Illustrated Daily News....*" The paper was
renamed the *Daily News* two years later. When the building
was opened, the large GLOBE in the lobby was found to be
revolving in the wrong direction. This mistake was hastily
rectified. The details on the globe are regularly updated as
the names and borders of the countries around the world are
changed.

## AROUND THE CHRYSLER BUILDING

The bronze
flooring in
the lobby of the
Chanin Building uses
typical Art Deco
motifs: boats, planes,
trains and cars.

**CHANIN BUILDING.** 122 E. 42ND ST. (1929, arch.
Sloan & Robertson, lobby designed by Jacques
Delamarre). Magnificent bas-reliefs,
composed of animal motifs, run the
length of the façade on the lower part of
this 56-story building. The breathtaking
Art Deco lobby, with its bronze screens and
richly decorated elevator doors and mailboxes,
is a "must". The building originally had a scenic
roof and a theater on the 50th floor; unfortunately
neither is now accessible. You can see
the top of the Chanin Building by walking
several blocks down Lexington Avenue.

**GRAYBAR BUILDING.** 420 LEXINGTON AVE.
(1927, arch. Sloan & Robertson). When this
was built, it was the largest office building in
the world, capable of accommodating twelve
thousand employees. Lines for Grand Central
Terminal ▲ *236* used to run through the
basement, and one of the three entrances
located on Lexington Avenue still serves as an
entrance to the station. One of the arches
along this corridor is decorated with frescoes
depicting trains, planes and building sites.

**BESTIARY**
The carved animal
forms that appear on
the capitals, cornices
and other places in
the former Bowery
Savings Bank include
squirrels, lions, and
bulls and bears which
symbolize
respectively thrift,
power and the world
of finance.

**HOME SAVINGS BANK, FORMER BOWERY
SAVINGS BANK.** 110 E. 42ND ST. (1923, arch.
York & Sawyer). Constructed in the style of a
Roman basilica, this imposing bank has a distinctive arched
entrance as well as a huge 65-foot-high banking hall with a
coffered ceiling, which should not be missed. The counters
are still positioned in the center of the hall, leaving exposed
large areas of the richly patterned mosaic floor. The huge
original solid bronze doors now adorn the east and west walls
of this splendid room.

**PERSHING SQUARE BUILDING.** 100 E. 42ND ST. (1914–23, arch.
York & Sawyer). Although the word "square" figures in the
building's name, the "square" is actually just an intersection
of 42nd Street and Park Avenue South, named in homage to
General John J. Pershing, who commanded the American
Expeditionary Forces in France in 1917–18. It was the last
skyscraper in New York to be built without setbacks, its plans
having predated the Zoning Resolution of 1916 ● *97*.

# AROUND
# ROCKEFELLER CENTER

**SUNSHINE AND ICE**
Since 1936, the lower Plaza has been a sunny terrace in summer but is transformed from October through April into a 957-square yard open-air skating rink.

**ATLAS**
The bronze Atlas by Lee Lawrie, placed at the entrance of the International Building in 1937, faces St. Patrick's Cathedral on 5th Ave. He holds an armillary sphere, decorated with the signs of the zodiac, whose axis points foward the North Star.

**THE MODERN AGE.** "This Titanesque composition of stone, concrete, glass and steel is symbolic of New York – it embodies its essence, trumpets its pride in the same way as the solemn splendor of cathedrals symbolized the very essence of urban communities in the Middle Ages, handing it down to future generations" (Klaus Mann, 1936). The image of the cathedral seems appropriate for Rockefeller Center, just as it was for the Woolworth Building, since it evokes time-honored tradition, though it fails to take account of the innovative nature of the project. The driving force behind the project, John D. Rockefeller Jr, was not attempting, like Chrysler or John Jakob Raskob – two patrons of the motor car, another symbol of modernity – to feed his ego by building a larger and more magnificent monument than that of his precursors. On the contrary, as Klaus Mann pointed out, his project was the very embodiment of quintessential New York and, more generally, of a type of modernity which was, by definition, American.

**A CLASSICAL MODEL.** Rockefeller Center is made up of a complex of fourteen buildings, built in the 1930's, plus another five buildings

> "THE BUILDINGS ARE A SHIMMERING VERTICALITY, A GOSSAMER VEIL, A FESTIVE SCENE-DROP HANGING THERE AGAINST THE BLACK SKY TO DAZZLE, ENTERTAIN, AMAZE"
> FRANK LLOYD WRIGHT

### A CITY WITHIN A CITY

The nineteen buildings that make up Rockefeller Center are arranged in a gridiron pattern. The main axis is composed of Rockefeller Plaza (1), then the Lower Plaza (2), and finally Channel Gardens (3), flanked by La Maison Française (4) and the British Empire Building (5); among other stores, this latter houses a Metropolitan Museum of Art shop. From its height of 850 feet (70 stories), the General Electric Building (6) towers above the complex which boasts altogether 557 stories, 67 elevators, 48,000 windows cleaned by 893 employees and 100,000 telephones. Sixty thousand people work there and every day Rockefeller Center welcomes 175,000 visitors.

completed after 1945, on the other side of 6th Avenue. It is currently home to a number of diverse businesses (Radio City Music Hall, NBC, General Electric – the former RCA Building), and links older nations (Maison Française and the British Empire Building) which were there from its inception. Its pleasing design provides the city with an open space, dotted with fountains and statues whose transparent symbolism reiterates American values by dint of a great many mythological allusions (*Prometheus* lording it over the Lower Plaza, for example). It is a strange mixture of idealism and pragmatism, inspired by functionalist theories similar to those of Le Corbusier but which yield to the constraints of New York's urban fabric. It is also a democratic, liberal American counterweight to the Imperial giganticism of Fascist and Communist totalitarian regimes, as well as an answer to the equally harsh challenge of the Great Depression.

Photograph of John D.
Rockefeller, taken in 1933.

Manhattan's largest-scale building project was financed by John
Davison Rockefeller Jr (1874–1960). He set his heart on three
large blocks between 48th and 51st streets, 5th and 6th avenues
and, in December 1929, he signed an eighty-year lease with their
owner, Columbia University. The lease has since been extended
until 2069, much to Mitsubishi's satisfaction, as this company is
currently the majority shareholder of Rockefeller
Center. The center owes the purity of its design to
Nelson Aldrich Rockefeller (1908–79),
the financier's second son, who was
a collector of modern art, future
governor of the State of New
York and vice president of the
United States.

### A COLOSSAL BUILDING SITE

The board of architects, headed by Raymond F
and Wallace K. Harrison, who were to be the ch
designers for the United Nations building,
made the best of continual changes to the
plans: the Rockefeller family fortune
went through a very rough time
which lasted until the end
of the 1930's.

### RCA Building
(since 1988, General Electric). Opened in 1933, this building took only sixteen months to build. Above, an RCA advertisement.

### A Depth of 85 feet
The parking lots, underground passages and shopping center, around Lower Plaza, were built below ground level, creating space for vast terraces at street level.

### After the crash
The collapse of the stock market in 1929 made the realization of the original plans for an opera house impossible and, while demolition work was being completed, in July 1931, the Rockefellers developed the plans for a commercial center. The extension, west of 6th Ave., was completed in 1973.

### Historic monuments
The smoking rooms (above) and powder rooms (opposite) of Radio City Music Hall still contain the original furniture.

### Radio City Music Hall
The auditorium, an homage to American Art Deco decoration, was opened on December 27, 1932. The décor was coordinated by Donald Deskey, and many painters contributed to the murals in the lobbies, lounges and stairways (above). These design features are designated as historic landmarks.

### In the clouds
The recently restored Rainbow Room, on the sixty-fifth floor of the RCA buildings, affords a spectacular view of the entire Manhattan skyline. Opposite, a poster from the 1930's, advertising this exceptional view. Today, Rockefeller Center has nearly forty restaurants and several theaters.

### A NEW CONCEPT IN TOWN PLANNING

The decoration is mainly restricted to the lower stories because the architects of Rockefeller Center felt it was less important to apply motifs to an architectural mass – which was, in this case, inordinately tall – than to create a landscaped environment whose variety would attract new tenants as well as sightseers. This was a revolutionary attitude for an urban complex composed mainly of office buildings. The Promenade overlooking 5th Ave. was nicknamed "Channel Gardens" because it separates the Maison Française from the British Empire Building. The gardens, which are re-planted several times a year, provide a setting for fountains that have tritons and nereids riding dolphins. The regular gridiron pattern of Manhattan is broken here by other axes, creating a geometrical effect that highlights the feeling of being in a "city within a city".

**THE MAJOR ART DECO COMPLEX IN NEW YORK.** At the center of Lower Plaza, a gilded bronze *Prometheus* by Paul Manship rises from the waves (opposite). The main entrance of the General Electric Building is crowned by *Genius* by Lee Lawrie which pays homage to the miracle of radio broadcasting. Everything in Lower Plaza – fountains, flags snapping in the wind, sunshades or a huge Christmas tree – combines to create a continual mood of festivity, an atmosphere more in keeping with world fairs than a traditional financial district.

The cladding of Rockefeller Center is white limestone, quarried in Indiana. It contains numerous fossils of tiny animals (left) which lived in the sea 300 million years ago.

## LOWER PLAZA

The former RCA Building is reached via the Lower Plaza, originally designed as the entrance to the underground shopping center.

At the height of the Depression, one by one the luxury stores around the plaza folded but, in 1936, an incredible publicity stunt diverted attention away from this commercial failure: the Lower Plaza was transformed into a skating rink or an elegant café depending on the time of year. This was one of the attractions which made Rockefeller Center so popular with all New Yorkers. It was the hub of this cosmopolitan quarter with its travel agencies, shipping companies, consulates, luxury stores and press offices. The New York Bound Bookshop, which specializes in books on the city's history, is situated on the ground floor of the Associated Press Building.

## A SLENDER SILHOUETTE

"A colossal structure, brazen in its height . . . graceful and monumental, sober and fantastic." (Klaus Mann). The squares and thoroughfares which lead to the General Electric Building provide the perfect vantage point to appreciate the tower's silhouette (above, illuminated at night). The tower's slenderness was dictated by the architect's aim of providing every work station with direct lighting. Each horizontal setback also corresponds to a reduction in the size of the elevator shafts.

### A MODERN FORUM

Rockefeller Center marks a return to classical tradition, to a collective style of architecture for use by the whole city, not just an individual (the Prince), a religious order (the Church) or the commercial sector. Its style of decoration also reflects a return to mythology, with its allegorical evocation of the key principles which govern the world it depicts. Inside as well as outside the building, clocks remind passers-by that "Time Is Money"

### A FANTASTIC BESTIARY

The treatment of the American eagle (below) irresistibly calls to mind the winged bulls found in Assyrian art, while Hermès, the god of commerce (right), is more in line with Greco-Roman tradition.

### THE AMERICAN IDEAL AS SEEN BY A SPANIARD

Even the name of the works that decorate the buildings' interiors show a desire to return to the world of myth; for example, the grandiloquent mural, *Triumph of Man's Accomplishments through Physical and Mental Labor*, by José Maria Sert in the General Electric Building.

### FROM EGYPT TO ASSYRIA VIA CLASSICISM

The mural with its shallow-carved characters (right) calls to mind bas-reliefs from Ancient Egypt, while the classical goddess in the allegory (opposite), who is a successful blend of the American eagle and an olive branch, bears an undeniable likeness to *La Marseillaise* by Rude which adorns the Arc de Triomphe in Paris.

### AN INTERNATIONAL STYLE OF ARCHITECTURE
Classical antiquity was a rich stylistic source during the 1930's in New York, Moscow, Rome or Berlin. The Allegory of Prosperity and Labor (left and right) are two examples.

### THE HAMMER AND THE SICKLE
The tools of the laborer and the peasant still seem to be the time-honored symbols of work, even in New York.

### SPACE AND MODERNITY
The imaginative and artistic interior decoration, glimpsed here, links modern and monumental references (as seen in the design and layout of the lobby) with a strong element of symbolism.

### THE PEOPLE IN NEW YORK
Pablo Picasso was asked to paint a new mural for the lobby of the RCA Building, but *Man at the Crossroads* was eventually commissioned from the Mexican Communist, Diego Rivera. When the fresco was unveiled the commissioners were stunned to see the face of Lenin, rather than the anonymous figure of the "leader of the worker's movement", as depicted in the sketch they had approved months before. Asked to remove Lenin, Rivera said he would rather see the painting destroyed. The managers of the Center did just that.

# ▲ FROM ROCKEFELLER CENTER THROUGH THE EAST SIDE

**1** ROCKEFELLER CENTER  **2** SWISS CENTER  **3** BRENTANO'S  **4** SAKS FIFTH AVE.  **5** ST. PATRICK'S CATHEDRAL  **6** OLYMPIC TOWERS  **7** NEW YORK PALACE HOTEL  **8** WALDORF-ASTORIA HOTEL  **9** ST. BARTHOLOMEW'S CHURCH  **10** GENERAL ELECTRIC BLDG.

✖ Six hours

> "When I am in New York, I never miss a visit to the basement of Brentano's, which contains catacombs of information. Here, you will find all the American periodicals, most of them published in New York. Their brightly colored covers resemble a flower display."
>
> Paul Morand
> New York

Midtown began to develop after the Civil War when new millionaires built luxurious mansions along that stretch of 5th Avenue. In the 1880's, the Vanderbilts, Whitneys, Goulds, Astors and other top families settled here. At the beginning of the 20th century the neighborhood began to change drastically, with many businesses moving into the area, and to escape this

invasion the wealthier residents began to migrate northward. Today, Midtown is the second-largest business center in the city after Downtown, with some 750,000 employees flocking into its offices every day. The area has been shaped by magnates such as Trump and Helmsley.

## AROUND ST. PATRICK'S CATHEDRAL

**BRENTANO'S.** 597 5TH AVE. (1913, arch. Ernest Flagg). For more than seventy years this building was the home of Charles Scribner's Sons bookshop – as the sign above its huge glass and iron storefront reminds one. The interior, which is listed as a landmark, has a vast single-story vaulted space, covered in fine wood paneling. Scribners, founded in 1846, published such authors as F. Scott Fitzgerald and Ernest Hemingway. The company was bought out by another publishing house and in 1989 the store was sold to the Brentano's chain of bookstores.

**SWISS CENTER, FORMER GOELET BUILDING.** 5TH AVE. AT 49TH ST. (1932, arch. E. H. Faile & Co.). This building occupies the site formerly occupied by the house of the Goelet family, who built up a fortune in real estate. It is a striking example of Art Deco with a façade juxtaposing green and white marble and aluminum. The lobby is worth a visit, especially for its elevator doors. The Swiss Center houses the Swissair offices and the Swiss National Tourist Board.

**SAKS FIFTH AVENUE.** 611 5TH AVE. BETWEEN 49TH AND 50TH STS. (1924, arch. Starrett & Van Vleck). The first Saks store opened in 1902 on 34th Street. The son of the founder,

**LOBBY OF THE SWISS CENTER**
The gold and silver Art Deco ● *98* elevator doors in the Swiss Center are decorated with floral motifs and nymphs.

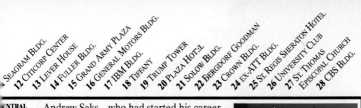

Andrew Saks – who had started his career as a peddler in Washington, D.C. – built this Renaissance-style palazzo when his wealthy clientele moved Uptown. Saks has built up an international reputation as a luxury department store, selling a choice range of furs, jewelry and designer clothing. The store's main restaurant on the eighth floor affords a magnificent view of St. Patrick's Cathedral, Rockefeller Center

**CONSTRUCTION**
The cathedral was built on a site owned by the Catholic Church since 1828. It was originally bought for a graveyard, but the land proved to be too rocky. At the time the cathedral was built, New York included nearly 200,000 Catholics – mainly Irish immigrants (peasants unaccustomed to city life, building workers, dockers and bar owners). Their propensity to drink did nothing to enhance their image with New York's Protestant bourgeoisie, and for this reason Archbishop Hughes added a clause to the building contract for the cathedral stipulating that workers were not allowed to drink during work hours.

▲ 274 and Channel the Gardens.
**ST. PATRICK'S CATHEDRAL ★.** 5TH AVE. BETWEEN 50TH AND 51ST STS. (1858–88, arch. James Renwick Jr.). Archbishop John Hughes commissioned James Renwick Jr. to design this church, which was inspired by the great Gothic cathedrals of Europe and follows the traditional cruciform plan, enriched with side chapels. When New Yorkers learned that the cathedral was to be built on a site that was then virtually out in the country, they nicknamed it "Hughes's Folly". But as the city expanded northward, St. Patrick's was soon enveloped by it. The cathedral was dedicated in 1879, twenty-one years after the first stone was laid. The construction of the building, interrupted by the Civil War, was completed under the aegis of John McCloskey, the first American cardinal. This is the largest Catholic cathedral in the United States. The Lady Chapel, situated behind the altar and completed in 1906, was constructed of Vermont marble. Its floor includes a mosaic of the arms of Pope Leo XIII and the stained glass windows over

Statue in St. Patrick's Cathedral.

283

**5TH AVENUE IN 1900**
"Sunday afternoon Fifth Avenue filed by rosily dustily jerkily. On the shady side there was an occasional man in top hat and frock coat. Sunshades, summer dresses, straw hats were bright in the sun that glinted in squares on the upper windows of the houses, lay in bright slivers on the hard paint of limousines and taxicabs."

John Dos Passos, *Manhattan Transfer*

the altar depict the mysteries of the rosary.

**OLYMPIC TOWER.** 645 5TH AVE., N. E. CORNER OF 51ST ST. (1976, arch. Skidmore, Owings & Merrill). This is one of the last of the "glass boxes" – as they are dismissively called these days – which typifies the International Style ● *100*. This skyscraper, built at the instigation of Aristotle Onassis, houses boutiques, offices and luxury apartments. One can visit the Olympic Place Gallery, which, despite its unremarkable décor, is a pleasant setting with its waterfall, trees and pianist.

**FORMER VANDERBILT RESIDENCE.** 647 5TH AVE. (1905, arch. Hunt & Hunt). In the late 1800's several private mansions belonging to the Vanderbilts clustered along 5th Avenue north of 51st Street and were nicknamed "the Vanderbilt Colony". The only house to survive is no. 647, George W. Vanderbilt's former residence. Around 1915, when the neighborhood was taken over by businesses, the Vanderbilts moved to the Upper East Side.

**VILLARD HOUSES/NEW YORK PALACE HOTEL** ● *92*. 451–457

**THE "VANDERBILT COLONY"**
The owner of one "Vanderbilt Colony" mansion, William H. Vanderbilt (a son of the "Commodore"), created an art gallery in his home (right and below) to which the public was admitted on Thursdays.

MADISON AVE. BETWEEN 50TH AND 51ST STS. (1883–6, arch. McKim, Mead & White). This brownstone structure, which suggests a great Renaissance palazzo, actually consists of six private mansions. They were built, beginning in 1883, for Henry Villard, the president of the Northern Pacific Railroad

and owner of the *New York Evening Post*. When Villard went bankrupt, he sold the unfinished mansions to several individuals. In recent years they were owned by the archdiocese of New York, who sold them to the Helmsley Corporation, for inclusion in the former HELMSLEY PALACE HOTEL (1980), only after the corporation had agreed to preserve the courtyard as well as the interior of the north and south wings. Tea and cocktails are served at appropriate hours in the Gold Room; its décor, supervised by Stanford White, includes murals by John La Farge and a gilded, barrel-vaulted ceiling.

The adjacent hallway features a gilt and marble clock by Augustus Saint-Gaudens and Tiffany stained-glass windows. The north wing houses the Urban Center, a group of organizations dedicated primarily to historic preservation. For example they have saved Grand Central Terminal ▲ *236* and Radio City Music Hall ▲ *275* from demolition. Step inside to consult the varied range of literature (including suggested historic and architectural tours of the city).

## ON PARK AND LEXINGTON AVENUES

**WALDORF-ASTORIA HOTEL.** 301 PARK AVE. BETWEEN 49TH AND 50TH STS. (1931, arch. Schultze & Weaver). Although it was constructed during the Great Depression, this Art Deco brick- and limestone-faced hotel, with its granite base, is a monument to luxury. It succeeded the first Waldorf-Astoria (5th Avenue and 33rd Street), owned by the Astor family, which had been demolished in 1929 to make way for the Empire State Building ▲ *242*. Rising above the hotel (below right) are the forty-two-story WALDORF TOWERS – which can be seen from several blocks to the north. These private apartments have had some famous tenants, including the Duke of Windsor, President Herbert Hoover, General MacArthur and "Lucky" Luciano ● *40*, once head of the New York Mafia. The lobby of the hotel's Park Avenue entrance is richly decorated with murals and a mosaic by Louis Rigal, *The Wheel of Life*. The clock in the lobby – made by the Goldsmith's Company (London) for the Chicago World's Fair of 1893 – was bought by the Astor family and stood in the first hotel. It is embellished with portraits of heads of state including George Washington, Abraham Lincoln and Queen Victoria. The chimes, which sound every quarter of an hour, are copies of those in Westminster Cathedral. Among the public rooms, the Silver Room and GRAND BALLROOM, which have been restored to their original splendor, are especially worth visiting.

**ST. BARTHOLOMEW'S CHURCH ★.** PARK AVE. BETWEEN 50TH AND 51ST STS. (1919, arch. Bertram G. Goodhue). The portico (1912) that graces this Episcopal church came from the first St. Bartholomew's, on Madison Avenue, designed by Stanford White, who modeled it on that of St. Gilles in Provence. The figures were commissioned from Daniel Chester French and Philip Martiny, among others. Inside the STAINED GLASS WINDOWS, some

**STARLIGHT ROOF**
In the 1930's and 1940's New York socialites used to dance to the music of Count Basie and Glenn Miller under the vaulted ceiling of the Waldorf-Astoria's famous Starlight Roof. Less fortunate fans of the big band sound tuned in at home to the Starlight Roof's regular radio broadcasts.

of which also were taken from the older church, are worth seeing.

**GENERAL ELECTRIC BUILDING, FORMER RCA VICTOR BUILDING ★.** 570 LEXINGTON AVE. S. W. CORNER OF 51ST ST. (1931, arch. Cross & Cross) ● *98*, ▲ *275*. This building towers above ST. BARTHOLOMEW'S, its proximity creating a visual shock. It has little in common with the church except for its limestone and pinkish brick, materials chosen by its architects. The crown – part neo-Gothic, part Art Deco – is one of the most spectacular on the Manhattan skyline. Walk down Lexington Avenue for several blocks to see the figures, facing the four cardinal points, which seem to watch over the city. Visit the Art Deco lobby with its aluminum-plated ceiling, decorated with sunburst motifs. The building was donated to Columbia University in 1993.

**LEVER HOUSE.** 390 PARK AVE. BETWEEN 53RD AND 54TH STS. (1952, arch. Skidmore, Owings & Merrill). Now a designated landmark, this building belonging to the Lever Brothers Company (a major soap manufacturer) is regarded as an exemplar of the minimalist, International Style skyscraper ● *100*. When this ultramodern office block first appeared on Park Avenue – then lined almost entirely with sedate masonry apartment houses – it provoked a storm of protest, but it seems rather subdued now.

**SEAGRAM BUILDING.** 375 PARK AVE. (1958, arch. Ludwig Mies van der Rohe and Philip Johnson). The design of this building owes much to the architect daughter of Samuel Bronfman, Seagram's president, who persuaded her father to abandon the original undistinguished design in favor of an innovative one by an internationally renowned architect. Mies' dramatic bronze tower, set back on its open plaza, met with unanimous approval when it was completed and for years it served as a model for the skyscraper design.

**CITICORP CENTER.** LEXINGTON AVE. BETWEEN 53RD AND 54TH STS. (1978, arch. Hugh Stubbins & Assocs.)● *101*. This monumental white aluminum structure, with its top sliced off at an angle (originally designed to accommodate solar

**ON PARK AVENUE**
The Four Seasons, one of the best restaurants in New York, is on the ground floor of the Seagram Building (above, center). In the entrance to the restaurant hangs Picasso's stage backdrop for the ballet The Three-Cornered Hat (1919). Opposite the Seagram Building, at 370 Park Ave., is the Racquet and Tennis Club ● *93* (above), a sports club for affluent New Yorkers. The Florentine Renaissance-style palazzo houses one of the few courts in the 'United States for playing real (indoors) tennis – the precursor of lawn tennis.

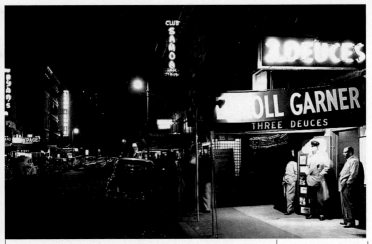

panels) has become one of the most distinctive landmarks on the New York skyline.

## 5TH AVENUE, 52ND AND 53RD STREETS

**CARTIER, INC.** 651 5TH AVE. AND 4 E. 52ND ST. (1905, arch. Robert W. Gibson). This mansion was built for Morton F. Plant, a banker and "Commodore" of the New York Yacht Club. William K. Vanderbilt had sold him the land, stipulating that the site remain residential for twenty-five years. Eleven years later, however, Plant sold the house. Legend has it that Cartier, the Parisian jeweler, bought it at the price of a pearl necklace, reputed then to be worth one million dollars.

**TISHMAN BUILDING.** 666 5TH AVE. BETWEEN 52ND AND 53RD STS. (1957, Carson, Lundin & Shaw). The red limestone that lines the lobby was quarried in the south of France. On close examination the stone is seen to contain fossils (brachiopods, crinoidea, goniatites). The shopping arcade boasts a waterfall designed by Isamu Noguchi. The top-floor restaurant, The Top of the Sixes, affords a panoramic view of Midtown.

**SWING STREET.** 52ND ST. BETWEEN 5TH AND 6TH AVES. At the end of the 1930's and during the 1940's, this part of 52nd Street (above left and right) was a mecca for jazz ● *60*. Audiences who wanted to hear Charlie Parker or Dizzie Gillespie flocked to such clubs as the Onyx, the Three Deuces, Kelly's Stables and the Famous Door. Performances often lasted all night and ended with jam sessions or occasionally with competitions between musicians.

**21 CLUB ★.** 21 W. 52ND ST. (1872, arch. Duggin & Crossman). During Prohibition this smart restaurant was a speakeasy called Jack and Charlie's Place. Of the many clandestine bars on this street, it was the only one to survive. The owners and their customers escaped police raids by disposing of their drinks into trapdoors under the tables and hiding behind concealed doors. The outside staircase and balcony

In the 1940's, at the *Three Deuces* (above, left and right) on 52nd St., Miles Davis (below) enjoyed top billing for several months.

**St. Thomas Church**
1 W. 53rd St. (arch. Richard Upjohn). In 1895 this Episcopal church on 5th Ave. was the scene of a glittering wedding – that of a local girl, Consuelo Vanderbilt, to the ninth Duke of Marlborough. Ten years later the church burned down; it was replaced by the present St. Thomas Church (1914, Cram, Goodhue & Ferguson), a fine example of neo-Gothic style, with magnificent reredos and stained-glass windows.

**University Club**
A carved panel in the hall, inspired by classical Rome.

The University Club's library is decorated with murals reminiscent of the frescoes by Pinturicchio in the Borgia apartments in the Vatican.

are decorated with cast-iron jockeys wearing the colors of the leading stables in the United States.

**CBS Building.** 51 W. 52nd St. at 6th Ave. (1965, arch. Eero Saarinen). This building, which was nicknamed "Black Rock" because it was built of dark gray granite, stands as a monument to the success and egocentricity of William S. Paley – founder (in 1929) of the Columbia Broadcasting System – who had a profound influence on media and entertainment in the United States ● *56*.

**Paley Park.** 5 E. 53rd St. (1967, landscape arch. Zion & Breen). William S. Paley donated the park in 1965 on the site of the defunct Stork Club (a popular nightclub in the 1950's) and named it after his father, Samuel Paley. This was the first public space to be created in Midtown after that of Rockefeller Center ▲ *274*. Although small, it is artfully designed, and the shade of its honey locust trees and the muffled roar of its waterfall, masking the noise of traffic, make it a haven of tranquility.

**University Club.** 1 W. 54th St. (1899, arch. McKim, Mead & White). The imposing façade of this Italianate palazzo appears to be three stories high but the building actually contains seven. The elegant interior is richly endowed with marble hallways, high ceilings and wood-paneled walls. Although the club is for members only, one can glimpse some of the rooms from the street, especially in the evenings, when they are illuminated.

**Rizzoli Building and former Coty Building.** 712 and 714 5th aves. (1908, arch. Adolf S. Gottlieb; 1909, arch. Woodruff Leeming). These office blocks were scheduled for demolition in the 1980's, but were saved when it was realized that some of the Coty Building's upper windows were the work of René Lalique, who created scent bottles for Coty, the French perfume company.

## Around the Sony Building

**St. Regis-Sheraton Hotel.** 2 E. 55th St. (1904, arch. Trowbridge & Livingston). Encouraged by the success of his first hotel, the original Waldorf-Astoria ● *285*, John Jacob Astor IV decided to create a second deluxe establishment. This elegant Beaux Arts-style hotel represents the height of opulence. Of the hotel's once-famous restaurants, all are gone, except for the King Cole Room. The name of this restaurant was derived from the mural painting, *King Cole*, previously commissioned from Maxfield Parrish to decorate the Knickerbocker, an Astor hotel on Times Square.

**SONY BUILDING, FORMER AT&T BUILDING.** 550 MADISON AVE. BETWEEN 55TH AND 56TH STS. (1984, arch. Philip Johnson & John Burgee). The grayish-pink granite, used here instead of glass as the facing, is one of the elements that mark the advent of Postmodernism ● *102*. At street level a Renaissance-style colonnade surrounds a pedestrian space, which adjoins the Sony Wonder, a store-cum-gallery, which displays and sells a range of the company's electronic products (such as camcorders, laser disks and computers).

**IBM BUILDING.** 590 MADISON AVE. BETWEEN 57TH AND 58TH STS. (1983, arch. Edward Larrabee Barnes Assocs.). The best view of this five-sided prism, faced with greenish-black polished granite, can be obtained from the intersection of 5th Avenue and 57th Street. On the southern side of the building is a large ATRIUM, planted with a forest of bamboo trees, open

The lobby of the St. Regis-Sheraton (top), where Dali stayed on his visits to New York, and (above) the atrium of the IBM Building.

**THE SONY BUILDING**
The construction of the former AT&T Building aroused a great deal of public debate. Certain architecture critics, referring to its unusual pediment, which can be seen from the southwest corner of 5th Ave., and 55th St., nicknamed the building "the Chippendale skyscraper". Not only did the AT&T Building open up new vistas for architects; it also served as a source of inspiration for some American painters. In 1987 Richard Haas ▲ *112* depicted the building with Trump Tower in the foreground (left).

When the Museum of Modern Art (MOMA) was founded in 1929, the intention was to make it the largest museum of modern art in the world. Its collections now form one of the most wide-ranging panoramas of modern art: paintings, sculpture, drawings, engravings and photographs, as well as films, architectural models and highstyle functional objects in eye-catching designs.

**PABLO PICASSO,** *Les Demoiselles d'Avignon* (1907). The rough, almost violent, brushstrokes, the heads turned to the right, their hypnotically staring eyes, the fragmented faces refuting the laws of symmetry and the angular hangings, all contribute to this work's expressive intensity. Picasso initially intended to add two male figures.

**AUGUSTE RODIN,** *Balzac* (1897–8). This bronze statue's full cloak and huge head give it a revolutionary appearance. This colossal being symbolizes much more than the writer – it is the universal embodiment of genius.

**PAUL CÉZANNE,** *The Bather* (c. 1885) Despite or because of a certain freedom in his treatment of line and scale, this monumental, formal work is extraordinarily powerful.

**VINCENT VAN GOGH,** *The Starry Night* (1889) This canvas is simultaneously stormy and transcendent. The stable geometry of the village acts as a foil for the flamelike cypress trees, the roiling sky and the vortex of the planets, rendered with coarse, vigorous brushstrokes, loaded with vision and feeling never before expressed in painting.

**HENRI MATISSE,** *The Red Studio* (1911) Everything but the painter's works appears in outline.

**HENRI ROUSSEAU,** *The Sleeping Gypsy* (1897). The central figure sleeps near a lion, as she has nothing to fear. The supernatural atmosphere of this scene is typical of this painter's work.

MOMA, built in 1939, was designed by Philip Goodwin and Edward Durrell Stone, and later extended by Philip Johnson, who also created the Sculpture Garden (Abby Aldrich Rockefeller). In 1984, Cesar Pelli was responsible for the final extension work.

Orson Welles' movie *Citizen Kane* (1941), which was suggestive of William Randolph Hearst, caused such a scandal that members of Hearst's empire tried to squash its release. But the film made it to the theater and won popular and critical acclaim.

**JOAN MIRÓ,** *Hirondelle/Amour* (1933–4). In this painting, the fluid lines of the abstract shapes move against an ethereal blue background, which gives the work a dream-like serenity.

The aerodynamic line of the Cisitalia "202" GT, body designed by Pininfarina (1946), create an impression that the car is moving even when stationary.

"UNTIL THE SECOND WORLD WAR, WHICH CAUSED EUROPEAN PAINTERS TO TAKE REFUGE IN NEW YORK, ABSTRACT ARTISTS WERE LITTLE MORE THAN A SMALL EXPERIMENTAL GROUP."

BARBARA ROSE

**CONSTANTIN BRANCUSI,** *The Fish* (1930). The artist is not interested in representing one particular fish but rather has distilled the creature's very essence, reducing it to its natural condition.

**PIET MONDRIAN**
*Broadway Boogie-Woogie* (1942–3). This painting (above) embodies the artist's search for rhythm, apparent in his later works, and is a dazzling interpretation of New York, where he was living at the time he painted it.

293

**MUSEUM GALLERY**
The collection retraces the history of
photography from its invention, around 1840.
Besides works by artists, it shows photographs
taken by journalists, scientists and amateurs.

**JASPER JOHNS,** *Flag*
(1954–5). Flag or
painting? The illusion
is almost perfect. The
artist has blurred the
traditional concept of
reality in painting by
merging the pictorial
form and space of his
subject – here, as
often, an everyday
object – with those of
his painting.

**WILLEM DE KOONING,**
*Woman, I* (1950–2).
The painter has given
this figure, with its
staring eyes and
artificial grin, a
sinister, ironic look.
This figurative work
was painted at a time
when critics favored
more abstract works.

**JACKSON POLLOCK,** *One (Number 31, 1950)*. Despite the illusion of complete spontaneity, Pollock never lost control of his line, thickening, thinning, spreading or layering its applications. The overall effect, although rhythmic and lyrical, is aggressive.

**ROBERT RAUSCHENBERG,** *Bed* (1955). This abstract expressionist work uses the components of a real bed, and is firmly rooted in "the gulf between art and life" – a phenomenon that Rauschenberg was exploring in his work.

**ANDY WARHOL,** *Gold Marilyn Monroe* (1962). The gold background of this portrait is reminiscent of Byzantine art, which surrounds its subject with an almost mystical aura. Andy Warhol, who painted the actress on many occasions, was clearly aware of the irony of this symbolism.

**MERET OPPENHEIM,** *Object, Fur Covered Cup* (1936). The Surrealists liked to invent bizarre, nightmarish objects. *Object*, a teacup, saucer and spoon covered in fur, is a good example of the surprise and unease they aimed to create by an unexpected juxtaposition of subject and material.

# Trump Trips Up

▲ 234

to the public. Concerts are sometimes given here. The IBM Gallery of Science and Art mounts temporary exhibitions.

**FULLER BUILDING. 41 E. 57TH ST. (1929, arch. Walker & Gillette).** This black, gray and white building, a fine example of restrained Art Deco style, formerly housed the offices of the Fuller Company, a large building firm which previously occupied the Flatiron Building▲ 234. The façade bears a sculpture by Elie Nadelman, depicting some idealized construction workers. The top of the building can be seen from the corner of 5th Avenue and 57th Street.

**TRUMP TOWER. 725 5TH AVE. (1983, arch. Der Scutt).** This tower, which houses six floors of shops and stores, including Galeries Lafayette, twenty floors of offices and forty of luxury apartments, is named after the real estate developer who built it, Donald J. Trump. Reactions to the building have been mixed, with some critics finding the ATRIUM's waterfall, its pink marble and sparkling brass trimmings too brash.

## TOWARD GRAND ARMY PLAZA

**TIFFANY & CO. 727 5TH AVE. AT S. E. CORNER OF 57TH ST. (1940, arch. Cross & Cross).** This famous jewelry store was founded by Charles Tiffany in 1837. Above the main entrance there is a carving of Atlas on bronzed wood, commissioned for an earlier store. Charles' son, Louis Comfort Tiffany ● 66, was renowned for his designs in jewelry, enamel and glass. The store's small windows, with their ingenious displays of jewels, acquired worldwide fame when Audrey Hepburn, as Holly Golightly (left), enjoyed "Breakfast at Tiffany's" in the film (1962) of that name.

**CROWN BUILDING ★. 730 5TH AVE. (1921, arch. Warren & Wetmore).** This was the first skyscraper to be built at the top of 5th Avenue and the first office block to be built after the 1916 ordinances. It housed the Museum of Modern Art when it opened in 1929, pending the construction of the museum at its current address (1939) ▲ 290. The Crown Building was once owned by Ferdinand and Imelda Marcos.

### AIR RIGHTS

In Manhattan, where a square foot of land can cost as much as several thousand dollars, each square inch is worth its weight in gold. Historic buildings, even functional buildings, have often been destroyed to make way for taller buildings simply because they were much lower than the permitted height for their surface area. A few years ago, an ingenious scheme was devised, enabling these buildings to be saved: their "air rights" can be transferred to a nearby building project. In other words, the available air space left unused by a low historic building legally can be used by a new building; the latter can therefore exceed current specifications, and the historic building need not be demolished. Thus, in recent years Tiffany sold its air rights to Trump Tower.

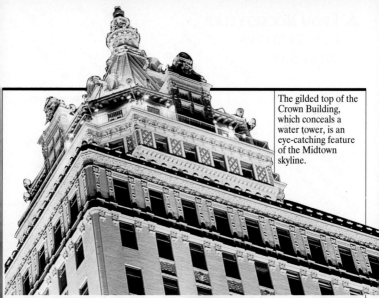

The gilded top of the Crown Building, which conceals a water tower, is an eye-catching feature of the Midtown skyline.

**BERGDORF GOODMAN.** 754 5TH AVE., AT S. W. CORNER OF 58TH ST. (1928, arch. Buchman & Kahn). Herman Bergdorf, a tailor of Alsatian extraction, founded a store in 1894 and sold his shares to his partner, Edwin Goodman, in 1901. The latter was responsible for assuring the store's reputation for a wide range of top-quality European clothing. In 1928 Bergdorf's moved to its present site.

**SOLOW BUILDING.** 9 W. 57TH ST. (1974, arch. Skidmore, Owings & Merrill). This is the twin of the Grace Building, opposite Bryant Park. The giant red 9 sculpture on the sidewalk was created by Ivan Chermayeff.

**GENERAL MOTORS BUILDING.** 767 5TH AVE. BETWEEN 58TH AND 59TH STS. (1968, arch. Edward Durell Stone, Emery Roth & Sons). The Savoy Plaza Hotel was demolished to make way for this tower, much to the chagrin of New Yorkers who loved the hotel both for its intrinsic merits and for its contribution to the architectural ensemble of Grand Army Plaza. General Motors cars are on display on the ground floor. The toyshop F.A.O. Schwarz, founded in 1862, moved here in 1986.

The Oak Room (above center) of the Plaza Hotel is named for its oak paneling. This watercolor (above, 1982) of the hotel is by the American artist A. Troubetzkoy.

**PLAZA HOTEL.** GRAND ARMY PLAZA, BETWEEN W. 58TH AND 59TH STS. (1907, arch. Henry J. Hardenbergh). Twenty years after the completion of his earlier masterpiece the Dakota Apartments, H. J. Hardenbergh designed this grand French Renaissance-style hotel. For nearly a century it has welcomed a succession of eminent guests, including Eleanor Roosevelt, Mark Twain, Groucho Marx, F. Scott Fitzgerald and Frank Lloyd Wright. Donald Trump bought the hotel in 1988.

**GRAND ARMY PLAZA.** Created in 1912, this plaza was the first European-style square in New York. It takes its name from the Northern army in the Civil War. The army is also commemorated by a statue of General William Tecumseh Sherman, famous for his victorious march through Georgia to the sea. This work, by Augustus Saint-Gaudens, is regarded as one of the finest equestrian statues in the United States. The PULITZER FOUNTAIN (1916), which is dominated by the statue of Pomona (goddess of Abundance) by Karl Bitter, was financed by the publisher Joseph Pulitzer. In 1919, on learning that his first book had been accepted for publication, F. Scott Fitzgerald joyfully leaped into this fountain.

Statue of William T. Sherman (1820–91), the famous Union general, which stands in Grand Army Plaza.

1 WORLDWIDE PLAZA
2 ST. MALACHY'S ROMAN CATHOLIC CHURCH
3 CITY CENTER OF MUSIC
4 OMNI PARK CENTRAL HOTEL
5 RUSSIAN TEA ROOM
6 CARNEGIE HALL
7 MANHATTAN LIFE INSURANCE BLDG.
8 HOTEL PARKER MERIDIEN
9 OSBORNE APARTMENTS AND ART STUDENT LEAGUE
10 ALWYN COURT
11 HEARST MAGAZINE BLDG.
12 N.Y. ATHLETIC CLUB

LINCOLN CENTER

W. 61ST ST.
W. 60TH ST.
W. 59TH ST.
W. 58TH ST.
W. 57TH ST.
W. 56TH ST.
W. 55TH ST.
W. 54TH ST.
W. 53RD ST.
W. 52ND ST.
W. 51ST ST.
W. 49TH ST.
W. 48TH ST.
E. 48TH ST.

AMSTERDAM AVE.
W. 64TH ST.
W. 63RD ST.
W. 62ND ST.

10TH AVE.
COLUMBUS AVE.
8TH AVE.
BROADWAY
7TH AVE.
6TH AVE.
5TH AVE.

CENTRAL PARK

ROCKEFELLER CENTER

DIAMOND DISTRICT

🏃 Six hours

"He blinked ... and suddenly, he could see. He was crouching in the middle of a large meadow fringed with trees. Beyond the trees, wreathed in fog and mist, dozens of giant buildings were thrusting towards a leaden sky. There was a sign at the top of one of them: Essex House."
George Chesbro, *Bone*

The rapid growth of harbor activity along the Hudson River that started in the late 19th century, created a more varied mix of neighborhoods on the West Side than on the East Side. The Midtown West Side welcomed all manner of businesses and industries – including the entertainment industry – and saw the construction of both tenements and private mansions.

After World War Two, air transportation became more popular than sea travel, and the decline in harbor activity had a correspondingly adverse effect on this part of town. In the early 1980's the city of New York endeavored to rehabilitate the area west of Broadway and north of Times Square, as can be seen in the recent crop of skyscrapers. The entertainment and arts sectors, long concentrated on the West Side, have undergone a shift to the north. While the legitimate theaters remain clustered in the 40's, just north of Times Square, and Carnegie Hall still stands on West 57th Street, the Metropolitan Opera, New York City Ballet, New York Philharmonic and other companies have moved to Lincoln Center ▲ *305* at 65th Street.

## THE DIAMOND DISTRICT

**DIAMOND AND JEWELRY WAY.** W. 47TH ST. BETWEEN 5TH AND 6TH AVES. Four hundred million dollars' worth of precious stones changes hands daily on this block. During the 1920's and 1930's, the diamond trade was concentrated among the Hassidim ▲ *194* on the Lower East Side; it moved to 47th Street around the outbreak of World War Two, when more Jewish gem traders and cutters arrived from Europe. The street is lined with stores; business transactions are carried out in rooms behind the stores and in clubs such as the Diamond Dealers Club. Until recently deals were also transacted on the sidewalk; the murder of two jewelers in the street in 1977 put an end to this informality.

**GOTHAM BOOK MART ★.** 41 W. 47TH ST. "Wise men fish here" is the motto of this bookshop, which was founded in 1920 by Frances Steloff. Her customers included T. S. Eliot, Henry

**THE DIAMOND DISTRICT EARLY IN THIS CENTURY**
At the beginning of the 1920's, about ten bookshops were gathered along this stretch of the street. Today only one remains: the Gotham Book Mart. "Gotham" was the nickname given to New York by Washington Irving around 1806 in his collection of essays and poems the *Salmagundi Papers*. According to a medieval legend, the people of the village of Gotham, in Nottinghamshire, pretended to be deranged in order to dissuade King John from collecting taxes there. In Irving's opinion New York, like Gotham, seemed inhabited by madmen.

Miller and Thornton Wilder, the novelist and playwright, whose most famous play is *Our Town*. Defying the censors, Frances Steloff stocked copies of *Lady Chatterley's Lover*, by D. H. Lawrence, a highly controversial work when published in 1928, which she secretly imported from England. She employed the poets Everett LeRoi Jones and Allen Ginsberg, as well as the playwright Tennessee Williams, as sales assistants when they were still struggling to make names for themselves. Woody Allen, Saul Bellow and the playwright John Guare, have been frequent visitors to the store. When Frances Steloff died in 1989, at the age of 101, letters and flowers poured in from all over the world. The shop supplies a wide range of books, antique and modern, and literary magazines, in particular those dealing with 20th-century poetry and prose. A gallery above the main floor displays a collection of art books and temporary exhibitions.

**DIAMOND DISTRICT DISPLAYS**
Firms selling precious stones and metals, antique and modern jewelry, now line both sides of 47th St. The lively trade being transacted in the diamond district brings a flavor of the Lower East Side to the otherwise cool commerce of Midtown.

299

ST. MALACHY'S – THE ACTORS' CHAPEL

## ST. MALACHY'S CATHOLIC CHURCH

Built in 1903, this small neo-Gothic church, at 239–245 W. 49th St., has long been the parish church of Broadway's Catholic actors, since its proximity to the theater district enables them to attend services between performances. In 1926 Rudolph Valentino's funeral took place in this church, attended by thousands of women.

*Window of the City Center of Music and Drama.*

## IN THE VICINITY OF ROCKEFELLER CENTER

Originally Rockefeller Center was intended to include a site between 47th and 52nd streets on the west side of 6th Avenue, but the El, which operated until 1938, checked its development. Work was not resumed until the 1960's, when a Modernist-style complex, including the new McGraw-Hill, Exxon and Time & Life buildings, was built.

**WORLDWIDE PLAZA.** 935 8TH AVE. BETWEEN 49TH AND 50TH STS. (1989, arch. Frank Williams). This commercial and residential complex, whose pyramidal top looms above the western side of 8th Avenue, is proof of the recent commercial recovery of this part of Midtown. It was built on the site of the second Madison Square Garden ▲ *249*. The northwest corner of 49th Street and Broadway was named JACK DEMPSEY CORNER in memory of the world boxing champion who defended his title at Madison Square Garden. At the end of his boxing career, he opened a restaurant in this district called Jack Dempsey's.

**ROSELAND BALLROOM.** 239 W. 52ND ST. BETWEEN BROADWAY AND 8TH AVE. The original Roseland, a club that opened on December 31, 1919, became a mecca for ballroom dancers of all ages; thousands of people came here to learn the new dances: the lindy, shag and jitterbug or, later, the cha-cha and twist. Many top entertainers have performed here, including Ella Fitzgerald ● *61*. The first Roseland was on 50th Street and moved in 1956 to the present location. Roseland boasts the largest dance floor in New York.

**CITY CENTER OF MUSIC AND DRAMA ★.** 135 W. 55TH ST. (1924, arch. Harry P. Knowles). This exotic-looking theater started life as the Mecca Temple of the *Ancient and Accepted Order of the Mystic Shrine* (a branch of Freemasonry). The institution foundered during the 1929 Wall Street crash. Fiorello La Guardia saved the building at the end of the 1930's by converting it into a theater. The City Center was the home of the New York City Ballet and the New York City Opera ● *62* until they moved to Lincoln Center in the 1960's. In recent years the City Center has offered performances by various companies including the Joffrey Ballet, the Paul Taylor Dance Company and the Dance Theater of Harlem.

**PARK CENTRAL HOTEL.** 870 7TH AVE. (1927, arch. Groneburg and Leuchtag). Throughout the Prohibition years this hotel was used by bootleggers ● *40* and small-time crooks. One of them, Arnold Rothstein, was thought to be the model for Meyer Wolfsheim in F. Scott Fitzgerald's novel *The Great Gatsby*.

TRISHA BROWN

**TRATTORIA
DELL'ARTE**

He was shot in 1928, in room 349,
for refusing to pay a poker debt. In 1957,
the gangster Albert Anastasia was murdered
in the hotel's barbershop. Both of these murders remain
unsolved because, as they say in New York, "nobody saw
anything."

**TRATTORIA DELL'ARTE.** 900 7TH AVE. One wall of this
restaurant displays the sculpted noses of famous Italians and
Italian-Americans, from Julius Caesar, Dante, and Verdi to
Joe DiMaggio, the legendary baseball player and husband of
Marilyn Monroe. Enormous sculptures representing different
parts of the human body adorn the others.

## 57TH STREET

Before World War Two, this street became one of the most
elegant in New York. A concert hall, art galleries, chic
boutiques and restaurants abounded. New structures such as
the SOLOW BUILDING (9
W. 57th St.) and the
METROPOLITAN TOWER
(140 W. 57th St.) have
altered the street's
appearance in recent
decades, although many
of its original attractions
remain.

**CARNEGIE HALL.** 156 W.
57TH ST. AT THE CORNER

OF 7TH AVE. (1891, arch. William B. Tuthill). This Italian
Renaissance-style building was financed by the steel magnate,
Andrew Carnegie, to house the Oratorio Society, a choir
founded by Leopold Damrosch and presided by Carnegie.
Tchaikovsky conducted the opening gala concert on May 9,
1891, and paid tribute to the concert hall's "magnificent"
acoustics. A year later the New York Philharmonic Orchestra,
also founded by Damrosch, took up residence here; it moved
to Lincoln Center in 1962. A campaign led by the violinist
Isaac Stern saved Carnegie Hall from demolition and it was
restored in 1986.

Sign from the
restaurant in
Carnegie Hall and
logo of the Russian
Tea Room.

**CARNEGIE HALL**
Carnegie Hall
welcomes the leading
performers of
orchestral music,
opera, pop and jazz.
Its halls and corridors
are decorated with
scores and
mementoes of the
artists who have
helped create its
legend.

**ANDREW CARNEGIE**
(1835–1919) He
ended his days in the
house now occupied
by the Cooper-Hewitt
Museum ▲ 320.

**RUSSIAN TEA ROOM**
This charming
restaurant (left),
situated at 150 W.
57th St., began life in
1927 as a little store,
which also served as a
meeting place for
Russian immigrants.
The Christmas
decorations, dating
from 1910,
commemorate the
tradition of Christmas
as celebrated before
the Revolution. Its
regular patrons have
included George
Balanchine, Rudolf
Nureyev and Leonard
Bernstein; Woody
Allen shot scenes
from *Manhattan* and
*New York Stories* here
in 1979 and 1989.

THE RUSSIAN TEA ROOM

Sign from Planet
Hollywood.

**HARD ROCK CAFÉ**
This New York
establishment
displays electric
guitars that used to
belong to Billy Joel
and Brian Jones.
Steinway piano
showroom.

Façade of the New
York Delicatessen.

❝ I have often
managed to dine for
about ten francs in an
Automat. . . . They
are popular, these
Automats with their
change machines for
nickels, people
walking along with
their trays, the
jostling, the soup
down the back of
your neck, the smiling
waitresses, blond
nurses, all those
ordinary people . . .❞
Paul Morand,
*New York*

**PLANET HOLLYWOOD.** 140 W. 57TH ST. This bar-restaurant is in
direct competition with the nearby HARD ROCK CAFÉ at no.
221 of the same street. It is regarded as the "Hollywood
Studio" of New York. Its owners, Sylvester Stallone, Arnold
Schwarzenegger and Bruce Willis used scenery from movies
such as *Indiana Jones, Rambo, Star Wars* and *Terminator* to
decorate the restaurant. The handprints of numerous stars
adorn the establishment's façade.

**HOTEL PARKER MERIDIEN.** 118 W. 57TH ST. (1981, arch Philip
Birnbaum). The main features of this Postmodern hotel are
the breathtaking marble lobby-atrium and the view from the
swimming pool terrace on the top floor.

**MANHATTAN LIFE INSURANCE BUILDING.** 111 W. 57TH ST.
(1925, arch. Warren & Wetmore). This neo-classical building,
not far from CARNEGIE HALL, used to belong to Steinway, the
famous piano manufacturer. The company had to sell the
building after the 1929 crash, although they retained the
superb ground floor space as a showroom. At 211 West 58th
Street, the MUSEUM OF THE AMERICAN PIANO exhibits 19th-
century American musical instruments.

**NEW YORK DELICATESSEN.** 104 W. 57TH ST. (1938,
arch. Ralph B. Bencker). The building originally
housed an "automat". The Automatic Food
Dispensing Systems, created in 1912 by Horn &
Hardart, flourished from the 1930's to the 1950's.
Customers inserted coins to open the glass flaps
of pigeonholes containing dishes of food. Fast-
food restaurants represented the kiss of death for
the automat; the last one, on the corner of 42nd
Street and 3rd Avenue, closed in 1991.

**OSBORNE APARTMENTS ★.** 205 W. 57TH ST. (1885,
arch. James E. Ware). The plain brownstone
façade of this building conceals an extravagant
marble lobby. Leonard Bernstein, who composed
the music for *West Side Story* ● *305*, was one of
the Osborne's illustrious residents. In 1978 the
actor Gig Young, who was awarded an Oscar for
his role in the film *They Shoot Horses, Don't They?*, with Jane
Fonda, was found dead beside his wife in one of the
apartments, a revolver in his hand.

**ART STUDENTS LEAGUE.** 215 W. 57TH ST. (1892, arch. Henry J.
Hardenbergh). This French Renaissance-style building
originally housed the AMERICAN FINE ART SOCIETY and was
built by the Art Students League, founded in 1875. Among
the eminent artists who have taught at this school are William
Merritt Chase and Robert Henri ● *107*, who influenced an
entire generation of students including Edward Hopper,
George Bellows and John Sloane.

Detail of the French Renaissance-style façade of Alwyn Court.

**HEARST MAGAZINE BUILDING.** 959 8TH AVE. (1928, Joseph Urban and George B. Post & Sons). This building was commissioned by William Randolph Hearst (1863–1951), the newspaper tycoon. At the height of his career, in 1935, Hearst – one of the pioneers of "yellow journalism"

● *54* – owned 28 newspapers and 18 magazines. He was immortalized on screen by Orson Welles in *Citizen Kane* (1941). This building, with its over-abundant decoration, including huge columns capped with urns, was intended to have seven more stories, but the 1929 crash forced Hearst to put a stop to the work. The building was never completed.

**ALWYN COURT ★.** 180 W. 58TH ST. (1909, arch. Harde & Short). This was designed as a luxury apartment building with no more than twenty-two apartments, each containing between fourteen and thirty-four rooms. In 1938 it was divided into seventy-five apartments of three to five rooms. The French Renaissance-style façade is covered with sculptures depicting dragons, crowns, leaves, flowers and crowned salamanders, the emblem of Francis I. A large interior courtyard, decorated with a mural by Richard Haas, is situated through the lobby and can be glimpsed through the glass front door.

The Hearst Magazine Building's classical sculptures symbolize music, comedy, tragedy, sport, industry, printing and the sciences.

# CENTRAL PARK SOUTH

**ESSEX HOUSE.** 160 CENTRAL PARK SOUTH (1930, arch. Frank Grad). This Art Deco hotel enjoys an exceptional view over Central Park. Its residents have included such diverse artists as Betty Grable and Igor Stravinsky. Ingrid Bergman stayed here in 1946, when she was performing *Joan of Lorraine* on Broadway.

**NEW YORK ATHLETIC CLUB.** 180 CENTRAL PARK SOUTH (1929, arch. York & Sawyer). The sculptures decorating the main entrance of this club, founded in 1868, represent athletes in training or playing their sport.

**THE GAINSBOROUGH STUDIOS.** 222 CENTRAL PARK SOUTH (1908, arch. Charles W. Buckham). Originally this was a block of artists' studios; later converted into apartments. Only the frieze by Isidore Konti and the bust of Gainsborough on the façade point to the building's original purpose. The jazz clarinettist Artie Shaw lived here during the 1940's.

**MAINE MEMORIAL**
The Maine Memorial was erected in 1913 at the behest of William Randolph Hearst, who covered the Spanish-American War extensively in the New York *Journal*.

Plan in perspective for Lincoln Center, displayed in the Avery Library at Columbia University.

## COLUMBUS CIRCLE

This traffic circle was given its present name in 1892 in celebration of the 400th anniversary of Europe's discovery of the New World. The marble column, topped by a statue of Christopher Columbus by Gaetano Russo, was a gift from America's Italian citizens.

**MAINE MEMORIAL.** S. W. CORNER OF CENTRAL PARK (1913, statue by Attilio Piccirilli and H. Van Bwen Magonigle). This monument commemorates the victims of the sinking of the *Maine* ▲ *174*, an American battleship which was blown up in Havana harbor in 1898, an event that helped to precipitate the Spanish-American War ● *28*.

**NEW YORK CITY DEPARTMENT OF CULTURAL AFFAIRS.** 2 COLUMBUS CIRCLE (1965, arch. Edward Durell Stone). The NEW YORK CONVENTION AND VISITORS BUREAU, a mine of information for tourists, can be found on the ground floor of this building.

**LINCOLN CENTER CAMPUS OF FORDHAM UNIVERSITY.**
COLUMBUS AVE., BETWEEN 60TH AND 62ND STS. This houses the Fordham Law School, part of a Jesuit university based in the Bronx, founded in 1841.

Some 1.5 million people attended the parade held on the day that the Columbus Circle monument was unveiled. It is situated an the southwest entrance to Central Park.

**KENT GARAGE.** 43 W. 61ST ST. (1930, arch. Jardine, Hill & Murdock). This garage, now converted into apartments, is considered an Art Deco gem. It was one of the first garages in New York with an elevator capable of transporting vehicles.

# LINCOLN CENTER ★

The plans for the Lincoln Center for the Performing Arts date from the 1950's, when the Metropolitan Opera and the New York Philharmonic needed new premises more urgently than ever. The work was directed by John D. Rockefeller III and Robert Moses, the New York property developer and parks commissioner. President Eisenhower laid the first stone in 1959. Although most architectural critics have judged it to be conventional and flashy, it has become an important cultural center. It now employs seven thousand people and attracts more than five million patrons to some three thousand performances each year. The construction of Lincoln Center was postponed to allow the slums on 62nd Street to be used as a backdrop for scenes in *West Side Story*. The film's director, Robert Wise, employed some members of neighborhood gangs to play the parts of policemen.

**NEW YORK STATE THEATER.** (1964, arch. Philip Johnson and Richard Foster). This is the home of the New York City

Opera and the New York City Ballet ● *62*. The New York City Ballet was founded in 1948 by George Balanchine, who built it into a world-famous company. The two large statues dominating the Grand Promenade, *Two Nudes* and *Two Circus Women*, are huge replicas of original works by Elie Nadelman.

**METROPOLITAN OPERA HOUSE.** (1966, arch. Wallace K. Harrison). This is the centerpiece of Lincoln Center. The Metropolitan Opera House was founded in 1883 by wealthy New Yorkers, such as J. P. Morgan and the Vanderbilts, who wanted to have their own opera house because the "old" New York aristocracy were monopolizing the Academy of Music on 14th Street. Although badly designed and cramped, the old house, on Broadway at 39th Street, was nevertheless used for eighty years, until the opera moved to Lincoln Center in September 1966.

**"AMERICA"**
Lincoln Center was built on a large plot of West Side land marked for urban renewal. The developers were able to purchase this land due to a law of 1949 which allowed dwellings to be demolished so long as the site thereby cleared was allocated for artistic purposes. Before being bulldozed, the neighborhood (above) served as the backdrop for *West Side Story*. This musical was inspired by *Romeo and Juliet*. The action of Shakespeare's tragedy is moved to 20th-century New York, portraying the conflict existing there between two communities, gangs who roam the streets: the Jets (white Americans) and the Sharks (Puerto Rican immigrants). The tragic outcome of the love story between Maria and Tony (one connected with the Sharks, the other with the Jets) shows the enemies how absurd their rivalry is. *West Side Story*'s musical score, by Leonard Bernstein, is generally considered a milestone in the history of the Broadway musical.

The interior, with its red carpeting, gold leaf and marble is a modern version of traditional opera house design. The crystal chandelier was a gift from the Austrian government. The main staircase is flanked by two huge murals by Chagall, *The Triumph of Music* and *The Sources of Music*, which can best be seen from outside at night.

**LINCOLN CENTER**
The name of the center was taken from the adjacent Lincoln Square, which marks the intersection of Broadway and Columbus Ave. The layout of Lincoln Center's three main

buildings – the Metropolitan Opera, the New York State Theater and Avery Fisher Hall – is modeled on Michelangelo's Piazza del Campidoglio in Rome. Instead of a statue, as in the original, a fountain (above) adorns the center of this plaza. The fountain was financed by a special donation from the Charles Revson Foundation. The huge pool in the northeast plaza contains a sculpture by Henry Moore, *Reclining Figure*. Two other buildings of the center, the Vivian Beaumont Theater and the Juilliard School of Music, are even better examples of the aesthetic trends that dominated architecture in the 1960's.

**DAMROSCH PARK AND GUGGENHEIM BANDSHELL.** (1969, arch. Eggers & Higgins). The park and its open-air theater are used for concerts in the summer. Every winter, in December, the BIG APPLE CIRCUS raises its tent here. The park takes its name from the conductor and composer Walter Damrosch, who conducted the NEW YORK SYMPHONY ORCHESTRA in the early part of the 20th century.

**AVERY FISHER HALL.** (1962, arch. Max Abramovitz). This is the home of the New York Philharmonic Orchestra.
Originally called Philharmonic Hall, it was renamed in 1973 after its principal patron, Avery Fisher. The acoustics in the hall were so poor that the interior was dismantled and reconstructed in 1976. The rebuilt hall was greeted warmly by performers and audiences alike. In the lobby areas are the *Tragic Mask of Beethoven* by Antoine Bourdelle and the bronze head of Mahler by Rodin.

**VIVIAN BEAUMONT THEATER.** 150 W. 65TH ST. (1965, arch. Eero Saarinen). This building is named after a philanthropist who made a large donation toward its construction. It has the largest stage of any legitimate theater in the city.

**LIBRARY AND MUSEUM OF THE PERFORMING ARTS.** 111 AMSTERDAM AVE. (1965, Skidmore, Owings & Merrill). The library and museum are part of the NEW YORK PUBLIC LIBRARY ▲ 252. The museum's archives include recordings made at the Metropolitan Opera House since the beginning of the century, the Rodgers and Hammerstein sound archives and several thousand theater programs.

**JUILLIARD SCHOOL OF MUSIC.** 144 W. 56TH ST. (1969, arch. Pietro Belluschi with Eduardo Catalano and Westermann & Miller). This prestigious school of music, dance and drama, which can take its pick from the most brilliant students in the world, was founded in 1904 by Frank Damrosch and James Loeb and named after its patron, the millionaire Augustus D. Juilliard.

# AROUND
# CENTRAL PARK

View of the Upper East Side (1907) taken from the north, showing Roosevelt Island and the banks of the East River.

E. 77TH ST.
E. 76TH ST.
E. 75TH ST.
E. 74TH ST.
E. 73RD ST.
E. 72ND ST.
E. 71ST ST.
E. 70TH ST.
E. 69TH ST.

The upper East Side has two natural boundaries – the East River and Central Park, and two urban limits, 60th and 96th streets – where the railroad tracks emerging from Park Avenue tunnel form an unmistakable border between the most elegant part of the city and Harlem. The first houses in the district were farms, built before 1860, to the east of Park Avenue, which was then named 4th Avenue and scored by above-ground railroad tracks. When the 3rd Avenue El was built in 1878, followed

❊ Five hours

**AN ATTRACTIVE NEIGHBORHOOD**
The sailing ships are long gone, the lawns no longer slope down to the river's edge, a highway runs along the banks, but the neighborhood is still one of the most desirable areas in New York. Its regular streets exude an air of financial ease and security. People still live the good life in this stylish, expensive neighborhood, with its aristocratic houses, luxury apartments, clubs, museums, galleries and churches, liberally interspersed with bars and cafés.

by the 2nd Avenue El ● *36*, a crop of tenements sprang up. However, in 1880, to the west, the situation changed again with the completion, finally, of Central Park. The wealthy started to move northward once again and, for the first time in the

GRAND ARMY PLAZA

MADISON AVE.

308

city's history, they put down roots and stayed in one neighborhood. They did not move again, particularly as, in 1907, Park Avenue – an attractive and uncluttered thoroughfare lined with sumptuous apartment buildings – was built over the 4th Avenue railroad tracks, which had been sunk beneath a planted center divider. Now the neighborhood runs along both sides of Lexington Avenue: to the west, residential and commercial prosperity; to the east, a more modest display of wealth dating from the 1950's. When the El was dismantled, the neighborhood regained its tranquility, attracting the middle classes. The side streets, with their carefully renovated workers' residences, are very attractive, while the many bars and movie houses at the foot of modern high-rises contribute to the vibrant bustle of 3rd, 2nd and 1st avenues, making them a favourite haunt for young people.

Since 1964, the children attending the Lycée Français, who come from 54 different countries, have studied here.

## FROM 5TH AVENUE TO ROOSEVELT ISLAND

**72ND STREET, A MARRIAGE OF OPPOSITES.** CORNER MADISON AVE. The profusion of styles and professions represented by the elegant ROSARIO CANDELA BUILDING (N. W. CORNER, 1936), the Beaux Arts façades of the LYCÉE FRANÇAIS next dòor at nos. 7 and 9 (1899, arch. Flagg & Chambers; 1896, arch. Carrère and Hastings) and THE MANSION (s. W. CORNER, 1898, arch. Kimball & Thompson), which houses RALPH LAUREN, was formerly the OLIVETTI BUILDING, and originally the Gertrude Rhinelander WALDO RESIDENCE, are characteristic of this stretch of Madison Avenue.

**ST. JAMES EPISCOPAL CHURCH.** 861 MADISON AVE., N. E. CORNER 71ST ST. (1884, arch. Robert H. Robertson). Founded in 1810 as a parish church during the summer months, when people come here on vacation, a simple wooden church was replaced in 1869 by a Victorian Gothic-style building which, in its turn, made way in 1884 for the present church. Note the TIFFANY stained-glass windows.

**71ST AND 70TH STREETS.** BETWEEN 5TH AND PARK AVES. The elegant streets that flank the Frick Collection ▲ *322*, although a little stiff in appearance, still boast a number of neo-classical ashlar mansions dating from the neighborhood's early days: too large to be converted into apartments, they house private colleges, foundations or galleries. The streets to the east of Madison Avenue, which are less ostentatious and more eclectic, still possess some fine residences. The many garages were once stables belonging to the palazzos on 5th Avenue.

**LUXURY ON MADISON**
The Ralph Lauren boutique (the Mansion) has retained the appearance of a private residence, with its wood-paneled rooms and fireplaces.

**UNION CLUB OF NEW YORK.** N. E. CORNER PARK AVE. AND 69TH ST. (1932, arch. Delano & Aldrich). This is the headquarters of the oldest club in the city, founded in 1836. Clubs have always played an important role in New York society, membership of specific clubs being taken as an accurate gauge of someone's social standing. The UNION CLUB is for affluent people of good family; the METROPOLITAN (1 E. 60th St., 1893, arch. McKim, Mead & White) places more importance on wealth, and the Knickerbocker (2 E. 62nd St., 1913, arch. Delano & Aldrich) insists on members having one ancestor dating directly back to colonial times. The CENTURY ASSOCIATION ( 7 W. 43rd St., 1891, arch. McKim, Mead & White) is more concerned with culture ▲ *251*. Walk down Park Avenue on the left-hand side, turning a blind eye to HUNTER COLLEGE's modern buildings, completed in 1940 – the old neo-Gothic style building (1913, arch. C. B. J. Snyder) is on Lexington – in order to concentrate on the avenue's only unspoiled block.

**PARK AVENUE ★.** WEST SIDE, BETWEEN 69TH AND 68TH STS. A cluster of Georgian houses provides a glimpse of how Park Avenue would have looked in the early 1900's. These are the CENTER FOR INTER-AMERICAN RELATIONS (1911, arch. McKim, Mead & White), the SPANISH INSTITUTE (1926, same arch.) the ITALIAN CULTURAL INSTITUTE (1919, arch. Delano & Aldrich) and the CONSULATE GENERAL OF ITALY (1916, arch. Walker & Gillette).

**LUXURY ON "FIFTH"**
The doorman, who performs the role of caretaker, doorkeeper and porter, is essential to the Upper East Sider's sense of well-being. A superintendent and elevator man who act as plumbers, electricians and general repairmen, take care of the residents continued comfort within the walls of these bastions of wealth.

**THE 7TH REGIMENT ARMORY**
The huge inner hall (187 feet by 270 feet), once used for military maneuvers, can be hired for private functions, exhibitions or shows. The interior is a museum, retracing the history of the unit, which defended Washington, D.C. during the Civil War. Tiffany was the interior designer for two rooms, which can be visited by appointment. On the fifth floor, the officers' mess – with its décor devoted to the sport of hunting – has been converted into a restaurant.

**ELEVATED RAILWAYS**
These were enthusiastically welcomed by New Yorkers.

### THE 7TH REGIMENT ARMORY ★. 643 PARK AVE.

BETWEEN 67TH AND 66TH STS. (1880, arch. Charles W. Clinton). This impressive brick fortress used to be the rallying point for the 7th Regiment of the NATIONAL GUARD.

**45 EAST 66TH STREET.** (1908, arch. Harde & Short). The façade, a staggering array of double windows separated by terracotta ogives, swelling into a tower at the corner of the avenue, is a monument to the sumptuousness of the first buildings on Madison Avenue.

**TEMPLE EMMANU-EL ★.** 840 5TH AVE. N. E. CORNER 65TH ST. (1929, arch Robert D Kohn, Charles Butler and Clarence Stein). This SYNAGOGUE, with its Moorish and Romanesque-style decoration, is one of the city's largest places of worship.

**ASIA HOUSE, RUSSELL SAGE FOUNDATION AND ROBERT STERLING CLARK FOUNDATION ★.** 112 E. 64TH ST. (1959, arch. Philip Johnson). This is one of the architect's great successes, with its tinted glass façade crisscrossed with white steel. It was built to house John D. Rockefeller's collection of art from the Far East, currently at the ASIA SOCIETY (725 PARK AVE.).

**LEXINGTON AVENUE.** CORNER 64TH ST. The view to the north is obstructed by the footbridge straddling the avenue linking the buildings of Hunter College. Farther south, it loses its residential character and takes on a more commercial aspect.

**BLOOMINGDALE'S.** LEXINGTON AND 3RD AVES. BETWEEN 59TH AND 60TH STS. There is a constant throng of pedestrians around the most famous store in the city. Founded in 1870, in what was a working-class area, Bloomingdale's started out as a humble store. After the El was dismantled, a middle-class clientele moved into the area and Bloomingdale's supplied them with fashion, food and furniture.

**ABIGAIL ADAMS SMITH MUSEUM.** 421 E. 61ST ST. (1799). Among the neighborhood's many garages, stands the vestiges of one of the finest properties in 18th-century New York. This Federal-style building ● 82, which once belonged to the daughter of President John Adams, is now a nine-room museum of period furniture set in a tiny garden, an unlikely spot in the shadow of Queensboro Bridge ▲ 188.

**ROOSEVELT ISLAND.** For two centuries this small island was owned by a family of farmers: it was bought by the city in 1828 to serve as the site for a PENITENTIARY, a MADHOUSE and an ALMSHOUSE. Most of these buildings have now disappeared, and in 1973 mixed rent housing was built. It can be reached by aerial tramway from 2nd Avenue.

**ROOSEVELT ISLAND TRAMWAY PLACE ★.** S. W. CORNER 2ND AVE. AND 60TH ST. A four-minute ride in the Swiss-made cable car (1976, eng. Prentice & Chan), affords breathtaking views of the eastern part of the city.

Their comfort and speed soon made them indispensable. Furthermore, they afforded a breathtaking view of the city, a fleeting and intimate bird's-eye view of neighboring houses. At night, the spectacle was even more dazzling, due to the myriad sparkle of the lights. But these railways were incredibly noisy and devastated long stretches of the city.

**45 EAST 66TH STREET**
This eye-catching façade has a twin: Alwyn Court, 180 W. 58th St. ▲ 303.

311

## FROM 5TH AVENUE TO GRACIE MANSION

**YORKVILLE**
In 1790 this was a village; and the name survived 19th-century urbanization.

**UKRAINIAN INSTITUTE.** 2 E. 79TH ST. (1899, arch. C. P. H. Gilbert). This residence, encircled by a moat, was built for Isaac D. Fletcher, a reclusive industrialist who donated his collection of paintings to the Metropolitan Museum. There used to be a Renaissance château opposite, on the northeast corner of the street. The demolition of this building caused such a storm of protest that the Landmark Preservation Law was passed (1965).

**HOTEL CARLYLE.** 35 E. 76TH ST. (1929, arch. Bien & Prince). Crossing Madison Avenue, you can glimpse the Hotel Carlyle's green pyramid in the south. This hotel's suites have accommodated a vast number of stars and politicians. President Kennedy occupied the penthouse suite when he came to New York. There are some fine murals in the two bars, *Bemelmans Bar* and *Café Carlyle*.

**80TH STREET, A REFUGE.** BETWEEN PARK AND LEXINGTON AVES. On this street stand the last private residences dating from before the Depression. They have all been converted into apartments except for the largest, no. 130 (1928, arch. Mott B. Schmidt), sold in 1947 to the JUNIOR LEAGUE, a philanthropic and social organization for young women.

**UNITARIAN CHURCH OF ALL SOULS.** S. E. CORNER 80TH ST. AND LEXINGTON AVE. (1931, arch. Hobart Upjohn). Look up to see small children playing on the terrace. Space on the ground is so expensive that playgrounds are sometimes built on the rooftops. The church, which plays an important role in community life, houses a school, a theater and a soup kitchen.

**YORKVILLE BRANCH, N. Y. PUBLIC LIBRARY.** 222 E. 79TH ST. The beautiful Palladian façade belongs to the neighborhood's first library. In 1901, Andrew Carnegie founded sixty-five branch libraries.

Until the 1950's, E. 86th St. was the main street in a prosperous German neighborhood.

**1356–1368 3RD AVENUE, A REMINDER OF THE EL.** BETWEEN 78TH AND 79TH STREETS (1938, eng. E. H. Faile). The windows of this building overlooking the avenue were glazed with triple-thick glass in an attempt to muffle the din from the El ● *36*. There is a terraced garden that can be reached via 78th Street.

**78TH STREET, A MIXED STREET.** BETWEEN 3RD AND 2ND AVES. This street's charm resides in the fact that houses built in the 1860's – nos. 208 to 218 are the most interesting – stand next to tenements built earlier, but so carefully maintained that the contrast is not displeasing. Beyond 2nd Avenue, leading down to the river, the neighborhood becomes more blue-collar. There are high-rises all along the avenues but the streets still have the five- and six-story worker's

Over one hundred breweries were built in the surrounding district, including the one owned by Jacob Ruppert, which occupied three blocks between 2nd and 3rd aves. and 90th and 93rd sts.

residences occupied by older inhabitants with low incomes, often from abroad, a reminder of the time when the neighborhood was nicknamed "little Europe", due to its many Czech, Hungarian, and German residents.

**CHEROKEE APARTMENTS.** 514 E. 78TH ST. AND 515 E. 77TH ST. (1910–11, arch. Henry Atterbury Smith). This bright, spacious six-story structure was built for families of patients suffering from tuberculosis. External staircases lead up to the apartments which are arranged around large courtyards, reached by paved passageways. .

**HENDERSON PLACE.** 86TH ST. BETWEEN YORK AND EAST END AVES. (1882, arch. Lamb & Rich). This group of Queen Anne-style buildings, with their many towers, turrets and gables ● *90*, was built on the site of a farm that once belonged to JOHN JACOB ASTOR.

**CARL SCHURZ PARK ★.** EAST END AVE. BETWEEN 84TH AND 90TH STS. (1876, reconstructed 1938, arch. Harvey Stevenson and Cameron Clarke). This park, which is small but has a variety of landscaping effects, affords a splendid view of the river.

**GRACIE MANSION ★.** (1799, arch. Ezra Weeks; modern wing, 1966, arch. Mott B. Schmidt). The mayor's private residence can be seen clearly from the park, especially in winter when trees are bare. Built for Archibald Gracie, a Scottish ship-owner whose guests included such famous figures as Louis-Philippe, the future king of France, and Lafayette, it is the only surviving 19th-century country home. The mayor has

Above, and opposite page, E. 86th St. in 1939.

lived here since 1942. Note the wooden floor of the entrance, painted to look like marble and decorated with a compass – a reminder of the first occupant's maritime connections.

**GRACIE MANSION**
Before the construction of the F.D.R. Drive, the East River was an ideal place for bathing, fishing and mooring boats. Now only the promenade overlooking the river gives an idea of what the view used to be. However, the private and attractive park around Gracie Mansion remains unspoiled, as the F.D.R. Drive passes underneath Carl Schurz Park.

# ▲ CENTRAL PARK

Central Park in spring, its cherry trees and magnolias laden with blossoms.

> "I reached Central Park, level with the street, and decided to walk across it to find Manhattan . . . The sky was pale green. Springtime was showering New York with flurries of damp blossom. . . . There was a river, boats, ducks . . . ."
>
> Pierre Bourgeade, *New York Party*

**HECKSCHER PLAYGROUND**

It took twenty years and ten million cartloads of rock and soil to make this park in the middle of Manhattan. Its 844 acres comprise gently sloping meadows, winding paths and natural-looking lakes, created from the water which originally flooded the swampy site.

**1 COLUMBUS CIRCLE**  **2 BIRD SANCTUARY**  **3 WOLLMAN RINK**  **4 THE DAIRY**  **5 THE LAKE**

Central Park in fall.

"They are walking up the Mall in Central Park . . . . She is walking in her wide hat in her pale loose dress that the wind now and then presses against her legs and arms, silkily, swishily walking in the middle of the great rosy and purple and pistachiogreen bubbles of twilight that smell out of the grass and trees and ponds, bulge against the tall houses sharp gray as dead teeth round the southern end of the park, melt into the indigo zenith."

John Dos Passos, *Manhattan Transfer*

**HECKSCHER PLAYGROUND**

**The Dairy**
Central Park's Administration welcomes visitors in this original, High Victorian Gothic-style structure. The Dairy contains a twelve-foot long model of the park showing various points of interest. Below, one of the park's several information kiosks.

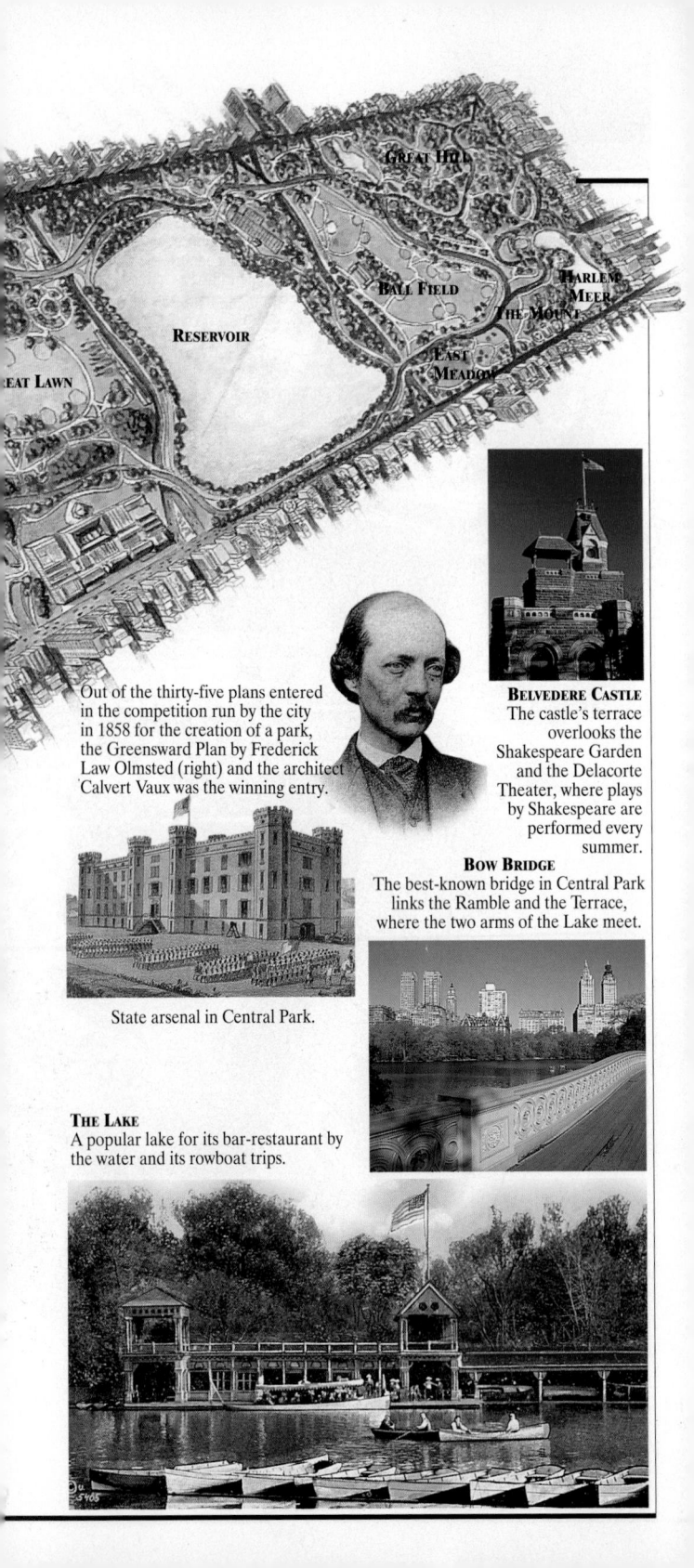

Out of the thirty-five plans entered in the competition run by the city in 1858 for the creation of a park, the Greensward Plan by Frederick Law Olmsted (right) and the architect Calvert Vaux was the winning entry.

State arsenal in Central Park.

**BELVEDERE CASTLE**
The castle's terrace overlooks the Shakespeare Garden and the Delacorte Theater, where plays by Shakespeare are performed every summer.

**BOW BRIDGE**
The best-known bridge in Central Park links the Ramble and the Terrace, where the two arms of the Lake meet.

**THE LAKE**
A popular lake for its bar-restaurant by the water and its rowboat trips.

1 COLUMBUS CIRCLE  2 THE POND  3 THE ZOO  4 BETHESDA FOUNTAIN AND TERRACE  5 CONSERVATORY WATER  6 ALICE IN WONDERLAND  7 THE LAKE  8 BELVEDERE CASTLE  9 SHAKESPEARE GARDEN

STRAWBERRY FIELDS

THE RAMBLE

CHERRY HILL

SHEEP MEADOW

BANDSHELL

EAST GREEN

Ornamental detail from the stone staircase of the Terrace, depicting nature and the seasons.

**SHEEP MEADOW**
Used for grazing until 1934, this "meadow" is a favorite haunt of New Yorkers in the summer.

**THE ZOO**
This boasts nearly one hundred species from three climatic regions - polar, temperate and tropical. In the 1880's, a pair of hippopotami bought for 5,000 dollars were the zoo's main attraction. Now people flock to see the polar bears.

**OBELISK**
The obelisk in Central Park, one of thirty-eight in the world, was a gift from Egypt to America in 1881.

The undergrowth in Central Park is a paradise for rodents. Rabbits, marmots, squirrels – there are nearly fourteen thousand – live on the thirty-seven acres of the Ramble, around the lake.

Resident and migratory birds nest in the Bird Sanctuary, where the vegetation is thickly planted.

EAST GREEN

THE MALL

BANDSHELL

SHEEP MEADOW

CHERRY HILL

THE RAMBLE

STRAWBERRY FIELDS

Map labels:
- 8
- GREAT HILL
- 11
- 7
- HARLEM MEER
- BALL FIELD
- THE MOUNT
- RESERVOIR
- EAST MEADOW
- 9
- GREAT LAWN
- 10
- 6

## GAPSTOW BRIDGE
This is one of the thirty-six bridges and arches which are an integral part of Central Park's traffic network. Take time out to watch the wild ducks that live on the Pond in winter.

**DARKISH DUCK**

**RUDDY STIFF-TAILED DUCK**

Female    Male          Female    Male
**BUFFEL-HEADED DUCK**      **WHITE-FRONTED DUCK**

## WOLLMAN RINK
Renovated with assistance from the developer Donald Trump, the skating rink (right, in 1919) is a popular site.

In 1858, Ignaz Anton Pilat, an Austrian gardener, oversaw the planting of nearly four million trees and plants in the park. There are now some 25,000 trees.

M useum Mile (5TH AVE., BETWEEN 70TH AND 104TH STS.) owes its name to the group of prestigious museums (Metropolitan Museum of Art ▲ 328, Guggenheim Museum ▲ 338, Frick Collection ▲ 322 and so on) which line the avenue (the Whitney Museum ▲ 326, a block to the east, is also close by). But this part of Upper East Side is a museum in itself, dedicated to the mansions built at the beginning of the century.

The Commonwealth Fund (1 E. 75TH ST., 1907, arch. Hale and Rogers), the N.Y.U. Institute of Fine Arts (1 E. 78TH ST., 1912, arch. Horâce Trumbauer) and the Duchesne Residence school facility, also known as the Convent of the Sacred Heart, originally the Kahn residence (1 E. 91ST ST., 1918, arch. J. Armstrong Stenhouse and C. P. H. Gilbert), formerly private residences, testify to past glory.

**FRENCH EMBASSY CULTURAL SERVICES .** 972 5TH AVE. BETWEEN 78TH AND 79TH STS. (1906, arch. McKim, Mead & White). When there is an exhibition in this building, you can see the circular entrance hall of Harry Whitney Payne's former mansion, with its border of pillars and marble floor.

**GOETHE HOUSE.** 1014 5TH AVE. BETWEEN 82ND AND 83RD STS. (1907, arch. Welch, Smith & Provot). This is the German cultural center. The libraries are open to the public.

**NATIONAL ACADEMY OF DESIGN.** 1083 5TH AVE. BETWEEN 89TH AND 90TH STS. (1914, arch. Ogden Codman). In 1825 some American artists got together to form an academy. Each member had to donate a work to the collection.

**COOPER-HEWITT MUSEUM ★.** 2 E. 91ST ST. (1901, arch. Babb, Cook & Willard). This is now the National Museum of Design, housed in the mansion built by Andrew Carnegie, the steel magnate. His wife lived here until 1946. The Carnegie Corporation gave the house to the Smithsonian Institution in 1972 and the Cooper-Hewitt moved here in 1977, the only branch of the Smithsonian located outside Washington. Taking its inspiration from the Musée des Arts Decoratifs in Paris and the Victoria and Albert Museum in London, the museum was founded in 1897 as the Cooper Union Museum for the Arts of Decoration, by the Hewitt sisters, who amassed an impressive collection of prints, textiles and furniture. The Smithsonian purchased the collection in 1967.

🏃 Two days

Although Washington is the political capital of the U.S., New York is its cultural capital. Recognizing this phenomenon, the French Embassy has restructured its departments accordingly. In 1952 the Republic bought this mansion, with its curved façade decorated with wave moldings, cherubs and lions' heads.

A little to one side, a plastic owl attached to the wall serves as a scarecrow to frighten off the pigeons.

Badge from the Metropolitan Museum.

**JEWISH MUSEUM.** 1109 5TH AVE., N. CORNER 92ND ST. (1908, arch. C. P. H. Gilbert; 1962, arch. Samuel Glazer; 1993, arch. Kevin Roche). The building, which is reminiscent of the Cluny Museum in Paris, was built for the banker Felix Warburg. It has now become the largest American museum devoted to the history and art of the Jewish people: it contains a collection of coins and medals, antique books and valuable manuscripts, objects of worship, and a collection of prehistoric archeological artifacts.

**INTERNATIONAL CENTER OF PHOTOGRAPHY ★.** 1130 5TH AVE., N. CORNER 94TH ST. (1914, arch. Delano and Aldrich). Built for the financier Willard Straight, this Federal-style residence was not remodeled when the Museum of Photography moved into the premises, so it is worth visiting for those interested in architecture as well as photography.

**MUSEUM OF THE CITY OF NEW YORK.** 1220 5TH AVE. BETWEEN 103RD AND 104TH STS. (1932, arch. Joseph H. Freedlander). This museum, founded in 1923,

Badges from the Jewish Museum, the Yivo Institute, El Museo del Barrio, Museum of the City of New York and the International Center of Photography.

**MUSEUM OF THE CITY OF NEW YORK**
Mrs John King van Rensselaer, a socialite who was shocked by how little New Yorkers knew about the history of their own city, was the driving force behind the foundation of this museum. The collection is highly instructive about past customs.

was first housed in Gracie Mansion ▲ 313. The city donated the present site in 1928 and 1,500 subscribers provided the two million dollars needed for the building. The museum, devoted to the city's history, with period rooms, dioramas, toys and dollshouses, not to mention a collection of old fire engines, is as fascinating for children as it is for adults.

**EL MUSEO DEL BARRIO.** 1230 5TH AVE. BETWEEN 104TH AND 105TH STS. (1934, arch. Frank N. Maynicke). Very popular with families living in this part of East Harlem, the museum is devoted to the art and culture of Puerto Ricans and other Latin Americans.

Museum Mile meets East Harlem at the Museo del Barrio, which is dedicated to the culture of Latin Americans.

**HENRY CLAY FRICK**
(1849–1919) This leading Pittsburgh
industrialist had been a collector from
childhood, but his passion
intensified during the last
twenty years of his life (bust
by Malvina Hoffman).

What is
most distinctive
about the Frick
Collection is that it sets
breathtaking works of art
against the backdrop of an early
20th-century bourgeois interior. A
visit to the museum, unique of its kind in
New York, offers a tour
of the history of art and
taste.

**ENTRANCE**
This monumental doorway,
crowned with a classical
inspired relief, has replaced
the original *porte-cochère*.
This was one of the changes
made by the architect
John Russell Pope in 1935
to transform Frick's
residence into a museum.

Designed in 1913 by
Thomas Hastings, the
architect of the New
York Public Library
● 92, Henry Clay
Frick's residence
resembles private
mansions built in
Paris at the end of the
18th century.

**VERMEER, OFFICER AND LAUGHING GIRL (1655–60).** There are only thirty–five authenticated paintings by the "Delft Sphinx". The Frick collection has three of them, including this radiant interior with its ambiguous subject.

**JEAN-HONORÉ FRAGONARD (1771–3),** *The Meeting* One of the four panels that make up "The Progress of Love", painted by Fragonard for Mme du Barry's residence in Louveciennes.

**GIOVANNI BELLINI (1480),** *Saint Francis in the Desert* This masterpiece by the *cinquecento* Venetian artist, long considered one of the finest paintings in America. It depicts Saint Francis of Assisi receiving Christ's stigmata in a lyrically rendered landscape in which the details (animals, plants, rocks) reflect the saint's emotions.

**JEAN-ANTOINE HOUDON (1741–1828),** *Diana the Huntress* A lifesize terracotta figure whose graceful appearance belies its technical virtuosity.

Wandering through the rooms of Mr Frick's residence, one finds works by Boucher, Bruegel, Chardin, Claude Lorrain, Constable, Drouais, Gainsborough, Goya, Greuze, Ingres, De La Tour, Memling, Monet, Rembrandt, Reynolds, Ruysdael and Watteau.

**REMBRANDT,** *Self-Portrait* (1658), as an Oriental potentate.

**JOHN CONSTABLE,** *The White Horse* (1819)
"One of my best efforts" said the artist, referring to this tranquil Suffolk landscape.

**MAIN STAIRCASE**
In response to Mr Frick's desire for a home that would be "simple, comfortable and unostentatious", his architect, Thomas Hastings, and the two interior designers, Sir Charles Allom and Elsie de Wolfe, applied themselves to designing a discreetly luxurious house. The predominantly classical style of decoration contains references to 17th- and 18th-century English decoration, Renaissance and 18th-century French decoration, while incorporating some modern touches, typical of the turn of the century. This residence was designed primarily as a setting for the various works of art collected by its owner. This pink marble staircase acts as a foil for the largest organ ever built for a New York residence, a neo-classical calendar clock (left) and a large sun-drenched painting by Renoir.

**LIVING HALL** Houses English, French, Italian, Spanish, Chinese and Japanese works.

**HANS HOLBEIN THE YOUNGER.** *Portrait of Sir Thomas More* (1527), the great English humanist.

**FURNISHINGS** There is a fine collection of tables, armchairs (above, 16th-century French chair), cassoni and carved cabinets from the Italian and French Renaissance, as well as furniture signed by great 18th-century French masters, including a chest of drawers and a secretaire made by Riesener for Marie-Antoinette.

**DUCCIO DI BUONINSEGNA,** *The Temptation of Christ on the Mountain* (c. 1308). This section of the famous reredos from the Maestà in Siena was one of the first pieces acquired by the museum after Frick's death. The beauty and historic importance of this panel makes it a worthy addition to the founder's collection, especially given his unflagging quest for excellence. His daughter, who took over from him as the museum's influential trustee, encouraged the purchase of works by Bastiani, Castagno, Gentile da Fabriano, Fra Filippo Lippi, Piero della Francesca and Paolo and Giovanni Veneziano.

In 1966 the Whitney Museum moved to its permanent address on the corner of Madison Ave., and 75th St., a building designed by Marcel Breuer, one of great masters of the Bauhaus. Practically all the leading figures in American art in the last fifty years are represented here. They bear witness to Gertrude Whitney's unremittingly non-conformist stance. **STUART DAVIS,** *The Paris Bit* (1959) This is a pastiche made up of remembered fragments of architecture and Parisian life and, according to Stuart, "There was simultaneously so much past and present there, in the same sphere, that you couldn't want for anything more."

The Whitney Museum of American Art, founded in 1931 by Gertrude Vanderbilt Whitney, a sculptor and an enlightened patron of the arts, now houses the largest collection of works by modern American artists in the world.

"Neither symbolism nor calligraphy" is how Franz Kline described his own mature abstract works, exclusively in black and white. In *Mahoning* (1956), as in Kline's later works, the black motifs touch at least two sides of the painting, giving the overall composition an architectural quality.

**ANDY WARHOL,**
*Green Coca-Cola Bottles* (1962)
Warhol was the first artist to use silk-screen techniques, hitherto reserved for advertising, in order to reproduce images of modern society for artistic purposes.

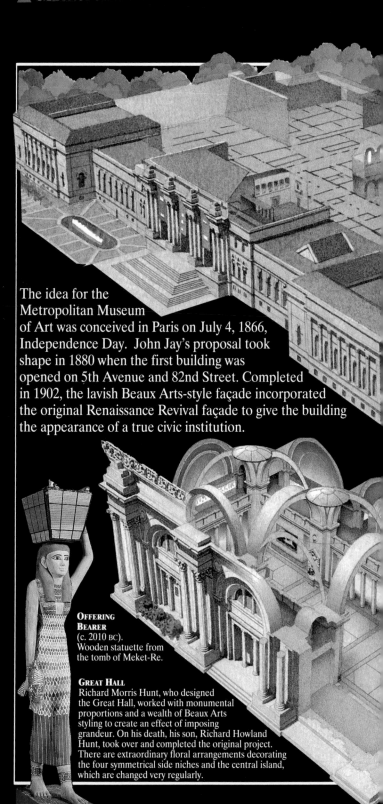

The idea for the
Metropolitan Museum
of Art was conceived in Paris on July 4, 1866,
Independence Day. John Jay's proposal took
shape in 1880 when the first building was
opened on 5th Avenue and 82nd Street. Completed
in 1902, the lavish Beaux Arts-style façade incorporated
the original Renaissance Revival façade to give the building
the appearance of a true civic institution.

**OFFERING
BEARER**
(c. 2010 BC).
Wooden statuette from
the tomb of Meket-Re.

**GREAT HALL**
Richard Morris Hunt, who designed
the Great Hall, worked with monumental
proportions and a wealth of Beaux Arts
styling to create an effect of imposing
grandeur. On his death, his son, Richard Howland
Hunt, took over and completed the original project.
There are extraordinary floral arrangements decorating
the four symmetrical side niches and the central island,
which are changed very regularly.

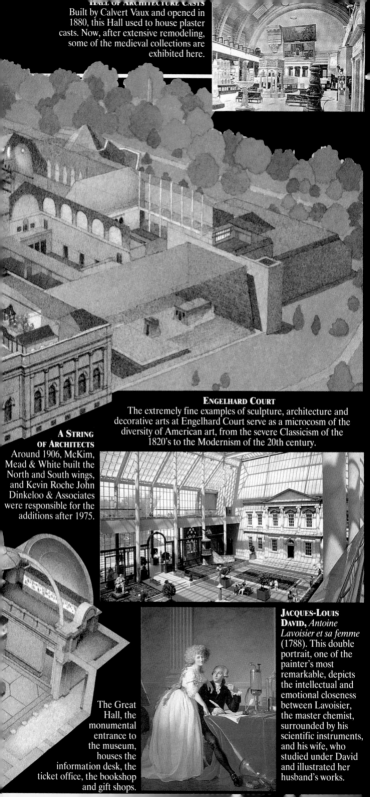

## HALL OF ARCHITECTURE CASTS
Built by Calvert Vaux and opened in 1880, this Hall used to house plaster casts. Now, after extensive remodeling, some of the medieval collections are exhibited here.

## ENGELHARD COURT
The extremely fine examples of sculpture, architecture and decorative arts at Engelhard Court serve as a microcosm of the diversity of American art, from the severe Classicism of the 1820's to the Modernism of the 20th century.

### A STRING OF ARCHITECTS
Around 1906, McKim, Mead & White built the North and South wings, and Kevin Roche John Dinkeloo & Associates were responsible for the additions after 1975.

The Great Hall, the monumental entrance to the museum, houses the information desk, the ticket office, the bookshop and gift shops.

### JACQUES-LOUIS DAVID, *Antoine Lavoisier et sa femme* (1788). This double portrait, one of the painter's most remarkable, depicts the intellectual and emotional closeness between Lavoisier, the master chemist, surrounded by his scientific instruments, and his wife, who studied under David and illustrated her husband's works.

**PENDANT MASK**
(early 16th century)
This extraordinary ivory and metal object is a typical example of the highly elaborate works of art which came out of the kingdom of Benin in Nigeria, usually from the royal court, and which astounded European travelers. The king probably wore this mask on his belt for ceremonies honoring the dead Queen Mother, of whom this may be a portrait.

**HEADDRESS**
(Nigeria)
Carved out of a single block of wood, this was worn by the Yorubas during masked invocations of the water spirits.

**YAISUHASHI SCREEN**
(Edo period, 1603–1867)
This screen is the work of the Japanese artist, Ogata Korin. Its design – a composition of irises, massed against a bridge made of eight planks of wood, and set against a gold background – unfolds across six sections.

## ASTOR COURT

The court of the famous Garden of the Master of the Fishing Nets at Suzhou, was reproduced by Chinese craftsmen who used ancient techniques and aboriginal materials to recreate this perfect microcosm of the natural world: water, rocks and plants, where the contrast of light and shade, softness and hardness, creates a feeling of serenity.

### RECEPTION ROOM FROM THE NUR AD-DIN HOUSE (1707)

This room comes from a residence in Damascus built during the reign of the Ottoman empire and its magnificent marble inlays, gilded and painted wood paneling, stained-glass windows and ceramic tiles encapsulate that period's harmonious luxury.

### MICHAEL C. ROCKEFELLER WING

This wing was inaugurated in 1982 and houses collections of African, Pacific and American art. Nelson Rockefeller donated this wing to the museum, in memory of his son, an explorer who died during a trip to New Guinea.

### MBIS TOTEM

(20th century) The Asmat tribe in New Guinea produces wood carvings, especially totem poles, which are reserved for ritual ceremonies associated with death.

# ▲ METROPOLITAN MUSEUM

**TEMPLE OF DENDUR**
A gift to the United States from the Egyptian government in recognition of American assistance in saving the monuments of Nubia, this small temple dedicated to Isis, built by Augustus around 15 BC, was reconstructed to look as it did on the banks of the Nile, with a pool in the foreground. It can be seen from the park and is illuminated at night.

**FUNERARY STELE**
(6th century BC)
This Attic sculpture shows a female sphinx watching over the tomb of two hieratic young men.

**"PORTRAIT OF A MAN"**
(Fayum, 2nd century BC)
Funerary portrait in the Egyptian tradition influenced by Greco-Roman art.

**"SEATED HARP PLAYER"**
(3rd millennium BC)
This Cycladic marble statue is beautifully simple and represents a male musician – a highly unusual subject.

**BOSCOREALE**
This town, which was buried by the eruption of Vesuvius in AD 79, left, like Pompeii, a superb legacy, including these trompe l'oeil paintings.

**"KING'S HEAD"**
(4th century AD). This engraved and embossed silver head shows the talent of Sassanian artists.

**"Queen's Head"**
(c. 1400 BC)
This fragment of jasper is a perfect illustration of art during the reign of Amenophis III.

**Chair belonging to the Scribe Renyseneb**
(c. 1450 BC)
This attractive chair, skillfully worked in wood and ivory, was used during the pharaoh's lifetime and probably engraved for his tomb after his death.

**Kneeling Man**
(6th century)
This Mayan wooden statue, from the border between Mexico and Guatemala, has miraculously survived the tropical climate.

**"Perseus with the Head of Medusa"**
(1808) Inspired by the *Apollo of the Belvedere* in the Vatican, this marble statue displays Antonio Canova's perfect mastery of the neo-classical style.

**JACKSON POLLOCK,**
*Autumn Rhythm*
(1950)
This painting was the last in a series of large "drip" paintings, an innovative technique which contributed to the development of Abstract Expressionism.

**LIVING ROOM FROM THE LITTLE HOUSE**
In 1914 Frank Lloyd Wright (1867–1959) designed a summer house for Francis W. Little in Wayzata, a suburb of Minneapolis. The ocher-colored walls, natural oak floor and brick fireplace contribute to the harmonious feeling of this room. The oak furniture, and even the way it is arranged, form an integral part of the overall architectural composition.

**CHARLES DEMUTH,**
*I Saw the Figure 5 in Gold* (1928)
This abstract impression of urban life is typical of the modernist American painter.

**ROOM FROM THE HEWLETT HOUSE**
(c. 1739)
The furniture and paneling of this room came from a farmhouse on Long Island at a time when English and European styles were being mixed. The large cupboard painted in grisaille, is typical of the Dutch colonial period.

**MARSDEN HARTLEY,**
*Portrait of a German Officer*
This powerful canvas was painted in November 1914, during a visit to Berlin.

Hartley's treatment of the military themes shows the influence of German Expressionism, as well as Cubism. This painting of an officer with its dense mass of symbols, insignias, medals and flags, enhanced by more personal references – letters and numbers – to a friend who had just been killed at the front, is intended to be a collective physical and psychological portrait.

**THOMAS EAKINS,**
*Max Schmitt in a Single Scull* (1871)
Between 1870 and 1874 Eakins painted a series of canvases devoted to rowing – clear evidence of his passion for sport. Note his treatment of light and space, as well as his great technical virtuosity and his immediate, analytical approach to the subject matter.

**WINSLOW HOMER,**
*The Gulf Stream*
Homer painted this canvas from sketches done during a trip to the Bahamas. It is a fine example of one of his favorite subjects, the reciprocal relationship between man and nature, a subject that is most powerfully expressed in his seascapes.

**SPANISH PATIO**
(1506–15)
This inner courtyard
came from a castle
near Almería (Spain).
It is lavishly sculpted
and a gem of
Renaissance-style,
Italo-Hispanic
architecture.

**JAN VAN EYCK,**
*The Last Judgment*
(c. 1425)
This painting, one of
the earliest by the
Flemish painter and a
masterpiece of the
new technique of oil
painting, foreshadows
Northern Realism.

**GEORGES DE LA TOUR,** *The Fortune*
(1616–39). This is one of the painter's rare
daylight scenes, depicting betrayed innocence.

**EL GRECO,**
*View of Toledo* (c. 1595)
This is one of the few surviving
landscapes by El Greco; he
limited himself to the use of
greens, grays and a dazzling
white, which gives the
painting an inner luminosity
and a mystical aura.

**PARADE ARMOR**
(c. 1550). Decorated
by the engraver
Étienne Delaune,
for Henry II, of
France, its superb
engravings depict
the themes of
Victory and Fame.

**PICASSO,** *Woman in White* (1923). This is a classical, monumental and monochromatic, if sentimental, portrait of Olga.

**SEURAT,** *The Side Show)* (1887–8). This painting is the artist's first magical evening scene showing a popular entertainment.

**MANET,** *Boating* (1874). All the elements of the burgeoning Impressionist movement are here: an open-air setting, color, atmosphere.

**MADONNA WITH CHILD** (Auvergne, 1200). Mary, Throne of Wisdom, holds Jesus, Divine Wisdom, depicted full-face with stylized features.

**GRAND SALON FROM THE HOTEL DE TESSÉ** (Paris, 1765–8) All the grace of the Louis XVI style.

# ▲ Guggenheim Museum

*Fernande with Black Mantilla* (1905) by Pablo Picasso.

The baroness Hilla Rebay von Ehrenwiesen, who inspired Solomon Guggenheim's collection and was its director, commissioned the architect Frank Lloyd Wright to build a museum to house it, with the instruction: "I want a temple of spirit." Solomon Guggenheim, a copper magnate and enlightened patron of the arts, was already the proud owner of a collection of Old Masters and had been introduced to modern art twenty years before when he met the baroness, who had opened his eyes to the work of

*Mountains at Saint-Rémy* (1889) by Vincent van Gogh, left to the museum in 1976 by Justin K. Thannhauser.

*King of Kings* (c. 1930), oak carving by Constantin Brancusi, and *Femme cuiller* (*Spoon in the form of a woman*), (1926), a bronze by Giacometti.

Delaunay, Gleizes, Chagall, Kandinsky and Bauer. He set up an award for modern artists and founded the Solomon Guggenheim Foundation, whose aim was "the promotion and encouragement of education in art". "I do not want to found another museum such as now exists in New York . . . No such building as is now customary for museums could be appropriate for this one."

### A Museum Illuminated by Natural Light.

The architect drew up plans which focused on the importance of natural light. As well as the glass dome over a central court – which figured in all the early proposals – Wright recommended a strip running along the walls, providing a constant source of daylight, modeled on his own studio Wisconsin. Another concept which figured prominently in Wright's plans was that of an open space, without partitions, which a wheelchair could traverse from one end to another. In his original plans, Wright wrote the words "constant ramp" – the idea of a building with a spiral ramp was born.

View of the dome from inside the museum.

*Preparedness* (1968), triptych by Roy Lichtenstein.

"Abstract painting is stronger than figurative art because it creates beauty instead of reproducing what already exists in the natural world."
    Jean Cocteau

*Painting with White Border* (May 1913), oil on canvas by the Russian artist Wassily Kandinsky, painted in Munich.

**A CONTROVERSIAL PROJECT.** It took sixteen years from the first plans to the final building. This was due to clashes with the building authorities and with the director of the Foundation, James Johnson Sweeney, who succeeded Baroness Rebay in 1952 and who felt that Wright's proposals might cause grave problems in terms of conserving and hanging the collections. Not only was Wright keen on having the paintings

illuminated by natural light, which would change with the movement of the sun and the seasons, but he he also wanted them to be displayed at an angle, as if on an easel. The following scheme was finally adopted: a spiral ramp, 1416 feet long, gently climbing up to a glass dome, about 92 feet higher, showering the whole building with light. Along the ramp, artificial lighting was used. In keeping with Wright's intentions, the paintings are exhibited without frames or with very simple frames, and are hung, "as if in an artist's studio", on the curved walls and partitions.

M U S E U M

**A** Main entrance to the Solomon
R. Guggenheim Museum, 1071
5th Ave.

**B** Entrance to the café
**C** Gift shops
**D** Thannhauser Collection
**E** Thannhauser Galleries
**F** Sculpture Terrace

**G** High Gallery
**I** Auditorium
**K** Rotunda

**H** Offices
**I** Auditorium
**J** Tower Gallery
**K** Rotunda

**"A Ship within the City".** Work started in August 1956. Wright visited his building site for the last time in January 1959 and died three months later,

*Composition I A* (1930), oil painting by Piet Mondrian.

without seeing his work completed. The museum opened in October of the same year and caused a storm of protest: people were considerably taken aback, not only by the concrete used for the façade (instead of marble as Wright had wanted) and the upended spiral defying the laws of balance, but also by the abstract works on display inside. Wright had already answered those who, well before it was completed, had called the museum a "washing machine" or a "monstrous mushroom" by saying: "One should no more judge a building from the outside than a car by its color."

**THE COLLECTION.** The Guggenheim Museum is essentially made up of five major private collections: SOLOMON

*Terremoto* (1981) Installation by Joseph Beuys composed of eighteen objects: a

GUGGENHEIM'S COLLECTION OF NON-OBJECTIVE PAINTINGS – Kandinsky, Bauer, Moholy-Nagy, Léger, Delaunay, Chagall, Modigliani; JUSTIN K. THANNHAUSER'S COLLECTION OF IMPRESSIONIST AND MODERN ART – including a large number of Picasso's early works; KARL NIERENDORF'S GERMAN EXPRESSIONIST PAINTINGS (including over 100 works by Paul Klee); KATHERINE S. DREIER'S HISTORIC AVANT-GARDE PAINTINGS AND SCULPTURES (Brancusi, Mondrian); COUNT GIUSEPPE PANZADI BIUMO'S COLLECTION

typewriter, a flag, some felt, nine paintings covered in chalk drawings and diagrams, a cask, a tape-recorder, a cassette and some brochures.

*Morning in the Village after a Snowstorm* (1912) oil painting by Kazimir Malevich.

OF AMERICAN "MINIMAL ART" FROM THE 1960's AND 1970's (Robert Ryman, Dan Flavin); as well as successive acquisitions by the museum's directors and curators – including works by Roy Lichtenstein and Joseph Beuys. Currently the Museum owns more than 5,000 paintings, sculptures and sketches ranging from the Impressionists to the present day. Many works have never been shown due to lack of space. An annex designed by Gwathmey Siegel and Associates was opened in 1992, inspired by the plans drawn up by Wright for artists' studios, intended to occupy the same site. At the same time, the museum opened a new exhibition space in SoHo ▲ *204*.

*Luminous Object* by Dan Flavin, exhibited from June 28, to August 27, 1992.

**✕ Six hours**

The Upper West Side did not actually become a popular residential area until 1879, when the El was built on 9th Avenue (Columbus Avenue). The section of 8th Avenue between 59th and 110th streets was called Central Park West to encourage property developers to build quality residences there. It is now the most prestigious area in the district, its arresting skyline forming a contrast with that of 5th Avenue when seen from the east side of Central Park. The population of the Upper West Side is, like its architecture, eclectic and non-

**HUDSON RIVER**

THE SOCIETY FOR ETHICAL CULTURE FOUNDED IN THE CITY OF NEW YORK MAY 1876

**N.Y. SOCIETY FOR ETHICAL CULTURE**
This society, founded by Felix Adler, made a name for itself primarily for its highly progressive teaching methods. It has established several schools (Ethical Culture Schools), one of which is nearby, at 33 Central Park West, on the corner of 63rd St. The N.Y. Society for Ethical Culture founded New York's first free kindergarten in 1878 and the first social work center in the United States.

conformist. Since the beginning of the 20th century, the district has acted as a magnet for intellectuals and artists, a trend which became even more marked when Lincoln Center was built in the 1960's ▲ 305. The Upper West Side is now a lively, fashionable neighborhood with stores and restaurants. It is also the home of another stylish enclave lining the Hudson from 72nd to 153rd streets – Riverside Drive and Riverside Park, both designed at the end of the 19th century as part of an ambitious development program for the Upper West Side. Some of the city's finest examples of "residential

**THE ELDORADO**
300 Central Park West (1931). This was designed by Margon & Holder in collaboration with Emery Roth, who was also responsible for the San Remo and the Beresford. Below, one of the

hotels" (apartment buildings which provide hotel facilities) can be found on the avenues and, on the side streets, there are some superb groups of rowhouses ● *90*.

three murals from the lobby.

## AROUND CENTRAL PARK WEST

**CENTURY APARTMENTS.** 25 CENTRAL PARK WEST (1931, arch. Irwin Chanin). This is the southernmost apartment building with twin towers of the five lining Central Park West. Heading northward, the others are, respectively, the *Majestic*, the *San Remo*, the *Beresford* (which actually has three towers) and the *Eldorado*. The group gives Central Park West its original and impressive skyline.

**NEW YORK SOCIETY FOR ETHICAL CULTURE.** 2 W. 64TH ST. (1910, arch. Robert D. Kohn). Founded in 1876, the aim of this humanist society was to encourage morality irrespective of religious principles and dogma. It now has twenty-three branches throughout the United States and three thousand members.

343

When it was opened the Hôtel des Artistes offered a communal kitchen, a squash court, a swimming pool, a ballroom and . . . the Café des Artistes.

*Café des Artistes*

**TAVERN ON THE GREEN**
Every year since 1970 the illuminated trees of the Tavern on the Green have marked the finishing line of the New York marathon. This 26.2 mile long race starts from Staten Island, at the entrance to the Verrazano Bridge, and takes in the city's five boroughs.

**LIBERTY WAREHOUSE.** 43 W. 64TH ST. (c. 1900). This is one of the most eccentric buildings on the Upper West Side. The owner built a fifty-five-foot-high replica of the Statue of Liberty on top of the warehouse roof. It used to be a prime attraction for visitors who would climb the mini-staircase inside to marvel at the view of the district. The site was closed in 1912, because the visits disturbed the workers. The statue can be seen clearly from the Lincoln Center plaza.

**AMERICAN BROADCASTING COMPANY TELEVISION STUDIOS.** 56 W. 66TH ST. (1901, arch. Horgan & Slattery). ABC restored the former First Battery Armory of the New York National Guard in 1978. Its television studios now occupy the building and many features have been filmed here.

**TAVERN ON THE GREEN.** CENTRAL PARK WEST AND 67TH ST. (c. 1870). This restaurant is in Central Park. It started life more modestly as a fold for the sheep grazing nearby in Sheep Meadow. Since first opening, in 1934, it has become a favourite haunt of celebrities. At night the surrounding trees are spectacularly festooned with lights.

**HÔTEL DES ARTISTES, CAFÉ DES ARTISTES.** 1 W. 67TH ST.

(1918, arch. George Mort Pollard). This was one of a number of residences built along this street at the beginning of the 20th century by groups of artists who had pooled their finances. The buildings contained studios as well as apartments which could be rented out. The revenues from rents helped the artists to eke out a living and to pay back the money they had borrowed for the construction work. Isadora Duncan, Noel Coward, Norman Rockwell and John Lindsay, one of New York's former mayors, were among the many celebrities who lived here. The painter, Howard Chandler Christy, one of the first residents, painted the murals in the charming Café des Artistes which can be reached via the hotel lobby.

**"CAFÉ DES ARTISTES"**
The murals by Howard Chandler Christy, a long-time resident at the Hôtel des Artistes, depict thirty-six willowy, naked beauties in a woodland setting. Most of the artist's models were well-known by the hotel's other residents. Christy, nicknamed the "pin-up artist", was renowned for this type of painting and his pin-ups were often used as magazine illustrations. This was why he was asked to be one of the judges for the first Miss America beauty contest.

**CONGREGATION SHEARITH ISRAEL.** 99 CENTRAL PARK WEST (1897, arch. Brunner & Tryon). The oldest Jewish congregation in New York, whose name means "remnant of Israel", was formed in 1655 by refugees from Brazil who were fleeing persecution. The Dutch governor, Peter Stuyvesant, wanted to prevent them from settling here, but was informed by his employer, the Dutch West India Company, that the company's Jewish shareholders would not tolerate such an attitude. The group was therefore allowed to stay and build its first synagogue in 1730 on Mill Street, in Lower Manhattan. That small Georgian-style synagogue has been recreated within the present building. It contains two millstones from a Dutch windmill that used to stand on Mill Street.

**THE PYTHIAN CONDOMINIUM, FORMER PYTHIAN TEMPLE.** 135 W. 70TH STREET (1927, arch. Thomas W. Lamb). This eye-catching building, west of Columbus Avenue, is worth making a detour to visit. It was created by Thomas Lamb, the theater designer, to house the headquarters of the brotherhood, the *Knights of Pythias*. In 1986 the building, whose décor evokes Hollywood epics of the 1920's, was remodeled and converted into apartments. Note the inscription above the front door: "If fraternal love held all men bound how beautiful this would be."

**WEST 71ST STREET.** BETWEEN CENTRAL PARK WEST AND COLUMBUS AVENUE (1890's). The rowhouses that line this stretch of 71st Street date from the time when the Upper West Side was just becoming established. Most of them were private houses.

**MAJESTIC APARTMENTS.** 115 CENTRAL PARK WEST (1930, arch. Jacques Delamarre). This apartment building was the successor to the sumptuous Majestic Hotel, built in 1893 and renowned for its *Roof Garden*. These hanging gardens, resplendent with fountains and waterfalls, were one of the fashionable haunts of New York's high society at the turn of the century. Fred Astaire stayed at the *Majestic Hotel* in 1919. Its successor, the Majestic

**WEST 71ST STREET**
The façade and main entrance of the houses lining the two sides of this street are decorated with carved ornamental motifs, including lions' heads, cupids and shells. The carved bas-relief of the first bay window of the house at no. 33 shows a fox holding a rabbit in its jaws, among other motifs.

"Once again, Stillman retreated to Riverside Park, this time to the edge of it, coming to rest on a knobby outcrop at 84th Street known as Mount Tom. On this same spot, in the summers of 1843 and 1844, Edgar Allan Poe had spent many long hours gazing out at the Hudson."
Paul Auster,
*City of Glass*

**THE FORMER PYTHIAN TEMPLE**
This building is one of the area's most interesting sights. Its façade offers a carefree mixture of ancient decorative styles (Sumerian, Assyrian, Egyptian) and has an unusual top, dominated by two colorful pharaohs.

## Dakota Apartments

Designed by the architect who later designed the Plaza, the Dakota is regarded as an architectural gem and one of the city's most desirable

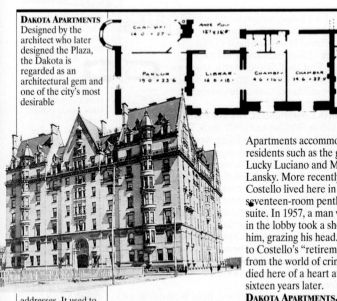

Apartments accommodated residents such as the gangsters Lucky Luciano and Meyer Lansky. More recently, Frank Costello lived here in a seventeen-room penthouse suite. In 1957, a man waiting in the lobby took a shot at him, grazing his head. This led to Costello's "retirement" from the world of crime. He died here of a heart attack sixteen years later.

addresses. It used to house an army of servants and provide a huge range of services to its rich residents. Roberta Flack, Leonard Bernstein and Judy Garland all lived here. Roman Polanski used it as the setting for his film *Rosemary's Baby* (1968). The Dakota was John Lennon's last address. In 1980 he was shot dead by a misfit as he stood under the hotel awning. His wife, Yoko Ono, still lives at the Dakota. The section of Central Park just opposite the hotel was landscaped at her request, including this mosaic (right) and is called Strawberry Fields, after the title of a Beatles song written by Lennon.

**Dakota Apartments.** 1 W. 72nd St. (1884, arch. Henry J. Hardenbergh). This was the first residential luxury apartment house in New York, built by Edward Clark, president of the Singer Sewing Machine company. When people found out that he had decided on an Uptown site, many nicknamed the project, "Clark's folly". Why not in Dakota, in the Far West? asked one of his friends. Clark kept the name and had the building decorated with arrowheads, ears of corn and an Indian head over the main entrance.

**San Remo Apartments.** 145–146 Central Park West (1930, arch. Emery Roth). The actress Rita Hayworth lived until she died in 1987 in this luxury apartment building. A boat trip on Central Park lake probably affords the best view of the *San Remo* and its spectacular towers, each topped with a cupola (opposite).

**New-York Historical Society.** 170 Central Park West (1908, arch. York & Sawyer). Founded in 1804 by New Yorkers keen to preserve the history of their city, the New-York Historical Society is a museum and reference library. Its permanent collections include three hundred watercolors by

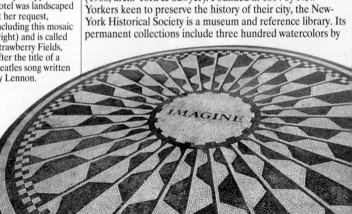

"HUDDLED TOGETHER ON THE NARROW ISLAND, THE BUILDINGS WITH THEIR THOUSAND WINDOWS WILL SOAR, SPARKLING . . . TOPS SURROUNDED BY WHITE CLOUDS, RISING ABOVE THE STORMS. . . ."

JOHN DOS PASSOS

Plans of the Dakota.

**THE MUSEUM OF NATURAL HISTORY**
This vast museum includes collections ranging from butterflies to dinosaurs, which are also shown in murals.

John James Audubon ▲ *361*, works by Thomas Cole and other members of the Hudson River School as well as a large collection of Tiffany glass and lamps ▲ *296*. Serious financial difficulties forced the museum to close temporarily in 1993.

**AMERICAN MUSEUM OF NATURAL HISTORY.** CENTRAL PARK WEST, BETWEEN 77TH AND 81 STS. (original wing 1872–7, arch. Calvert Vaux and J. Wrey Mould). Opened by President Ulysses S. Grant, the museum's original wing is now lost among an array of twenty-one later buildings. THE THEODORE ROOSEVELT MEMORIAL (1936, arch. John Russell Pope) now forms the main entrance of the museum, on Central Park West. The interior is decorated by murals depicting scenes

from the life of the former president, a great explorer who campaigned for the preservation of natural sites in the United States (such as the Grand Canyon). An equestrian statue standing outside (1940, James Earle Fraser) shows Roosevelt flanked by an Indian and an African to symbolize his "friendship for all races". This is one of the most visited museums in New York. The collections documenting Indian, African and Pacific civilizations, the dioramas of animal habitats, the lifesize reproduction of a blue whale and the Dinosaur Hall are particularly popular. THE HAYDEN PLANETARIUM (1935, arch. Trowbridge & Livingston) occupies the north wing of the museum, on 81st Street.

**THE BERESFORD.** 211 CENTRAL PARK WEST (1929, arch. Emery Roth). This huge luxury apartment building, designed by the architect who was responsible for the *San Remo* replaced a hotel of the same name on this site. Its main distinguishing characteristics are its three Baroque-style towers, which loom above Central Park.

**THE ANSONIA HOTEL**
"It looks like a baroque palace from Prague or Munich enlarged a hundred times, with towers, domes, huge swells and bubbles . . . Under the changes of weather it may look like marble or like sea water, black as slate in the fog, white as tufa in sunlight."
Saul Bellow, *Seize the Day*

## FROM BROADWAY TO RIVERSIDE PARK

**ANSONIA HOTEL.** 2109 BROADWAY (1904, arch. Graves and Duboy). This Beaux Arts building has a sophisticated exterior, designed primarily by the French architect and sculptor Paul E. Duboy. Note the corner towers topped with domes and the many balconies. As a luxury hotel, it represented the height of modernity and was the first air-conditioned building in New York. Its excellent sound-proofing has attracted many musicians, including Stravinsky, Toscanini, Caruso, Chaliapin and Menuhin. Step into the lobby to see the display of photos retracing the Ansonia's glamorous history. These show that it once had two swimming pools, several shops, a fountain in the lobby with seals swimming in its basin and a roof garden

**RIVERSIDE PARK**
Riverside Drive, first developed in the 1880's, has never seriously rivaled 5th Ave. as a fashionable address, but the proximity of Riverside Park (right, at the beginning of the century) and its magnificent views of the Hudson River, have ensured its appeal for many New Yorkers.

**STATUE OF JOAN OF ARC**
Riverside Drive and W. 93rd St. This statue, designed in 1915 by Anna Vaughn Hyatt Huntington, stands at the center of Joan of Arc Park. Some of the stones of its pedestal come from Rheims Cathedral and others from the tower in Rouen where Joan of Arc was imprisoned.

with a henhouse built by the owner who provided his guests with fresh eggs.

**COLLEGIATE CHURCH AND COLLEGIATE SCHOOL.** 241 W. 77TH ST. (1893, arch. Robert W. Gibson). The Collegiate Church's gables, steeples and intricately worked dormer windows are a reminder that it used to belong to the Dutch Reformed Church, established in the United States in 1628. The Collegiate School is no longer directly connected with the church. This prestigious private boys' school is one of the oldest schools in the United States.

**APTHORP APARTMENTS.** 2211 BROADWAY (1908, arch. Clinton & Russell). Built by William Waldorf Astor, this Italian Renaissance-style residential hotel, which covers an entire block, attracted wealthy boarders who wanted to live on the Upper West Side. Its two large arched gateways lead into a vast inner court with a decorative central fountain.

**RIVERSIDE DRIVE WEST 80TH–81ST STREETS HISTORIC DISTRICT** (c. 1890). The thirty-two rowhouses that make up this historic district were built by developers who were reluctant to emulate the prevailing trend for residential hotels. Note the embellishment of the ridgepoles and the varied array of bow windows.

**RIVERSIDE PARK.** RIVERSIDE DRIVE, FROM 72ND TO 153RD STS. (1873–1910, Frederick Law Olmsted). This is Manhattan's other major park, after Central Park, designed by the same landscape gardener. It covered the disued tracks of the New York Central Railroad for a stretch of seventy blocks. The riverside promenade, with its small marina at 79th Street, running along the Hudson between 72nd and 86th streets, is a worth a visit.

**YESHIVA CHOFETZ CHAIM/FORMER VILLA JULIA.** 346 W. 89TH ST. (1901, arch. Herts & Tallant). The former home of Isaac L. Rice, who called it Villa Julia after his wife, is one of the few private mansions still standing on Riverside Drive. Rice made his fortune selling electric batteries and made a name for himself, in his later years, as an outstanding chess player. His house is now occupied by a Jewish seminary (*Yeshiva* in Hebrew).

# Off the beaten track

🕐 Four hours

"I remember …
when you had to
change trains at
Washington and had
to travel in a car for
Blacks only – when
you could not go to
the dining car until
all the Whites had
finished. . . . I don't
mean that I want to
eat with the Whites.
It just makes life a

little easier – it may
make my children's
life a little easier.
Perhaps that is all I
want."

James Baldwin,
*Harlem*

This itinerary includes
Morningside Heights
and Harlem – two adjacent neighborhoods which lie north of
110th Street and together run the width of Manhattan. The
two areas present a dramatic contrast. Morningside Heights
has various educational and religious
establishments, notably Columbia
University, Barnard College, Riverside
Church and the huge and splendid
Cathedral of St. John the Divine,
reflecting the movement, that began in
the 1890's, to make this part of town a
spiritual and intellectual center.
Harlem's history is more checkered; it
has a rich and varied past which dates
back to the 17th century.

**HISTORY.** In 1658 Dutch farmers, attracted by the fertile soil,
built the village of Nieuw Haarlem – named after a town in
Holland – about 10 miles north of the main settlement, New
Amsterdam. In the next century wealthy New Yorkers built
country residences here. In 1837 the New York and Harlem
railroad opened on 4th Avenue. This link, which ran from
City Hall to the Harlem River transformed the village into a
thriving suburb, whose western area acquired some fine

116TH ST.

MORNINGSIDE AVE.

MORNINGSIDE PARK

MANHATTAN AVE.

110TH ST.

COLUMBUS AVE.

AMSTERDAM AVE.

CATHEDRAL PARKWAY

The trompe l'oeil façade of this Harlem house is a remnant of the elegance that prevailed here at the beginning of the 19th century.

"Harlem, in New York, soon became the largest black community in the world; it became the symbol and the model of the city lifestyle that the Blacks, victims of segregation, were creating within their new group. Harlem . . . formed a sort of urban frontier zone."

D. Boorstin

rowhouses. The building of the 3rd- and 2nd-Avenue elevated railways in 1879 led to the development of its eastern area with blocks of tenements inhabited by immigrants. The opening of the Lenox Avenue IRT subway in 1901gave another boost to Harlem's growth.

**THE BLACK COLONIZATION OF HARLEM.** Toward the end of the 1880's plummeting prices in this new district, caused by overly optimistic speculation by real estate developers, attracted an influx of poor Blacks. By 1920 200,000 Blacks were living in Harlem. This decade was the neighborhood's golden age, known to many as the "Harlem Renaissance"; Black musicians, intellectuals and writers came here in droves. However, the 1929 crash put an end to this revival.

**THE 1960'S.** During this period Harlem became a center of political and social activism. The Black Muslims, led by Elijah Mohammed, founded the Temple of Islam on Lenox Avenue at 116th Street. Malcolm X worked there until 1964 before setting up his own organization. He was assassinated in February 1965 at the Audubon Ballroom on 165th Street. In 1968 Harlem was the scene of rioting by the Black residents, who were seeking social and economic justice.

351

## COLUMBIA UNIVERSITY

**STATUE OF THE ALMA MATER**
Daniel Chester French's statue, completed in 1903, presides over the majestic staircase outside the Low Memorial Library. It personifies learning and knowledge.

**SETH LOW**
(1850–1916)
He was the Mayor of Brooklyn and, from 1890, President of Columbia University. He built the Low Memorial Library. In 1901, he was elected Mayor of New York.

Columbia University at the beginning of the century.

**HISTORY.** Founded in 1754 as King's College and renamed Columbia College after the War of Independence, Columbia University is now one of the oldest and largest universities in the country and one of the largest private landowners in New York, after the Catholic Church. Even in its infancy the college produced some distinguished citizens. Alexander Hamilton, the first secretary of the treasury; John Jay, the first chief justice of the Supreme Court, and Robert Livingston, the first secretary of foreign affairs, all graduated from King's College. More recently, both Theodore and Franklin D. Roosevelt attended the university's Law School. Dwight D. Eisenhower was president of the university from 1948 to 1953, before becoming President of the United States.

Columbia University now has nearly 18,000 students and a faculty of 5,000. The campus is open to the public and guided tours can be arranged.

**SEVERAL SITES.** The first site of King's College was near Trinity Church ▲ *154* in Lower Manhattan. In 1857, it moved to Madison Avenue between 49th and 50th streets. It moved to its present site, bounded by 114th and 121st streets, Broadway and Amsterdam Avenue, in 1897. The plan and most of the original buildings on the campus were designed by McKim, Mead & White.

**LOW MEMORIAL LIBRARY.** (1897, arch. McKim, Mead & White). Low Memorial Library, standing in the middle of the campus and built in the

> **"IT WAS REALLY HARLEM, AND ALL THE STORIES I HAD HEARD ABOUT THE CITY WITHIN THE CITY FLASHED INTO MY MIND."**
> RALPH ELLISON

**"OUR COUNTRY AND OUR CULTURE"**
In the 1950's, the universities, and primarily Columbia University, were the driving force behind intellectual activity. In 1952, the *Partisan Review* published a synthesis of the new approach adopted by thinkers, defined during a symposium called "Our Country and Our Culture". It forecast America's intellectual emancipation from Europe and the birth of an American intellectual hegemony.

shape of a Greek cross, was the first building to be constructed on the campus. It has an exquisite Beaux Arts interior, featuring a vast rotunda capped with a dome, reminiscent of the Pantheon in Rome. The library was superseded by the Butler Library in 1934, and the building now houses the university's central administrative offices, as well as the COLUMBIANA LIBRARY COLLECTION, an assortment of documents, books and portraits relating to the university's history.

**BUTLER LIBRARY.** (1934, arch. James Gamble Rogers). Columbia University's main library is opposite the Low Memorial Library, on the southern side of the campus. Butler Library owes its name to Nicholas Murray Butler, president of the university from 1902 to 1945. With more than six million volumes, it is one of the largest libraries in the United States. Rogers was inspired by the Bibliothèque Sainte-Geneviève in Paris, designed by Henri Labrouste.

**ST. PAUL'S EPISCOPAL CHAPEL.** (1907, arch. Howells & Stokes). This nondenominational (formerly Episcopal) chapel, in the shape of a Greek cross, is situated east of Low Memorial Library. Its construction was financed by the family of Anson Phelps Stokes, a wealthy financier and philanthropist. Below the chapel, there is the Postcrypt, a small café-concert hall where students in the 1960's discovered the *Beat Generation* poet Jack Kerouac and the songs of the young Robert Zimmerman (Bob Dylan).

**EAST HALL.** BETWEEN LOW LIBRARY AND ST. PAUL'S EPISCOPAL CHAPEL (1878). This building, part of a former insane asylum, now houses the TEMPLE HOYNE BUELL CENTER FOR THE STUDY OF AMERICAN ARCHITECTURE as well as the MAISON FRANÇAISE OF COLUMBIA. On the lawn between East Hall and the Philosophy Department stands a replica of Rodin's *Thinker*, executed in 1930. Opposite stands Avery Hall and AVERY LIBRARY, the largest architecture library in the country. Although the campus as a whole is open to the public, you must have a Columbia University student card to get into the Butler and Avery libraries.

**A FRENCH CULTURAL CENTER**
Columbia University's Maison Française, established in 1910, is the oldest foreign language study center attached to an American university. Its artistic and literary events attract a lively French contingent. Sartre and Ionesco, among others, have given lectures here.

## ▲ MORNINGSIDE HEIGHTS AND HARLEM

1 GREEK AMPHITHEATER  2 GRAPHIC ARTS STUDIO  3 OMEGA LITURGICAL DANCE COMPANY  4 ENSEMBLE FOR EARLY MUSIC  5 HORIZON CONCERTS  6 SCULPTURE STUDIO  7 BIBLICAL GARDEN

At the beginning of the century, people were already impressed by the size of the cathedral, shown (below) under construction. When finished, Saint John the Divine will be the largest Gothic cathedral in the world, 601 feet long and 177 feet high under the nave.

## ST. JOHN THE DIVINE ★

**THE EPISCOPAL CATHEDRAL OF NEW YORK.** This majestic cathedral stands on Amsterdam Avenue at 112th Street in Morningside Heights. Near this spot, on September 16, 1776, the patriot forces, under George Washington, defeated the British in the Battle of Harlem Heights, which took place during the War of Independence. In 1887, wishing to build a cathedral on a par with the finest in Europe, the Episcopal Diocese of New York paid an exorbitant sum of money for 15 acres of land and launched a competition for its design. Of the sixty entries, the winning plan was one for a Romanesque-style building submitted by the firm of Heins & La Farge.

**A LONG AND DIFFICULT TASK.** Work began on the cathedral in 1892, under the guidance of Bishop Henry Codman Potter; today, a century later, it still remains unfinished. The first phase, constructing the choir and the four arches of the great dome, took nearly twenty years. In 1916 the plans underwent radical changes; following the death of the two architects and Bishop Potter, it was decided to adopt plans by Cram & Ferguson for a Gothic-style cathedral. The construction of the nave did not start until 1925 after an appeal for contributions from the public, which

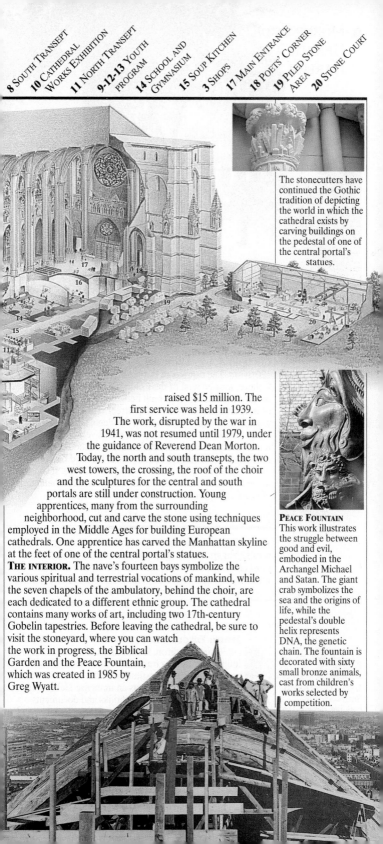

The stonecutters have continued the Gothic tradition of depicting the world in which the cathedral exists by carving buildings on the pedestal of one of the central portal's statues.

raised $15 million. The first service was held in 1939. The work, disrupted by the war in 1941, was not resumed until 1979, under the guidance of Reverend Dean Morton. Today, the north and south transepts, the two west towers, the crossing, the roof of the choir and the sculptures for the central and south portals are still under construction. Young apprentices, many from the surrounding neighborhood, cut and carve the stone using techniques employed in the Middle Ages for building European cathedrals. One apprentice has carved the Manhattan skyline at the feet of one of the central portal's statues.

**The interior.** The nave's fourteen bays symbolize the various spiritual and terrestrial vocations of mankind, while the seven chapels of the ambulatory, behind the choir, are each dedicated to a different ethnic group. The cathedral contains many works of art, including two 17th-century Gobelin tapestries. Before leaving the cathedral, be sure to visit the stoneyard, where you can watch the work in progress, the Biblical Garden and the Peace Fountain, which was created in 1985 by Greg Wyatt.

**Peace Fountain**
This work illustrates the struggle between good and evil, embodied in the Archangel Michael and Satan. The giant crab symbolizes the sea and the origins of life, while the pedestal's double helix represents DNA, the genetic chain. The fountain is decorated with sixty small bronze animals, cast from children's works selected by competition.

"But when I opened my eyes we were turning into Riverside Drive. . . . To my right and ahead the church spire towered high, crowned with a red light of warning. And now we were passing the hero's tomb (Grant's Tomb) and I recalled a visit there. You went up the steps and inside and you looked far below to find him, at rest, draped flags . . ."
Ralph Ellison,
*Invisible Man*

### BARNARD COLLEGE.
BETWEEN BROADWAY AND CLAREMONT AVE., 116TH AND 120TH STS. The campus of Barnard College, located west of the Columbia University campus, consists of nine buildings built between 1896 and 1988. The oldest wing is at 606 West 120th Street. The establishment was founded in 1889 as a women's college, affiliated with Columbia, which was at that point exclusively male (the first female students were admitted in 1983). Although Columbia now welcomes members of both sexes, Barnard College has proudly preserved its status as a women's college. It owes its name to Frederick A. P. Barnard, one of the first champions of equal rights for women in higher education.

## NORTHERN MORNINGSIDE HEIGHTS

**UNION THEOLOGICAL SEMINARY.** BROADWAY, BETWEEN 120TH AND 122ND STS. (1910, arch. Allen & Collens). Some of the most eminent Protestant pastors in the United States – including Reinhold Niebuhr, who was professor of Christian ethics here between 1928 and 1960 – have been associated with this seminary, which was founded in 1836. Ask to visit the small garden within the cloisters and see the magnificent staircase.

**JEWISH THEOLOGICAL SEMINARY.** 3080 BROADWAY (1930, arch. Gehron, Ross, Alley). This seminary, founded in 1886 to train rabbis and theologians, has become the central institution of the American Jewish conservative movement. It boasts an immense Hebrew and Jewish library, a collection of rare books and documents relating to the Jewish community during the colonial period.

**UNION THEOLOGICAL SEMINARY.** This building, designed by the architect of Riverside Church and Teachers College (on 120th St.), is based on the same theme with neo-Gothic ● *86* variations. It is one of the finest examples of the English Gothic style in New York.

**RIVERSIDE CHURCH ★.** 490 RIVERSIDE DRIVE AND W. 120TH ST. (1930, arch. Allen & Collens, Henry C. Pelton). This neo-Gothic ● *86* church was founded by a Baptist congregation. It is now interdenominational and renowned for its liberalism and active involvement in community affairs. It was here, in 1967, that the Rev. Martin Luther King, Jr, gave his famous sermon, "It is time to break the silence", protesting against American intervention in Vietnam. Nelson Mandela was

## GENERAL GRANT NATIONAL MEMORIAL.

The Baptist Church, introduced in North America in the 17th century, became very popular, especially among Blacks. Here (left) a baptism in 1834 in the waters of the Hudson River.

honored here in 1990, for his work in bringing an end to apartheid in South Africa. The interior of the church contains many remarkable works of art including some fine stained glass and a huge sculpture, *Christ in Majesty* by Jacob Epstein.

**GENERAL GRANT NATIONAL MEMORIAL.** RIVERSIDE DRIVE, NEAR W. 122ND ST. (1891–7, arch. John H. Duncan). Erected with funds raised by subscription, this tomb is the final resting place of Ulysses S. Grant (1822–85), commander-in-chief of the Union Armies during the Civil War and President of the United States from 1869 to 1877, and of his wife Julia. This shrine is a reconstruction of the tomb of King Mausolus in Halicarnassus (in modern-day Turkey), one of the seven wonders of the ancient world. The words spoken by Grant when he was nominated for President ("Let us have peace") are engraved above the entrance, flanked by allegories of Victory and Peace. The design of the tomb itself, clad in red marble, was modeled on Napoleon's tomb at the Hôtel des Invalides in Paris. The five busts on the colonnade, carved in 1938, portray the generals who served under Grant during the Civil War: Sherman, Thomas, McPherson, Ord and Sheridan. Three mosaics (1966, Allyn Cox) represent the Battle of Vicksburg, his first great victory; the Battle of Chattanooga, his first as commander of all the armies in the West and, between them, Grant and Lee shaking hands to seal the surrender of the Confederacy at Appomattox. More than one million people followed Grant's funeral procession on August 8, 1885. He has gone down in history as the man who saved the nation and restored peace; but he was more successful as a general than as President, as he failed in his attempts to rebuild the South and integrate Blacks into American society. His term of office was tainted by corruption.

**CARILLON OF RIVERSIDE CHURCH**
At the top of the church's bell tower is the Laura Spelman Rockefeller Memorial Carillon.

Its 20-ton great bell, the largest in the world, and its 74 other bells cover a range of more than five octaves.

**BLACK LEADERS**
The clergy has often provided political leaders for the Black community, such as, in New York, Adoui Clayton Powell Jr. of the Abyssinian Baptist Church in Harlem and, more recently, Reverends Calvin O. Butts, Al Sharpton and Herbert Daughtry (below).

Tom-toms in the African Market, along 125th St., between Adam Clayton Powell Jr. Blvd. and 5th Ave.

The African Market, which sells a wide variety of Afro-American products.

"We have not lost the habit of jostling in the market place, buying and selling, selling and buying. We like trading. We are born with the gift. We love it. The city is itself a huge market. You can't go more than a few steps without finding a store of some sort. We are all potential entrepreneurs, looking to make a deal in this country of commerce."
Jerome Charyn,
*Metropolis*

## THE HEART OF HARLEM

**APOLLO THEATER.** 253 W. 125TH ST. (1914, arch. George Keister). When this theater first opened it was a burlesque house for Whites only. In 1934, when its new owners, Leo Brecher and Frank Schiffman, opened it to Blacks, it became extremely popular, offering top-flight entertainment. Bessie Smith, "the Empress of the Blues", and Billie Holiday performed here in the 1930's. Duke Ellington and Count Basie played here in the 1940's as did Charlie Parker and Dizzie Gillespie, the fathers of bebop ● *60*. Many other artists, including Aretha Franklin and the Jackson Five, have since appeared on the bill. The Apollo Theater closed in 1976 for financial reasons, but reopened ten years later.

**THERESA TOWERS, FORMER THERESA HOTEL.** 2090 ADAM CLAYTON POWELL JR. BD. (1910, arch. George and Edward Blum). Built at a time when racial segregation was still widely practiced in New York, this establishment was reserved for Black customers, since Blacks, however wealthy, could not stay at most other New York hotels. It soon became one of the most popular haunts in Harlem. Years later it welcomed Fidel Castro, who stayed here in 1960, when he came to New York to speak before the United Nations General Assembly, and also Nikita Khrushchev. Malcolm X moved his offices into the hotel shortly before he was assassinated in 1965. The hotel was converted into offices in 1971.

**MARCUS GARVEY MEMORIAL PARK.** BETWEEN MOUNT MORRIS PARK W. AND MADISON AVE., 120TH AND 124TH STS. This was called Mount Morris Park when it was opened in 1839, and renamed in 1973 in homage to Marcus Garvey, the West Indian leader of the *Back to Africa* movement in the early 20th century. This park was built when it proved impossible to move the enormous central rock obstructing 5th Avenue. A fire watchtower, then visible from Madison Avenue, was built in 1855 on top of this promontory. This is the last of the city's many fire towers.

**SYLVIA'S RESTAURANT.** 328 LENOX AVE. This Harlem institution has been serving Afro-American cooking for thirty years now. Its walls are covered with photos of famous Black Americans and with murals. The riot of August 1, 1943 broke out in this area when a White policeman shot a Black soldier. Thousands of Blacks poured into the streets, overturning cars, ransacking stores belonging to Whites and starting a number of fires.

**"WEDNESDAY AMATEUR NIGHTS"**
On Wednesday nights the Apollo Theater runs its famous amateur nights, in which young musicians are judged by an audience of afficionados.

**SCHOMBURG CENTER FOR RESEARCH IN BLACK CULTURE.** 515 LENOX AVE. (1978, arch. Bond Ryder Assocs.). This is one of the largest branches of the New York Public Library ▲ 252 . It owes its name to Arthur A. Schomburg (1874–1938), a Black Puerto Rican who collected documents on Afro-American culture after being told at school that the Blacks had no history. THE CARNEGIE CORPORATION OF NEW YORK bought his collection in 1926 and employed him as the curator. The Schomburg Center is now – with some 75,000 books, 300,000 photographs and a collection of musical recordings – the largest historical collection devoted to all peoples of African descent in the world.

**ABYSSINIAN BAPTIST CHURCH.** 132 W. 138TH ST. (1923, arch. Charles W. Bolton). The church, whose name is a constant reminder to parishioners of their African heritage, was founded in 1808 on Worth Street, and was moved when the congregation migrated northward. Its main claim to fame is its former preacher, Adam Clayton Powell Jr (1908–72), elected to the House of Representations in 1945. He presented bills in favor of education and civil rights, campaigning in particular for a minimum wage and the abolition of racial segregation in the army. This church boasts one of the finest gospel choirs in Harlem.

**ST. NICHOLAS HISTORIC DISTRICT.** 138TH AND 139TH STS., BETWEEN ADAM CLAYTON POWELL, JR, AND FREDERICK DOUGLASS BLVDS. These rowhouses from 1891, grouped around a communal backyard, were built for middle-class Whites, but began to be occupied by Black middle-class families from 1919. As a result the district was nicknamed "Striver's Row". W. C. Handy, Noble Sissle and Eubie Blake – all famous jazz musicians – lived here.

THE AMERICAN NEGRO THEATRE
PRESENTS

**"ANGEL STREET"**
by Patrick Hamilton
Staged and Directed by Stanley Greene

**"ANGEL STREET"**
In 1943, at the same time as rioting broke out in the Black ghettos, a new style of music was born. It spread throughout the country and all over the world. Below, from left to right: Coleman Hawkins, Benny Harris, Don Byas, Thelonius Monk, Denzil Best, Eddie Robinson, photographed in 1944.

▲ HAMILTON AND WASHINGTON HEIGHTS

1 ST. JOHN THE DIVINE
2 LOW MEMORIAL LIBRARY
3 BARNARD COLLEGE
4 RIVERSIDE CHURCH
5 GENERAL GRANT NATIONAL MEMORIAL
6 THERESA TOWERS
7 APOLLO THEATER
8 HAMILTON GRANGE
9 THE CLOISTERS
10 DYCKMAN HOUSE
11 MORRIS-JUMEL MANSION
12 ABYSSINIAN BAPTIST CHURCH
13 SCHOMBURG CENTE
14 HARLEM STA OFFICE B

## HAMILTON AND WASHINGTON HEIGHTS

These two neighborhoods occupy the northmost strip of Manhattan, between the Hudson and Harlem rivers. At the north end of Washington Heights is Fort Tryon Park, with its museum, the Cloisters.

**CITY UNIVERSITY OF NEW YORK.** BETWEEN 130TH AND 140TH STS., ST. NICHOLAS TERRACE AND AMSTERDAM AVE. Founded in 1849 to provide free university education for New Yorkers, City College of New York (as it then was) was nicknamed the "Harvard of the people".

**HAMILTON GRANGE NATIONAL MONUMENT.** 287 CONVENT AVE. BETWEEN 141ST AND 142ND STS. (1801, arch. John McComb, Jr). Hamilton Grange was the home of

✂ Two hours

**CITY COLLEGE**
At the heart of the university's original campus – now the North Campus – which is located between 135th and 140th sts., stands Shepard Hall, a neo-Gothic pile dominating Hamilton Heights. Some alumni of City College, which was originally founded to provide a free college education for New York's working-class students, have been Nobel Prize winners.

Alexander Hamilton ▲ *154*. This Federal-style ● *82* residence, built by the architect of City Hall ▲ *168*, is situated in the heart of the HAMILTON HEIGHTS HISTORIC DISTRICT. This district contains some very attractive rowhouses, built between 1886 and 1906 and clustered along Convent Avenue between 141st and 145th streets. No. 6 Hamilton Terrace (Edgecombe Ave., north of

145th Street) is occupied by Aunt Len's Doll and Toy Museum (temporarily closed).

**SUGAR HILL.** SUGAR HILL BETWEEN ST. NICHOLAS AND EDGECOMBE AVES., 143RD TO 155TH STS. This district used to be called Sugar Hill because its affluent Black residents had finally earned their place in the sun and the right to a "sweet life in Harlem". Duke Ellington and Cab Calloway, the Black leader W. E. B. DuBois and the writer Langston Hughes all lived along Edgecombe Avenue.

## FROM AUDUBON TERRACE TO THE CLOISTERS

**TRINITY CEMETERY.** BETWEEN AMSTERDAM AVE. AND RIVERSIDE DRIVE, 153RD AND 155TH STS. This cemetery ▲ *154*, straddles Broadway. The entrance, on Riverside Drive, leads into the western part, which affords a magnificent view of the Hudson River and the George Washington Bridge. Clement Clarke Moore, author of "A Visit from Saint Nicholas", is buried in the eastern part of the cemetery and every Christmas eve a children's choir sings carols around his tomb.

**TRINITY CEMETERY**
This covers a section of the land that once belonged to the naturalist and artist John James Audubon (1785–1851), who is buried in the eastern part, behind the Church of the Intercession.

**AUDUBON TERRACE HISTORIC DISTRICT.** BROADWAY, BETWEEN 155TH AND 156TH STS. (1908–30, arch. Charles Pratt Huntington and others). This is a group of museums clustered around a central courtyard in which stands a statue of El Cid (1927, Anna Hyatt Huntington). The AMERICAN ACADEMY OF ARTS AND LETTERS houses manuscripts, paintings, sculpture, and musical scores by its members, who are some of America's most respected artists. The HISPANIC SOCIETY OF AMERICA, devoted to the art, culture and history of Spain and Latin America, contains works by El Greco, Velázquez, Goya and Picasso. The AMERICAN NUMISMATIC SOCIETY is a museum of coins and civil and military decorations. Audubon Terrace was once the site of the MUSEUM OF THE AMERICAN INDIAN, founded in 1916, which possesses a magnificent collection of art and crafts made by America's Indian cultures. This is moving to the former U. S. Custom House ▲ *157* at Bowling Green.

**MORRIS-JUMEL MANSION**
This house has one of the finest Georgian interiors in New York. In 1810 Stephen Jumel, a wealthy merchant of French origin, related to Bonaparte's family, bought the house and remodeled it. In particular, he added the Federal-style entrance. After his death, his widow, Eliza Jumel, married Aaron Burr. She lived here until her death in 1865.

**MORRIS-JUMEL MANSION ● *82* ★.** N. W. CORNER OF 160TH ST. AND EDGECOMBE AVE. (1765, remodeled in 1810). This superb residence gives an impression of the way rich New Yorkers lived two centuries ago. It was built in the Georgian style ● *82* by a British colonel, Roger Morris. During the War of Independence Washington used it briefly as his headquarters before it fell into British hands.

**DYCKMAN HOUSE. ● *82* ★.** 4881 BROADWAY AT N. W. CORNER OF 204TH ST. (1784). East of the Cloisters stands the last colonial farmhouse in Manhattan. It once belonged to a family of Dutch settlers, the Dyckmans, who settled here in 1661. After the War of Independence, during which the British burned down the original farmhouse, the Dyckmans built the house that stands today. Saved from demolition in 1916, it is now a museum, evoking rural life during the colonial period.

A part of the Metropolitan Museum of Art, the Cloisters was established in 1938 and is devoted exclusively to European art of the Middle Ages. On entering this building, with its powerful medieval style of architecture, the visitor is immediately immersed in the past. Here, medieval treasures, notably the architectural fragments, are sympathetically installed.

The flexible plan enabled the architects to incorporate the Romanesque apse from the escheated church of Fuentadueña in Spain. Composed of nearly three thousand slabs of pale limestone, it was dismantled stone by stone, brought back to New York and carefully reassembled.

This 14th-century Italian diptych, entitled *Crucifixion and Lamentation*, is one of t many works of medieval painting in the Cloisters.

The museum has many precious works of art such as *Saint John the Evangelist*, a Carolingian ivory (c. 800).

This silver ewer is a gem of medieval decorative art. (German, c. 1500).

**COLLECTOR AND PATRON OF THE ARTS** John D. Rockefeller, Jr, financed this building, which stands on top of a hill in Fort Tryon Park, (above), in Upper Manhattan. His own gifts and the acquisition, in 1925, of the collection owned by George Grey Barnard, an American sculptor living in France, formed the nucleus of the museum's collection, which has grown considerably since then.

Another masterpiece of European art, a *Virgin and Child* from 12th-century Burgundy.

The museum is so called because fragments of four medieval cloisters have been incorporated into the modern structure. The floral gardens in the cloisters of Cuxa, Bonnefont and Trie often include the same plants as those listed in inventories compiled in the Middle Ages. The cloister of Saint-Guilhem-le-Désert encloses a winter garden.

**THE ANNUNCIATION**
*The Annunciation*, a triptych by Robert Campin (c. 1425), clearly illustrates the convergence of religious and secular themes.

Although the symbolism of the *Annunciation* is still medieval, the treatment anticipates the Renaissance.

Manuscript from the end of the 15th century (below).

The 12th-century cloister from Saint-Michel-de Cuxa (left), in the Pyrenees, is completely made of marble.

The rosary bead above, made of boxwood, dates back to the early 16th century.

J. P. Morgan's generosity was not limited to financing the construction of the Cloisters; he also endowed the museum with more than forty pieces from his own collection. Among the most important of these are the Unicorn Tapestries (right).

The famous Unicorn Tapestries, seven hangings (above, the *Unicorn at the Fountain*) probably designed in Paris and woven in Brussels c. 1500, represent the symbolic quest for this mythical animal.

One of the capitals from the cloister of Saint-Michel-de-Cuxa.

**LIGHT AND COLOR**
The nucleus of the building is made up of fragments of cloister arcading from Barnard's collection. The Cloisters' many windows are glazed with stained glass, resplendent when bathed in natural light, like the panels from Saint Leonhard, in Austria, created c. 1340–50, or these Rhenish stained-glass windows (left) dating from 1440–7.

George Grey Barnard bought medieval architectural elements from farmers and magistrates who had salvaged them in monasteries and churches damaged during the 16th-century wars of religion, then abandoned during the French Revolution. Although Barnard sold some of his acquisitions to subsidize his work as a sculptor, he exhibited the others in New York to introduce Americans to the mastery of what he called the "patient Gothic chisel".

❝If those who come under the influence of this place go out to face life with a new courage and restored faith because of the peace, the calm, the loveliness they have found here . . . those who have built here will not have builded [sic] in vain.❞

John D. Rockefeller

View of the Fulton Ferry Building in Brooklyn, in June 1857.

**WILLIAMSBURG SAVINGS BANK TOWER** This skyscraper, which was erected during the 1929 crisis and is the tallest building in Brooklyn, is reminiscent of a Byzantine church, with its mosaics, carved capitals and its vault (below) three stories high. The counters on the ground floor are small votive chapels. Where the altar would be a large mosaic depicts an aerial view of the city of New York with Brooklyn and the Williamsburg Savings Bank Tower in the center.

**BROOKLYN HEIGHTS ESPLANADE.** (1951) Built to cover the Brooklyn-Queens expressway and lined with houses and gardens, this promenade affords a magnificent view of Manhattan, the bay of New York and the Brooklyn Bridge.

Founded in 1657 by Dutch settlers, Brooklyn (after Breuckelen, a small town in the Utrecht region) is now the most densely populated borough of New York after Manhattan. The district of Brooklyn Heights, a headland that overlooks the East River, grew considerably after 1814, when Robert Fulton established a steam ferry service, which allowed people to cross the river more quickly than via the existing boats. The wealthy inhabitants moved out of Brooklyn Heights after the Brooklyn Bridge ▲ *186* was opened in 1883; Brooklyn was joined with Manhattan in 1898 and the first subway line was created in 1908. The elegant mansions were converted into apartments and the area lost some of its former charm. Today, about half of the houses date from before 1860 and most were restored some fifteen years ago.

**BROOKLYN BOROUGH HALL, FORMER BROOKLYN CITY HALL** 209 JORALEMON ST. AND CADMAN PLAZA (1846–51, Gamaliel King). Brooklyn's former city hall was designed by a carpenter; at the time, few public buildings were designed by architects. When Brooklyn became part of New York in 1898, the city hall was renamed Borough Hall and given a cupola, after the fashion of City Hall ▲ *168*.

**MONTAGUE STREET ★.** With its many restaurants, stores, office buildings, small houses, and its church – ST. ANN'S AND THE HOLY TRINITY at no. 157 – Montague Street has an almost European-style charm. It was once nicknamed "Bank Avenue" because of the predominance of financial establishments. Note in particular, at no. 185, the FORMER NATIONAL TILE GUARANTY BUILDING, in Art Deco style (1930, arch. Corbett, Harrison and MacMurray). By the early 1920's, at the intersection of Flatbush and Atlantic avenues, there were so many trolley lines that all Brooklynites were called "trolley dodgers", thus the name of the legendary baseball team, the Dodgers (now in Los Angeles).

**BROOKLYN HISTORICAL SOCIETY** 128 PIERREPONT ST. AT S. W. CORNER OF CLINTON ST. (1878, arch. George B. Post). This society was founded in 1863 and opened to the public in 1880. It contains a remarkable collection documenting the history of Brooklyn, the city and the State of New York, and has one of the best genealogical research libraries in the country. Busts of Christopher Columbus and Benjamin Franklin decorate the façade.

## TOWARD PROSPECT PARK

**BROOKLYN MUSEUM.** EASTERN PARKWAY AND WASHINGTON AVE. (1897, arch. McKim, Mead & White). This museum possesses a large collection of documents and various objects relating to the American Indians, as well as a magnificent collection of Egyptian art, which is considered one of the best collections in the States. The entrance to this neo-classical building is through a superb porch that is embellished with statues (depicting Manhattan and Brooklyn) designed by Daniel Chester French (1916).

# PRACTICAL
# INFORMATION

# ◆ Useful Information

Even though for most visitors New York City is synonymous with Manhattan, the city has, since 1898, been made up of five boroughs: Manhattan, Brooklyn, the Bronx, Queens and Staten Island. (A poll carried out on November 2, 1993, however, showed that Staten Islanders have begun to question whether their borough should be part of New York City at all.) Although the 13-mile-long island of Manhattan is the geographical heart of New York City, its 1.5 million inhabitants account for less than 20 percent of New York's total population.

## CONSULATES

◆ **CANADA**
1251 Ave of the Americas
Tel. 596-1700

◆ **CHINA**
520 12th Ave
Tel. 868-7752

◆ **FRANCE**
934 5th Ave
Tel. 606-3600

◆ **GERMANY**
460 Park Ave
Tel. 308-8700

◆ **ITALY**
690 Park Ave
Tel. 737-9100

◆ **JAPAN**
299 Park Ave
Tel. 371-8222

◆ **SPAIN**
150 East 58th St
Tel. 355-4090

◆ **UK**
845 3rd Ave
Tel. 745-0202

## FORMALITIES

United Kingdom citizens do not need a visa for holidays and business trips under 90 days. You must hold a valid passport and a return ticket (not essential for anyone entering the city overland), as well as adequate financial resources for their proposed stay in the United States. No vaccinations are needed for entry. You must have a visa for visits over 90 days, whether for study or business.

## NEW YORK CITY MARATHON

This takes place in early November. New Yorkers line the race course to cheer on the 26,000 competitors, who run from Staten Island to the Tavern on the Green in Central Park, crossing the Verrazano Bridge, parts of Brooklyn, Queens and the Bronx. Domestic applicants should send a check for $6 payable to "New York Road Runners Club", along with a self-addressed envelope to: Marathon Entries, P.O. Box 1388 GPO, New York, NY 10116. Foreign applicants should send a self-addressed envelope to Int'l Entries, P.O. Box 1766 GPO, New York, NY 10116. Some travel agencies are authorized to sell "competitor's number included" deals: more pricy, but a safer bet.

## INTERNATIONAL STUDENT CARDS

An international student membership card enables students to obtain reductions on the price of airline tickets and admission to museums and various cultural events. It also ensures reimbursement for some kinds of medical treatment. For information contact:
**US:**
Tel. (800) 777-0112
**UK:**
STA TRAVEL
Priory House,
6 Wrights Lane,
London W8
Tel. 0171 937 9971

## MEDICAL INSURANCE

It is advisable to take out a personal medical insurance policy before your departure to cover you for the duration of your stay in the US. Medical treatment is prohibitively expensive in the United States. Many hospitals will not treat uninsured patients and no agreement exists with the Social Security office in the UK. Cover may be provided as an extra by your Visa or MasterCard accounts. Banks and travel agencies also have their own policies.

## SPRING
**March to May**

*The city is flooded with light, its inhabitants are invigorated by the sea air. The season of street fairs and parades begins.*

| | |
|---|---|
| MARCH 17 | **ST. PATRICK'S DAY PARADE,** 5th Ave. and Saint Patrick's Cathedral |
| **EASTER SUNDAY** | **EASTER PARADE,** 5th Ave., 44th-59th sts. |
| **LAST MON. MAY,** public holiday | **MEMORIAL DAY** |

★ Have lunch in the South St. Seaport.

MARCH 30° / 76°
APRIL 43° / 61°
MAY 54° / 70°

## SUMMER
**June to August**

*The weather is hot and humid, New Yorkers escape to Long Island, the streets are packed with tourists and musicians perform in the parks.*

| | |
|---|---|
| **2ND TUES., JUNE (6-9PM)** | **MUSEUM MILE FESTIVAL, FREE** admission to Museums, 5th Ave. (82nd–105th sts.) |
| JUNE, JULY AND AUGUST | **FREE CONCERTS BY THE METROPOLITAN OPERA AND THE NEW YORK PHILHARMONIC,** Parks and Great Lawn of Central Park |
| JUNE, JULY AND AUGUST | **SHAKESPEARE IN THE PARK** Delacorte Theater, Central Park (free) |
| **END JUNE, BEGINNING JULY** | **JAZZ FESTIVAL** |
| **JULY 4,** public holiday | **INDEPENDENCE DAY,** fireworks display on the tip of Manhattan alternates between East and West sides of the island |

★ Visit the Cloisters or the Botanical Garden.

JUNE 63° / 81°
JULY 70° / 82°
AUGUST 66° / 79°

## FALL
**September to November**

*An incredible wave of energy is unleashed by the mild fall weather in New York. There is no better time of year to fall under New York's spell.*

| | |
|---|---|
| **SEPTEMBER** | **US OPEN TENNIS TOURNAMENT,** Flushing Meadows |
| **1ST MON., SEPTEMBER,** public holiday | **LABOR DAY** |
| | **WEST INDIAN AMERICAN DAY CARNIVAL,** Departs from the Brooklyn Museum |
| **2ND MON., OCTOBER,** public holiday | **COLUMBUS DAY** |
| **OCTOBER 31** | **HALLOWEEN,** Fancy dress parade in Greenwich Village. "Trick or treat" – free candy for the children. |
| **EARLY NOVEMBER** | **NEW YORK CITY MARATHON** |
| **NOVEMBER 11,** public holiday | **VETERANS' DAY** |
| **4TH THURS. NOVEMBER,** public holiday | **THANKSGIVING DAY,** Parade along Central Park West and Broadway |

★ The Thanksgiving turkey is eaten at this family occasion.

SEPTEMBER 61° / 73°
OCTOBER 54° / 63°
NOVEMBER 43° / 52°

## WINTER
**December to February**

*The East Coast is besieged by cold weather and snow and legendary storms occasionally bring everything to a standstill. But this city never sleeps!*

| | |
|---|---|
| **DECEMBER 25,** public holiday | **CHRISTMAS** |
| **JANUARY 1,** public holiday | **DROPPING THE "BIG APPLE",** midnight |
| **END JANUARY, BEGINNING FEBRUARY** | **CHINESE NEW YEAR,** Chinatown |
| **3RD MON. JANUARY,** public holiday | **MARTIN LUTHER KING'S DAY** |
| **3RD MON. FEBRUARY,** public holiday | **PRESIDENT'S DAY** |

★ An ideal time to visit the museums!

DECEMBER 30° / 39°
JANUARY 28° / 39°
FEBRUARY 28° / 41°

 warm and sunny    changeable to cloudy   rainy    cold, possible snow

*The minimum and maximum temperatures for each month are given in degrees Fahrenheit.*

## AIR TRAVEL

**US:**
For reservations for flights within the US, the following major domestic carriers offer flights to Kennedy, Newark, and La Guardia airports.
◆ American Airlines Tel. (800) 433-7300
◆ Delta Airlines Tel. (800) 221-1212

◆ United Airlines Tel. (800) 241-6522
◆ US Air Tel. (800) 428-4322

**UK:**
The main carriers from the UK are British Airways (including Concorde), Continental, United, Virgin Atlantic, American Airlines and Air India. Flights are from various major UK cities.
◆ British Airways 156 Regent Street London W1R 5TA Tel. (0181) 897 4000 C'tral Booking Office: Tel. (0345) 222111
◆ American Airlines 23–59 Staines Rd, Hounslow, TW3 Tel.0181 572 5555

◆ Virgin Atlantic Unit 8, Radius Park, Faggs Road, Feltham, TW14 Tel. 0181 890 0090 or 0181 890 4411
◆ United Airlines United House Building, 451 Southern Perimeter Rd, Heathrow Airport, London TW6. Tel. 0181 990 9900

## BY SEA

The *Queen Elizabeth II*, last of the great liners, crosses the Atlantic five times a year, leaving from Cherbourg, Liverpool and Southampton. The journey takes five days (from £1245 return per person). The Cunard Line Ltd, 30 Pall Mall, London SW1. Tel. 0171 839 1414 or 0171 930 4321. In New York: (800) 221-4770.

## BY AIR

New York City is serviced by three main airports: John F. Kennedy International Airport, Newark International Airport and La Guardia Airport, which handles internal flights exclusively. Many London–New York flights leave London around lunchtime and land in New York in the early afternoon, local time, after a journey of eight hours. Return flights tend to leave New York in the evening and arrive in London in the early hours of the following morning. The price of a standard economy-class return ticket from London to New York is rarely under $600. Charter flights are cheaper (between $300 and $450). Economy-class or excursion return tickets to New York from other areas can generally be found at the following rates (given in dollars): Paris $800; Rome $1050; Bonn $920; Tokyo $1380; Ottawa $285.

## BY CONCORDE

This prestigious airplane leaves London's Heathrow airport daily (Terminal 4). The flight takes only four hours and a roundtrip ticket costs $6558. Air France's Concorde travels between Charles de Gaulle airport in Paris and J.F.K. airport daily. The least expensive one-way ticket costs $2203, while round trip costs $6405.
For reservations:
**US:**
Tel. 212-247-0100 or (800) 237-2747
**UK:**
Tel. 0345 222100

## BUS–SHUTTLE SERVICE

The three New York airports are all situated within a 16-mile radius of Manhattan and can all be reached by bus. Carey Transportation (718-632-0550) provides a regular shuttle service (every 20–30 minutess; no service between 1am and 5am) between Kennedy and La Guardia, and six drop-off points in Midtown

Manhattan: opposite Grand Central Terminal (125 Park Avenue), the Hilton, Sheraton Manhattan, Holiday Inn Crown Plaza and Marriott Marquis hotels, and the Port Authority Bus Terminal. The Olympia Airport Express provides a similar service (every 20–30 minutess; no service between

11pm and 5am) between Newark and Manhattan. Buses stop at Pennsylvania Station, Grand Central Terminal and the World Trade Center. The Gray Line Air Shuttle is slightly more expensive but provides a door-to-door service between these three airports and Manhattan, from 23rd Street to 63rd Street. Heading out to the airports from Manhattan it picks up passengers from sixty different hotels across Midtown.

| | |
|---|---|
| 1. JOHN F. KENNEDY AIRPORT | |
| 2. LA GUARDIA AIRPORT | |
| 3. NEWARK AIRPORT | |

Montreal

Montpellier

Concord

Albany

Boston

Hartford

Providence

**NEW YORK**
Kennedy Airport

Long Island

Philadelphia

antic City

*Delaware Bay*

*To: Liverpool, Southampton, Cherbourg*

*Atlantic Ocean*

*To: Panama, Recife, Rio de Janeiro*

| | |
|---|---|
| 🛣 80 | US Interstate Highway |
| | Railway |
| | Sea links |

M o u n t a i n s

### BY CAR

From the east, take the Lincoln or the Holland Tunnels (into Midtown), and from the north, take the George Washington Bridge. The New England Thruway (I-95) connects the Triborough Bridge and the Cross Bronx Expressway. Highway I-87, from the north, also connects with the Triborough Bridge, the other bridges over the Harlem and the East River. Two expressways run the length of Manhattan: the West Side Highway along the Hudson and Franklin D. Roosevelt Drive, along the East River.

### BY BUS

All "long distance" buses terminate at the Port Authority Bus Terminal (W. 41st St/8th Ave, Tel. 564-8484).

Greyhound Trailways (tel. 1-800-231-2222) is the best company to use for long bus journeys to Manhattan.

### BY TRAIN

Manhattan has two stations: Pennsylvania Station (7th Ave/W. 34th St) and Grand Central Terminal (42nd St/Park Ave South). Amtrak trains run between Pennsylvania Station and many cities in the United States and Canada. An express train, the Metroliner, links New York to Washington and Boston. A one-way (single) ticket from Chicago to New York costs about $141, from Washington or Montreal about $75, and from Boston $43.
♦ Amtrak Tel. (800) USA-Rail (toll free 381). Trains from Grand Central Terminal run to all stations in Westchester County and Connecticut.

At first glance visitors may find Manhattan overwhelmingly large and confusing, but most of its streets and avenues have numbers, not names, forming a straightforward, logical system. Above 14th Street the avenues, which run north to south, form a right angle with the streets, which run east to west. Only in the older part of Manhattan, below 14th Street, where the streets twist and turn as they do in European cities, will you need a map to find your way around.

### AVENUES

Most avenues are numbered from east to west, although there are exceptions. On the East Side, Lexington, Park and Madison avenues are sandwiched, in that order, between 3rd and 5th avenues. In the East Village, four small avenues (A, B, C and D) lead to the neighborhood east of 1st Avenue. On the West Side, 6th Avenue is officially called the Avenue of the Americas, and on the Upper West Side, 8th, 9th, 10th and 11th avenues become, respectively, Central Park West, Columbus, Amsterdam and West End avenues. Building numbers increase from south to north, but because of the avenues' length, addresses will also give the relevant cross street.

### THE SUN

On a sunny day it is easy to get your bearings in Manhattan (above 14th Street). In the morning, if the sun is to your right, you are facing uptown; in the afternoon, if it is to your right, you are facing downtown.

### STREETS

Streets are numbered from south to north. 5th Avenue is the dividing line between the West Side and the East Side in Manhattan, so that a street with a given number is designated "West" or "East" to either side of it. It is easy to find a street address: apartment building numbers start on 5th Avenue, and increase by a hundred for every block, whatever the direction. 244 W. 38th Street, therefore, is between 7th and 8th avenues. Traffic generally travels eastward on even-numbered streets and westward on odd-numbered streets. On few, wider crosstown streets traffic moves in both directions. As a rule, even-numbered buildings line the south side of the street and odd-numbered buildings the north.

### UPTOWN, MIDTOWN AND DOWNTOWN

When New Yorkers refer to Uptown, they are talking about neighborhoods north of 59th Street (the Upper East Side, Upper West Side and Central Park). Heading uptown means going north. Midtown is the part of the city between 14th and 59th streets. Downtown covers the south of the city from 14th Street (from Greenwich Village to the Financial District). Heading downtown means going south.

### EAST SIDE/WEST SIDE

North of 59th Street and south of 110th, Central Park divides the Upper East Side from the Upper West Side. On the south side of 59th Street the dividing line between East Side and West Side is 5th Avenue.

### BLOCKS

Distances are estimated in blocks (shorter north-south than east-west). There are about twenty blocks (north-south) to one mile.

### STREET SIGNS

Most street names are given in white on a green background. Streets or squares named after famous figures or particular activities may appear on blue or brown signposts.

BUSES, TAXIS, LIMOUSINES ◆

Although traffic can be a nightmare in Manhattan, particularly between 8am and 6pm, traveling by bus, taxi or perhaps limousine, is a fascinating way to see the city at close quarters. The buses (usually air-conditioned in summer) are a welcome alternative to the subway. They are extremely handy for traveling from east to west (via the wide crosstown streets), which is not so easy by subway. The yellow taxis – there are nearly 12,000 licensed by the city – are easy to find and not overly expensive. People traveling in a group or wishing to cover fairly extensive distances can hire a chauffeur-driven limousine for an affordable price.

### BUSES

Traveling by bus in Manhattan will take you close to your destination because buses travel both crosstown (east-west), uptown and downtown (north-south), stopping every two or three blocks. Bus stops are indicated by a yellow mark on the curb, showing a stylized bus and line number, and occasionally by a bus shelter. Several lines may stop at one bus stop: check the number of the bus indicated on the front and back of the vehicle. Bus drivers are generally friendly and helpful.

### FARES, TRANSFERS

The bus fare is the same as the subway fare and is paid by token or with the exact money in coins (no change is given). If you need to change buses to reach your destination, the driver will give you a transfer paper on request.

### LIMOUSINES

Taxi-limousines are also licensed by the New York City Taxi and Limousine Commission, but can only pick up passengers by prior arrangement. A private chauffeur-driven car can be hired by the hour or by contract for a tour around the city. You can even travel by limousine from the airport to the city center.

### TAXI FARES

Medallion taxis have a meter fixed to the dashboard which indicates the exact cost of the ride. The minimum fare is $2, then 30¢ for every additional ⅛ mile. When the taxi is stationary, every 90-second waiting period costs 30¢. You must also allow for an additional 50¢ for rides between 8pm and 6am. Check that the driver has re-set the meter to zero when you get in the cab. The vehicle's identity number (4 digits at the side of the meter) can be used to track down lost property or, if necessary, to file a complaint with the Taxi and Limousine Commission, 220 W. 41st Street. Tel. 302-8294

### HAILING A TAXI

In Manhattan finding a taxi is easy (except on rainy days). The yellow cabs are the only ones authorized to pick up passengers in the street and are hailed from the sidewalk (there are few taxi stands). They can carry up to a maximum of four passengers, unless they are the larger Checker cabs, which can carry five.

### TRAVELING BY CAR

It is not a good idea to drive a car around Manhattan. Finding on-street parking is a lottery and garages are expensive. However, you may want to rent a car to visit the surrounding countryside. The main rental car companies in Midtown are:
Avis:
1-800-331-1212
Hertz:
1-800-654-3131
National:
1-800-328-4567
Dollar:
1-800-421-6868
Budget:
1-212-807-8700
1-800-527-0700

Green globe: ticket office open at all times.

Red globe: restricted opening times.

Graffiti have practically disappeared. The din remains, however…

With 710 miles of track, 469 stations and 5,950 trains, the New York subway is the largest urban transportation system in the world. It provides a reliable and efficient service, enabling you to travel quickly north or south. The network operates 24 hours a day, 7 days a week, but certain lines run only a part-time service (6am–12pm, at the very least). The authorities have made every effort to improve passenger safety and most subway cars are now clean and air-conditioned.

## EXPRESS TRAINS AND LOCAL SLOW TRAINS

Lines are referred to by their original name (IRT, IND, BMT), by letters (A, B, C, etc.) or by numbers (1, 2, 3, 4, 5, 6, 9). Many lines have two tracks and operate a dual service: express or local. Local trains make all the stops, while express trains stop only at the larger stations, indicated by a rectangle on the maps. To change trains, just cross over the platform in the larger stations.

## TAKING THE RIGHT TRAIN

To enter the subway system, deposit a token or a MetroCard in the turnstile then follow the signs for the line you wish to take. Once on the platform, you will find other signs indicating the type of train (local or express) and its direction. The line and destination also appear on the train.

## SAFETY

As in any large city, certain precautions should be taken when traveling on the subway, especially at night: beware of pickpockets and stand well back from the yellow line at the edge of the platform. It is not advisable to travel "after hours" (between 11pm and 7am). During this period, wait for your train in the areas indicated by a yellow sign (Off-Hour Waiting Areas), where the ticket clerks can see the passengers. Never get into an empty car.

## STATIONS

Stations are generally named after streets. Subway entrances are indicated by green or red globes. The green globe signifies that the ticket office at that entrance is open 24 hours a day, but a red one means that this is not the case. All stations have at least one entrance and ticket office that is always open. Signs at the entrance indicate the lines running through that station, their direction and, if relevant, the type of train. Uptown and downtown trains often have separate entrances, one on either side of the street.

## TOKENS

A token ($1.50) covers one journey, whatever its length or duration (but does not cover transfers by bus). Tokens are sold at ticket booths (notes larger than $20 are not accepted), by automatic ticket machines in some stations, at drugstores and at McDonalds, as well as in several major museums. MetroCards are now available and are good for $10, $20 or more worth of rides. MetroCards do not save any money on travel but they do allow you to avoid standing in long lines at the token booth. Tokens are also valid for travel on buses (◆ 375).

## DISCOUNT FARES

Children shorter than 3½ feet travel free. To obtain reduced fares at certain times of the day, senior citizens (over 65) should call 442-3000 and disabled people should call 878-7294. Weekly or monthly cards are available in some locations.

## INFORMATION

Free subway maps are available from most ticket offices. A large-scale map of the system as well as information about how it operates are usually displayed nearby. The New York City Transit Authority can also be contacted 24 hours a day at 718-330-1234.

New York is the financial capital of the United States as well as its largest business center. The city is home to two of the nation's major stock markets (the New York Stock Exchange and the American Stock Exchange), and also of many international institutions and some of the most prestigious banks in the world. Successful business deals and large amounts of money changing hands are daily features of a world which also offers free rock concerts and plays in Central Park yet has one of the most expensive hotel industries on earth. The consumer is king in this city if he or she does the "job" of comparing prices, asking questions and – in some cases – haggling before making a purchase.

### CHANGING FOREIGN MONEY

Banks are generally open Monday to Friday, 9am to 3pm (some also open on Saturday mornings). Most large banks will change currency, as will many of the best hotels (but at a less competitive rate).

### USEFUL ADDRESSES

**AMERICAN EXPRESS**
World Financial Center Tower C
Tel. 640-2000
374 Park Ave.
Tel 421-8240

**BLOOMINGDALE'S**
Corner of 59th St./Lexington Ave.
Tel. 705-3171

**MACY'S**
Herald Square
Tel. 695-8075

**BANK OF AMERICA INTERNATIONAL**
355 Madison Ave.
Tel. 503 7000

**CHECKPOINT**
609 Madison Ave.
Tel. 750-2255

**DEAK INTERNATIONAL**
Kennedy Airport
Tel. 718-656-8444
630 5th Ave.
Tel. 757-6915

**THOMAS COOK CURRENCY SERVICES**
Kennedy Airport
Tel. 1-718-656-8444
511 Madison Ave
Tel. 753-0132
41 E. 42nd Street
Tel. 883-0400
29 Broadway
Tel. 363-6208

### EXCHANGE RATE

The dollar fluctuates depending on the policy of the Federal Reserve Bank. In 1996, it tends to be around Canadian $1.27, UK £0.63, FF4.99, DM1.47 and Yen 102.82.

### DOLLARS AND CENTS

The United States dollar is divided into 100 cents. The bills in circulation are $1, $5, $10, $20, $50, $100. You will occasionally come across $2 bills but these are rare. Coins in circulation are the penny (1¢), the nickel (5¢), the dime (10¢), the quarter (25¢), the half dollar (50¢) and the $1 coin, although the last two are rarely used.

### TRAVELERS' CHECKS

Dollar travelers' checks are extremely useful: they are accepted as hard currency in most hotels, restaurants and shops and can be replaced if lost or stolen.

### BANK CARDS
The United States leads the field in the use of plastic money as legal currency. Debit or credit cards are therefore widely accepted in hotels, restaurants and stores, the most popular being Visa and MasterCard, (Access), American Express and Diner's Club (the latter two being more exclusive). Due to the wider availability of cash machines, cards are now a more practical method of payment than travelers' checks.

### CASH DISPENSERS
There are several networks of Automatic Teller Machines (ATM), the largest of which are Cirrus, affiliated to Visa, and Plus, affiliated to MasterCard. These cash dispensers are open 24 hours a day and can be found at branches of Citibank and Chase Manhattan as well as at other banks in Manhattan.
**LISTING OF ATMs:**
Cirrus:
1-800-424-7787.
Plus:
1-800-843-7587.

### TIPPING
Tipping is obligatory, but a service charge is rarely added to the check (bill). Use the following scale to work out your tip:
Restaurants: 15–20 percent (double the local tax of 8.25 percent)
Bars: 15 percent
Taxis: 15 percent (minimum of 25¢).

### SALES TAX
Most goods bought in Manhattan are taxed at 8.25 percent. This tax is not generally included in the marked price. In hotels it can vary from 13.25 percent to 19.25 percent on top of the fixed hotel tax of $2. With the exception of confectionery and soft drinks, food bought at a grocery store is not taxed.

## WHAT THINGS COST...

**COFFEE: $1 TO $1.50**

**ALCOHOL: $3**

**BAGEL: $0.50 TO $1.50**

**MUSEUM ADMISSION: $3 TO $7**

**CONCERT: $5 TO $30**

**MOVIE: $8.50**

**TOP-CLASS RESTAURANT: $35 TO $60**

**BUDGET HOTEL: $60 TO $75 PER NIGHT**

379

## CONVERSION TABLES FOR MEASUREMENTS

### LIQUIDS

| | | |
|---|---|---|
| 1 fluid ounce (fl. oz.) | = 0.03 l | *To convert liters into US gallons, multiply the number of liters by 0.26 (e.g.: 50 liters x 0.26 = 13 gal.). To convert gallons into liters, multiply the number of gallons by 3.79 (e.g.: 12 gal. x 3.79 = 45.48 liters)* |
| 1 pint = 16 fl. oz. | = 0.47 l | |
| 1 quart = 2 pints | = 0.94 l | |
| 1 gallon (gal.) = 4 quarts | = 3.785 l | |

### LENGTHS AND DISTANCES

| | | |
|---|---|---|
| 1 inch (in.) | = 2.54 cm | *To convert miles into kilometers, multiply the number of miles by 1.61 (e.g.: 50 miles x 1.61 = 80.5 km). To convert kilometers into miles, multiply the number of kilometers by 0.62 (e.g.: 25 km x 0.62 = 15.5 miles)* |
| 1 foot (ft.) = 12 in. | = 30.48 cm | |
| 1 yard (yd.) = 3 ft. | = 0.915 m | |
| 1 mile (mi.) | = 1.609 km | |

### WEIGHTS

| | | |
|---|---|---|
| 1 ounce (oz.) | = 2.54 cm | *To convert pounds into kilograms, multiply the number of pounds by 0.45 (e.g.: 90 lb. x 0.45 = 40.5 kg). To convert kilos to pounds, multiply the kilos by 2.2 (e.g.: 75 kg x 2.2 = 165 lb.)* |
| 1 pound (lb.) = 16 oz. | = 30.48 cm | |
| 1 ton = 2000 lb. | = 907 kg | |

### TEMPERATURES

-18°C  -10   0   10   20   30   40
0°F  10  20  32  40  50  60  70  80  90  100

*To convert degrees Fahrenheit into degrees Celsius, subtract 32 from the degrees F, multiply by 5, then divide by 9 (example: 85°F − 32 = 53/53 x 5 = 265/265 ÷ 9 = 29.4°C)*
*To convert degrees Celsius into degrees Fahrenheit, multiply the degrees Celsius by 9, divide by 5 then add 32 (example: 20°C x 9 = 180/180 ÷ 5 = 36/36 + 32 = 68°F).*

### ELECTRICITY

The electric current is 110 V and 60 Hz and the sockets have two flat pins. A transformer and an adaptor are needed to use European appliances in the United States.

### EQUIVALENT MEN'S SIZES

| FRANCE | US (UK) |
|---|---|
| **JACKETS** | |
| 44 | 36 |
| 46 | 36/38 |
| 48 | 38 |
| 50 | 40 |
| 52 | 42 |
| 54 | 42/44 |
| 56 | 44 |
| **TROUSERS** | |
| 44 | 36 |
| 46 | 38 |
| 48 | 40 |
| 50 | 40/42 |
| 52 | 42 |
| 54 | 44 |
| **SHOES** | |
| 40½ | 8 (7½) |
| 41 | 8½ (8) |
| 42 | 9½ (9) |
| 43 | 10½ (10) |
| 44 | 11 (10½) |
| 45 | 11½ (11) |

### EQUIVALENT WOMEN'S SIZES

| FRANCE | US (UK) |
|---|---|
| **SKIRTS AND DRESSES** | |
| 34 | 4 (8) |
| 36 | 8 (10) |
| 38 | 10 (12) |
| 40 | 12 (14) |
| 42 | 14 (16) |
| 44 | 16 (18) |
| 46 | 18 (20) |
| **JACKETS** | |
| 36 | 6 (8) |
| 38 | 10 (12) |
| 40 | 12 (14) |
| 42 | 14 (16) |
| 44 | 16 (18) |
| 46 | 18 |
| 48 | 20 |
| 50 | 22 |
| **SHOES** | |
| 36½ | 5½ (4) |
| 37 | 6 (4½) |
| 37½ | 6½ (5) |
| 38½ | 7 (5½) |
| 39 | 7½ (6) |
| 39½ | 8 (6½) |
| 40 | 8½ (7) |

### THE TIME

In the United States, the 12-hour clock (as opposed to the 24-hour clock) is used: time in the afternoon is described as *post meridiem* or pm (eg. 2pm) and time in the morning is described as *ante meridiem*, or am (eg. 2am). Relative time zones: London: midnight New York: 6pm (of the previous day) Tokyo: 8am (of the following day).

### TOBACCO

Smoking is strictly regulated in New York. It is illegal to smoke in any enclosed public area, on public transportation, in theaters, stores and office lobbies. Fewer and fewer restaurants have smoking areas, and the smoking of pipes and cigars is prohibited. You can usually smoke in bars.

### ALCOHOL

In New York, you cannot buy alcohol or be served in a bar before the age of twenty-one. Age is quite often checked. Restaurants that display a "No liquor license" sign are not allowed to serve alcohol, but you can generally bring your own wine or beer in with you, if this is the case. On the other hand, some bars generally operate a "happy hour" between 5pm and 7pm on weekdays, when you can buy doubles for the price of a single or half-price cocktail.

*All phone boxes have their own numbers, so you can be called back.*

*Letters to Europe cost 60¢ and postcards 50¢.*

### PUBLIC TELEPHONES

A local call in New York City costs 25¢. Public telephones accept 5, 10, and 25¢ cent pieces and do not give change. If you have not inserted the right amount, an electronic message will cut in, informing you how much more you need to insert; if you do not do this, the conversation will be cut off. Some telephones accept credit and debit cards.

### THE POSTAL SYSTEM

"US Mail" appears on all American mailboxes. When sending a letter anywhere in the United States, you pay 32¢ for the first ounce, then 23¢ for every additional ounce. Sending a letter abroad costs 60¢ for the first half ounce and 45¢ for every additional half ounce; sending a postcard costs 40¢ or 15¢ first-class within the U.S. The General Post Office is open 24 hours a day. General Post Office: 8th Ave./33rd St., Tel: 967-8585.

### LONG DISTANCE CALLS

To make a phone call from New York to anywhere else in the United States, dial 1 + the area code + the number you require (7 digits).
To make a call through the operator, dial 0. If making international calls, first dial 011, then the country + city code + rest of number. To call the US from overseas, dial 0101 + area code + local number. To call Manhattan from the UK, for example, dial 00 1 212 plus the 7 digit number. To call central London from New York, dial 011 44 171 plus the 7-digit number.

### TELEGRAMS AND MONEY ORDERS

In the United States, the telegram service is handled by private companies. Contact Western Union at 1-800-325-6000

### NEW YORK AREA CODES

New York City is divided into three different codes, depending on whether you are calling Manhattan (212), the other boroughs (718), a radiophone or various services which carry special charges (900, 917, etc). When calling from Manhattan to another borough in the city, dial 1-718 and the 7 digits of the number you require. Unless otherwise indicated, the numbers mentioned in this book are all preceded by 212.

### INFORMATION DIRECTORY INQUIRIES

Dial 411. The cost is 45¢ for every number required, unless you make the call from a public phone booth (when the service is free).

| THE COST OF A PHONE CALL (AT&T RATES) | | | |
|---|---|---|---|
| NEW YORK | cost in $ for the first minute then every minute thereafter: | | |
| | 7am | 1pm | 6pm |
| FRANCE | 1.71 / 1.08 | 1.39 / 82c | 1.15 / 67c |
| UK | 1.44 / 96c | 1.15 / 73c | 98c / 62c |
| GERMANY | 1.77 / 1.09 | 1.42 / 87c | 1.15 / 69c |
| JAPAN | 2.16 / 81c | 3.05 / 1.24 | 2.55 / 99c |
| Local call: 25c min | | | |

### TOLL-FREE CALLS

Numbers preceded by 1-800 are free. Many hotels and companies have "toll-free" numbers. Unfortunately, you cannot dial these numbers from outside the United States. For further information, dial 1-800-555-1212, after you arrive in the United States.

The Pierre Hotel (second from left) and its neighbors, seen from Central Park.

The Woolworth Building, seen from the top of the World Trade Center.

Manhattan's jagged skyscraper skyline is infinitely varied; depending on your location, the time of day or season, its buildings are transformed by a constantly shifting panoply of light and shadow. And although nothing beats the view from the top of the city's highest buildings, there are many other places at street level that show the multifaceted building tops to good advantage.

## SKY-HIGH VIEWS

### INITIATION
The observation deck of the Empire State Building or of the World Trade Center is a "must" for the visitor to New York. The views they provide, however, are completely different: the Empire State Building, which is more central and not quite so tall, gives a better idea of the city's layout and the regular Midtown and Uptown grid pattern, whereas the World Trade Center affords a giddy view of the tangle of streets in Downtown Manhattan, as well as a wider view of the surrounding area.

### CONTEMPLATION
Several other skyscrapers were built with observation decks. Although none of these are now accessible, there is a breathtaking view from some bars and restaurants, such as the *Rainbow Room* (65th floor of the RCA Building), especially at night.

### OBSERVATION
You can see the city from an unusual angle from the terrace of the Clocktower Gallery, the former skylobby of the Equitable Building on Broadway, or the terrace of the Dia Center in Chelsea.

## VIEWS FROM OTHER PLACES

### AROUND THE EDGES
The boat trip to Liberty Island or Staten Island is another form of initiation: as the ferry pulls out into the bay, the "prow" of Manhattan gradually takes shape. Likewise, a stroll across the Brooklyn Bridge's pedestrian walkway affords a splendid, ever-changing view, through the mesh of cables, of the island's eastern profile, with its most renowned skyscrapers thrusting skyward.

### IN THE CENTER
One of Manhattan's most heart-stopping cityscapes can be seen from the reservoir in Central Park (90th Street).

The buildings lining the two thoroughfares bordering the park – 5th Avenue and Central Park West (dominated by the twin peaks of the Eldorado) – come into view from this inland sea.

### FROM AFAR
For an unusual perspective on Manhattan, take the short, breathtaking journey through the air above the roofs of Midtown, the Queensboro Bridge and then the East River, by aerial tramway to Roosevelt Island. The view from the top of the tower of Riverside Church, above the banks of the Hudson (120th Street), affords a good view of Harlem and the Bronx.

### THE HEIGHT OF SOME STRUCTURES IN MANHATTAN
From left to right:
Dutch windmill
1664, 39 feet
Saint Paul's Chapel
1796, 220 feet
Federal Hall
1842, 56 feet
Pier of Brooklyn Bridge
1883, 436 feet
Flatiron Building
1902, 312 feet
Pulitzer Building
1903, 377 feet
Metropolitan Life Tower
1909, 699 feet
Woolworth Building
1913, 792 feet
Equitable Building
1915, 515 feet
Chrysler Building
1930, 1048 feet
Empire State Building
1931, 1250 feet
Seagram Building
1958, 476 feet
World Trade Center
1973–7, 1350 feet
Citicorp Building
1978, 915 feet
Sony Building former
ATT Building, 650 feet

## LIBERTY HELICOPTER TOURS

The highest building in New York . . . seen from above. A flight over Manhattan is a memory that will stay with you forever. It is a relatively affordable luxury (between $54 and $160) and most hotels will take care of reservations. Most trips include a bird's-eye view of the Statue of Liberty, then a flight northward, often as far as Central Park. West 30th St., at Hudson River. Tel. 967-6464 9am–9pm daily throughout the year. Fax 487-4781.

### Circle Line
#### Sightseeing Cruises
WEST 42ND STREET AT THE HUDSON RIVER
NEW YORK, NY
SOUTH PIER, HARBORSIDE FINANCIAL CENTER
JERSEY CITY, NJ
212-563-3200

Nobody gets around New York like

"The views were spectacular, even inspiring."

## CIRCLE LINE

This company offers excursions around the island up to eleven times a day. The trip lasts three hours and there is a commentary describing all the sites shown on the map. It is possible to organize a corporate mini-cruise or a social gathering on the company's boats. Pier 83, West 42nd St., Hudson River. Tel. 563-3200

CIRCLE LINE
W. 42nd Street at the Hudson River,
New York, NY
Park on our pier.
By bus:
34th Street M16, 49/50th Street M50,
42nd Street M42
Westbound right to our pier.
South Pier,
Harborside Financial Center,
Jersey City, New Jersey, NJ
Park on our pier.
By train:
PATH to Exchange Place
Northbound right to our pier.

**Enjoy the only sightseeing cruise that sails all the way around Manhattan.**

# ◆ PARKS AND GARDENS

The beautiful landscape described by Verrazano, with its thickly wooded hills, has irrevocably changed. However, nature has not been chased out of Manhattan entirely, as can be seen by the vast expanses of Central Park or, on a more modest scale, by the city's waterside promenades, community gardens and lush atriums. Then again, the other boroughs, which also boast some wonderful gardens, are within easy reach.

## AT THE WATER'S EDGE

Surrounded by Midtown's towers, you could easily forget that Manhattan is an island. The riverside highways, too, with their heavy traffic, form a barrier between the city and its rivers. In a few spots, however, this barrier is breached by a park or a promenade running along the water's edge:
◆ Battery Park's esplanade and the peace of South Cove
◆ Riverside Park Marina (79th St. Boat Basin)
◆ The north tip of Roosevelt Island and

its old lighthouse towering above the waters of Hell's Gate (where the East River meets the Long Island Sound).
◆ The terraces of Fort Tryon Park and the Cloisters museum, opposite the Hudson Palisades, sheer cliffs dramatically dropping away into the Hudson. Here, in the unexpected setting of medieval buildings brought over from France and Spain, green vistas and tranquillity reign supreme. It is hard to believe you are still in Manhattan.

## MINIATURE GARDENS

"Community gardens" are small oases, wrested from the concrete and asphalt and lovingly tended by people living in the neighborhood who can be seen on weekends, digging and hoeing, dressed in their gardening clothes. These small gardens, which are well worth a visit, thrive in Manhattan

and are particularly common in the East Village. They grow in vacant plots between the blind walls of two apartment blocks or rowhouses. The oldest (1973), Liz Christy Community Garden, at the corner of Bowery and Houston is a wonderful refuge in summer.

## ATRIUMS

On a very different scale, several office towers provide pedestrians with a cool, quiet sanctuary in vast atriums decked out with plants, trees and

fountains. The most stunning of these is the one in the Ford Foundation Building, at the easternmost end of 42nd Street (321 East 42nd St.).

## BREAKAWAY

The four other boroughs of New York City, which are larger and less built-up, offer numerous parks and gardens. The Bronx has two of the city's outstanding treasures: the New York Botanical Garden and the Bronx Zoo. The Botanical Garden's 40-acre forest, through which the Bronx River runs, is the only vestige of the forest that used to cover all of New York City before the

Europeans settled here. The zoo, the largest city zoo in the United States, has re-created the natural habitats of animals from all over the world – among others an astonishing rain forest from southeast Asia. These two parks, close to each other, can be easily and safely reached by bus or subway.

Café terrace east of Times Square.

Water tanks standing on three-legged metal stands can be seen all over the city.

Tennis at the top! Every square yard of Manhattan is used, including the roofs . . .

At apartment entrances, policemen main reassuring presence

**"**Taxis . . . spent their time hooting or squealing to a halt, then nipping in and out of the traffic . . .**"** Donald Westlake

Daily newspapers are also sold in automatic vending machines. Magazines, on the other hand, are still sold only at newsstands

You have to be fit and athle be a messenger in New Here, bicycles are used in of motorcycles (as in Lor

The New York firemen, city guardians, are an integral part of daily life. The City Fire Museum is devoted to their work.

The positioning of the traffic lights in the middle of a junction or on the other side, may surprise more than one European driver.

...rush hour, wave after wave of New Yorkers ...ur out of the elevators onto the subway ...tforms.

Fire escapes in SoHo.

For a long time, the New York "cop" carried a Python 357.

Playing with water in New Riverfront Park (Riverside Drive/138th St.)

"The square is also a small world: little old men, chess players, policemen on horseback watching the chess games from their high vantage point . . ." Edgar Morin, New York

After taxis, limousines reign supreme in New York . . .

The Metropolitan Opera House at night (Lincoln Center).

Street ball.
All day long, behind the wire fences around the small basketball courts, teams of three players compete against each other.

A familiar sight in Manhattan: the dogwalker and his/her charges.

Typical urban furniture: New York's metal garbage cans.

Chinatown, a city within the city . . .

Many New York chil
learn to play baseb.
the streets.

*School buses are yellow.*

*A trompe l'oeil view of the Brooklyn Bridge from the South Street Seaport.*

In summer, when the sidewalks sizzle, some residents in poorer neighborhoods cool off by opening a fire hydrant.

Newsstands are traditionally found at street corners, near the "Walk/Don't Walk" signs.

*In the garment district racks of "ready-to-wear" roll by.*

*The city is punctuated by the intermittent din of police and fire engine sirens.*

*You can get a quick snack anywhere in the city, at any time of day.*

*The horse-drawn carriages in Central Park are a relic of the 19th century.*

## RESTLESS

"New York was to become the restless city," wrote Jerome Charyn, "past, present and future seemed to merge into one single time zone, a different age altogether, nervy, jangling. . . .The Dutch merchants were never to put down firm roots here. The city has become a victim of incurable amnesia. It is the city of oblivion."

Although the writer of these words may have overstated his case, it is undeniable that New York is pre-eminently a city of the present. Time, as they say, is money; and a city that makes no apology for its dedication to the pursuit of money keeps its eye on the clock. Lots of clocks. They adorn buildings – inside and out – all over the town; some even stand commandingly on street corners, like temporal policemen, helping to organize one's time as efficiently as the grid street layout organizes the traffic. Many of them have a secondary purpose: advertising. Clocks vie for attention, outdoing each other in originality – a rivalry taken to extremes by Robert Venturi's 98-foot-diameter clock, which will crown the new Whitehall Ferry Terminal on the tip of Manhattan and will be visible from out in the harbor.

# LISTINGS

| | MAJOR MUSEUMS |
|---|---|
| 15 | American Museum of Natural History |
| 54 | Brooklyn Museum of Art |
| 2 | The Cloisters |
| 11 | Cooper-Hewitt National Design Museum |
| 17 | Frick Collection |
| 11 | Solomon R. Guggenheim Museum |
| 41 | Guggenheim Museum of SoHo |
| 14 | Metropolitan Museum of Art |
| 21 | Museum of Modern Art |
| 29 | Pierpoint Morgan Library |
| 16 | Whitney Museum of American Art |
| 28 | Whitney Museum of American Art (annexe) |
| | HISTORY |
| 1 | Dyckman House Museum |
| 53 | Ellis Island (Immigration Museum) |
| 47 | Federal Hall National Memorial |
| 51 | Fraunces Tavern Museum |
| 23 | Intrepid Sea-Air-Space Museum Pier |
| 42 | Lower East Side Tenement Museum |
| 3 | Morris Jumel Mansion Museum |
| 50 | Museum of American Financial History |
| 8 | Museum of the City of New York |
| 40 | New York City Fire Museum |
| 48 | South Street Seaport Museum |
| 33 | Theodore Roosevelt Birthplace Museum |
| | ARTS, CULTURE |
| 44 | Chinatown History Museum |
| 32 | Dia Center for the Art |
| 36 | Forbes Magazine Galleries |
| 10 | International Center of Photography Uptown |
| 30 | Jacob K. Javits Convention Center |
| 7 | El Museo dei Barrio |
| 18 | Museum of American Folk Art |
| | ARCHITECTURE |
| 5 | Columbia University |
| 12 | Gracie Mansion |
| 28 | Grand Central Terminal |
| 52 | Statue of Liberty Ferry |
| 26 | United Nations |
| | PLACES OF WORSHIP |
| 6 | Cathedral Church of St. John the Divine |
| 35 | Church of the Ascension |
| 31 | Church of the Incarnation |
| 51 | Church of Our Lady of the Rosary |
| 37 | Grace Church |
| 9 | Islamic Cultural Center of New-York |
| 39 | Judson Memorial Baptist Church |
| 45 | Mariner's Temple |
| 43 | Most Holy Crucifix Church |
| 4 | Riverside Church |
| 25 | St. Bartholomew's Church |
| 45 | St. James Church |
| 38 | St. Mark's Church in The Bowery |
| 24 | St. Patrick's Cathedral |
| 46 | St. Paul's Chapel |
| 22 | St. Thomas Church |
| 20 | Temple Emmanu-El |
| 49 | Trinity Church |
| | LIBRARIES |
| 13 | Gœthe House |
| 27 | New York Public Library |
| | MISCELLANEOUS |
| 19 | 7th Regiment Armory |
| 34 | Con Edison Energy Museum |
| 49 | New York Stock Exchange (Visitors' Center) |
| 24 | Radio City Music Hall |

| Central Park West, 79th Street | 769-5100 | Upper West Side |
| 200 Eastern Parkway | 718-638-5000 | Brooklyn |
| Fort Tyron Park | 923-3700 | Harlem, Uptown |
| 2 E. 91st Street | 860-6868 | Upper East Side |
| 1 E. 70th Street | 288-0700 | Upper East Side |
| 1071 5th Avenue | 423-3500 | Upper East Side |
| 575 Broadway (Prince Street) | 423-3500 | Washington Square |
| 5th Avenue and 82nd Street | 535-7710 | Upper East Side |
| 11 W. 53rd Street | 708-9480 | Rockefeller Center |
| 29 E. 36th Street | 685-0610 | Grand Central |
| 945 Madison Avenue (75th Street) | 570-3676 | Upper East Side |
| 120 Park Avenue (42nd Street) | 878-2550 | Grand Central |
| | | |
| 4881 Broadway (204th Street) | 360-8123 | Harlem, Uptown |
| New York Harbor | 363-7620 | World Trade Center |
| 26 Wall Street | 264-8711 | World Trade Center |
| 54 Pearl Street | 425-1778 | World Trade Center |
| 86, 12th Avenue and W. 46th Street, Pier 86 | 245-0072 | Grand Central |
| 90 Orchard Street | 431-0233 | Lower East Side |
| W. 160th Street and Edgecombe Avenue | 923-8008 | Harlem, Uptown |
| 26 Broadway | 908-4519 | World Trade Center |
| 5th Avenue and 103rd Street | 534-1672 | Upper East Side |
| 278 Spring Street | 691-1303 | Washington Square |
| 207 Front Street | 748-8600 | City Hall |
| 28 E. 20th Street | 260-1616 | Union Square |
| | | |
| 70 Mulberry St., 2nd floor | 619-4785 | Chinatown |
| 548 W. 22nd Street | 989-5912 | Washington Square |
| 62 5th Avenue (12th Street) | 206-5548 | Washington Square |
| 1130 5th Avenue, 94th St | 860-1777 | Upper East Side |
| 655 W. 34th Street | 216-2000 | Grand Central |
| 1230 5th Avenue, 104th St | 831-7272 | Upper East Side |
| 2 Lincoln Square (Columbus Avenue and 65th Street) | 977-7298 | Upper West Side |
| | | |
| 114th and 120th sts, Broadway and Amsterdam avenues | 854-4900 | Harlem, Uptown |
| 88th Street (in Carl Schurz Park) | 570-4751 | Upper East Side |
| 42nd Street (Park and Lexington avenues) | 935 3960 | Grand Central |
| Liberty Island (New York Harbor) | 269-5755 | World Trade Center |
| 1st Avenue (46th Street) | 963-7713 | Grand Central |
| | | |
| Amsterdam Avenue (112th Street) | 316-7540 | Harlem, Uptown |
| 5th Avenue (10th Street) | 254-8620 | Washington Square |
| 209 Madison Avenue (35th Street) | 689-6350 | Grand Central |
| 7-8 State Street | 269-6865 | World Trade Center |
| 800–804 Broadway (10th Street) | 254-2000 | Union Square |
| 1711 3rd Avenue (97th Street) | 722-5234 | Upper East Side |
| 55 Washington Square South | 447-0351 | Washington Square |
| 3 Henry Street and 12 Oliver Street | 233-0423 | Lower East Side |
| 378 Broome Street | 226-2556 | Lower East Side |
| 490 Riverside Drive | 222-5900 | Harlem, Uptown |
| 109 E. 50th Street | 751-1616 | Rockefeller Center |
| 32 James Street | 233-0161 | Lower East Side |
| 131 E. 10th Street | 674-6377 | Union Square |
| 5th Avenue (50th Street) | 753-2261 | Rockefeller Center |
| Broadway (Fulton Street) | 602-0800 | City Hall |
| 1 W. 53rd Street | 757-7013 | Rockefeller Center |
| 1 E. 65th Street | 744-1400 | Upper East Side |
| Broadway (Wall Street) | 602-0872 | World Trade Center |
| | | |
| 1014 5th Avenue (83rd Street) | 439-8700 | Upper East Side |
| 5th Avenue (42nd Street) | 930-0800 | Grand Central |
| | | |
| 643 Park Avenue (67th Street) | 744-4107 | Upper East Side |
| 145 E. 14th Street | 460-6244 | Union Square |
| 20 Broad Street | 654-5165 | World Trade Center |
| Rockefeller Center, Avenue of the Americas (50th Street) | 632-4041 | Rockefeller Center |

# ◆ SHOPPING

## ANTIQUES

| Christie's | ◆ 420 | 502 Park Avenue / Rockefeller Center |
|---|---|---|
| Darrow's Fun Antiques | ◆ 424 | 1101 1st Avenue / Upper East Side |
| Lost City Arts | ◆ 409 | 275 Lafayette Street / Washington Square |
| Sotheby's | ◆ 424 | 1334 York Avenue / Upper East Side |
| William Doyle Galleries | ◆ 424 | 175 East 87th Street / Upper East Side |

## JEWELRY STORES

| Cartier | ◆ 420 | 653 5th Avenue / Rockefeller Center |
|---|---|---|
| Harry Winston | ◆ 421 | 718 5th Avenue / Rockefeller Center |
| Tiffany and Co. | ◆ 421 | 727 5th Avenue / Rockefeller Center |

## DEPARTMENT STORES

| Barneys | ◆ 424 | 660 Madison Avenue (61st Street) / Upper East Side |
|---|---|---|
| Barneys New York | ◆ 408 | 106 7th Avenue / Washington Square |
| Bergdorf Goodman | ◆ 420 | 754 5th Avenue (58th Street) / Rockefeller Center |
| Bloomingdale's | ◆ 420 | 1000 3rd Avenue (59th and 60th streets) / Rockefeller Center |
| Century 21 Department Store | ◆ 404 | 22 Cortland Street / City Hall |
| Henri Bendel | ◆ 421 | 712 5th Avenue / Rockefeller Center |
| Lord and Taylor | ◆ 414 | 424 5th Avenue (38th Street) / Grand Central |
| Macy's | ◆ 414 | 151 West 34th Street (Broadway) / Grand Central |
| Pier 17 Pavilion | ◆ 404 | 89 South Street (South Street Seaport) / City Hall |
| Saks Fifth Avenue | ◆ 421 | 611 5th Avenue (49th and 50th streets) / Rockefeller Center |
| Stern's | ◆ 414 | 899 Avenue of the Americas / Grand Central |
| Takashimaya | ◆ 421 | 693 5th Avenue |

## BOOKSTORES

| Barnes & Noble | ◆ 426 | 2289 Broadway at 82nd Street / Upper West Side |
|---|---|---|
| The Biography Bookshop | ◆ 409 | 400 Bleecker Street / Washington Square |
| Books & Co. | ◆ 422 | 939 Madison Avenue / Upper East Side |
| Coliseum Books | ◆ 420 | 1771 Broadway (57th Street) / Rockefeller Center |
| Drama Bookshop | ◆ 420 | 723 7th Avenue (48th and 49th streets) / Rockefeller Center |
| Forbidden Planet | ◆ 411 | 840 Broadway / Union Square |
| Gotham Book Mart | ◆ 421 | 41 West 47th Street / Rockefeller Center |
| Hagstrom Map and Travel Center | ◆ 412 | 57 West 43rd Street / Grand Central |
| Librairie de France / Libreria Hispanica | ◆ 421 | 610 5th Avenue / Rockefeller Center |
| Rizzoli | ◆ 421 | 31 West 57th Street / Rockefeller Center |
| Strand Book Store | ◆ 411 | 828 Broadway (12th Street) / Union Square |

## MUSIC

| Colony Records | ◆ 420 | 1619 Broadway (49th Street) / Rockefeller Center |
|---|---|---|
| Footlight Records | ◆ 409 | 113 East 12th Street |
| J&R Computer/Music World | ◆ 404 | 15–33 Park Row / City Hall |
| Manny's Musical Instruments | ◆ 414 | 156 West 48th Street / Grand Central |
| Sam Goody | ◆ 414 | 666 3rd Avenue (43rd Street) / Grand Central |
| Tower Records | ◆ 411 | 692 Broadway (4th Street) / Union Square |

## COMPUTERS, PHOTOGRAPHY, VIDEO

| | | |
|---|---|---|
| B. & H. Photo-Video | ◆ 411 | 119 West 17th Street / Union Square |
| Harvey Electronics | ◆ 414 | 2 West 45th Street / Grand Central |
| J&R Computer/Music World | ◆ 404 | 15 –33 Park Row / City Hall |
| Detective Store | ◆ 409 | 164 Christopher Street / Washington Square |
| Uncle Steve's | ◆ 409 | 343 Canal Street / Washington Square |

## SHOES

| | | |
|---|---|---|
| Billy Martin | ◆ 424 | 812 Madison Avenue / Upper East Side |
| Cole-Haan | ◆ 424 | 667 Madison Avenue (61st Street) / Upper East Side |
| Diego della Valle | ◆ 420 | 41 East 57th Street |
| Harry's Shoes | ◆ 426 | 2299 Broadway (83rd Street) / Upper West Side |
| Joan and David | ◆ 424 | 816 Madison Avenue / Upper East Side |
| Stride Rite | ◆ 424 | 1241 Lexington Avenue / Upper East Side |
| Susan Bennis/Warren Edwards | ◆ 421 | 22 West 57th Street / Rockefeller Center |
| Timberland | ◆ 424 | 709 Madison Avenue (63rd Street) / Upper East Side |
| Tootsie Plohound | ◆ 409 | 413 West Broadway / Washington Square |

## MEN'S FASHIONS

| | | |
|---|---|---|
| Brooks Brothers | ◆ 414 | 346 Madison Avenue  (44th Street) / Grand Central |
| J. Press | ◆ 414 | 7 East 44th Street / Grand Central |
| New Republic | ◆ 409 | 93 Spring Street / Washington Square |

## WOMEN'S FASHIONS

| | | |
|---|---|---|
| Agnès B | ◆ 408 | 116 Prince Street / Washington Square |
| Ann Taylor | ◆ 420 | 645 Madison Avenue / Rockefeller Center |
| Charivari | ◆ 420 | 18 West 57th Street / Rockefeller Center |
| Express | ◆ 414 | 7 West 34th Street / Grand Central |
| Henri Bendel | ◆ 421 | 712 5th Avenue / Rockefeller Center |
| Norma Kamali | ◆ 421 | 11 West 56th Street / Rockefeller Center |
| Victoria's Secret | ◆ 421 | 34 East 57th Street / Rockefeller Center |

## UNISEX FASHIONS, CLASSIC SPORTSWEAR

| | | |
|---|---|---|
| Banana Republic | ◆ 420 | 130 East 59th Street / Rockefeller Center |
| Betsey Johnson | ◆ 408 | 130 Thompson Street / Washington Square |
| Burberry Limited | ◆ 420 | 9 East 57th Street / Rockefeller Center |
| Canal Jeans | ◆ 409 | 600 Madison Avenue (58th Street) / Rockefeller Center |
| Eddie Bauer | ◆ 420 | 504 Broadway / Washington Square |
| Gap | ◆ 414 | Broadway and 34th Street / Grand Central |
| Original Levi's Store | ◆ 421 | 750 Lexington Avenue / Rockefeller Center |
| Polo-Ralph Lauren | ◆ 424 | 867 Madison Avenue and 72nd Street / Upper East Side |
| Pop Shop | ◆ 409 | 292 Lafayette Street / Washington Square |
| Replay Country Store | ◆ 409 | 109 Prince Street / Washington Square |
| Screaming Mimi's | ◆ 409 | 382 Lafayette Street / Washington Square |
| Timberland | ◆ 424 | 709 Madison Avenue (62nd Street) / Upper East Side |

## MISCELLANEOUS, ACCESSORIES

| | | |
|---|---|---|
| Coach | ◆ 420 | 342 Madison Avenue (57th Street) / Rockefeller Center |
| Cole-Haan | ◆ 424 | 667 Madison Avenue (61st Street)  / Upper East Side |
| J.J. Hat Center | ◆ 414 | 310 5th Avenue and 32nd Street / Grand Central |
| Paul Stuart | ◆ 414 | Madison Avenue and 45th Street / Grand Central |
| Susan Bennis / Warren Edwards | ◆ 421 | 22 West 57th Street / Rockefeller Center |

| TIMBERLAND | ◆ 415 | 709 Madison Avenue (63rd Street) / Upper East Side |
| WORTH AND WORTH | ◆ 414 | 709 Madison Avenue (63rd Street) / Upper East Side |
| **SPORTS** | | |
| EDDIE BAUER | ◆ 420 | 600 Madison Avenue / Rockefeller Center |
| LOCKER | ◆ 414 | 43–45 West 34th Street / Grand Central |
| POLO SPORT | ◆ 424 | 888 Madison Avenue / Upper East Side |
| POLO-RALPH LAUREN | ◆ 424 | 867 Madison Avenue / Upper East Side |
| PARAGON | ◆ 411 | 867 Broadway ( 18th Street) / Union Square |
| YANKEE CLUBHOUSE SHOP | ◆ 421 | 110 East 59th Street / Rockefeller Center |
| **TOYS, USEFUL GADGETS, NOVELTIES** | | |
| THE COMPLEAT STRATEGIST | ◆ 414 | 11 East 33rd Street / Grand Central |
| DARROW'S FUN ANTIQUES | ◆ 424 | 1101 1st Avenue / Upper East Side |
| DETECTIVE STORE | ◆ 409 | 164 Christopher Street / Washington Square |
| THE ENCHANTED FOREST | ◆ 409 | 85 Mercer Street / Washington Square |
| F.A.O. SCHWARZ | ◆ 421 | 767 5th Avenue  (58th–59th sts) / Rockefeller Center |
| HAMMACHER SCHLEMMER | ◆ 421 | 147 East 57th Street / Rockefeller Center |
| LOVE SAVES THE DAY | ◆ 411 | 119 2nd Avenue and 7th Street / Union Square |
| MAXILLA & MANDIBLE | ◆ 426 | 451 Columbus Avenue / Upper West Side |
| THE SHARPER IMAGE | ◆ 421 | 4 West 57th Street / Rockefeller Center |
| **FOR CHILDREN** | | |
| BLADES EAST | ◆ 424 | 160 East 86th Street / Upper East Side |
| BLADES-WEST | ◆ 426 | 120 West 72nd Street / Upper West Side |
| LOUIS TANNEN | ◆ 414 | 24 West 25th Street (2nd Floor) / Grand Central |
| TOYS R US | ◆ 414 | 1293 Broadway (34th Street) / Grand Central |
| WARNER BROS, STUDIO STORE | ◆ 421 | 1 East 57th Street / Rockefeller Center |
| **FLEA MARKETS** | | |
| ANNEX ANTIQUES FAIR AND FLEA MARKET | ◆ 411 | 6th Avenue and W. 26th Street / Union Square |
| CANAL STREET FLEA MARKET | ◆ 409 | 335 Canal Street / Washington Square |
| GREEN FLEA MARKET (IS 44 FLEA MARKET) | ◆ 426 | Columbus Ave (76th–77th sts) / Upper West Side |
| **GROCERY STORES** | | |
| BALDUCCI'S | ◆ 408 | 424 Avenue of the Americas / Washington Square |
| DEAN AND DELUCA | ◆ 409 | 560 Broadway / Washington Square |
| ZABAR'S | ◆ 426 | 2245 Broadway / Upper West Side |
| **HOME FURNISHINGS** | | |
| ABC CARPETS | ◆ 411 | 888 Broadway (East 19th Street) |
| JACQUES CARNCANAGUES | ◆ 409 | 106 Spring Street |
| URBAN ARCHEOLOGY | ◆ 409 | 285 Lafayette Street |
| **SHOPPING STREETS** | | |
| ELECTRONIC | ◆ 404 | Canal Street / China Town |
| SHOES | ◆ 404 | Canal Street / China Town |
| GENERAL GOODS | ◆ 405 | Mott, Pell, Bayard and Doyers streets / Chinatown |
| | ◆ 404 | Grand Street / Little Italy |
| CLOTHES AND LEATHER | ◆ 405 | Orchard Street / Lower East Side |
| **GALLERIES** | | |
| 303 GALLERY | ◆ 405 | 89 Greene Street (2nd floor) / Washington Square |
| A/D | ◆ 405 | 560 Broadway / Washington Square |
| A.I.R. | ◆ 405 | 40 Wooster Street / Washington Square |
| ARTISTS' SPACE | ◆ 405 | 38 Greene Street (3rd floor) / Washington Square |

| AMERICAN FINE ARTS CO. | ◆ 405 | 22 Wooster Street / Washington Square |
|---|---|---|
| BARBARA GLADSTONE | ◆ 405 | 99 Greene Street / Washington Square |
| CURT MARCUS GALLERY | ◆ 406 | 578 Broadway (Prince St) / Washington Square |
| THE DRAWING CENTER | ◆ 406 | 35 Wooster Street / Washington Square |
| EXIT ART / THE FIRST WORLD | ◆ 406 | 548 Broadway (2nd floor) / Washington Square |
| FEATURE GALLERY | ◆ 406 | 76 Greene Street (2nd floor) / Washington Square |
| GAGOSIAN GALLERY | ◆ 422 | 980 Madison Avenue / Upper East Side |
| GALERIE ST ETIENNE | ◆ 415 | 24 West 57th Street |
| HIRSCHL & ADLER MODERN | ◆ 422 | 21 East 70th Street (2nd Floor) / Upper East Side |
| HOLLY SOLOMON GALLERY | ◆ 406 | 172 Mercer Street / Washington Square |
| JAMES DANZIGER GALLERY | ◆ 406 | 130 Prince Street / Washington Square |
| JANET BORDEN INC. | ◆ 406 | 560 Broadway (6th floor) / Washington Square |
| JAY GORNEY MODERN ART | ◆ 406 | 100 Greene Street / Washington Square |
| JOHN GIBSON | ◆ 406 | 568 Broadway / Washington Square |
| JOHN WEBER GALLERY | ◆ 406 | 142 Greene Street (3rd floor) / Washington Square |
| JOSEPH HELMAN GALLERY | ◆ 415 | 20 West 57th Street (2nd floor) / Rockefeller Center |
| KNOEDLER AND COMPANY | ◆ 422 | 19 East 70th Street / Upper East Side |
| LEO CASTELLI GALLERY | ◆ 406 | 420 W. Broadway (2nd fl) & 578 B'way / Washington Sq. |
| LOWINSKY GALLERY | ◆ 406 | 578 Broadway / Washington Square |
| LUHRING/AUGUSTINE GALLERY | ◆ 406 | 130 Prince Street (2nd floor) / Washington Square |
| MARIAN GOODMAN GALLERY | ◆ 415 | 24 West 57th Street (4th floor) / Rockefeller Center |
| MARLBOROUGH GALLERY | ◆ 415 | 40 West 57th Street |
| MARY BOONE GALLERY | ◆ 415 | 745 Fifth Avenue at 57th Street |
| MAX PROTETCH | ◆ 406 | 560 Broadway (2nd floor) / Washington Square |
| METRO PICTURES | ◆ 406 | 150 Greene Street / Washington Square |
| MICHAEL WERNER | ◆ 422 | 21 East 67th Street (3rd floor)/ Upper East Side |
| O.K. HARRIS WORKS OF ART | ◆ 406 | 383 West Broadway / Washington Square |
| P.P.O.W. | ◆ 406 | 532 Broadway (3rd floor) / Washington Square |
| PACE WILDENSTEIN/MACGILL GALLERY | ◆ 416 | 32 East 57th Street (9th floor) / Rockefeller Center |
| PACE WILDENSTEIN GALLERY | ◆ 415 | 32 East 57th Street / Rockefeller Center |
| PACE WILDENSTEIN GALLERY | ◆ 406 | 142 Greene Street / Washington Square |
| PAT HEARN | ◆ 406 | 530 W. 22nd Street / Washington Square |
| PAULA COOPER GALLERY | ◆ 406 | 155 Wooster Street / Washington Square |
| ROBERT MILLER GALLERY | ◆ 416 | 41 East 57th Street (3rd floor) / Rockefeller Center |
| RONALD FELDMAN FINE ARTS | ◆ 407 | 31 Mercer Street / Washington Square |
| SIDNEY JANIS GALLERY | ◆ 416 | 110 West 57th Street (6th Floor) / Rockefeller Center |
| SONNABEND GALLERY | ◆ 407 | 420 West Broadway (3rd floor) / Washington Square |
| SPERONE WESTWATER | ◆ 407 | 142 Greene Street & 121 Greene St / Washington Square |
| STALEY-WISE GALLERY | ◆ 407 | 560 Broadway (6th floor) / Washington Square |
| THREAD WAXING SPACE | ◆ 407 | 476 Broadway (2nd floor) / Washington Square |
| TONY SHAFRAZI GALLERY | ◆ 407 | 119 Wooster Street / Washington Square |
| ZABRISKIE GALLERY | ◆ 416 | 41 E. 57th Street / Rockefeller Center |

# ◆ CHOOSING A HOTEL

**Price legend:**
- ♦ under $100
- ♦♦ $100 to $150
- ♦♦♦ $150 to $200
- ♦♦♦♦ over $200

| | PAGE | PRICE | CHILDREN'S RATE | WEEKEND RATE | VIEW | QUIET | PARKING | HOTEL RESTAURANT | SPORTS | CONFERENCES | NO. OF ROOMS |
|---|---|---|---|---|---|---|---|---|---|---|---|
| **WASHINGTON SQUARE** | | | | | | | | | | | |
| CHELSEA HOTEL* | 408 | ♦♦ | | | | | | ● | | | 400 |
| WASHINGTON SQUARE HOTEL** | 408 | ♦♦ | ● | | ● | ● | | ● | ● | | 160 |
| **UNION SQUARE** | | | | | | | | | | | |
| ARLINGTON HOTEL** | 410 | ♦ | | | | ● | | ● | | | 120 |
| GRAMERCY PARK HOTEL** | 410 | ♦♦ | | ● | ● | | | ● | | ● | 509 |
| **GRAND CENTRAL, THEATER DISTRICT** | | | | | | | | | | | |
| THE ALGONQUIN HOTEL*** | 412 | ♦♦♦ | ● | | | | | ● | | ● | 165 |
| BEST WESTERN MANHATTAN | 412 | ♦ | ● | | | | | ● | | | 150 |
| THE CARLTON*** | 412 | ♦♦ | ● | ● | ● | ● | ● | ● | | ● | 280 |
| COMFORT INN, MURRAY HILL** | 412 | ♦♦ | ● | ● | | | | ● | | | 125 |
| DORAL PARK AVENUE*** | 412 | ♦♦♦ | ● | | | | | ● | | ● | 188 |
| GRAND HYATT*** | 413 | ♦♦♦♦ | ● | ● | | | | ● | ● | ● | 1407 |
| HERALD SQUARE HOTEL* | 413 | ♦ | ● | ● | ● | | | | | | 114 |
| HOLIDAY INN, CROWNE PLAZA** | 413 | ♦♦♦♦ | ● | ● | ● | | | ● | ● | ● | 770 |
| HOTEL INTER-CONTINENTAL | 413 | ♦♦♦♦ | | ● | | | | ● | ● | ● | 691 |
| HOTEL IROQUOIS* | 413 | ♦ | ● | | | | | ● | | | 100 |
| HOTEL MANSFIELD* | 413 | ♦ | | | | | ● | ● | | | 200 |
| MARRIOTT EAST SIDE | 413 | ♦♦♦♦ | ● | ● | | | | ● | ● | ● | 683 |
| MARRIOTT MARQUIS*** | 413 | ♦♦♦♦ | ● | ● | ● | | | ● | ● | ● | 1874 |
| MILLENNIUM BROADWAY**** | 413 | ♦♦♦♦ | | ● | ● | | | ● | | ● | 638 |
| MORGANS**** | 413 | ♦♦♦♦ | | ● | | | | ● | | | 113 |
| NY'S HOTEL PENNSYLVANIA** | 413 | ♦♦ | ● | | | | | ● | | ● | 1670 |
| PARAMOUNT*** | 413 | ♦♦♦ | ● | ● | | ● | | ● | | ● | 610 |
| RENAISSANCE NY HOTEL*** | 413 | ♦♦♦♦ | | ● | ● | | | ● | | ● | 305 |
| ROYALTON**** | 413 | ♦♦♦♦ | | ● | | | | ● | | | 205 |
| SHELBURNE MURRAY HILL*** | 414 | ♦♦♦♦ | ● | | | | | ● | | ● | 253 |
| SOUTHGATE TOWER*** | 414 | ♦♦♦ | ● | | | | | ● | ● | ● | 523 |
| TUDOR HOTEL*** | 414 | ♦♦♦♦ | ● | | | | | ● | | ● | 300 |
| UN PLAZA PARK HYATT**** | 414 | ♦♦♦♦ | | ● | ● | | | ● | ● | ● | 428 |
| **ROCKEFELLER CENTER** | | | | | | | | | | | |
| BEEKMAN TOWER*** | 418 | ♦♦♦♦ | ● | ● | ● | | | ● | ● | ● | 171 |
| BOX TREE**** | 418 | ♦♦♦♦ | | | | ● | | ● | | | 12 |
| DOUBLE TREE GUEST SUITES HOT. | 418 | ♦♦♦♦ | ● | ● | | | | ● | ● | ● | 460 |
| ESSEX HOUSE (NIKKO)*** | 418 | ♦♦♦♦ | ● | ● | | | | ● | ● | ● | 591 |
| THE GORHAM*** | 418 | ♦♦♦ | ● | ● | | ● | | ● | | | 120 |
| HELMSLEY MIDDLETOWNE*** | 418 | ♦♦♦ | ● | ● | | ● | ● | | | | 190 |
| HELMSLEY WINDSOR*** | 418 | ♦♦♦ | ● | | | ● | ● | | | | 243 |
| HOLIDAY INN, CROWNE PL.*** | 418 | ♦♦♦♦ | ● | ● | ● | | ● | ● | ● | ● | 770 |
| HOTEL BEVERLY*** | 418 | ♦♦ | ● | ● | | | | ● | | ● | 186 |
| HOTEL DORSET*** | 418 | ♦♦♦♦ | ● | | | | | ● | | ● | 320 |
| HOTEL EDISON** | 418 | ♦ | ● | | | | ● | ● | | | 1000 |
| HOTEL ELYSEE*** | 418 | ♦♦♦ | ● | ● | | ● | | ● | ● | | 99 |
| HOWARD JOHNSON PLAZA** | 419 | ♦♦♦♦ | ● | ● | | | ● | | | | 300 |
| INN ON 57TH STREET** | 419 | ♦♦♦ | ● | ● | | ● | | ● | ● | ● | 596 |
| LOEWS NEW YORK*** | 419 | ♦♦♦ | ● | ● | ● | | | ● | ● | ● | 726 |
| LYDEN HOUSE*** | 419 | ♦♦ | | ● | | ● | | ● | | | 81 |

| | Page | Price | Children's Rate | Weekend Rate | View | Quiet | Parking | Hotel Restaurant | Sports | Conferences | No. of Rooms |
|---|---|---|---|---|---|---|---|---|---|---|---|
| **NY Hilton & Towers*** | 419 | ♦♦♦ | | ● | | | ● | | ● | ● | 2000 |
| **The New York Palace**** | 419 | ♦♦♦♦ | | ● | ● | ● | | ● | ● | ● | 963 |
| **Novotel New York*** | 419 | ♦♦ | ● | ● | ● | | ● | ● | | ● | 474 |
| **Omni Berkshire Place*** | 419 | ♦♦♦♦ | | ● | ● | | ● | ● | ● | ● | 416 |
| **Park Central Hotel*** | 419 | ♦♦♦♦ | | ● | | | ● | ● | | ● | 1269 |
| **Park Lane (Helmsley)**** | 419 | ♦♦♦♦ | | ● | ● | ● | ● | ● | | ● | 626 |
| **The Parker Meridien*** | 419 | ♦♦♦♦ | | ● | ● | | ● | ● | ● | ● | 700 |
| **The Peninsula***** | 419 | ♦♦♦♦ | | ● | ● | | ● | ● | ● | ● | 242 |
| **Pickwick Arms Hotel*** | 419 | ♦ | ● | | | | ● | | | | 300 |
| **The Plaza**** | 419 | ♦♦♦♦ | | ● | ● | | ● | ● | ● | ● | 820 |
| **Plaza 50*** | 419 | ♦♦♦ | | ● | ● | ● | ● | ● | | ● | 206 |
| **Rihga Royal Hotel**** | 419 | ♦♦♦♦ | | ● | ● | | ● | ● | ● | ● | 500 |
| **The Ritz-Carlton**** | 419 | ♦♦♦♦ | | ● | ● | | ● | ● | | ● | 330 |
| **The Roger Smith*** | 420 | ♦♦♦♦ | | ● | ● | ● | ● | ● | | | 136 |
| **St Moritz on Central Pk*** | 420 | ♦♦♦ | | ● | ● | ● | ● | | | ● | 680 |
| **St Regis ***** | 420 | ♦♦♦♦ | | ● | ● | ● | | ● | | ● | 434 |
| **Salisbury Hotel** | 420 | ♦♦ | | ● | ● | | | ● | | ● | 320 |
| **San Carlos Hotel*** | 420 | ♦♦ | ● | ● | ● | ● | ● | | | ● | 149 |
| **Sheraton Hotel Tower*** | 420 | ♦♦♦ | ● | ● | ● | | ● | ● | ● | ● | 1750 |
| **The Shoreham** | 420 | ♦♦♦ | | ● | ● | | | ● | | ● | 84 |
| **The Waldorf-Astoria & Waldorf Towers**** | 420 | ♦♦♦♦ | | ● | | ● | ● | ● | | ● | 1500 |
| **The Warwick*** | 420 | ♦♦♦ | | ● | | | ● | ● | | ● | 425 |
| **The Wyndham*** | 420 | ♦♦ | ● | ● | ● | ● | | ● | | | 204 |
| **YMCA, Vanderbilt*** | 420 | ♦ | | ● | | | | | ● | ● | 430 |
| **YMCA, West Side*** | 420 | ♦ | | ● | | | | ● | ● | ● | 550 |
| **UPPER EAST SIDE** | | | | | | | | | | | |
| **The Barbizon*** | 423 | ♦♦♦ | | ● | ● | ● | ● | | ● | ● | 350 |
| **The Carlyle***** | 423 | ♦♦♦♦ | | ● | ● | ● | ● | ● | ● | ● | |
| **Hotel Pierre***** | 423 | ♦♦♦♦ | | ● | ● | ● | ● | ● | ● | | 206 |
| **Hotel Plaza Athénée**** | 423 | ♦♦♦♦ | | ● | ● | ● | ● | ● | | | 160 |
| **Hotel Wales*** | 423 | ♦♦ | | ● | ● | ● | | ● | | | 100 |
| **Hotel Westbury**** | 423 | ♦♦♦♦ | | ● | | | ● | ● | ● | ● | 179 |
| **The Lowell (Landmark)**** | 423 | ♦♦♦♦ | | | ● | ● | ● | ● | ● | | 60 |
| **Lyden Gardens*** | 424 | ♦♦ | | ● | ● | ● | ● | | | | 133 |
| **The Mark**** | 424 | ♦♦♦ | ● | ● | ● | ● | ● | ● | | ● | 120 |
| **Mayfair Hotel**** | 424 | ♦♦♦♦ | | ● | | | ● | ● | ● | | 201 |
| **Regency Hotel**** | 424 | ♦♦♦♦ | | ● | ● | | ● | ● | ● | ● | 380 |
| **The Stanhope***** | 424 | ♦♦♦♦ | | ● | ● | | ● | ● | ● | ● | 141 |
| **Surrey Hotel*** | 424 | ♦♦♦♦ | | ● | ● | | ● | ● | | ● | 130 |
| **UPPER WEST SIDE** | | | | | | | | | | | |
| **Excelsior Hotel** | 425 | | ● | | ● | | | | | | | |
| **Mayflower Hotel*** | 426 | ♦♦♦ | ● | ● | ● | ● | ● | ● | ● | ● | 577 |
| **Milburn Hotel** | 426 | ♦♦ | ● | | ● | | | | | | 80 |
| **Olcott ** | 426 | ♦♦ | | | ● | | | ● | | | 100 |
| **Radisson Empire*** | 426 | ♦♦♦ | | ● | ● | | ● | ● | ● | ● | 375 |

# ◆ CHOOSING A RESTAURANT

| | PAGE | PRICE | AMERICAN CUISINE | FRENCH CUISINE | ORIENTAL CUISINE | EASTERN EUROPEAN CUISINE | ITALIAN CUISINE | WINE CELLAR | GARDEN, TERRACE | SETTING | "INSTITUTION" |
|---|---|---|---|---|---|---|---|---|---|---|---|
| **WORLD TRADE CENTER** | | | | | | | | | | | |
| **FRAUNCES TAVERN** | 403 | ♦♦♦♦ | ● | | | | | | | ● | ● |
| **HUDSON RIVER CLUB** | 403 | ♦♦♦♦ | ● | | | | | ● | | ● | |
| **CITY HALL** | | | | | | | | | | | |
| **SLOPPY LOUIE'S** | 404 | ♦♦♦ | ● | | | | | | | ● | ● |
| **LOWER EAST SIDE, LITTLE ITALY, CHINATOWN** | | | | | | | | | | | |
| **KATZ'S DELICATESSEN** | 404 | ♦ | | | | ● | | | | | ● |
| **MANDARIN COURT** | 404 | ♦ | | | ● | | | | | | |
| **NEW ORIENTAL PEARL REST.** | 404 | ♦♦ | | | ● | | | | | | |
| **SAMMY'S ROUMANIANO** | 404 | ♦♦♦♦ | | | | ● | | | | | ● |
| **WASHINGTON SQUARE** | | | | | | | | | | | |
| **ALISON ON DOMINICK** | 407 | ♦♦♦♦ | | | | | | ● | | ● | |
| **ARQUÁ** | 407 | ♦♦♦♦ | | | | | ● | | | ● | |
| **AU TROQUET** | 407 | ♦♦♦ | | ● | | | | | | ● | |
| **BENNY'S BURRITOS** | 407 | ♦ | | | | | | | | | |
| **LA BOHÊME** | 407 | ♦♦♦ | | ● | | | | | ● | ● | |
| **BOULEY** | 407 | ♦♦♦♦ | | ● | | | | ● | ● | ● | |
| **CAPSOUTO FRÈRES** | 407 | ♦♦♦♦ | | ● | | | | ● | | ● | |
| **CHANTERELLE** | 407 | ♦♦♦♦ | | ● | | | | ● | | ● | |
| **CHELSEA TRATTORIA** | 407 | ♦♦♦♦ | | | | | ● | | | ● | |
| **DA SILVANO** | 407 | ♦♦♦♦ | | | | | ● | ● | ● | | |
| **EMPIRE DINER** | 407 | ♦♦ | ● | | | | | | | ● | ● |
| **ENNIO & MICHAEL** | 407 | ♦♦♦♦ | | | | | ● | | | | |
| **FÉLIX** | 407 | ♦♦♦ | | ● | | | | | | ● | |
| **FLORENT** | 407 | ♦♦♦ | | ● | | | | | | | |
| **GOTHAM BAR & GRILL** | 407 | ♦♦♦♦ | | | | | | ● | | | ● |
| **JEAN-CLAUDE** | 408 | ♦♦♦ | | ● | | | | | ● | | |
| **JERRY'S** | 408 | ♦♦♦ | ● | | | | | | | ● | |
| **JOHN'S PIZZERIA** | 408 | ♦ | | ● | | | ● | | | | |
| **LA LUNCHONETTE** | 408 | ♦♦♦ | | ● | | | | ● | | | |
| **LA METAIRIE** | 408 | ♦♦♦ | | ● | | | | ● | | ● | |
| **LE MADRI** | 408 | ♦♦♦♦ | | | | | ● | ● | ● | | |
| **LE PESCADOU** | 408 | ♦♦♦ | | ● | | | | ● | | | |
| **MESA GRILL** | 408 | ♦♦♦ | ● | | | | | ● | | ● | |
| **MEZZOGIORNO** | 408 | ♦♦♦♦ | | | | | ● | | | ● | |
| **MONTRACHET** | 408 | ♦♦♦♦ | | ● | | | | ● | | ● | |
| **THE ODEON** | 408 | ♦♦♦♦ | | | ● | | | ● | | ● | |
| **OMEN** | 408 | ♦♦♦ | | | ● | | | | | | |
| **PERIYALI** | 408 | ♦♦♦ | | | | | | | | | |
| **PROVENCE** | 408 | ♦♦♦ | | ● | | | | | | ● | |
| **SOHO KITCHEN AND BAR** | 408 | ♦♦♦ | ● | | | | | ● | | | |
| **TRIBECA GRILL** | 408 | ♦♦♦ | | | | | | ● | | ● | |
| **ZOÉ** | 408 | ♦♦♦ | | | | | | ● | | ● | |
| **UNION SQUARE** | | | | | | | | | | | |
| **AN AMERICAN PLACE** | 410 | ♦♦♦♦ | ● | | | | | ● | | ● | |
| **CIRCA** | 410 | ♦♦♦ | ● | | | | | | | | |
| **COFFEE SHOP** | 410 | ♦♦ | | | | | | | ● | | |
| **LA COLOMBE D'OR** | 410 | ♦♦♦♦ | | ● | | | | ● | | | |
| **LOLA** | 410 | ♦♦♦ | | | | | | | | | |
| **MITALI EAST** | 410 | ♦♦ | | | ● | | | | | | |
| **PARK BISTRO** | 411 | ♦♦♦♦ | | ● | | | | ● | | | |
| **UNION SQUARE CAFÉ** | 411 | ♦♦♦♦ | ● | | | | | ● | | ● | ● |
| **GRAND CENTRAL, THEATER DISTRICT** | | | | | | | | | | | |
| **"44"** | 412 | ♦♦♦♦ | | | | | | ● | | ● | |
| **AMBASSADOR GRILL** | 412 | ♦♦♦ | | | | | | ● | | ● | |
| **BARBETTA** | 412 | ♦♦♦♦ | | | | | ● | ● | ● | ● | |
| **BECCO** | 412 | ♦♦♦ | | | | | ● | ● | | | |
| **IPANEMA** | 412 | ♦ | | ● | | | | | | | |
| **CHEZ JOSÉPHINE** | 412 | ♦♦♦ | | ● | | | | | | ● | |
| **JEZEBEL** | 412 | ♦♦♦ | ● | | | | | | | ● | |
| **JOE ALLEN** | 412 | ♦♦♦ | ● | | | | | | | | |
| **ORSO** | 412 | ♦♦♦ | | | | | ● | | | ● | |
| **OYSTER BAR** | 412 | ♦♦♦ | ● | | | | | | | | ● |
| **PALM** | 412 | ♦♦♦♦ | ● | | | | | | | | ● |
| **SPARKS STEAK HOUSE** | 412 | ♦♦♦♦ | ● | | | | | ● | | | |

♦ $10
♦♦ $20
♦♦♦ $30
♦♦♦♦ $40 and over

| | PAGE | PRICE | AMERICAN CUISINE | FRENCH CUISINE | ORIENTAL CUISINE | EASTERN EUROPEAN CUISINE | ITALIAN CUISINE | WINE CELLAR | GARDEN, TERRACE | SETTING | "INSTITUTION" |
|---|---|---|---|---|---|---|---|---|---|---|---|
| **ROCKEFELLER CENTER** | | | | | | | | | | | |
| "21" CLUB | 416 | ◆◆◆◆ | ● | | | | | | | ● | ● |
| AL BUSTAN | 416 | ◆◆◆ | | | | | ● | | | ● | |
| AQUAVIT | 416 | ◆◆◆◆ | | | | | | | | ● | |
| LE BERNARDIN | 417 | ◆◆◆◆ | | | | | | ● | | ● | |
| BICE | 416 | ◆◆◆◆ | | | | | ● | ● | | ● | |
| LA CARAVELLE | 417 | ◆◆◆◆ | | | | | | ● | ● | ● | ● |
| CARNEGIE DELI | 416 | ◆◆ | | ● | | | | ● | | | |
| LE CIRQUE | 416 | ◆◆◆◆ | | | | | | ● | | ● | ● |
| DAWAT | 416 | ◆◆◆ | | | ● | | | | | ● | |
| FELIDIA | 416 | ◆◆◆◆ | | | | | ● | | | ● | |
| THE FOUR SEASONS | 416 | ◆◆◆◆ | ● | | | | | ● | | ● | ● |
| HARD ROCK CAFÉ | 416 | ◆◆ | ● | | | | | | | ● | |
| HARRY CIPRIANI | 417 | ◆◆◆◆ | | | | | ● | | | ● | |
| LESPINASSE | 417 | ◆◆◆◆ | | | | | | ● | | ● | |
| LUTÈCE | 417 | ◆◆◆◆ | | ● | | | | ● | | ● | |
| MICKEY MANTLE'S | 417 | ◆◆◆ | ● | ● | | | | ● | ● | ● | |
| IL NIDO | 417 | ◆◆◆◆ | | | | | ● | | | ● | |
| PETROSSIAN | 417 | ◆◆◆◆ | | | | | | ● | | ● | |
| P.J. CLARKE'S | 417 | ◆◆ | ● | | | | | ● | | ● | |
| PLANET HOLLYWOOD | 417 | ◆◆ | ● | | | | | | | ● | |
| RAINBOW ROOM | 417 | ◆◆◆◆ | | | | | | | | ● | ● |
| REMI | 417 | ◆◆◆◆ | | | | | ● | ● | | ● | ● |
| ROYAL CAN. PANCAKE HOUSE | 417 | ◆◆ | ● | | | | | ● | | | |
| RUSSIAN TEA ROOM | 417 | ◆◆◆◆ | | | | | | | | ● | ● |
| SAN DOMENICO | 417 | ◆◆◆◆ | | | | ● | ● | ● | | ● | ● |
| SHUN LEE PALACE | 417 | ◆◆◆◆ | | | ● | | | | | ● | |
| SMITH & WOLLENSKY | 417 | ◆◆◆◆ | ● | | | | | ● | ● | ● | |
| TRATTORIA DELL'ARTE | 418 | ◆◆◆◆ | | | | | ● | | | ● | |
| VONG | 418 | ◆◆◆◆ | | | ● | | | | | ● | |
| ZARELA | 418 | ◆◆◆ | | | | | ● | | | | |
| **UPPER EAST SIDE** | | | | | | | | | | | |
| ARIZONA 206 AND CAFÉ | 422 | ◆◆◆ | ● | | | | | | | ● | |
| AURÉOLE | 423 | ◆◆◆◆ | ● | | | | | ● | ● | ● | |
| BISTRO DU NORD | 423 | ◆◆◆ | | | | | | ● | ● | ● | |
| CAFÉ CROCODILE | 423 | ◆◆◆◆ | | ● | | | | ● | | | |
| CONTRAPUNTO | 423 | ◆◆◆ | | | | | ● | | | ● | |
| DANIEL | 423 | ◆◆◆◆ | | | | | | ● | | ● | |
| JOJO | 423 | ◆◆◆◆ | | ● | | | | ● | | ● | |
| MARK'S RESTAURANT | 423 | ◆◆◆◆ | | ● | | | | ● | | ● | |
| MEZZALUNA | 423 | ◆◆◆ | | ● | | | ● | | | ● | |
| MOCCA HUNGARIAN | 423 | ◆◆ | | | | | | | | | |
| MORTIMER'S | 423 | ◆◆◆◆ | ● | | | ● | | ● | | | ● |
| PAPAYA KING | 423 | ◆ | | | | | | | | | ● |
| PARK AVENUE CAFÉ | 423 | ◆◆◆◆ | ● | | | | | | | ● | |
| SETTE MEZZO | 423 | ◆◆◆◆ | | | | | ● | ● | | ● | |
| THREE GUYS | 423 | ◆◆ | ● | | | | ● | | | | |
| **UPPER WEST SIDE** | | | | | | | | | | | |
| CAFÉ DES ARTISTES | 425 | ◆◆◆◆ | | | | | | | | ● | |
| CAFÉ LUXEMBOURG | 425 | ◆◆ | | ● | | | ● | | | ● | |
| EJ'S LUNCHONETTE | 425 | ◆◆ | ● | ● | | | | | | ● | |
| SARABETH'S | 425 | ◆◆◆ | ● | | | | | | | ● | |
| TAVERN ON THE GREEN | 425 | ◆◆◆◆ | | | | | | | ● | ● | ● |
| VINCE & EDDIE'S | 425 | ◆◆◆◆ | ● | | | | ● | ● | | ● | |
| **HARLEM, UPTOWN** | | | | | | | | | | | |
| SYLVIA'S | 427 | ◆◆ | ● | | | | | | | ● | ● |
| THE TERRACE | 427 | ◆◆◆◆ | | | | | | | ● | ● | |
| **BROOKLYN** | | | | | | | | | | | |
| THE RIVER CAFÉ | 427 | ◆◆◆◆ | | | | | | ● | ● | ● | ● |

1. WORLD TRADE
   CENTER, CITY HALL
2. LOWER EAST SIDE,
   LITTLE ITALY,
   CHINATOWN
3. WASHINGTON
   SQUARE
4. UNION SQUARE
5. GRAND CENTRAL,
   THEATER DISTRICT
6. ROCKEFELLER
   CENTER
7. UPPER EAST SIDE
8. UPPER WEST SIDE
9. HARLEM,
   UPTOWN

# GENERAL

## USEFUL INFORMATION

### CONSULATES

UK
845 3rd Avenue
Tel. 745-0202
CANADA
1251 Ave of the
Americas
Tel. 596-1700
JAPAN
299 Park Avenue
Tel. 371-8222

### HOSPITALS

BETH ISRAEL
MEDICAL CENTER
1st Ave and 16th St
Tel. 420-2840
(emergencies)
LENOX HILL HOSPITAL
100 E. 77th St
Tel. 434-2000
MOUNT SINAI
MEDICAL CENTER
5th Ave and 100th St
Tel. 241-6500
ROOSEVELT
HOSPITAL CENTER
1111 Amsterdam Ave
Tel. 523-3335
(emergencies)
SAINT LUKE'S HOSPITAL
1000 10th Ave
Tel. 523-6800
(emergencies)
SAINT VINCENT'S
HOSPITAL
153 W. 11th St
Tel. 604-7000

### NEW YORK
CONVENTION AND
VISITORS' BUREAU

2 Columbus Circle
New York, NY 10019
Tel. 484-1200
Open Mon.–Fri.
9am–6pm. Open Sat.,
Sun. and public holidays
10am–3pm
*Multilingual reception
desk.*

### EMERGENCY SERVICES

POLICE, FIRE AND
AMBULANCE
Tel. 911
DOCTORS ON CALL
Tel. 737-2333
DENTAL SERVICE
Tel. 679-3966

### 24-HOUR PHARMACY

KAUFMAN PHARMACY
557 Lexington Ave
(at 50th St)
Tel. 755-2266

### TRAVELERS' AID
SOCIETY

1451 Broadway (2nd fl.)
Tel. 944-0013
Open Mon., Tue., Thur.,
Fri. 9am–6pm, Wed.
9am–noon
*Emergency assistance
for tourists. Same
service and general
information at JFK
Airport, International
Arrivals Building*
Tel. 718-656-4870

## TOURISM

### CIRCLE LINE

W. 42nd St, Pier 83
Tel. 563-3200
*Boat trip around
Manhattan island
(3 hours).*

### GRAY LINE
NEW YORK TOURS

900 8th Ave (between
53rd and 54th sts.)
Tel. 397-2600
*Twenty different guided
tours of the city.*

### HARLEM SPIRITUALS

1697 Broadway and
53rd St (Suite 203)
Tel. 757-0425
*Tours of Harlem
(including soul food
and gospel choirs),
around Brooklyn and
the Bronx.*

### LIBERTY
HELICOPTERS

12th Ave at W. 30th St
(on the Hudson)
Tel. 967-6464
(lines open:
Mon.–Fri. 9am–6pm)
Tours 9am–9pm
*Second location:*
Pier 6, near South Street
Seaport (on East River);
open Mon.–Fri.
9am–6pm

### THE LIMO TOUR

1636 3rd Ave
(Suite 420)
Tel. 423-0101
*Limousine rental.*

### NEW YORK
APPLE TOURS

Double-decker buses
Tel. 348-5300
*Bus tours leave from
the corner of 50th
Street and 8th
Avenue.*

## WORLD TRADE CENTER

### CULTURE

**CHURCH OF
OUR LADY OF THE
ROSARY**
Shrine of St Elizabeth
Ann Seton
7–8 State St

Tel. 269-6865
Open Mon.–Fri.
6.30am–6.30pm
Open Sat.–Sun.
for Mass ▲ 157

**ELLIS ISLAND**
New York Harbor
Tel. 363-7620
Open daily 9.30am–5pm
(ferry service to the
island stops at 3.30pm)
*Ferry every 30 minutes
(9.30am–3.30pm)
from Battery Park for
Ellis Island and the
Statue of Liberty.
Extraordinary
Museum of Immigration.
Ferry ride lasts
approximately 3 hours.*
▲ 148

**FEDERAL RESERVE
BANK OF NEW YORK**
33 Liberty St
Tel. 720-6130
Open Mon.–Fri. Tours
10.30am, 11.30am,
1.30pm, 2.30pm
Guided tours: 45 mins
*Limited number of
places. Reserve several
days in advance.
Contact the Public
Information Division*
▲ 158.

**FRAUNCES TAVERN
MUSEUM**
54 Pearl St
Tel. 425-1778
Open Mon.–Fri.
10am–4.45pm
Open Sat. noon–4pm
Closed Sun., public
holidays.
*18th- and 19th-century
American history, with
reconstructions of
period interiors* ▲ 166.

**HOBOKEN FERRY**
Battery Park City
(at the foot of the
World Financial Center,
on the Hudson River).
Tel. 1-908-GO FERRY
*Daily departures,
virtually every half
hour on weekends.
Weekday schedule
varies. The journey
(8 minutes) affords a
fine view of New York
and the bay.*

**JOHN STREET
METHODIST
CHURCH**
44 John St
Tel. 269-0014
Museum open Mon.,
Wed., Fri. noon–4pm
▲ 158

**MUSEUM OF AMERICAN
FINANCIAL HISTORY**
26 Broadway
Tel. 908-4519
Open Mon.–Fri.
11.30am–2.30pm but
hours can vary so call
ahead
*Temporary exhibitions*
▲ 156.

**NATIONAL MUSEUM OF
THE AMERICAN INDIAN**
Smithsonian Institution
Alexander Hamilton
US Custom House
1 Bowling Green
Tel. 668-6624
Open daily 10am–5pm
Closed Dec. 25
*Major collection of
photographs and
American-Indian objects*
▲ 157.

**NEW YORK STOCK
EXCHANGE (N.Y.S.E.)**
20 Broad St
Tel. 656-5165
Open Mon.–Fri. 9.15am–
4pm. Closed Sat., Sun.,
public holidays.
*Free admission if there
is enough room; it is
advisable to get there
early (tickets available
from 9am).*

**STATEN ISLAND FERRY**
Battery Park,
South Ferry
Tel. 806-6940
Departures every
30–60 minutes, 24 hours
a day. Length of journey:
30 minutes
*Superb view of lower
Manhattan, the Statue
of Liberty and the bay.*

**STATUE OF LIBERTY**
Liberty Island
New York Harbor
Tel. 363-8340
Same times and place of
departure as for
Ellis Island.
*Tickets available from
Castle Clinton, in
Battery Park. The tour
lasts a total of 4 hours.
Extremely popular in
summer and at
weekends* ▲ 144.

**TRINITY CHURCH**
Broadway and Wall St
Tel. 602-0872
CHURCH
Tours Mon.–Fri. 2pm
MUSEUM
Open Mon.–Fri.
9–11.45am and
1–3.45pm, Sat. 10am–
3.45pm, Sun. 1–3.45pm
▲ 154

**WORLD FINANCIAL
CENTER**
West St
Entry through the World
Trade Center via North
or South Bridge
Tel. 945-0505
*Entertainment at the
Winter Garden.
Shopping mall* ▲ 141.

**WORLD TRADE
CENTER**
Between Church, Vesey,
West and Liberty sts.
Tel. 323-2340
Open daily
9.30am–9.30pm,
9.30am–11.30am in
summer
*Breathtaking view from
the top of the
Observatory (Tower Two,
110th floor)* ▲ 138.

### RESTAURANTS

**FRAUNCES TAVERN**
54 Pearl St
Tel. 269-0144
Closed Sat., Sun.
*A quintessentially
American restaurant.
Grills and seafood*
▲ 166.

**HARRY'S AT HANOVER
SQUARE**
1 Hanover Square
Tel. 425-3412
*A typical Wall Street
scene where brokers
eat hamburgers with
their eyes glued to an
electronic display board
in the center of the
restaurant, with its
relentless stream of
stock exchange prices
at breakneck speed.*

**HUDSON RIVER CLUB**
250 Vesey St (4 World
Financial Center)
Tel. 786-1500
Closed Sat. lunchtime,
Sun. evening
*In season, Hudson
River valley products.
Overlooking the mouth
of the Hudson. Brunch.*

**WINDOWS ON
THE WORLD**
One World Trade Center
107th floor
Tel. 524-7000
Open weekdays
lunchtime and evenings,
and for brunch on Sun.
*Choice of three
restaurants and a bar.
Magnificent view.*

## CITY HALL

### CULTURE

**CITY HALL**
City Hall Park (between Broadway and Park Row)
Tel. 788-3000
Opening times vary; call ahead to check
*Information on tours of the city. New York's City Hall ▲ 168.*

**ST PAUL'S CHAPEL**
Broadway and Fulton St
Tel. 602-0874
Open Mon.–Fri. 9am–3pm
*Concerts and operas every Mon. and Thur. at noon ▲ 176*

**SOUTH STREET SEAPORT MUSEUM**
207 Front St
Tel. 748-8600
Open Mon., Wed., Fri.–Sun. 10am–6pm, closed Tue., open Thur. until 8pm
*Maritime museums. Ships tours. Boat trips. Tour of the fish market Apr.–Oct. 6am (reserve a week in advance Tel. 669-9416) ▲ 172.*

### RESTAURANTS

**SLOPPY LOUIE'S**
92 South St
Tel. 509-9694
Open daily
*Charming old restaurant, polite service. Wide range of freshly caught fish and shellfish. Closes early.*

### SHOPPING

**CENTURY 21 DEPARTMENT STORE**
22 Cortlandt St
Tel. 227-9092
*Three floors of "end of line" and marked-down goods: a very popular store.*

**J&R MUSIC WORLD**
15–33 Park Row
Tel. 238-9000

*Photography, computers, records, videos. A wide choice, well-informed sales assistants.*

**PIER 17 PAVILION**
89 South St
(South Street Seaport)
*Shopping center. Enormous number of restaurants and cafés, some with terraces.*

## LOWER EAST SIDE LITTLE ITALY CHINATOWN

### CULTURE

**CATHOLIC CHURCH OF THE TRANSFIGURATION**
29 Mott St
Tel. 962-5157
*Open only for services ▲ 192.*

**K'HAL ADATH SYNAGOGUE**
(Eldridge St Synagogue)
12 Eldridge St
Tel. 219-0888
*Visits by previous arrangement ▲ 194.*

**LOWER EAST SIDE TENEMENT MUSEUM**
90 Orchard St
Tel. 431-0233
Open Tue.–Sun. 11am–5pm
*Exhibitions on immigrant life on the Lower East Side. Guided walks and tour of a restored tenement building.*

**MARINERS' TEMPLE BAPTIST CHURCH**
3 Henry St and 12 Oliver St
Tel. 233-0423
Open Sun. 10am
*Service with gospel choir ▲193.*

**MOST HOLY CRUCIFIX CHURCH**
378 Broome St
Tel. 226-2556
Open for services.
▲ 196.

**MUSEUM OF CHINESE IN THE AMERICAS**
70 Mulberry St (2nd fl.)
Tel. 619-4785
Open Tue.–Sun. 10.30am–5pm
*Exhibition rooms and archives ▲191.*

**ST JAMES CHURCH**
32 St James St
Tel. 233-0161
*Refectory open Mon.–Sat. 10am–9pm ▲193.*

### RESTAURANTS

**BIG WONG**
67 Mott St
Tel. 964-0540
*Uninviting décor, but its grilled pork specialty draws the crowds. A good way to absorb the atmosphere of Chinatown. No credit cards.*

**HONG KONG EGG CAKE COMPANY**
Mott St
*Small cabin on Mott street selling delicious freshly made pancakes.*

**ISO**
175 2nd Ave (11th St)
Tel. 777-0361
*The fresh sushi makes this one of the best Japanese restaurants in New York.*

**KATZ'S DELICATESSEN**
205 E. Houston St
Tel. 254-2246
*Entertaining and friendly. The place to go if you like real Jewish delis.*

**MANDARIN COURT**
61 Mott St
Tel. 608-3838
Open daily
*Very popular dim sum restaurant, specializing in steamed dishes. Brunch. No alcohol.*

**NEW ORIENTAL PEARL RESTAURANT**
103–105 Mott St
Tel. 219-8388
*Recommended for its steamed dumplings. Dim sum served on trolleys until 3.30pm. À la carte menu in the evenings.*

**SAMMY'S ROUMANIANO**
157 Chrystie St
Tel. 673-0330
Open daily
*Fairly heavy Central European Jewish cuisine, huge helpings in a rather noisy setting.*

### CAFÉS

**CAFFÈ ROMA PASTRY**
385 Broome St
Tel. 226-8413
*Traditional Italian café.*

**FERRARA**
195 Grand St
Tel. 226-6150
Open daily
*Ice cream and a wide range of delicious pastries of Southern Italy. No alcohol.*

### SHOPPING

**CANAL STREET (CHINATOWN)**
*Electronic goods, clothes, perfume, shoes and jewelry.*

**GRAND STREET (LITTLE ITALY)**
*An interesting array of grocery stores.*

## KAN MAN FOOD PRODUCTS, INC.
200 Canal St
Tel. 571-0171
*The best supermarket in Chinatown.*

## MOTT, PELL, BAYARD AND DOYERS STS (CHINATOWN)
*South of Canal St
Lined with small stores and restaurants.*

## MULBERRY STREET (LITTLE ITALY)
*A choice of restaurants and terraces with tables on the sidewalk in summer.*

## ORCHARD STREET (LOWER EAST SIDE)
*Closed Sat.
Clothes and leather goods.*

## PEARL
308 Canal St
Tel. 431-7932
*Art and graphic furniture at low prices. Enormous choice on eight stories.*

## WASHINGTON SQUARE

### CULTURE

### ALTERNATIVE MUSEUM
594 Broadway
(Houston St)
Tel. 966-4444
Open Tue.–Sat.
11am–6pm
*Exhibitions of contemporary and avant garde works.*

### CHURCH OF THE ASCENSION
5th Ave at 11th St
Tel. 254-8620
*Visits by previous arrangement ▲ 218.*

### CIRCLE IN THE SQUARE THEATRE
1633 Broadway
Tel. 239-6200
*The birthplace of "Off-Broadway" productions.*

### CLOCKTOWER GALLERY
108 Leonard St (14th fl.)
Tel. 233-1096
*Open for temporary exhibitions ▲ 182, ◆ 382*

### DIA CENTER FOR THE ARTS
548 W. 22nd St
Tel. 989-5912
Open Thur.–Sun.
noon–6pm
Closed Jul.–Aug.
*Modern art ▲ 220.*

### THE FORBES MAGAZINE GALLERIES
62 5th Ave (12th St)
Tel. 206-5548
Open Tue.–Wed. and Fri.–Sat. 10am–4pm
Also open Thurs. if reserved in advance.
*Malcolm Forbes' collections (Fabergé eggs, 12,000 toy soldiers, etc.) ▲ 219.*

### GENERAL THEOLOGICAL SEMINARY
175 9th Ave
Tel. 243-5150
Open Mon.–Fri.
noon–3pm, Sat.
11am–3pm
*Exhibition in the lobby. Garden. The library is closed to the public ▲ 220.*

### GUGGENHEIM MUSEUM SOHO
575 Broadway
(Prince St)
Tel. 423-3500
Open Sun., Mon.–Fri.
11am–6pm, Sat.

11am–8pm (public holidays; 5pm)
*Annex of the Guggenheim Museum ▲ 204.*

### JUDSON MEMORIAL BAPTIST CHURCH
55 Washington Square South
Tel. 477-0351
*Visits by previous arrangement. ▲ 200*

### MUSEUM FOR AFRICAN ART
593 Broadway
Tel. 966-1313
Open Tue.–Fri.
10.30am–5.30pm
Open Sat. and Sun.
noon–6pm
*African art ▲ 204.*

### NEW MUSEUM OF CONTEMPORARY ART
583 Broadway
(Prince and Houston sts)
Tel. 219-1222
Open Wed.–Fri. and Sun. noon–6pm
Open Sat. noon–8pm
Closed in summer
*Contemporary artists ▲ 204.*

### NEW YORK CITY FIRE MUSEUM
278 Spring St
Tel. 691-1303
Open Tue.–Sat.
10am–4pm
*▲ 205*

### PUBLIC THEATER
425 Lafayette St
Tel. 598-7150
*Six theaters grouped together. Half-price tickets one hour before performance, Tuesday to Sunday.*

### GALLERIES

### 303 GALLERY
89 Greene St (2nd floor)
Tel. 966-5605
Open Tue.–Sat.
10am–6pm
*Liz Larner and Thomas Ruff made a name for*

*themselves here. The gallery continues to be on the lookout for young talent.*

### A/D
560 Broadway
Tel. 966-5154
Open Tue.–Sat.
11am–6pm
*A/D commissions limited editions of decorative everyday objects from various artists (Arman, Gerhard Richter, Donald Sultan, etc.)*

### A.I.R.
40 Wooster St
Tel. 966-0799
Open Tue.–Sat.
11am–6pm
*First women's cooperative, non-profit gallery founded in 1972.*

### AMERICAN FINE ARTS CO.
22 Wooster St
Tel. 941-0401
Open Tue.–Sat.
11am–6pm
*A fascinating, unconventional gallery which mounts provocative exhibitions. A showcase for up-and-coming young artists.*

### ARTISTS' SPACE
38 Greene St (3rd floor)
Tel. 226-3970
Open Tue.–Sat.
10am–6pm
*Voluntary organization exhibiting avant-garde works. The curators also organize thematic exhibitions.*

### BARBARA GLADSTONE
99 Greene St
Tel. 431-3334
Open Tue.–Sat.
10am–6pm
*The most radical masterpieces of politicized conceptualism (Acconci, Faigenbaum, Holzer, Mullican, Trockel, etc.).*

### BROOKE ALEXANDER EDITIONS
59 Wooster St
Tel. 925-4338
Open Tue.–Sat.
10am–6pm
*Luxurious art gallery designed by Max Gordon, and interesting talents such as Yvonne Jacquette and Nuno Ramos.*

405

### CURT MARCUS GALLERY
578 Broadway
(Prince St, 10th floor)
Tel. 226-3200
Open Tue.–Sat.
10am–6pm
*The cream of up-and-coming artists as well as those who have already acquired some measure of renown.*

### DOLGENOS, NEWMAN AND CRONIN
96 Spring St (8th floor)
Open Tue.–Sat.
10am–5pm
Tel. 925-2800
*A group of lawyers with offices in an art gallery.*

### THE DRAWING CENTER
35 Wooster St
Tel. 219- 2166
Open Tue., Thur., Fri.
10am–6pm
Open Wed. 10am–8pm
Open Sat. 11am–6pm
*Four or five times a year, this center exhibits the work of artists who have yet to make a name for themselves. It also possesses an index of slides, covering recent works by nearly 5,000 artists, which is open to the public by appointment only.*

### EXIT ART THE FIRST WORLD
548 Broadway (2nd fl.)
Tel. 966-7745
Open Mon.–Fri.
10am–6pm
Open Sat. 11am–10pm
*Mainly exhibitions of works by established artists.*

### FEATURE GALLERY
76 Greene St (2nd floor)
Tel. 941-7077
Open Tue.–Sat.
11am–6pm
*A highly distinctive group of artists whose works run the gamut from conceptual installations to expressive drawing.*

*A gallery where you are most likely to discover new artists.*

### HOLLY SOLOMON GALLERY
172 Mercer St
Tel. 941-5777
Open Tue.–Sat.
10am–6pm, summer hours Memorial Day–Labor Day Tue.–Fri.
10am–5pm.
*Holly Solomon has a flair for discovering important artists yet to make a name for themselves.*

### JAMES DANZIGER GALLERY
130 Prince St
Tel. 226-0056
Open Tue.–Fri.
11am–6pm
*Represents some of the big contemporary names in fashion photography, 19th-century prints, and launches young unknowns.*

### JANET BORDEN INC.
560 Broadway (6th floor)
Tel. 431-0166
Open Tue.–Sat.
11am–5pm
*Large-scale, color photographs.*

### JAY GORNEY MODERN ART
100 Greene St
Tel. 966-4480
Open Tue.–Fri.
10am–6pm, Sat.
11am–6pm
*Gallery exhibiting works by contemporary painters and sculptors.*

### JOHN GIBSON
568 Broadway
Tel. 925-1192
Open Tue.–Sat.
11am–6pm
*Unpretentious gallery which has faithfully reflected all the new artistic trends to appear over the past thirty years.*

### JOHN WEBER GALLERY
142 Greene St (3rd fl)
Tel. 966-6115
Open Tue.–Sat.
10am–6pm
*Primarily conceptual art. Artists interested in minimalism (Buren); others inspired by the soil (Fulton, Smithson), an entire group (Burgin,*

*Haacke, Piper) with a penchant for strident political comment.*

### LEO CASTELLI GALLERY
420 West Broadway and 578 Broadway (2nd fl.)
Tel. 431-6279
Open Tue.–Sat.
10am–6pm
*Leo Castelli was the man who introduced Johns, Rauschenberg, Lichtenstein, Warhol, Rosenquist, Stella, Judd and Nauman and he continues to exhibit their works. His influence has shaped the world of modern art for the past thirty years. Also at 578 Broadway (3rd floor), Soho.*

### LOWINSKY GALLERY
578 Broadway
Tel. 226-5440
Open Tue.–Sat.
11am–6pm
*An array of 19th-century works and contemporary photography.*

### LUHRING AUGUSTINE
130 Prince St (2nd floor)
Tel. 219-9600
Open Tue.–Sat.
10am–6pm
*Exhibits mainly contemporary work by established German, American and Japanese artists.*

### MAX PROTECH
560 Broadway (2nd fl.)
Tel. 966-5454
Open Tue.–Sat.
10am–6pm
*This gallery contains ancient and modern architectural drawings (Isozaki, Tschumi, Frank*

*Lloyd Wright, etc.) and detailed and architectonic works by artists.*

### METRO PICTURES
150 Greene St
Tel. 925-8335
Open Tue.–Sat.
10am–6pm

*In a vast gallery, artists tackle socio-cultural issues, pulling no punches with their playful and provocative stance.*

### O.K. HARRIS WORKS OF ART
383 West Broadway
Tel. 431-3600
Open Tue.–Sat.
10am–6pm
*A gallery opened by Ivan C. Karp, the originator of the 1970's photo-realist movement.*

### P.P.O.W.
532 Broadway (3rd fl.)
Tel. 941-8642
Open Tue.–Sat.
10am–6pm
*Photography, painting, and works of up-and-coming artists with a keen awareness of social issues and a sense of irony.*

### PACE WILDENSTEIN GALLERY
142 Greene St
Tel. 431-9224
Open Tue.–Sat.
10am–6pm
*A key player in the contemporary art world. After showing Picasso, Noguchi and Joseph Cornell, Pace made inroads into the contemporary art market with Martin, Richard Serra and Louise Nevelson. Another gallery at 32 E. 57th St Tel. 421-3292.*

### PAT HEARN
530 W. 22nd St
Tel. 727-7366
Open Wed.–Sun.
11am–6pm
*Pat Hearn was one of the first artists to settle in the East Village, before moving to SoHo. She exhibits emerging American and European contemporary artists.*

### PAULA COOPER GALLERY
155 Wooster St
Tel. 674-0766

Open Tue.–Sat.
10am–6pm
*Exhibits works by
contemporary artists.
Women artists are given
more consideration here
than in other
comparable galleries.*

### RONALD FELDMAN FINE ARTS
31 Mercer St
Tel. 226-3232
Open Tue.–Sat.
10am–6pm
*Contemporary artists.*

### SONNABEND GALLERY
420 West Broadway
(3rd floor)
Tel. 966-6160
Open Tue.–Sat.
10am–6pm

*Monumental art often
goes hand in hand with
a quaint, almost kitsch
sensibility in this gallery.
Ileana Sonnabend
knows artistic quality
when she sees it and
has a keen, ironic eye.*

### SPERONE WESTWATER
121 and 142 Greene St
Tel. 431-3685
Open Tue.–Sat.
10am–6pm
*Exhibits a group of
young Italians, better-
known artists and
established names
(Long, Richter,
Rothenberg, etc.) and
also seeks out young
talent.*

### STALEY-WISE GALLERY
560 Broadway (6th floor)
Tel. 966-6223
Open Tue.–Sat.
11am–5pm
*Commercial
photographs used to
create artistic effects.
Striking and amusing.*

### THREAD WAXING SPACE
476 Broadway (2nd fl.)
Tel. 966-9520
Open Tue.–Sat.
10am–6pm

*A former factory, now a
cultural center. A multi-
disciplinary visual arts
and performing art
space.*

### TONY SHAFRAZI GALLERY
119 Wooster St
Tel. 274-9300
Open Tue.–Sat.
10am–6pm, mid-June
through Labor Day
Mon.–Fri. 10am–6pm
*Tony Shafrazi achieved
notoriety for defacing
Picasso's "Guernica"
with graffiti at the
Museum of Modern
Art. He now exhibits
contemporary artists,
some of whom (e.g.
Basquiat, Keith Haring
and Kenny Scharf)
started out as graffitists.*

## RESTAURANTS

### ALISON ON DOMINICK
38 Dominick St
Tel. 727-1188
*Elegant décor and
romantic atmosphere.
Provençale-inspired
American cuisine.*

### ARQUÁ
281 Church St
Tel. 334-1888
Closed Sat. and Sun.
lunchtime
*Stylish and convivial
trattoria. Attractive
menu.*

### AU TROQUET
328 W. 12th St
Tel. 924-3413
Open every evening.
*Romantic bistro with a
charming atmosphere.*

### BAROCCO
301 Church St
Tel. 431-1445
*Very lively, informal
clientèle.*

### BENNY'S BURRITOS
113 Greenwich Ave
Tel. 727-0584
Open daily
*Mammoth tortillas with
a huge variety of fillings,
from cheese to
guacamole. No credit
cards.*

### LA BOHÈME
24 Minetta Lane
Tel. 473-6447
Open Tue.–Sun.
*Provençale cuisine and
excellent pizzas
(artichokes and snails).*

### BOULEY
In the process of moving
Tel. 608-3852
Open lunchtime and
evening
Closed Sat. lunchtime,
Sun.
*Inventive cuisine (try the
grilled prawns with wild
mushrooms). "The"
place to eat in New York.
Reservation essential,
well in advance.*

### CAPSOUTO FRÈRES
451 Washington St
Tel. 966-4900
Open lunchtime and
evening
Closed Mon. lunchtime
*Excellent contemporary
French cuisine and very
good service. Housed in
a splendid old protected
building. Brunch.*

### CHANTERELLE
2 Harrison St
Tel. 966-6960
Open lunchtime and
evening
Closed Sun., Mon.
*The lunchtime set-price
menu makes this
magnificent restaurant
much more affordable.*

### CHELSEA TRATTORIA
108 8th Ave
Tel. 924-7786
Closed Sat. lunchtime,
Sun.
*Highly regarded, yet
unpretentious
(florentine soup with
haricot beans, sea food
"al cartoccio" and
delicious tiramisu).*

### DA SILVANO
260 Ave of the Americas
Tel. 982-2343
Closed Sat. and Sun.
lunchtime
*Italian specialties and
game dishes in season.
Terrace in summer.*

### EMPIRE DINER
210 10th Ave
Tel. 243-2736
Open 7 days a week,
24 hours a day. Closed
Tue. 4am–8am.
*Magnificent restored Art
Deco monument. Menu
for eclectic tastes,
ranging from chicken
wings, nachos or
Chinese wontons to
bacon, lettuce and
tomato sandwiches and
ice-cream sundaes
seasoned with chili*
▲ 220.

### ENNIO & MICHAEL
539 LaGuardia Pl.
Tel. 677-8577
Open daily
*Nourishing and delicious
dishes, such as fried
zucchini, seafood salad,
gnocchi in tomato sauce
and gamberi à la diable.
Outdoor café in summer.
American Express only.*

### FÉLIX
340 West Broadway
Tel. 431-0021
Open lunchtime and
evening
Closed Mon. lunchtime
*A lively, fashionable
bistro. No credit cards.*

### FLORENT
69 Gansevoort St
Tel. 989-5779
Open Mon.–Fri.
9am–5am, Sat. and
Sun. 24 hours
*The food could be
more exciting, but the
restaurant is not lacking
customers (Madonna is
occasionally seen here).
Order a taxi to get back.
No credit cards.*

### GOTHAM BAR & GRILL
12 E. 12th St
Tel. 620-4020
Open lunchtime and
evening
Closed Sat. and Sun.
lunchtimes
*Don;t miss. Sample their
ravioli "à la caponata"
and with goat's cheese,
and their wheat-free
chocolate cake. Fixed-
price menu at lunchtime.*

### HONMURA AN
170 Mercer St
Tel. 334-5253
*Original, very refined
Japanese cuisine
specializing in soba
dishes. Elegant, modern
space.*

### JEAN-CLAUDE
137 Sullivan St
Tel. 475-9232
Open every evening.
*A good place to have a
drink and savor
excellent, reasonably
priced bistro dishes.
Noisy and frequently
packed. No reservations
or credit cards.*

### JERRY'S
101 Prince St
Tel. 966-9464
Closed Sun. evening.
*A former diner which
has come up in the
world. Delicious
sandwiches, whole
meals in themselves.
Brunch.*

### JOHN'S PIZZERIA
278 Bleecker St
Tel. 243-1680
*The best Neapolitan
pizza house in
Manhattan. Brunch.
No credit cards.*

### LA LUNCHONETTE
130 10th Ave (18th St)
Tel. 675-0342
Closed Sat. lunchtime

*Impressive menu: leek
and lentil salad, snails in
cognac, grilled lamb
sausages, brains in
black butter and
cassoulet.*

### LE MADRI
168 W. 18th St
Tel. 727-8022
Closed in summer:
Sat.–Sun. lunchtime
*The fashion and
publishing worlds flock
here to savor delicious
pizzas cooked in a
traditional wood-fired
oven and imaginative
pasta dishes.*

### MESA GRILL
102 5th Ave (15th St)
Tel. 807-7400
Open daily
*Picturesque and friendly.
Specialties from
southwest America.
Ideal for family meals,
as well as for brunch.*

### LA METAIRIE
189 W. 10th St
Tel. 989-0343
*Friendly atmosphere.
Cooking with a
Provençal touch.
Seafood sausage, quail
stuffed with foie gras
and spinach.*

### MEZZOGIORNO
195 Spring St
Tel. 334-2112
Open lunchtime and
evenings
*Fine, light Italian
cooking, if a little
expensive, in relaxed
surroundings. No credit
cards.*

### MONTRACHET
239 West Broadway
Tel. 219-2777
Open evenings and Fri.
lunchtime
Closed Sun.
*Elegant French
restaurant. Mouth-
watering dishes and an
impressive wine list.*

### NOBU
105 Hudson St
Tel. 219-0500
*Nobu Matsuhisa has
now hit New York with
his new-style Japanese
cuisine with its
extraordinary flavors.
Reserve in advance.*

### THE ODEON
145 West Broadway
Tel. 233-0507
*This Art Deco bistro was
a favorite haunt of Andy
Warhol's group. The
food is now rather
commonplace.*

### OMEN
113 Thompson St
Tel. 925-8923
*Traditional Kyoto dishes
in a sensual, calm
atmosphere.*

### PERIYALI
35 W. 20th St
Tel. 463-7890
Closed Sat. lunchtime
and Sun.
*The most original Greek
restaurant in New York.
Greek salad with feta
cheese, grilled charcoal
octopus.*

### LE PESCADOU
18 King St
Tel. 924-3434
*A combination of fish
and Provençal dishes.
Food also served at the
bar for less.*

### PROVENCE
38 MacDougal St
Tel. 475-7500
*Authentic Provençal
cuisine in a lively bistro.
Superb garden.*

### SOHO KITCHEN AND BAR
103 Greene St
Tel. 925-1866
*Excellent wine bar with
more than 100 vintages
from all over the world,
served by the glass.
Pizzas, pasta and grills.*

### TRIBECA GRILL
375 Greenwich St
Tel. 941-3900
Closed Sat. lunchtime
*A spacious restaurant
opened by Robert de
Niro in a former
warehouse. A lively
establishment where
you can sample fine
food and rub shoulders
with celebrities.*

### ZOË
90 Prince St
Tel. 966-6722
Closed Mon.
*Superb all-American
cuisine: crisp noodle
wrapped shrimp, grilled
salmon with Moroccan
and basil mash
potatoes, Mexican
pecan pie with caramel
icing. Reserve well in
advance for brunch on
weekends.*

## ACCOMMODATION

### CHELSEA HOTEL*
222 W. 23rd St
Tel./Fax 243-7000
*Frequented by artists.
Relaxed service, simple,
fairly well-kept rooms.
Negotiate special rates
for long stays ▲ 220.*

### WASHINGTON SQUARE HOTEL**
103 Waverly Pl.
Tel. 777-9515
or 1-800-222-0418
Fax 979-8373
*Ideal for young people
who are not too fussy
about accommodation.
In the heart of
Greenwich Village.
Reserve in advance.*

## SHOPPING

### AGNÈS B
116 Prince St
Tel. 925-4649
*Great basics and
separates with a
French flair.*

### ASTOR PLACE HAIRSTYLIST, INC.
2 Astor Place
Tel. 475-9854
*One of the hundred hair-
stylists in this lively
basement, they will give
you a fast and funky
haircut for a just a few
dollars.*

### BALDUCCI'S
424 6th Ave
Tel. 673-2600
*Italian grocery store
which moved to the
Village in 1948. Not just
excellent caterers: an
institution. Worth a visit
for the décor and the
people who shop there.*

### BARNEYS NEW YORK
106 7th Ave
Tel. 593-7800
*Department store. One
of the leading menswear
outlets. From the most
original designs to
classic cuts. Also caters
to women and children.
Chic and expensive.
Renowned for its
window displays,
especially at Christmas.*

### BETSEY JOHNSON
130 Thompson St
Tel. 420-0169
*Teenage fashions,
inspired by the 1960's.*

## THE BIOGRAPHY BOOKSHOP
400 Bleecker St
Tel. 807-8655
*Specializes in biographies, letters, autobiographies, and memoirs by famous and unknown authors.*

## CANAL JEAN
504 Broadway
Tel. 226-1130
*Four floors of jeans and clothes for the young, often at rock-bottom prices. One whole floor of secondhand clothes.*

## CANAL STREET FLEA MARKET
335 Canal St
Open Sat.–Sun.
Closed Jan.–Feb.

## DEAN AND DELUCA
560 Broadway
Tel. 431-1691
*SoHo's main quality grocery store. Even if you don't want to buy anything, it is worth visiting this store for its décor. Espresso bar serving snacks at the entrance.*

## DETECTIVE STORE
164 Christopher St
Tel. 366-6466
*Everything for those iinterested in surveillance equipment.*

## THE ENCHANTED FOREST
85 Mercer St
Tel. 925-6677
*Wonderful plush toys in delightful surroundings.*

## FOOTLIGHT RECORDS
113 E. 12th St
Tel. 533-1572
*Records. Old, new, out of print.*

## JACQUES CARNCANAGUES, INC.
106 Spring St
Tel. 925-8110
*Furniture from India, Burma, Ethiopia...*

## LOST CITY ARTS
275 Lafayette St
Tel. 941-8025
*Secondhand goods; mainly advertising articles and other ephemera.*

## NEW REPUBLIC
93 Spring St
Tel. 219-3005
*Classic men's sportswear and tailored clothing.*

## POP SHOP
292 Lafayette St
Tel. 219-2784
*Designs by Keith Haring and prints of his work on T-shirts, books, posters, etc.*

## REPLAY COUNTRY STORE
109 Prince St
Tel. 673-6300
*Jeans and "western"-style clothing. Interesting décor. Basement bar*

## SCREAMING MIMI'S
382 Lafayette St
Tel. 677-6464
*Clothes for young people, caters for all tastes.*

## TERRA VERDE
120 Wooster St
Tel. 925-4533
*The first wholly ecological store: organic clothing and bedlinen, aromatherapy, environmentally-friendly furniture.*

## TOOTSIE PLOHOUND
413 West Broadway
Tel. 925-8931
*Fashionable men's and women's shoes.*

## UNCLE STEVE'S
343 Canal St
Tel. 226-4010
*Electronic goods at discount prices.*

## URBAN ARCHEOLOGY
285 Lafayette St
Tel. 431-6969
*An enormous store filled with fragments of New York: lamps, bar counters, old baths, signs, Art Deco wall lights. A very impressive collection.*

## VILLAGE CHESS SHOP
230 Thompson St
Tel. 475-9580
*A wide range of chess sets in all shapes and sizes.*

## NIGHTLIFE

## THE BACK FENCE
155 Bleecker St
Tel. 475-9221
*Simply a bar.*
Open 4pm–4am
*Live music every evening from 8.30pm: country, rock, folk.*

## THE BITTER END
149 Bleecker St
Tel. 673-7030
*Music club.*
Open 7.30pm–4am.
*Bob Dylan, Joan Baez and Neil Young started out here, as did Woody Allen. Sets between 10pm and 2am.*

## BLUE NOTE
131 W. 3rd St
Tel. 475-8592
*Bar-restaurant.*
Open 7pm–3am
*A jazz mecca. The musical fare is of a consistently high standard, with great classic performers such as Ray Charles, Dave Brubeck and Lionel Hampton. Brunch.*

## BOTTOM LINE
15 W. 4th St
Tel. 228-6300
*This fast-food joint, located in a student quarter, is an excellent place for rock music. All the big names in pop and country music play here.*

## BRADLEY'S
70 University Pl.
Tel. 473-9700
*Bar-restaurant.*
Open 5.30pm–4am
*One of the top jazz clubs. Shows at 10pm, midnight and 2am.*

## EAR INN
326 Spring St
Tel. 226-9060
*Music Mon.–Thur. 11pm–3.30am
The house is allegedly haunted. You can have lunch or supper at this bar, which is extremely lively in the evenings.*

## LIMELIGHT
47 W. 20th St
Tel. 807-7850
Open Wed.–Sat. nights
*A deconsecrated church, now a venue for the New York smart set who enjoy wild evenings here, with masquerade parties and shows.*

## PECULIAR PUB
145 Bleecker St
Tel. 353-1327
Open from 5pm
*Deservedly renowned for its wide range of beers from all over the world.*

## S.O.B.'s (SOUNDS OF BRAZIL)
204 Varick St
Tel. 243-4940
Closed Sun.
*Bar-restaurant. Brazilian and Caribbean cuisine. South American and African music is performed in the evenings, from 9pm to 11pm.*

## SWEET BASIL
88 7th Ave South
Tel. 242-1785
*Bar-restaurant. Open daily from noon, music from 2pm Brunch Sat.–Sun. Jazz sets at 9pm and 11pm.*

## TRAMPS
51 W. 21st St
Tel. 727-7788
or 544-1666
*Only open on days of with performances Cajun restaurant. Blues, soul and music with a sunny beat. There is also a restaurant, open daily for lunch and dinner. Tel. 633-9570.*

## VILLAGE VANGUARD
178 7th Ave South
Tel. 255-4037
Open 9.30pm–1am
*The spirit of John Coltrane is still kept very much alive in this club frequented by the jazz old guard.*

## WETLANDS
161 Hudson St
Tel. 966-4225
Open Mon.–Fri. 5pm–4am, Sat.–Sun. 9pm–4am

This venue comes alive with African rhythms, punk music, rock or jazz, depending on the evening.

## CAFÉ-BARS

### CAFÉ BORGIA
185 Bleecker St
Tel. 674-9589

### CAFÉ DANTE
79 MacDougal St
Tel. 982-5275

### CAFFÈ REGGIO
119 MacDougal St
Tel. 475-9557
*The most famous café in the Village. It boasts the oldest coffee percolator in New York and still has the original Italian décor which dates from its opening in 1927.*

### CHUMLEY'S
86 Bedford St
Tel. 675-4449
Bar-restaurant
Open Sun.–Thur.
5–11pm
Open Fri., Sat.
5pm–1am. ▲ 214

### FIGARO CAFFÈ
184 Bleecker St
Tel. 677-1100
*The original décor of this establishment, a meeting place for beatniks and café society during the 1950's, has been restored. Brunch.*

### WHITE HORSE TAVERN
567 Hudson St
Tel. 243-9260
Bar-restaurant
*Terrace in the summer. No credit cards.*
▲ 215

## UNION SQUARE

### CULTURE

### APPELLATE DIVISION OF STATE SUPREME COURT
25th Street and Madison Ave
Tel. 340-0477
Open Mon.–Fri.
9am–5pm
*You can attend when the courts are in session: Tue.–Thur., starting at 2pm; Fri., starting at 10am.*
▲ 234

### THE BROTHERHOOD SYNAGOGUE
28 Gramercy Park South
Tel. 674-5750
▲ 230.

### CHURCH OF THE TRANSFIGURATION
1 E. 29th St
Tel. 684-6770
Open 8am–6pm.

### CON EDISON ENERGY MUSEUM
145 E.14th St
Tel. 460-6244
Open Tue.–Sat.
9am–5pm
*Reconstruction of New York's underground wiring system* ▲ 229.

### GRACE CHURCH
802 Broadway and 10th St
Tel. 254-2000
Open Mon.–Fri.
10am–5.45pm, Sat.
noon–4pm
▲ 224.

### POLICE ACADEMY MUSEUM
235 E. 20th St
Tel. 477-9753
Open Mon.–Fri. 9am–3pm. Closed Sat., Sun. and public holidays. Always call first.
*The history of the New York police force.*

### ST MARK'S CHURCH IN THE BOWERY
131 E. 10th St
Tel. 674-6377
*Visit by appointment*
▲ 224

### THEODORE ROOSEVELT'S BIRTHPLACE
28 E. 20th St
Tel. 260-1616
Open Wed.–Sun.
9am–5pm ▲ 233

### UKRAINIAN MUSEUM
203 2nd Ave and 12th St
Tel. 228-0110.
Open Wed.–Sun. 1–5pm
*Cultural heritage of Ukrainian people. Exhibitions.*

### RESTAURANTS

### AN AMERICAN PLACE
2 Park Ave
Tel. 684-2122
Closed Sat. and Sun.
*American cuisine. All the inventiveness of a famous chef: Larry Forgione.*

### CIRCA
103 2nd Ave (6th St)
Tel. 777-4120
*American cuisine with a Mediterranean influence.*

### COFFEE SHOP
29 Union Square W.
Tel. 243-7969
Open 7am–6am
*Pre-1940's style and fashionable clientele. At full swing around midnight. South-American cuisine.*

### LA COLOMBE D'OR
134 E. 26th St
Tel. 689-0666
Open lunchtime and evenings
Closed Sat.–Sun. lunchtime
*Intimate and unpretentious. Provençal cuisine.*

### LOLA
30 W. 22nd St
Tel. 675-6700
*You can sample Cajun-style onion-rings or 100-spiced chicken against an increasingly noisy backdrop of conversation and live music. Brunch on Sun.*

### LOLA BOWLA
30 W. 22nd St
Tel. 675-5544
Open at lunchtime only

### MITALI EAST
336 E. 6th St
Tel. 533-2508
Open daily
*Good cuisine from the north of India at unbeatable prices. Brunch on Sundays.*

### PARK BISTRO
414 Park Ave South
Tel. 689-1360
*Probably the best bistro in New York. Provençal-style dishes. Pétatou au chèvre, shelfish soup, rabbit with salsify, medallions of beef.*

### UNION SQUARE CAFÉ
21 E. 16th St
Tel. 243-4020
Closed Sun. lunchtime
*Reserve well in advance to sample the Union Square's oysters, salmon grilled with corn and chocolate marble brownies. One of New York's best restaurants.*

### ACCOMMODATION

### ARLINGTON HOTEL**
18 W. 25th St
Tel. 645-3990
Fax 633-8952
*Well-maintained hotel. Good value.*

### GRAMERCY PARK HOTEL**
2 Lexington Ave (21st St)
Tel. 475-4320
or (800) 221-4083
Fax 505-0535
*The small rooms would benefit from redecoration. But the neighborhood is attractive and you are*

right on Gramercy Park. European clientèle.
▲ 230

## NIGHTLIFE

**C.B.G.B. A.O.M.F.U.G.**
315 Bowery
Tel. 982-4052
Open 7pm–3am
From the Ramones to Talking Heads, many groups who have since shot to fame once played at this strange little elongated club.
▲ 224

**CONTINENTAL DIVIDE**
25 3rd Ave
Tel. 529-6924
Open 4pm–4am
A rival of C.B.G.B. All the East Village's punk denizens come to listen or perform at this club.

**KNITTING FACTORY**
74 Leonard St
Tel. 219-3055
Open every evening
A tiny place where you can hear musicians who were once household names as well as a new generation of rising stars. An enthusiastic audience and a welcoming atmosphere.

## CAFÉ-BARS

**McSORLEY'S OLD ALE HOUSE**
15 E. 7th St
Tel. 473-9148
Open Mon.–Sat. 11am–1am, Sun. 1pm–1am
One of the oldest bars in New York (1854), serving a wide range of fine beers. No credit cards.

**PETE'S TAVERN**
129 E. 18th St
Tel. 473-7676
or (800) 286-3049
Open 11am–12.45am

O. Henry apparently wrote "The Gift of the Magi" sitting at the second booth on the left in this bar-restaurant, which is still a nice place to have a beer ▲ 229.

## SHOPPING

**ABC CARPETS**
888 Broadway
(E. 19th St)
Tel. 473-3000
Two buildings devoted to decoration (linen, antiquities, carpets).

**ANNEX ANTIQUES FAIR AND FLEA MARKET**
6th Ave and W. 26th St
Tel. 243-5343
Open Sat. and Sun. 9am–5pm
The largest flea market in the city.

**B. & H. PHOTO-VIDEO**
119 W. 17th St
Tel. 807-7474
One of New York's biggest photography stores.

**FORBIDDEN PLANET**
840 Broadway (13th St)
Tel. 473-1576
Wide assortment of science fiction, fantasy and comic art books plus toys and videos.

**LOVE SAVES THE DAY**
119 2nd Ave (7th St)
Tel. 228-3802
Secondhand clothing and collectible toys.

**PARAGON**
867 Broadway (18th St)
Tel. 255-8036
Three floors devoted to sporting goods.

**STRAND BOOK STORE**
828 Broadway (12th St)
Tel. 473-1452
Secondhand books and rare editions.

**TOWER RECORDS**
692 Broadway (4th St)
Tel. 505-1500
Music chain store. There is also a department selling books and videos.

## GRAND CENTRAL THEATER DISTRICT

## CULTURE

**CIRCLE LINE**
Pier 83, W. 42nd St
Tel. 563-3200
Closed Jan., Feb.
A three-hour boat trip around Manhattan. Cruises throughout day 9.30am–5pm. During the summer, 9am–7pm.

**EMPIRE STATE BUILDING**
350 5th Ave (34th St)
Tel. 736-3100
9.30am–11.30pm
Magnificent view over New York from the 86th and 102nd floors ▲ 242.

**GENERAL SOCIETY OF MECHANICS AND TRADESMEN MUSEUM**
20 W. 44th St
Tel. 840-1840
Open Mon.–Fri. 9am–5pm

**GRAND CENTRAL TERMINAL**
42nd St (between Park and Lexington aves)
Tel. 935-3960
Guided tour every Wed. at 12.30pm.
Wait in front of the Chemical Bank, in the Main Concourse ▲ 236.

**INTREPID SEA-AIR-SPACE MUSEUM**
Pier 86, 12th Ave and W. 46th St
Tel. 245-0072
Open daily 10am–5pm
Closed Mon.–Tue. in winter
The chance to see one of the famous aircraft carriers of World War Two, a submarine, a lightship and a destroyer ▲ 257.

**JACOB K. JAVITS CONVENTION CENTER**
655 W. 34th St
Tel. 216-2000
Opening times depend on the exhibitions ▲ 248.

**MADISON SQUARE GARDEN**
7th Ave (between W. 31st and W. 33rd sts)
Tel. 465-6741
Open daily
Vast sports and entertainment complex. Home to the NHL's New York Penguins and NBA's New York Knicks. Also a forum for other sports events, shows and concerts. Guided tours of the auditorium and behind the scenes are available.
▲ 249

**NEW YORK PUBLIC LIBRARY**
5th Ave and 42nd St
Tel. 930-0831
Open Tue., Wed. 11am–6pm; Mon., Thur.–Sat. 10am–6pm
New York City's main reference library. Guided tours at 11am and 2pm (tel. 930-0555)
▲ 252.

**NEW YORK SKYRIDE**
In the Empire State Building
Tel. 279-9777
Open 10am–10pm
Air tours of New York with the aid of a flight simulator.

**PIERPONT MORGAN LIBRARY**
29 E. 36th St
Tel. 685-0610
Open Tue.–Fri. 10.30am–5pm, Sat. 10.30am–6pm, Sun. noon–6pm. Closed Mon., public holidays.

Rare books (including 3 Gutenberg Bibles), manuscripts from the Middle Ages and the Renaissance, drawings, pictures, etc. Also mounts temporary exhibitions ▲ 241.

**UNITED NATIONS**
1st Ave and 46th St
Tel. 963-7713
Open daily,
9.15am–4.45pm
*Headquarters of the United Nations Organization.
Guided tours in many languages. Cafeteria, gifts stores, post office ▲ 264.*

**WHITNEY MIDTOWN**
120 Park Ave
and 42nd St
(Philip Morris Building)
Tel. 878-2550
Open Mon.–Fri.
11am–6pm (Thur. until 7.30pm)
Closed Sat., Sun.
*Branch of the Whitney Museum of American Art ▲ 240.*

## RESTAURANTS

**"44"**
44 W. 44th St
(Royalton Hotel)
Tel. 944-8844
Open daily
*Theatrical décor designed by Philip Stark for this branch of the Condé Nast publishing house. Reservation essential. Brunch.*

**AMBASSADOR GRILL**
1 United Nations Plaza
(U.N. Plaza Park Hyatt Hotel)
Tel. 702-5014
Open daily
*American grill cuisine.*

**BARBETTA**
321 W. 46th St
Tel. 246-9171
*The oldest family-owned and operated Italian restaurant in New York. A family concern renowned for its risotto and pasta dishes. Superb garden.*

**BECCO**
355 W. 46th St
Tel. 397-7597
*A trattoria where the menu changes everyday.*

**CHEZ JOSÉPHINE**
414 W. 42nd St
Tel. 594-1925
Open in the evening.
Closed Sun.
*Dedicated to Josephine Baker and Paris in the 20's. The charm of this restaurant is definitely the décor, the atmosphere and the music rather than the food.*

**IPANEMA**
13 W. 46th St
Tel. 730-5848
*Delicious Brazilian cuisine at low prices.*

**JEZEBEL**
630 9th Ave
Tel. 582-1045
Open only in the evenings.
Closed Sun.
*Friendly atmosphere and cheerful surroundings. Genuine food for the soul.*

**JOE ALLEN**
326 W. 46th St
Tel. 581-6464
Open daily
*For those who like a quick snack before or after the theater. Hamburgers and*
spareribs, often served by young actors.

**ORSO**
322 W. 46th St
Tel. 489-7212
Open daily
*The most popular restaurant in the theater district. Reservation essential.*

**OYSTER BAR**
Grand Central Terminal,
Lower Level
Tel. 490-6650
Open 11.30am–9.30pm.
Closed Sat. and Sun.
*Eye-catching surroundings, fresh fish and seafood.*

**PALM**
837 2nd Ave
Tel. 687-2953
Open lunchtime and evenings. Closed Sat. lunchtime, Sun.
*This quintessential steakhouse dates from the 1920's. Huge slabs of meat, lobster, fried onion rings and cheesecake.
Reservations needed for parties of more than four.*

**SPARKS STEAK HOUSE**
210 E. 46th St
Tel. 687-4855
Closed Sat. lunchtime, Sun.
*A restaurant for connoisseurs and lovers of fine wines. New York-style cheesecake is a specialty.*

## ACCOMMODATION

**THE ALGONQUIN HOTEL***
59 W. 44th St
Tel. 840-6800
Fax 944-1419
A host of writers have stayed here, assuring its fame. The worlds of literature and publishing still use this hotel. Restored in 1990. Small rooms and Edwardian décor ▲ 252.

**THE BEST WESTERN MANHATTAN**
17 W. 32nd St
Tel. 736-1600
or 1-800-551-2303
Fax 563-4007
*Simply decorated rooms in a lively neighborhood packed with restaurants and Korean wholesalers. Beauty salon, travel agency, and Japanese restaurant.*

**THE CARLTON***
22 E. 29th St
Tel. 532-4100
or 1-800-542-1502
Fax 889-8683
*A nice family hotel, with spacious rooms. Recently redecorated. The lobby is an attractive meeting place. Well-located for the big department stores.*

**COMFORT INN, MURRAY HILL****
42 W. 35th St
Tel. 947-0200
or 1-800-228-5150
Fax 594 3047
*Ongoing renovations. Continental breakfast.*

**DORAL PARK AVE ****
70 Park Ave
Tel. 687-7050
or 1-800-22-DORAL
Fax 808-9029
*A chic hotel with an intimate, secluded atmosphere. Marble bathrooms and Scandinavian-style furniture.*

### GRAND HYATT***
42nd St (Park Ave and Grand Central Terminal)
Tel. 883-1234
or 1-800-833-1234
Fax 697-3772
*Thirty-four stories sheathed in black glass in one of the busiest areas of Manhattan. Frequented by the business community. 1,407 rooms, functional but somewhat lacking in character.*

### HERALD SQUARE HOTEL*
19 W. 31st St
Tel. 279-4017 or 1-800-727-1888
Fax 643-9208
*Comfortable, with a friendly atmosphere. Cosmopolitan clientèle.*

### HOLIDAY INN, CROWNE PLAZA**
1605 Broadway (49th St)
Tel. 977-4000
or 1-800-2 CROWNE
Fax 333-7393
*Traditional rooms, some with an unbeatable view of Times Square. Swimming pool.*

### HOTEL INTER-CONTINENTAL
111 E. 48th St
Tel. 755-5900
Fax 644-0079
*Just been renovated. Good facilities for people with disabilities. Sumptuous lobby with plush sofas and leather armchairs.*

### HOTEL IROQUOIS*
49 W. 44th St
Tel. 840-3080
or 1-800-332-7220
Fax 398-1754
*Plain and simple. Suites with kitchenettes.*

### HOTEL MANSFIELD*
12 W. 44th St
Tel. 944-6050
or 1-800-255-5167
Fax 764-4477
*W.B. Yeats once lived in this building. Good for students.*

### MARRIOTT EAST SIDE
525 Lexington Ave (49th St)
Tel. 755-4000
Fax 751-3440
*Sedate, functional rooms. Frequented by the business community.* ▲ 261

### MARRIOTT MARQUIS ***
1535 Broadway
Tel. 398-1900
or 1-800-228-9290
Fax 704-8930
*Spacious rooms. Always a hive of activity. The best hotel for conferences in the Times Square area.*

### MILLENNIUM BROADWAY****
145 W. 44th St
Tel. 768-4400
or 1-800-622-5569
Fax 768-0847
*Small but stylish rooms. Jacuzzi in presidential suites.*

### MORGANS****
237 Madison Ave
Tel. 686-0300
or 1-800-334-3408
Fax 779-8352
*An elegant hotel with no sign outside. It can be recognized by the arched entrance flanked by impressive columns and a doorman standing on duty. A favorite with the world of show-business*

### NEW YORK'S HOTEL PENNSYLVANIA**
7th Ave and 33rd St
Tel. 736-5000
or 1-800-736000
Fax 502-8799
*An old hotel, with an imposing, rather uninviting appearance, frequented by overseas tourists.*

### PARAMOUNT***
235 W. 46 St
Tel. 764-5500
or 1-800-225-7474
Fax 575-4892

*In the heart of the Theater District, an extraordinary mixture: a Renaissance-style building dating from the 1930's, redesigned by Philip Stark. Average-sized rooms.*

### RENAISSANCE NEW YORK HOTEL***
714 7th Ave (47th St)
Tel. 765-7676
Fax 765-1962
*Unbeatable view of Times Square from the restaurant in this small, new tower of gleaming black glass. The huge bay windows give you the impression of floating in space.*

### ROYALTON****
44 W. 44th St (between 5th and 6th avenues)
Tel. 869-4400
or 1-800-635-9013
Fax 869-8965

*A fashionable hotel whose theatrical interior design is again the work of Philip Stark: cobalt blue carpeting, polished green granite, steel. Same management as the Morgan and Paramount hotels* ▲ 252.

### SHELBURNE MURRAY HILL***
303 Lexington Ave
Tel. 689-5200
or 1-800-ME-SUITE
Fax 779-7068

*Large comfortable rooms with kitchens. Hotel's rooftop garden open for reservations in summer. An affordable priced base for family holidays in an attractive and peaceful district.*

### SOUTHGATE TOWER***
371 7th Ave
Tel. 563-1800
or 1-800-ME-SUITE
Fax 643-8028
*Simply decorated suites, some with sofa-beds. Clientele primarily from the business community.*

### TUDOR HOTEL***
304 E. 42nd St
Tel. 986-8800
or 1-800-TRY-TUDOR
Fax 986-1758
*A bright, red-brick comfortable hotel surrounded by the bedlam of 42nd Street. Fairly simple rooms, but comfortable. Traditional*

30. DORAL PARK AVENUE HOTEL
29. MORGANS
30. SHELBURNE MURRAY HILL
31. COMFORT INN MURRAY HILL
32. HERALD SQUARE HOTEL
33. THE CARLTON

*British interior and afternoon tea is served* ▲ 264.

## UNITED NATIONS PLAZA PARK HYATT HOTEL★★★★

1 United Nations Plaza
Tel. 758-1234
or 1-800-228-9000
Fax 702-5051
*Many diplomats stay here. Huge rooms, most have a view of the New York skyline. Health and fitness center with indoor swimming pool, tennis, massage parlor.*

## SHOPPING

### BROOKS BROTHERS
346 Madison Ave
(44th St)
Tel. 682-8800
*Men's fashions. The place to go for shirts.*

### THE COMPLEAT STRATEGIST
11 E. 33rd St
Tel. 685-3880
*All kinds of games.*

### EXPRESS
7 W. 34th St
Tel. 629-6538
*Women's casual wear. Very popular chain with outlets all over the city.*

### LOCKER
45 W. 34th St
Tel. 971-9449
*Sports goods. Numerous other branches.*

### GAP
Broadway and 34th St
Tel. 643-8960
*Classic sportswear for children and adults. Outlets of this chain can be found all over the city.*

### HAGSTROM MAP AND TRAVEL CENTER
57 W. 43rd St
Tel. 398-1222
*Map and travel guide specialists.*

### HARVEY ELECTRONICS
2 W. 45th St
Tel. 575-5000
*Audio, video, home entertainment equipment. From the inexpensive to top of the line.*

### J.J. HAT CENTER
310 5th Ave
and 32nd St
Tel. 239-4368
*From stetsons to top hats, every type of hat for men and for women.*

### J. PRESS
7 E. 44th St
Tel. 687-7642
*Men's fashions.*

### LORD AND TAYLOR
424 5th Ave (40th St)
Tel. 391-3344
*Department store mainly for women's fashions.*

### LOUIS TANNEN
24 W. 25th St (2nd floor)
Tel. 929-4500
*For sixty-one years this has been the largest store for magicians' supplies for children, enthusiasts and professionals.*

### MACY'S
151 W. 34th St
Tel. 695-4400
*"The world's largest store".*

### MANNY'S MUSICAL INSTRUMENTS & ACCESSORIES
156 W. 48th St
Tel. 819-0576
*A comprehensive range of musical instruments. The walls are lined with photos of stars who have bought their instruments here.*

### PAUL STUART
Madison Ave and
45th St
Tel. 682-0320
*Clothes and accessories for men and women.*

### SAM GOODY
666 3rd Ave (46th St)
Tel. 986-8480
*Wide range of cassettes, records, CDs. Specialist chain of stores.*

### STERN'S
899 Ave of the Americas
Tel. 244-6060
*Department store. Less chic and less expensive than the others.*

### TOYS R US
1293 Broadway
and 34th St
Tel. 594-8697
*Store selling a vast assortment of children's toys and video games.*

### WILLOUGHBY'S
136 W. 32nd St
Tel. 564-1600
*Video and photography equipment.*

### WORTH AND WORTH
331 Madison Ave
(43rd St)
Tel. 867-6058
*The number-one men's hat shop since 1918.*

## ROCKEFELLER CENTER

## CULTURE

### AMERICAN CRAFT MUSEUM
40 W. 53rd St
Tel. 956-3535
Open Wed.–Sun.
10am–5pm, Tue.
10am–8pm. Closed
Mon.
*Arts and crafts from 1900 to the present day: glassware, pottery, metalwork, etc.*

### CARNEGIE HALL
152 W. 57th St (7th Ave)
Tel. 247-7800
Open Mon., Tue., Thur., and Fri 11am–4.30pm
CONCERT HALLS
Guided tours (Mon., Tue., Fri.) at 11.30am, 2pm and 3pm
▲ 301

### CENTRAL SYNAGOGUE
123 E. 55th St
Tel. 838-5122
Open Mon.–Thur. noon–2pm.

### LINCOLN CENTER
Broadway and 65th St
Tel. 875-5400
Guided tours daily,
10am–5pm. Call in advance to make reservations
(Tel. 875-5350)
*An enormous cultural center which houses a library and various auditoria for dance performances, opera, concerts and drama.*
ALICE TULLY HALL
Tel. 875-5050
AVERY FISHER HALL
Tel. 875-5030
JUILLIARD THEATER
Tel. 799-5000
LIBRARY AND MUSEUM OF THE PERFORMING ARTS
40 Lincoln Center Plaza
Tel. 870-1600

METROPOLITAN OPERA
HOUSE
Tel. 362-6000
Backstage tours, Mon.,
Tue., Thur., Fri. 3.45pm,
Sat. 10am
Telephone reservations
(769-7020)
NEW YORK STATE
THEATER
Tel. 870-5570
▲ 305

**MUSEUM OF THE
AMERICAN PIANO**
211 W. 58th St
Tel. 246-4646
*Open for temporary
exhibitions.*

**MUSEUM OF MODERN
ART (MOMA)**
11 W. 53rd St
Tel. 708-9480
Open Sat.–Tue.
11am–6pm
Open Thur.–Fri.
noon–8.30pm
Closed Wed.
*One of the largest
collection of modern art
in the world. Permanent
and temporary
exhibitions ▲ 290.*

**MUSEUM OF
TELEVISION
AND RADIO**
25 W. 52nd St
Tel. 621-6600
Open Tue., Wed.
Fri.–Sun. noon–6pm,
Thur. noon–8pm
*Extensive archives
containing recordings
of television and radio
broadcasts.*

**RADIO CITY
MUSIC HALL**
Ave of the Americas
(50th St)
Tel. 632-4041
*Tours of the auditorium
and backstage
Mon.–Sat. 10am–5pm,
Sun. 11am–5pm*

**ROCKEFELLER CENTER**
5th and 6th aves,
47th and 52nd sts
Tel. 632-3975
NBC STUDIOS
6th Ave (between 49th
and 50th sts)
Tel. 664-4000
Closed public holidays.
*Daily tours from
9.30am–5pm, Sun.
4.45pm ▲ 274*

**ST BARTHOLOMEW'S
CHURCH**
109 E. 50th St
Tel. 751-1616
Open Mon.–Fri. 9am–
6pm, Sat. 8am–3pm
▲ 285

**ST PATRICK'S
CATHEDRAL**
5th Ave (50th St)
Tel. 753-2261
Open daily
8.30am–8.45pm
*New York's Roman
Catholic cathedral*
▲ 282.

**ST THOMAS
EPISCOPAL CHURCH**
1 W. 53rd St
Tel. 757-7013
Open daily 9am–5.30pm
▲ 288.

**SONY**
550 Madison Ave
(between 55th and
56th sts)
Tel. 833-8830
ATRIUM: open
7am–11pm
SONY STORE: open
Mon.–Sat. 10am–7pm,
Sun. noon–6pm
SONY WONDER
TECHNOLOGY LAB:
entrance free
Tel. 833-8100
Open Tue.–Sat.
10am–6pm, Sun.
noon–6pm
*New technology
exhibitions ▲ 289.*

**URBAN CENTER**
457 Madison and
51st St
Tel. 935-3960
*Organizes thematic
tours of the city (history
and architecture). Its
bookstore stocks many
works on architecture.
(Tel. 935-3595).*

## GALLERIES

**GALERIE ST ETIENNE**
24 W. 57th St (8th floor)
Tel. 245-6734
*Specializes in historical
documents (letters from
Rilke, Einstein,
Roosevelt) and high-
quality modern painters
(Klimt, Schiele, etc.).*

**JOSEPH HELMAN
GALLERY**
20 W. 57th St (2nd floor)
Tel. 245-2888
Open Mon.–Fri.
10am–6pm
*Specialist in American
and European
contemporary art.*

**MARIAN GOODMAN
GALLERY**
24 W. 57th St (4th floor)
Tel. 977-7160
Open Mon.–Sat.
10am–5.30pm
*All the key figures in the
American and European
conceptual movement.*

**MARLBOROUGH
GALLERY**
40 W. 57th St (2nd floor)
Tel. 541-4900
Open Mon.–Sat.
10am–5.30pm
*Exhibits painters,
sculptors and
photographers: Henry
Moore, Francis Bacon,
Brassaï. The terrace
with its sculptures is
worth seeing.*

**MARY BOONE GALLERY**
745 Fifth Ave (58th St)
Tel. 752-2929
Open Tue.–Sat.
10am–6pm
*Mary Boone launched
the most outstanding
artists of the 1980's:
Eric Fischl, David Salle,
Julian Schnabel . . .*

**PACE WILDENSTEIN
GALLERY**
32 E. 57th St (4th floor)
Tel. 421-3292
Open Tue.–Fri.
9.30am–10pm,
Sat. 10am–6pm
*Sections devoted to
African art as well as to
ancient and modern
graphic art. The gallery
also has a branch on
Washington Square.*
▲ 406.

1. YMCA, WEST SIDE
2. HARRY CIPRIANI
3. SAN DOMENICO
4. THE ESSEX HOUSE HOTEL NIKKO NEW YORK
5. THE RITZ-CARLTON
6. SAINT MORITZ ON THE PARK
7. MICKEY MANTLE'S
8. THE PARK LANE
9. THE PLAZA
10. PETROSSIAN
11. HELMSLEY WINDSOR
12. THE WYNDHAM
13. DAWAT
14. FELIDIA
15. HARD ROCK CAFÉ

### PACE WILDENSTEIN/ MACGILL GALLERY

32 E. 57th St (9th floor)
Tel. 759-7999
Open Tue.–Fri.
9.30am–5.30pm
and Sat. 10am–6pm
in winter; Mon.–Thur.
9.30am–5.30pm and Fri.
9.30am–4pm in
summer.
*The gallery exhibits some of the leading contemporary photographers.*

### ROBERT MILLER GALLERY

41 E. 57th St (3rd floor)
Tel. 980-5454
Open Tue.–Sat.
10am–6pm; Mon.–Fri.
10am–6pm in summer
*A gallery with a "Downtown" feel, despite its location. Contemporary painters, sculptors and photographers.*

### SIDNEY JANIS GALLERY

110 W. 57th St
(6th floor)
Tel. 586-0110
Open Tue.–Sat.
10am–5.30pm
*Founded in 1948. The gallery has exhibited Mondrian, Brancusi, Giacometti, Léger and Albers in the past. It was the first to show the Abstract Expressionists in the 1950's.*

### ZABRISKIE GALLERY

41 E. 57th St (4th floor)
Tel. 752-1223
Open Tue.–Sat.
10am–5.30pm,
Sept.–May; Mon.–Fri.
10am–5.30pm,
June–Aug.

*This gallery has made a name for itself primarily as a showcase for photography: old prints or works by artists such as Man Ray and Nicolas Nixon.*

### RESTAURANTS

### "21" CLUB

21 W. 52nd St
Tel. 582-7200
Closed Sat. lunchtime in summer, Sun.
*Formerly a speakeasy. Renowned, among other things, for its chicken hash.*
▲ 287

### AL BUSTAN

827 3rd Ave
Tel. 759-8439
Open daily
*Excellent Lebanese cuisine.*

### AQUAVIT

13 W. 54th St
Tel. 307-7311
Open lunchtime and evenings. Closed Sat. brunch, Sun.
*Scandinavian cuisine. Sample a mouthwatering array of herring, salmon and venison dishes, downstairs near a waterfall.*

### LE BERNARDIN

155 W. 51st St
Tel. 489-1515
Closed Sat. lunchtime, Sun.
*Excellent French restaurant specializing primarily in fish and seafood dishes under the direction of its expert new chef, Eric Ripert.*

### BICE

7 E. 54th St
Tel. 688-1999
Open daily
*Lively trattoria, serving very varied cuisine. Expensive.*

### LA CARAVELLE

33 W. 55th St
Tel. 586-4252
Closed Sat. lunchtime, Sun.
*Romantic décor and gastronomic delights.*

### CARNEGIE DELI

854 7th Ave
Tel. 757-2245
Open daily
*Feast on enormous sandwiches, frankfurters, hamburgers and french fries. No credit cards.*

### LE CIRQUE

455 Madison Ave
(in New York Palace Hotel)
Tel. 888-7000
Closed Sun.
*A veritable institution. French chef Sylvain Poray continues to concoct imaginative and elegant dishes: pappardelle with foie gras, veal kidneys, curry with halibut. Superb desserts. This celebrated restaurant is due to reopen in a larger space in January 1997 and promises to be better than ever. Lunchtime menu: $30.*

### LE COLONIAL

149 E. 57th St
Tel. 752-0808
*French-Vietnamese cuisine: ravioli pancakes, spicy beef salad, shrimp beansprout roll.*

### DAWAT

210 E. 58th St
Tel. 355-7555
Closed Sun. lunchtime
*The best Indian restaurant in New York.*

### FELIDIA

243 E. 58th St
Tel. 753-1479
Closed Sat. lunchtime and Sun.
*The wood-paneled, flower-filled dining room is housed in a brownstone building. Refined, imaginative and mouth-watering dishes from Northern Italy's Trieste.*

### THE FOUR SEASONS

99 E. 52nd St
(Seagram Building)
Tel. 754-9494
Closed Sat. lunchtime and Sun.
*The Grill Room is good for business lunches, the Pool Room is more romantic.*

### LA GRENOUILLE

3 E. 52nd St
Tel. 752-1495
Closed Sun., Mon.and the end of July.
*Famous for the fresh floral arrangements and French haute cuisine.*

### HARD ROCK CAFÉ

221 W. 57th St
Tel. 459-9320
Open daily
*Packed with teenagers who come as much for the for the boisterous atmosphere and the loud music as for the sandwiches and hamburgers, which are very tasty nonetheless. No reservations.*

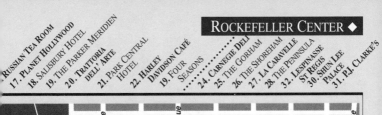

16. RUSSIAN TEA ROOM
17. PLANET HOLLYWOOD
18. SALISBURY HOTEL
19. THE PARKER MERIDIEN
20. TRATTORIA DELL'ARTE
21. PARK CENTRAL HOTEL
22. HARLEY DAVIDSON CAFÉ
19. FOUR SEASONS
24. CARNEGIE DELI
25. THE GORHAM
26. THE SHOREHAM
27. LA CARAVELLE
28. THE PENINSULA
32. LESPINASSE
ST REGIS
30. SHUN LEE PALACE
31. P.J. CLARKE'S

ROCKEFELLER CENTER ◆

## HARLEY DAVIDSON CAFÉ
1370 Ave of the Americas and 56th St
Tel. 245-6000
Open daily
*Have a meal or a drink here merely to sample the atmosphere and the décor: Harley Davidsons in photos. Gift store.*

## HARRY CIPRIANI
781 5th Ave (Sherry-Netherland Hotel)
Tel. 753-5566
Open daily
*Branch of Venice's legendary Harry's Bar. Simple dishes (risotto prima-vera) at exorbitant prices. Stick to set menu.*

## JEKYLL & HYDE
1409 Ave of the Americans (between 57th and 58th sts)
Tel. 255-5388
*An enormous restaurant with a lively décor (smoke machines, coffins hanging from the ceiling). Special effects somewhat reminiscent of Disneyland. Good American food, large portions and 250 types of beer.*

## LESPINASSE
2 E. 55th St
(St Regis Hotel)
Tel. 339-6719

*This impressive Louis XV dining room is ideal for business lunches and dinners. The Franco-Asian cuisine is delicate and inventive.*

## LUTÈCE
249 E. 50th St
Tel. 752-2225

Closed Sun.
*Bastion of the great tradition of French cuisine . Chef Eberhard Müller mixes traditional with innovation.*

## MICKEY MANTLE'S
42 Central Park South
Tel. 688-7777
Open daily
*The restaurant of the celebrated baseball player for the Yankees, Micky mantle. Children seem to like it here; you can devour enormous hamburgers, french fries and salads while watching a huge television screen.*

## IL NIDO
251 E. 53rd St
Tel. 753-8450
Closed Sun.
*Cuisine from central and northern Italy: ravioli with truffles, chicken à la toscana with pine kernels and mint, game, zabaglione with raspberries.*

## PETROSSIAN
182 W. 58th St
Tel. 245-2214
*This restaurant's claim to fame is its caviar, foie gras and smoked salmon (which are also on sale to take away). Reasonably priced lunch menus.*

## P.J. CLARKE'S
915 3rd Ave and 55th St
Tel. 759-1650
*Saloon with a somewhat faded reputation.*

## PLANET HOLLYWOOD
140 W. 57th St
Tel. 333-7827
Open daily
*Mediocre fast-food but an impressive décor inspired by the movies.*
▲ 302

## RAINBOW ROOM
30 Rockefeller Plaza (65th cloor)
Tel. 632-5000
Open in the evening.
*This sky-high restaurant serves classic dishes with a passing nod to "nouvelle cuisine".*
▲ 277

## REMI
145 W. 53rd St
Tel. 581-4242
Closed Sat. lunchtime, Sun. lunchtime
*The cuisine and the décor of this restaurant re-create a piece of Venice in the middle of New York.*

## ROYAL CANADIAN PANCAKE HOUSE
1004 2nd Ave
Tel. 980-4131
Open daily
*Despite a stern décor, a hive of cheerful activity*

*with more than sixty types of huge pancakes and waffles on the menu: children love it. Brunch. No alcohol.*

## RUSSIAN TEA ROOM
150 W. 57th St
Tel. 265-0947
*This New York institution is currently closed for renovations. Due to reopen in fall 1997.*
▲ 301

## SAN DOMENICO
240 Central Park South
Tel. 265-5959
Closed Sat. and Sun. lunchtimes
*Luxurious décor. Exquisite Bolognese cuisine. Each dish is an astonishing combination of flavors.*

## SHUN LEE PALACE
155 E. 55th St
Tel. 371-8844
Open daily
*The wonderful Cantonese, Mandarin and Szechwan dishes make up for the fact that you are being jostled on all sides as you eat.*

## SMITH & WOLLENSKY
201 E. 49th St
Tel. 753-1530
*Typical New York fare (steaks, lobster). A wide selection of fine wines.*

## SUSHISAY
38 E. 51st St
Tel. 755-1780
*One of the best Japanese restaurants in New York: fresh fish, pleasant décor and impeccable service.*

417

**TRATTORIA DELL'ARTE**
900 7th Ave (between
56th and 57th sts)
Tel. 245-9800
Open daily
*Somewhere to go before
and after a concert at
Carnegie Hall. Its
famous décor is more
interesting than the
cuisine.*
▲ 301

**VONG**
200 E. 54th St
Tel. 486-9592
Closed Sat. and Sun.
lunchtimes
*Very popular French-
Thai restaurant.*

**ZARELA**
953 2nd Ave
Tel. 644-6740
Closed Sat. and Sun.
lunchtime
*Adventurous Mexican
cuisine in pleasant
surroundings.*

## ACCOMMODATION

**BEEKMAN TOWER***
3 Mitchell Pl.
Tel. 355-7300
or 1-800-ME-SUITE
Fax 753-9366
*Secretarial services,
Fax and other
equipment are available
for use by guests. Suites
with self-catering
facilities are available for
families. Fixed monthly
rates.*

**BOX TREE****
250 E. 49th St
Tel. 593-9810
Fax 308-3899
*Two brownstones dating
from the 1840's and
crammed to overflowing
with antiques. Suites with
individual styles of
decoration – by turns,
English, Egyptian,
Japanese or Chinese.
Guests may have the
use of the hotel's
chauffeur-driven
Rolls-Royces and
Bentleys. Credit of
$100 for the
restaurant included in
the price of the room.
American Express only.
No children under 10.*

**DOUBLE TREE GUEST
SUITES HOTEL**
1568 Broadway
Tel. 719-1600
or 1-800-222-8733
Fax 921-5212
*Well equipped for
business people and
practical for families with
two-room suites fitted
with self-catering
facilities. Its "Kid's Club"
organizes activities for
children.*

**THE ESSEX HOUSE
HOTEL NIKKO
NEW YORK***
160 Central Park South
Tel. 247-0300
or 1-800-NIKKO-US
Fax 315-1839
*Elegant Art Deco
building opposite*

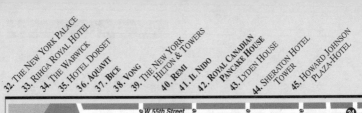

*Central Park.elements.
Luxurious rooms, some
with a view over the
park. Business center.
Transportation to Wall
Street provided. Two
good restaurants.* ▲ 303

**THE FOUR SEASONS**
57 E. 57th St
Tel. 758-5700
Fax 758-5711
*Designed by I.M. Pei
and opened in June
1993, this is the tallest
hotel in New York, with
52 floors, affording
breathtaking views over
the city. Expensive.*

**THE GORHAM***
136 W. 55th St
Tel. 245-1800
or 1-800-735-0710
Fax 582-8332
*Art Deco style. An
intimate and congenial
atmosphere.*

**HELMSLEY
MIDDLETOWNE***
148 E. 48th St
Tel. 755-3000
or 1-800-221-4982
Fax 832-0261
*Recently renovated.
Quiet. Rooms are
simple, fairly large,
some with a terrace.
This hotel is a favorite
among business
travelers.*

**HELMSLEY
WINDSOR***
100 W. 58th St
Tel. 265-2100
                    or 1-800-143-
                              2157

Fax 315-0371
*Business clientele:
special rates for
companies.*

**HOLIDAY INN,
CROWNE PLAZA***
1605 Broadway
Tel. 977-4000
or 1-800-243-NYNY
*Gleaming public
lounges with floor
lighting. A superb
view of Times Square
from some of the
rooms. Translation
service. Large
swimming pool.*

**HOTEL BEVERLY***
125 E. 50th St
Tel. 753-2700
or 1-800-223-0945
Fax 759-7300
*Bright rooms, simple
décor, with kitchenettes.*

**HOTEL DORSET***
30 W. 54th St
Tel. 247-7300
or 1-800-227-2348
Fax 581-0153
*Often full, because
some guests live there
all year round. Large,
bright rooms.
Competitive special
rates.*

**HOTEL EDISON****
228 W. 47th St
Tel. 840-5000
Fax 51-6868
*Art Deco-style building.
Big rooms decorated in
pastel colors.*

**HOTEL ELYSEE***
60 E. 54th St
Tel. 753-1066
Fax 980-9278
*Small, but luxurious
hotel. Recently
renovated. Popular
restaurant.*

46. NOVOTEL NEW YORK
47. "21" CLUB
48. OMNI BERKSHIRE PLACE
49. THE FOUR SEASONS
50. LE BERNARDIN
51. LOEWS NEW YORK
52. PICKWICK ARMS HOTEL
53. HOTEL BEVERLY
54. SAN CARLOS HOTEL
55. PLAZA 50
56. AL BUSTAN
57. LUTÈCE
58. ZARELA
59. THE WALDORF ASTORIA & WALDORF TOWERS
60. SMITH & WOLLENSKY
61. BOX TREE
62. BEEKMAN TOWER
63. HOLIDAY INN CROWNE PLAZA
64. RAINBOW ROOM

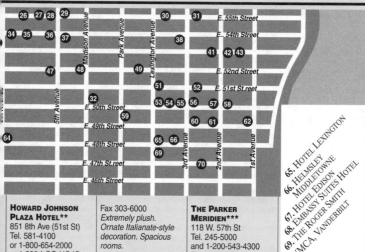

**HOWARD JOHNSON PLAZA HOTEL\*\***
851 8th Ave (51st St)
Tel. 581-4100
or 1-800-654-2000
or 1-800-I-GO-HOJO
Fax 974-7502
*Cleaner and safer than many other budget hotels in New York. In a rather run-down neighborhood.*

**INN ON 57TH ST\*\***
440 W. 57th St
Tel. 581-8100
or 1-800-231-0405
Fax 581-7733
*Very simple rooms in an industrial-style building, originally built to be a nursing home.*

**LOEWS NEW YORK\*\*\***
569 Lexington Ave
Tel. 752-7000
or 1-800-23-LOEWS
Fax 758-6311
*Famous for its bar/ restaurant in the lobby.*

**LYDEN HOUSE\*\*\***
320 E. 53rd St
Tel. 888-6070
Fax 935-7690
*Small hotel in a tree-lined street.*

**THE NEW YORK HILTON & TOWERS\*\*\***
1335 Ave of the Americas
Tel. 586-7000
or 1-800-HILTONS
Fax 261-5946
*Unequalled for conferences and meetings. Facilities for the disabled.*

**THE NEW YORK PALACE HOTEL\*\*\*\***
455 Madison Ave
Tel. 888-7000
or 1-800-657-2522
Fax 303-6000
*Extremely plush. Ornate Italianate-style decoration. Spacious rooms.*

**NOVOTEL NEW YORK\*\*\***
226 W. 52nd St
Tel. 315-0100
or 1-800-221-4542
Fax 765-5369
*Perfectly situated for theatergoers. Large, clean, quiet rooms, some with a view over the Hudson River. Breakfast included.*

**OMNI BERKSHIRE PLACE\*\*\***
21 E. 52nd St
Tel. 753-5800
or 1-800-843-6664
Fax 754-5020
*Atrium flooded with daylight, friendly atmosphere.*

**PARK CENTRAL HOTEL\*\*\***
870 7th Ave
Tel. 247-8000
or 1-800-843-6664
Fax 484-3374.
*For the business community and groups.*

**THE PARK LANE HELMSLEY HOTEL\*\*\*\***
36 Central Park South
Tel. 371-4000
or 1-800-221-4982
Fax 521-6666
*Breathtaking view of Central Park from the upper floors of this 46-story hotel. Bright and airy rooms. Pleasant hotel restaurant, and the celebrated Harry's Bar. Special weekend rates.*

**THE PARKER MERIDIEN\*\*\***
118 W. 57th St
Tel. 245-5000
and 1-200-543-4300
Fax 307-1776
*Many rooms available with self-catering facilities. View of the New York skyline from the swimming pool on the top floor.* ▲ 302

**THE PENINSULA\*\*\*\*\***
700 5th Ave
Tel. 247-2200
Fax 903-3949
*Justly proud of its "oriental-style" hospitality. Rooms decorated in Art Nouveau style. View of Midtown from the rooftop bar.*

**PICKWICK ARMS HOTEL\***
230 E. 51st St
Tel. 355-0300
or 1-800-PICKWIK
Fax 755-5029
*Very competitive prices for people traveling alone. Small, gloomy rooms.*

**THE PLAZA\*\*\*\***
5th Ave (Central Park South)
Tel. 759-3000
or 1-800-228-3000
Fax 527-4727
*A highly renowned hotel, the lobby of which is always thronged with people. Sumptuous rooms with marble bathrooms and European-style décor. The afternoon teas and morning brunches are superb. More formal meals are available in the Oak and Edwardian rooms. Polynesian lounge-bar: the Trader Vic's* ▲ 297.

**PLAZA 50 SUITE HOTEL\*\*\***
155 E. 50th St
Tel. 751-5710
or 1-800-ME-SUITE
Fax 753-1468
*Suites available with self-catering facilities. Lacking in charm but functional and good location. Special fixed monthly rates negotiable.*

**RIHGA ROYAL HOTEL\*\*\*\***
151 W. 54th St (between 6th and 7th aves)
Tel. 307-5000
or 1-800-937-5454
Fax 765-6530
*Brand new 54-story building. Luxurious suites (the "Grand" suites have saunas and jacuzzis). Panoramic view of skyscrapers from the restaurant and many of the rooms.*

**THE RITZ-CARLTON\*\*\*\***
112 Central Park South
Tel. 757-1900
Fax 757-9620
*Recently renovated in the style of an English-club with marble and elegant Tuscany colors. Fitness center, and fine Italian restaurant. Complimentary shuttle service to Wall Street.*

419

**THE ROGER SMITH\*\*\***
501 Lexington Ave
(47th St)
Tel. 755-1400
or 1-800-445-0277
Fax 758-4000
*Both more fashionable
and more comfortable
than its neighbors the
Waldorf, the Lexington
or the Intercontinental.
Piano-bar decorated
with comic strips.*

**ST MORITZ ON
CENTRAL PARK\*\*\***
50 Central Park South
Tel. 755-5800
Fax 752-5097
*A lively hotel opened in
1932. European-style
décor. Lovely suites with
a view of Central Park.
Café on the terrace.
On the first floor is
Rumplemeyer's, famous
for its ice cream and
French toasts.*

**ST REGIS\*\*\*\*\***
2 E. 55th St
Tel. 753-4500
Fax 787-3447
*One of the city's most
sumptuous hotels, in a
building dating from
1904, built by John
Jacob Astor and
restored at great cost.
Financial information
service and secretarial
facilities available.
Major-domo attached to
each floor.* ▲ 288

**SALISBURY HOTEL\*\***
123 W. 57th St
Tel. 246-1300
or 1-800-223-0680
Fax 977-7752
*Sturdy furniture in old
English style. Rooms
available with
kitchenettes.*

**SAN CARLOS HOTEL\*\*\***
150 E. 50th St
Tel. 755-1800
or 1-800-722-2012
Fax 688-9778
*Warm friendly welcome.
Rooms with fully fitted
kitchens. Special rates
for families are often
available. No restaurant.*

**SHERATON HOTEL
TOWER AND
SHERATON
MANHATTAN\*\*\***
811 and 790 7th Ave
(between 52nd and
53rd sts)
Tel. 581-1000
or 1-800-223-6550
Fax 262-4410

*The two hotels, located
opposite each other,
share the same
management. Specialize
in business clientele,
conferences.*

**THE SHOREHAM\*\***
33 W. 55th St
Tel. 247-6700
or 1-800-553-3347
Fax 765-9741
*Small hotel, recently
completely redecorated
in a refined and modern
style. Rooms have
refrigerators and video
players. Good location.*

**THE WALDORF-
ASTORIA & WALDORF
TOWERS\*\*\*\***
301 Park Ave (between
49th and 50th sts)
Tel. 355-3000
or 1-800-WALDORF
Fax 872-7272
*World-famous. The
building dating from
1931, has been restored
and now basks in its
original elegance.
Different décor in every
room. Very good
Japanese restaurant.*
▲ 285

**THE WARWICK\*\*\***
65 W. 54th St (between
5th and 6th aves)
Tel. 247-2700
Fax 957-8915
*More comfortable than
the Hilton, its close
neighbor. But it can be
gloomy and a little
lackluster. It offers
particularly competitive
weekend rates and
promotions.*

**THE WYNDHAM\*\*\***
42 W. 58th St (between
5th and 6th aves)
Tel. 753-3500
or 1-800-257-1111
Fax 754-5638
*Peaceful and attractive.
Much frequented by the
world of entertainment.*

**YMCA, VANDERBILT\***
224 E. 47th St
Tel. 756-9600
Fax 752-0210
*For the over 18's.
Friendly, up-beat
atmosphere. Shared
bathroom facilities.*

**YMCA, WEST SIDE\***
5 W. 63rd St
Tel. 787-4400
Fax 580-0440
*The largest youth hostel
in the world. Probably*

*the best value in New
York. Reserve in
advance. Shared
bathroom facilities.
No credit cards.*

## SHOPPING

**47TH STREET PHOTO**
67 W. 47th St
and 115 W. 45th St
Tel. 921-1287
Closed Fri. afternoon
and Sat.
*Video and photography
equipment. No
demonstrations, no
advisory staff, but very
good prices.*

**ANN TAYLOR**
645 Madison Ave
(60th St)
Tel. 832-2010
*Women's ready-to-wear
clothes.*

**BANANA REPUBLIC**
130 E. 59th St
(Lexington St)
Tel. 751-5570
*One of the casual wear
and fashion chains.*

**BERGDORF GOODMAN**
754 5th Ave and 58th St
Tel. 753-7300
*Department store.
Luxury clothing for men
and women (the men's
store is opposite the
main building). A home
decoration department.*
▲ 297

**BLOOMINGDALE'S**
Lexington Ave, 3rd Ave
and 59th St
Tel. 705-2000
*"Bloomie's" sells
everything: clothes,
perfume, furniture, fine
foods . . .* ▲ 311

**BURBERRY LIMITED**
9 E. 57th St
Tel. 371-5010

**CARTIER**
653 5th Ave (52nd St)
Tel. 446-3459
*The famous Parisian
jewelry store.* ▲ 287

**CHARIVARI**
18 W 57th St
Tel. 333-4040
*Ready-to-wear women's
clothes. Very chic and
very expensive.*

**CHRISTIE'S**
502 Park Ave
Tel. 546-1000
*One of the world's most
famous auction rooms.*

**COACH**
342 Madison Ave
(57th St)
Tel. 599-4777
*Exquisite leather goods.*

**COLISEUM BOOKS**
1771 Broadway (57th St)
Tel. 757-8381
*Wide range of books.*

**COLONY RECORDS**
1619 Broadway (49th St)
Tel. 265-2050
*Records, CDs, cassettes
and musical scores.
Competent, helpful
sales assistants.*

**COSMETIC PLUS**
875 3rd Ave (53rd St)
Tel. 838-6804
*A chain of drugstores
selling cosmetics and
beauty products (carries
over 100 brands of
shampoo) at very good
prices. Tel. 319-2120 for
addresses of other
branches.*

**DIEGO DELLA VALLE**
41 E. 57th St
Tel. 644-5945
*Superb Italian shoes
for men and women,
among them the famous
Todd's.*

**DOUBLEDAY BOOK
SHOP**
724 5th Ave (57th St)
Tel. 397-0550
*Large bookstore. A
good selection of books
and guides about New
York.*

**DRAMA BOOKSHOP**
723 7th Ave (2nd floor)
(between 48th and
49th sts)
Tel. 944-0595
*Bookstore specializing
in the theater.*

**EDDIE BAUER**
600 Madison Ave
(58th St)
Tel. 421-2450
*Sportswear.*

**F.A.O. SCHWARZ**
767 5th Ave
(between 58th and
59th sts.)
Tel. 644-9400
*The most stylish toy
shop in New York.
Don't miss its animated
clock.*

**GOTHAM BOOK MART**
41 W. 47th St
Tel. 719-4448
*Gallery and bookstore.
New and antique books,
especially literature.*
▲ 299

**HAMMACHER
SCHLEMMER**
147 E. 57th St
Tel. 421-9000
*All sorts of gadgets,
from the large to small.*

**HARRY WINSTON**
718 5th Ave
Tel. 245-2000
*The jewelry store that
Marilyn Monroe sang
about in "Diamonds are
a Girl's Best Friend".*

**HENRI BENDEL**
712 5th Ave (56th St)
Tel. 247-1100
*Chic women's boutique.*

**LIBRAIRIE DE FRANCE
LIBRERIA HISPANICA**
610 5th Ave
(Rockefeller Center
Promenade Store)
Tel. 581-8810
*French and Spanish
books, cassettes, guides
and posters.*

**THE MANHATTAN
ARTS AND ANTIQUES
CENTER**
1050 2nd Ave (55th St)
Tel. 355-4400
*More than 100 antiques
dealers.*

**NORMA KAMALI**
11 W. 56th St
Tel. 957-9797
*Ready-to-wear clothes
for women.*

**ORIGINAL LEVI'S
STORE**
750 Lexington Ave
(between 59th and
60th sts)
Tel. 826-5957
*Jeans from floor to
ceiling. There are
2 other outlets.*

**RIZZOLI**
31 W. 57th St
Tel. 759-2424
*Books on art, fashion
and photography
published in the United
States and in Europe.*

**SAKS FIFTH
AVENUE**
611 5th Ave
Tel. 753-4000
*Luxury department
store.* ▲ 282

**THE SHARPER IMAGE**
4 W. 57th St
Tel. 265-2550
*Gadgets.*

**SUSAN BENNIS
WARREN EDWARDS**
22 W. 57th St
Tel. 755-4197
*Shoes, boots, luggage
made of exotic skins.
Sometimes extravagant,
often expensive.*

**TAKASHIMAYA**
693 5th Ave (between
54th and 55th sts)
Tel. 350-0100
*The new Japanese
department store. Chic
and expensive. Five
stories of clothes,
furniture, art and
flowers. Very refined. In
the basement, a
Japanese café where
they serve delicious and
unusual dishes, and
have tea of course
(The Tea Box).*

**TIFFANY AND CO.**
727 5th Ave (57th St)
Tel. 755-8000
*In a class of its own for
jewelry. Also, a small
souvenir department.*
▲ 296

**VICTORIA'S SECRET**
34 E. 57th St
Tel. 758-5592
*Stylish, silk lingerie at
very interesting prices.*

**WARNER BROS,
STUDIO STORE**
1 E. 57th St
Tel. 754-0300
*Currently (the store is
expanding) 3 floors of T-*

shirts, toys, crockery,
gadgets . . . and a
unique theme: the
Warner Studio's heros.
It is worth a visit for the
décor alone.

**YANKEE CLUBHOUSE
SHOP**
110 E. 59th St
Tel. 758-7844
*Outlet for New York's
famous baseball team.
Also sells T-shirts and
caps representing other
teams. Also sells tickets
for matches.*

## NIGHTLIFE

**LE BAR BAT**
311 W. 57th St
Tel. 307-7228
Open Mon.–Sat.
midnight–4am
*A former chapel with
funky décor. Several
levels. Dancing, live
music, Vietnamese and
American cuisine.*

**ROSELAND BALLROOM**
239 W. 52nd St
Tel. 247-0200
*Dance the hours away
here between 2.30 and
11pm, Thur. and Sun.
Older age group.
Chinese cafeteria.*
▲ 300

## UPPER EAST
SIDE

## CULTURE

**ABIGAIL ADAMS SMITH
MUSEUM**
421 E. 61st St (between
1st and York aves)
Tel. 838-6878
Open Tue.–Sun. 11am–
4pm, Wed. 11am–8pm
(June and July). Closed
Aug.
*18th-century house*
▲ 311.

**THE ASIA SOCIETY**
725 Park Ave
Tel. 288-6400
Open Tue.–Wed. and

Fri.–Sat. 11am–6pm,
Thur. 11am–8pm, Sun.
noon–5pm. Closed Mon.
*Shows, lectures,
conferences and
contemporary Asian art
exhibitions.*

**COOPER-HEWITT
NATIONAL DESIGN
MUSEUM**
2 E. 91st St
Tel. 860-6868
Open Tue. 10am–9pm
Open Wed.–Sat.
10am–5pm
Open Sun. noon–5pm
Closed Mon.
*Decorative arts and
applied ornaments.*
▲ 320

**FRICK COLLECTION**
1 E. 70th St
Tel. 288-0700
Open Tue.–Sat.
10am–6pm
Open Sun. 1–6pm
Closed Mon. and
public holidays.
No admission for
children under ten.
*Henry Clay Frick's
house and art collection.*
▲ 322

**GOETHE HOUSE**
1014 5th Ave and
83rd St
Tel. 439-8700
*German cultural center.
Library, exhibitions,
lectures. Telephone for
programs.* ▲ 320

**GRACIE MANSION**
88th St and East End
Ave (in Carl Schurz
Park)
Tel. 570-4751
Tours on Wed., Mar.
15–Nov. 15, by
appointment.
*The residence of the
Mayor of New York.*
▲ 313

**INTERNATIONAL
CENTER OF
PHOTOGRAPHY
UPTOWN**
1130 5th Ave (94th St)
Tel. 860-1777
Open Tue. 11am–8pm
Open Wed.–Sun.
11am–6pm
Closed Mon. and public
holidays.
▲ 321

**ISLAMIC CULTURAL
CENTER OF NEW YORK**
1711 3rd Ave (97th St)
Tel. 722-5234
Open Sun.–Fri.
Closed Sat.

*New York's mosque. Call to visit.*

## THE JEWISH MUSEUM

1109 5th Ave (92nd St)
Tel. 423-3200
Open Mon., Wed., Thur.
11am–5.45pm, Tue.
11am–9pm, Sun. from
10am (Tue. until 9pm).
Closed Fri.–Sat. and
public holidays.
▲ 321.

## METROPOLITAN MUSEUM OF ART

5th Ave (82nd St)
Tel. 535-7710
Open Tue.–Thur., Sun.
9.30am–5.15pm, Fri.,
Sat. 9.30am–8.45pm
Closed Mon. and public
holidays. ▲ 328

## EL MUSEO DEL BARRIO

1230 5th Ave
and 104th St
Tel. 831-7272
Open Wed.–Sun.
11am–5pm
*Recently re-opened*
▲ 321.

## MUSEUM OF THE CITY OF NEW YORK

1220 5th Ave (103rd St)
Tel. 534-1672
Open Wed.–Sat.
10am–5pm, Sun. 1–5pm
Closed Mon., Tue.
▲ 321

## NATIONAL ACADEMY OF DESIGN

1083 5th Ave (between
89th and 90th sts)
Tel. 369-4880
Open Wed.–Sun.
noon–5pm, Fri.
noon–8pm
Closed Mon., Tue.
▲ 320

## ROOSEVELT ISLAND TRAMWAY

2nd Ave and 60th St
Tel. 832-4543
Open daily, 6am–2am,
Fri.–Sat. 6am–3.30am
Leaves every 15 mins.
*Buy return tokens before
departure, in Manhattan.*
▲ 311

## 7TH REGIMENT ARMORY

643 Park Ave (67th St)
Tel. 744-4107
Tour by appointment.
*The mess is open as
a restaurant in the
evenings.* ▲ 310

## SOLOMON R. GUGGENHEIM MUSEUM

1071 5th Ave (88th St)
Tel. 423-3500
Open Sun.–Wed.
10am–6pm, Fri.–Sat.
10am–8pm
Closed Thur.
*One of the finest
collections of modern
art in the world on
display.* ▲ 338

## TEMPLE EMANU-EL

1 E. 65th St
Tel. 744-1400
Open Sun.–Fri.
10am–5pm
Closed to the public on
Jewish holidays.
▲ 311

## WHITNEY MUSEUM OF AMERICAN ART

945 Madison Ave
and 75th St
Tel. 570-3676
Open Wed., Fri., Sat.,
Sun. 11am–6pm
Open Thur. 1–8pm
Closed Mon.–Tue.,
public holidays.
*In the basement of the
museum is Sarabeth's
café.* ▲ 326

## GALLERIES

## ALLAN STONE

113 E. 90th St
Tel. 988-6870
Open Tue.–Fri.
10am–6pm, Sat.
10am–5pm; summer,
Mon.–Fri. 10am–6pm

## GAGOSIAN GALLERY

980 Madison Ave
Tel. 744-2313
Open Tue.–Sat.
10am–6pm
*Exhibits established
contemporary artists as
well as key works by
great 20th-century
masters such as
Beckman and
Giacometti. A sculpture
terrace has recently
been added.*

## HIRSCHL & ADLER MODERN

21 E. 70th St (2nd floor)
Tel. 535-8810

Open Tue.–Sat.
9.30am–4.45pm;
Mon.–Fri. 9.30am–
4.45pm (summer)
*This gallery offers
a range of
contemporary art.
The main gallery
contains works by
19th-century and early
20th-century American
and European masters.*

## KNOEDLER AND COMPANY

19 E. 70th St
Tel. 794-0550
Open Tue.–Fri.
9.30am–5.30pm Open
Sat. 10am–5.30pm;
Mon.–Fri. 9.30am–5pm
(summer)
*Many well-known
American artists.
Specialists in Abstract
Expressionism,
Rauschenberg, Franck
Stella, David Smith,
Robert Motherwell.*

## MICHAEL WERNER

21 E. 67th St (3rd floor)
Tel. 988-1623
Open Mon.–Sat.
10am–6pm. Closed Sat.
in summer
*Contemporary artists
from Europe, especially
from Germany (Michael
Werner also has a
gallery in Cologne), and
older works by 20th-
century masters.*

## RESTAURANTS

## ARCADIA

21 East 62nd St
Tel. 223-2900
*Exquisite intimate
setting with chef/owner
Anne Rosenzweig.
Specializes in lobster
club sandwiches and
crab cakes.*

## ARIZONA 206

206 E. 60th St
Tel. 838-0440
Closed Sun. lunchtime
*Spicy cuisine from
southwest America, as
colorful as the
surroundings and
the atmosphere.*

## AURÉOLE

34 E. 61 St
Tel. 319-1660
Closed Sat. lunchtime
and Sun.
*Gastronomic restaurant
in a townhouse duplex.
Splendid and original
floral arrangements and
an equally magnificent
menu devised by
Charlie Palmer.
Impeccable service.
Lunchtime menu $32 is
a bargain.*

## BISTRO DU NORD

1312 Madison Ave
Tel. 289-0997
Open daily
*Bustling but congenial
atmosphere. Highly
inventive brasserie
dishes.*

## CAFÉ CROCODILE

354 E. 74th St
Tel. 249-6619
Open evenings only.
Closed Sun., Mon.
*Cheerful atmosphere.
American Express only.*

## COCO PAZZO

23 E. 74th St
Tel. 794-0205
*Luxurious East-side
décor with Tuscan
cuisine. Specialties
include grilled rib-eye
steak florentine-style
and fresh pasta with
tomatoes and fresh
herbs.*

## CONTRAPUNTO

200 E. 60th St
Tel. 751-8616
*Close to
Bloomingdale's.
Conveniently placed for
delicious pasta dishes and
substantial grills when
you are feeling hungry.*

## DANIEL

20 E. 76th St
Tel. 288-0033
Closed Sun. and Mon.
lunchtime
*Daniel Boulud's
gastronomic restaurant.
Menu offers such
culinary delights as
Oregon mushrooms
stuffed with pigeon and
fois gras, escalope of
sea bass with red
burgundy. Fixed price
lunchtime menu: $33.*

## ELAINE'S

1703 2nd Ave (between
88th and 89th sts)
Tel. 534-8103

*An establishment
immortalized by Woody
Allen. Clientele is
peppered with writers,
actors and New York
society figures.*

## JOJO

160 E. 64th St
Tel. 223-5656
Closed Sat. lunchtime,
Sun.
*The most fashionable
bistro in New York.*

## MARK'S RESTAURANT

Madison Ave (77th St)
(Mark Hotel)
Tel. 879-1864
*Varied menu with
creations by talented
chef Christophe Barbier.
Brunch.*

## MEZZALUNA

1295 3rd Ave (between
74th and 75th sts)
Tel. 535-9600
Open daily
*Frequented by
fashionable Europeans.
Lively and convivial.
Extremely simple
dishes.
No credit cards.*

## MOCCA HUNGARIAN

1588 2nd Ave (between
82nd and 83rd sts)
Tel. 734-6470
Open daily
*Satisfying specialties in
a restaurant that evokes
bygone times: gulyas,
chicken with paprika
and sweet pancakes.
No credit cards.*

## MORTIMER'S

1057 Lexington Ave
(75th St)
Tel. 517-6400
Open daily
*Fairly exclusive
restaurant for New
York's beautiful people,
who come here to
gossip over rather basic
dishes.*

## PAPAYA KING

179 E. 86th St
Tel. 369-0648
Open daily
*The bizarre combination
of hot dogs and papaya*

*juice, invented in the
1920's, has become a
real New York tradition.
No reservations.
No alcohol. No credit
cards.*

## PARK AVENUE CAFÉ

100 E. 63rd St
Tel. 644-1900
Closed Sat. lunchtime
*Highly imaginative décor
and menu. Brunch.*

## SETTE MEZZO

969 Lexington Ave
(between 70th and
71st sts)
Tel. 472-0400
*Long waits before you
can savor this
fashionable restaurant's
stuffed mozzarella and
other house specialties.
No credit cards.*

## THREE GUYS

960 Madison Ave
(75th St)
Tel. 628-8108
Open daily, in the
evenings.
*An excellent Greek café.
Popular with Madison
Ave gallery owners.
Good sandwiches and
hamburgers.*

## ACCOMMODATION

## THE BARBIZON***

140 E. 63rd St
Tel. 838-5700
or 1-800-223-1020
Fax 223-3287
*Small rooms but one of
the best hotels in New
York in terms of value. In
a stylish commercial
neighborhood.*

## THE CARLYLE*****

35 E. 76th St
Tel. 744-1600
or 1-800-227-5737
Fax 717-4682
*Perhaps the best hotel
in New York. Large
rooms in exquisite taste.
The bar boasts murals
by Ludwig Bemelmans.
Renowned for its
afternoon teas and the
equally famous Café
Carlyle.* ▲ 312

## HOTEL PIERRE*****

5th Ave (E. 61st St)
Tel. 838-8000
or 1-800-332-3442
Fax 940-8109
*A tall tower with a
mansard roof dating
from 1929. Furniture
made of inlaid wood,
antiques and
featherbeds in every
room. One of New York's
classic hotels
for the past 60 years.
A few extremely
expensive suites have a
view over Central Park.*
▲ 132

## HOTEL PLAZA ATHÉNÉE****

37 E. 64th St (between
Madison and Park aves)
Tel. 734-9100
or 1-800-447-8800
Fax 772-0958
*Similar style to that of
the Carlyle. French fin
de siècle furniture and
French gourmet cuisine.*

## HOTEL WALES***

1295 Madison Ave
(betwen 92nd and
93rd sts)
Tel. 876-6000
or 1-800-428-5252
Fax 860-7000
*This hotel has recently
been restored to its
original turn-of-the-
century Edwardian-style
splendor. Relaxed,
friendly atmosphere.
Tea is served to the
accompaniment of a
harpist from 3pm to 6pm
and Sarabeth's
restaurant in the
basement is famous for
is brunches.*

## HOTEL WESTBURY****

Madison Ave (69th St)
Tel. 535-2000
or 1-800-321-1569
Fax 535-5058
*The effect is
intentionally very British:
walls decorated with
hunting scenes,
tapestries, floral
bedspreads.*

## THE LOWELL****

28 E. 63rd St
Tel. 838-1400
or 1-800-221-4444
Fax 319-4230
*An extremely romantic,
elegant hotel in a
quiet residential area.
All the rooms come with
wine rack and books,
and many have a
fireplace.*

### LYDEN GARDENS***
215 E. 64th St
Tel. 355-1230
or 1-800-ME-SUITE
Fax 758-7858
*On an attractive tree-lined street. Rooms with extra sofa-beds and self-catering facilities. Ideal for families. Weekly rates negotiable.*

### THE MARK****
E. 77th St
Tel. 744-4300
or 1-800-THE MARK
Fax 744-2749
*Outside, Art Deco elements. Inside, antiques, paintings, architectural drawings. Large, elegant and comfortable rooms. Impeccable service. Very good restaurant.*

### MAYFAIR HOTEL PARK AVENUE****
Park Ave (65th St)
Tel. 288-0800
Fax 737-0538
*Elegantly restored turn-of-the-century lobby. Large bright rooms.*

### REGENCY HOTEL****
540 Park Ave
Tel. 759-4100
or 1-800-233-2356
Fax 826-5674
*This feels more like an elegant mansion than a hotel, since its rooms are furnished with 18th-century-style furniture and plush carpets. Ideal venue for business breakfasts.*

### THE STANHOPE*****
995 5th Ave
Tel. 288-5800
or 1-800-828-1123
Fax 517-0088

*This building, which dates from 1926, has the atmosphere of an English club. Spacious, luxurious rooms, many of which have a view over Central Park. Terrace restaurant overlooking 5th Ave is very pleasant in summer.*

### SURREY HOTEL***
20 E. 76th St
Tel. 288-3700
or 1-800-ME-SUITE
Fax 628-1549
*Mainly suites with self-catering facilities. Secretarial services. Fax and modems for use by guests on business. Sofa-beds for families. Negotiable weekly rates.*

## NIGHTLIFE

### HOTEL CARLYLE
Madison Ave and 76th St
Tel. 744-1600
– BEMELMAN'S BAR
Open noon–1am
piano from 9.30pm
– CAFÉ CARLYLE
Open Tue.–Sat.
6pm–1am
Shows at 8.45pm and 10.45pm
Brunch on Sundays.
Closed in summer.

### MANNY'S CAR WASH
1558 3rd Ave
(between 87th and 88th sts.)
Tel. 369-2583
Open daily 5pm–2am
*An excellent blues club with a different show every evening at 9.30pm. A limited number of tables are available.*

## SHOPPING

### BARNEYS
660 Madison Ave
(61st St)
and 61st St
Tel. 826-8900
*The famous Chelsea store has set up shop on the Upper East Side. Clothes for men and women.*

### BILLY MARTIN
812 Madison Ave
(68th St)
Tel. 861-3100
*All kinds of cowboy boots, affordable prices to suit every pocket.*

### BLADES EAST
160 E. 86th St
Tel. 996-1644
*Roller skates to buy or rent (Central Park is quite close).*

### BOOKS & CO.
939 Madison Ave
(61st St)
Tel. 737-1450
*Strong in literature and fine arts. Celebrated author readings upstairs.*

### COLE-HAAN
667 Madison Ave
(61st St)
Tel. 421-8440
*Shoes, fancy leather goods.*

### DARROW'S FUN ANTIQUES
1101 1st Ave (between 60th and 61st sts)
Tel. 838-0730
*American toys, jukeboxes, slot machines, signs. Very entertaining and unusual.*

### JOAN AND DAVID
816 Madison Ave
(68th St)
Tel. 772-3970
*Shoes.*

### POLO SPORT
888 Madison Ave
(72nd St)
Tel. 434-8000
*Ralph Lauren's second outlet. Specializes in sportswear.*

### POLO-RALPH LAUREN
867 Madison Ave
(72nd St) and 72nd St
Tel. 606-2100
*Casual wear and stylish clothing in a splendid building.* ▲ 309

### SOTHEBY'S
1334 York Ave
(72nd St)
Tel. 606-7000
*Antiques. Considered to be one of the most famous auction rooms in the world.*

### STRIDE RITE
1241 Lexington Ave
(84th St)
Tel. 249-0551
*A wide range of shoes for children.*

### TIMBERLAND
709 Madison Ave
(63rd St)
Tel. 754-0434
*Shoes, clothes, accessories.*

### WILLIAM DOYLE GALLERIES
175 E. 87th St
Tel. 427-2730
*Antiques from 18th–20th century. Auction every other Wednesday.*

### WILLIAM GREENBERG JR DESSERTS, INC.
1100 Madison Ave
(82nd St)
Tel. 744-0304
*One of the best patisseries in New York. Specialist in cheese-cake and honey buns.*

## CENTRAL PARK

### BOAT HOUSE CAFE IN CENTRAL PARK
E. 72nd St
Tel. 517-4723
*Bar, Italian restaurant closed in winter. Bicycle and boat rental, Mar.–Nov. Gondola trips around the lake. Shuttle from 5th Ave.*

### CARRIAGES
5th Ave (Central Park South)
*Trips around the park.*

### CENTRAL PARK ZOO
5th Ave
(E. 64th St)
Tel. 861-603
Open Mon.–Fri. 10am–5pm, Sat. and Sun. 10.30am–5.30pm

**THE DAIRY**
64th St
Tel. 794-6564
Open Tue.– Sun.
11am–4pm (until 5pm in summer)
*Park information center. Videos.*

**URBAN PARK RANGERS**
65th St
Tel. 772-0210
*Guided tours of the park.*

**WOLLMAN RINK**
59th St
Tel. 396-1010
*Ice skating rink (Nov.–Mar.). Roller-skating rink (Apr.–Oct.). Rental of rollerskates and rollerblades for skating through the park.*

## UPPER WEST SIDE

### CULTURE

**AMERICAN MUSEUM OF NATURAL HISTORY**
Central Park West and 79th St
Tel. 769-5100
Open Sun.–Thur.
10am–5.45pm, Fri.–Sat. until 8.45pm
▲ 347.

**BEACON THEATER**
2124 Broadway
(between 74th and 75th sts)
Tel. 496-7070
*Concert hall (rock, pop, jazz, etc.).*

**CHILDREN'S MUSEUM OF MANHATTAN**
212 W. 83rd St
Tel. 721-1234
Open Mon., Wed., Thur.
1.30–5.30pm
Open Fri.–Sun.
10am–5pm
*Exhibitions for children. including some interactive pieces.*

**HAYDEN PLANETARIUM**
W. 79th St and Central Park West
Tel. 769-5920
Open Sun.–Thur.
10am–5.45pm, Fri.–Sat. until 8.45pm
Closed Thanksgiving and Christmas
*Planetarium is housed in the American Museum of Natural History.*

**MUSEUM OF AMERICAN FOLK ART**
2 Lincoln Square
(between Columbus Ave and 65th St)
Tel. 977-7298
Open Tue.–Sun.
11.30am–7.30pm
*Museum of popular art.*

**NEW YORK HISTORICAL SOCIETY**
170 Central Park West
(77th St)
Tel. 873-3400
MUSEUM: open
Wed.–Sun. noon–5pm

LIBRARY: open Wed.–Fri.
noon–5pm
*Archives and photos of the city. Temporary exhibitions.* ▲ 346.

**SONNY THEATRE**
1992 Broadway
(68th St)
Tel. 336-5000
*Seven movie theaters, superb décor and one IMAX screen (extraordinary quality giant screen).*

**SYMPHONY SPACE**
2537 Broadway
(95th W. St)
Tel. 864-5400
*Auditorium.*

### RESTAURANTS

**CAFÉ DES ARTISTES**
1 W. 67th St
Tel. 877-3500
Open daily
*Howard Chandler Christy's delightful murals add to the enjoyment of the meal: gravlax (raw sea salmon), pot-au-feu, chicken flan, cassoulet and tarte Ilona. Brunch.*
▲ 344

**CAFÉ LUXEMBOURG**
200 W. 70th St
Tel. 873-7411
*A marvelous place for dining late into the night.*

**EJ's LUNCHONETTE**
447 Amsterdam Ave
(between 81st and 82nd sts)
Tel. 873-3444
*This diner, with its pre-1940's appearance and simple but appetizing dishes, is ideal for family meals. There are branches of the same establishment at E. 73rd St and 3rd Ave Brunch. No credit cards.*

**IRIDIUM**
44 W. 63rd St (opposite the Lincoln Center)
Tel. 582-2121
*Trendy restaurant with a "Dali-meets-Disney" style décor. Good American food. Jazz club in the basement (sets Fri. and Sat. at 8.30pm, 10.30pm and midnight). Live jazz Sat. and Sun. brunch.*

**SARABETH'S**
423 Amsterdam Ave
(between 80th and 81st sts)
Tel. 496-6280
Open daily
*This is a comfortable, family tearoom filled with the mouthwatering aroma of pastries, omelettes, pasta. Brunch is very popular, can be a long wait. The East Side branches are at 1295 Madison Ave at the Hotel Wales and the basement of the Whitney Museum, 945 Madison Ave.*

**TAVERN ON THE GREEN**
Central Park West and 67th St
Tel. 873-3200
*This caters mainly for tourists and is very kitsch. The dishes are nevertheless delicious. And there are some very reasonably priced set menus. Brunch.*
▲ 344

**VINCE & EDDIE'S**
70 W. 68th St
Tel. 721-0068
Open daily
*A taste of the countryside, substantial food, inexpensive menu: onion flan, fried oysters, knuckle of lamb with dried cherries, apple pie. Often crowded.*

### ACCOMMODATION

**EXCELSIOR HOTEL**
45 West 81st St
Tel. 362-9200
Fax 721-2994
*A clean, comfortable hotel, opposite Central Park and the Natural History Museum. Excellent value (offers suites for families). Reserve well in advance.*

1. SYLVIA'S
2. THE TERRACE

145th Street

Harlem River

BRONX

141st Street

Broadway

125th Street

119th Street

117th Street

110th Street

9th Avenue

Lenox Avenue

8th Ave

5th Ave

Park Avenue

3rd Avenue

1st Avenue

CENTRAL PARK

**MAYFLOWER HOTEL\*\*\***
15 Central Park West
(between 61st and
62nd sts)
Tel. 265-0060
or 1-800-223-4164
Fax 265-2026
*Less expensive than the
hotels near Central Park
South. Splendid view
from the rooms
overlooking the park.*

**MILBURN HOTEL\*\***
242 W. 76th St (between
West End Ave and
Broadway)
Tel. 362-1006
or 1-800-833-9622
Fax 721-5476
*Small rooms, but with
microwaves and
refrigerators. Washing
machines and driers in
the building.*

**THE OLCOTT\*\***
27 W. 72nd St
Tel. 877-4200
Fax 580-0511
*A simple hotel right
next to Central Park.
Special reduced rates
for long stays.*

**RADISSON EMPIRE\*\*\***
44 W. 63rd St
Tel. 265-7400
or 1-800-333-3333
Fax 315-0349
*Good hotel near Lincoln
Center. Recently
renovated. Well
equipped rooms. A
number of facilities:
swimming pool and
health club, conference
rooms. Don't miss the
restaurant jazz-club,
Iridium.*

## SHOPPING

**BARNES AND NOBLE**
2289 Broadway
Tel. 362-8835
*The most extensive
bookstore in New York.
Several other outlets.
Also has a café
upstairs.*

**BLADES-WEST**
120 W. 72nd St
Tel. 787-3911
*Roller skates for sale or
for rent (Central Park is*

*very close).*

**HARRY'S SHOES**
2299 Broadway
and 83rd St
Tel. 874-2035
*All the leading makes of
shoe (Timberland,
Sebago, etc.) for men,
women and children.*

**GREEN FLEA MARKET**
IS 44 Flea Market
Columbus Ave
(77th Ave)
Tel. 721-0900
Open Sun.

**MAXILLA
AND MANDIBLE**
451 Columbus Ave
(between 81st and
82nd sts)
Tel. 724-6173
*Weird and wonderful:
human skeletons,
animal skulls, insects,
fossils and minerals.*

**ZABAR'S**
2245 Broadway (80th St)
Tel. 787-2000
*Started out as a "deli".
Now it is a renowned
food store, the least
expensive of its kind.
A "must", if only for the
atmosphere and the
wonderful aromas.*

## HARLEM UPTOWN

### CULTURE

**ABYSSINIAN BAPTIST CHURCH**
132 W. 138th St
Tel. 862-7474
Office open Mon.–Fri.
10am–6pm
*Service on Sundays at
9am and 11am with
gospel choir. Memorial
Room in memory of
Adam Clayton Powell,
Jr.* ▲ 359

**AMERICAN
ACADEMY AND
INSTITUTE OF
ARTS AND LETTERS**
633 W. 155th St
(Audubon Terrace)
Tel. 368-5900
*Opens only for the
three annual exhibitions,
or by appointment
for the library.* ▲ 361

**AMERICAN
NUMISMATIC SOCIETY**
Broadway and 155th St
Tel. 234-3130
Open Tue.–Sat. 9am–
4.30pm, Sun. 1–4pm
*Museum of coins and
medals.* ▲ 361

**BUDDHIST CHURCH
OF NEW YORK**
332 Riverside Drive
(106th St)
Tel. 678-0305
*Open for services Sun.
morning.* ▲ 51

**CATHEDRAL CHURCH
OF ST JOHN
THE DIVINE**
Amsterdam Ave
and 112nd St
Tel. 316-7540
Open 7am–6pm, Sun.
7am–8pm
*New York's Episcopal
Cathedral.* ▲ 354

**THE CLOISTERS**
Fort Tryon Park
Tel. 923-3700
Open 9.30am–4.45pm
Closed Mon.
Free admission
with a Metropolitan
museum pass for the
same day
*Museum of medieval art
housed within old
cloisters; part of the
Metropolitan Museum.
Easily reached by bus
M4 on Madison Ave*
▲ 362.

**COLUMBIA
UNIVERSITY**
114th and 120th sts.
(Broadway and
Amsterdam Ave)
Guided tours: Mon.–Fri.
10am and 3pm.
Tours start from the
Visitor Center:
213 Low Library
Tel. 854-4900. ▲ 352

**DYCKMAN HOUSE
MUSEUM**
4881 Broadway and
204th St
Tel. 304-9422
Open Tue.–Sun.
11am–4pm
*17th-century house
belonging to Dutch
settlers. Entrance free.*
▲ 361

**GENERAL GRANT
NATIONAL
MEMORIAL**
Riverside Drive
(122nd St)
Tel. 666-1640
Open daily 9am–5pm
*Tomb of President
Grant and his wife.*
▲ 357

**HISPANIC SOCIETY
OF AMERICA**
Broadway (155th St)
Tel. 690-0743
Open Tue.–Sat. 10am–
4.30pm, Sun. 1–4pm,
Closed Mon. and public
holidays.
*Spanish art, literature
and culture. Entrance
free.* ▲ 361

**MORRIS-JUMEL
MANSION**
1765 Jumel Terrace,
corner W. 160th St and
Edgecombe Ave
Tel. 923-8008
Open Wed.–Sun.
10am–4pm
Closed Mon., Tue.
▲ 361.

**RIVERSIDE CHURCH**
490 Riverside Drive
Tel. 222-5900
Open daily 9am–5pm
Tower Sun. 12.30–4pm
*Climb the tower to see
the city from an unusual
angle. Carillon recitals
Sun. noon and 3pm.*
▲ 356

The hotels and restaurants in the address book were selected by Peter MELTZER, author of *Passport to New York restaurants*, Passport Press Ltd, New York 1994.

## SCHOMBERG CENTER FOR RESEARCH IN BLACK CULTURE
135th St and
Malcolm X Blvd
Tel. 491-2200
Open Mon.–Wed.
noon–8pm, Thur.–Sat.
10am–6pm, Sun. 1–5pm
*A branch of the New York Public Library specializing in the Black culture of the United States.* ▲ 359

## STUDIO MUSEUM IN HARLEM
144 W. 125th St
Tel. 864-4500
Open Mon.–Fri.
9am–5pm
*African, African-American and Caribbean art exhibitions.*

## RESTAURANTS

### SYLVIA'S RESTAURANT
328 Lenox Ave (between
126th and 127th sts)
Tel. 996-0660
*People come here in droves to sample a cuisine combining barbecue with soul. An after-dinner stroll in the vicinity is dangerous. Brunch on Sunday with gospel music is very popular.* ▲ 358

### THE TERRACE
400 W. 119th St
Tel. 666-9490
Open lunchtime and evenings
Closed Sat. lunchtime and Sun.–Mon.
*The delicious French cuisine is as memorable as the view.*

## NIGHTLIFE

### APOLLO THEATER
253 W. 125th St
Tel. 749-5838

*The mecca for rhythm-and-blues and soul music. Making a record, "Live at the Apollo", is considered the hallmark of success. Don't miss: the amateur nights, Wed. at 7.30pm. The shows also take place in the auditorium.* ▲ 358

### BIRDLAND
2745 Broadway
(105th St)
Tel. 749-2228
*Afro-American cuisine. Music (jazz, blues, etc.) from 10.30pm until midnight.*

### WEST END GATE
2911 Broadway
(114th St)
Tel. 662-8830
Open until 4am
*Bar, restaurant, and concert hall. Popular haunt of Columbia University students.*

## BROOKLYN

### CULTURE

#### BROOKLYN ACADEMY OF MUSIC
30 Lafayette Ave
Tel. 718-636-4100
*Organizes theatrical and musical shows as well as highly regarded dance events. Take the shuttle from Manhattan.*

### BROOKLYN BOTANIC GARDEN
1000 Washington Ave
Tel. 718-622-4433
Open Tue.–Fri.
8am–4.30pm (6pm in summer).
Open Sat.–Sun.
10am–4.30pm
(6pm in summer)
*Botanical garden within an enormous park. Greenhouses, cafeteria. Shuttle from Manhattan.*

### BROOKLYN CHILDREN'S MUSEUM
145 Brooklyn Ave
(St Mark's Ave)
Tel. 718-735-4432
Open Wed.–Fri. 2–5pm,
Sat. and Sun.
noon–5pm
*Free movies and shows for children interested in natural sciences.*

### BROOKLYN MUSEUM OF ART
200 Eastern Parkway
Tel. 718-638-5000
Open Wed.–Sun.
10am–5pm
Closed Mon.–Tue. and
public holidays.
*The second-largest museum in New York. Includes works by Rodin, Toulouse-Lautrec, Modigliani, Chagall, Monet, Sargent, Homer, etc. Renowned for its department of Egyptian antiquities (recently renovated). Shuttle from Manhattan.* ▲ 366

### NEW YORK TRANSIT MUSEUM
Boerum Place and
Schermerhorn St
(Brooklyn Heights)
Tel. 718-243-3000
Open Tue.–Fri.
10am–4pm, Sat. and
Sun. 11am–5pm
*History of public transportation in New York.*

### RESTAURANTS

#### PETER LUGER STEAK HOUSE
178 Broadway (between
Driggs and Bedford
aves) Williamsburg-
Brooklyn
Tel. 718-387-7400
*For 109 years this establishment has served the best steaks in the US. No credit cards. Don't hang around this area.*

### THE RIVER CAFÉ
1 Water St
Tel. 718-522-5200
*Unbeatable view over Manhattan. Desserts are always delectable. Some dishes are better than others. Brunch.*

## BRONX

### NEW YORK BOTANICAL GARDEN
200th St and
Southern Blvd, Bronx
Tel. 718-817-8700
Open Tue.–Sun.
and public holidays,
10am–6pm, Apr.–Oct.
10am–4pm Nov.–Mar.
Guided tours on Sat.
and Sun. only.
*Subway: line D, Bedford Park station, line 4, Bedford Bld. Train: Metro North at Grand Central Terminal, Botanical Garden station.
Bus: BX12, BX19, BX41. The bus stops in front of the entrance to the gardens.*

### NEW YORK ZOOLOGICAL PARK (BRONX ZOO)
Bronx River Parkway
(Fordham Road)
Tel. 718-367-1010
Open daily, 10am–
4.30pm, Nov.–Feb.;
Mon.–Fri. 10am–5pm,
and Sat.–Sun.
10am–5.30pm,
Mar.–Oct.
Free on Wed.
*Subway: line 2, Pelham Parkway station.
Bus: BX9 and M11 from Madison Ave (Liberty Lines 7, Tel. 18-652-8400).*

## NOTES

# APPENDICES

# ◆ BIBLIOGRAPHY

## ◆ ESSENTIAL READING ◆

◆ ALLEN (Oliver E.): *New York, New York*, Atheneum, NY, 1990

◆ CARO (Robert): *Power Broker, Colin Robert Moses and the Fall of New York*, Alfred A. Knopf, NY, 1974

◆ WHITE (E. B.): *This is New York*, Warner Books, NY, 1988

◆ WILLENSKY (Elliot) and WHITE (Norval) eds.: *AIA Guide to New York City*, Harcourt Brace Jovanovich, Publishers, NY, 1988

## ◆ GENERAL READING ◆

◆ ALLEN (Irving Lewis): *The City in Slang: New York Life and Popular Speech*, Oxford University Press, NY, 1993

◆ BOORSTIN (Daniel): *The Americans*, 3 vols, Random House, NY, 1975

◆ CHARYN (Jerome): *Metropolis: New York as Myth, Marketplace, and Magical Land*, Avon, NY, 1987

◆ COHN (Nik): *Heart of the World*, Alfred A. Knopf, NY, 1992

◆ DIAMONSTEIN (Barbaralee): *Landmarks: Eighteen Wonders of the New York World*, Harry Abrams, NY, 1992

◆ FONER (NANCY): *New Immigrants in New York*, Columbia University Press, NY, 1987

◆ GOLD (Joyce): *From Windmills to the World Trade Center: A Walking Guide to Lower Manhattan History*, Old Warren Road Press, NY, 1988

◆ GLUECK (Grace) and GARDNER (Paul): *Brooklyn: People, Places, Past and Present*, Harry Abrams, NY, 1991

◆ GRAFTON (John): *New York in the Nineteenth Century*, Dover, NY, 1992

◆ HORNUNG (Clarence P.): *The Way It Was, New York, 1850–1890*, Schocken Books, NY, 1977

◆ JOHNSON (Harry) and LIGHTFOOT (Frederick S.): *Maritime New York in Nineteenth Century Photographs*, Dover, NY, 1980

◆ KINKEAD (Gwen.): *Chinatown: A Portrait of a Closed Society*, Harper Collins, NY, 1992

◆ KOUWENHOVEN (John A.): *The Columbia Historical Portrait of New York*, Harper & Row, NY, 1972

◆ MANGIONE (Jerre) and MORREALE (Ben): *La Storia: Five Centuries of the Italian American Experience*, Harper Collins, NY, 1992

◆ PLOTCH (Batia) ed. with MORSE (John) et al.: *New York walks*, Henry Holt, NY 1992

◆ SANTE (Luc): *Low Life: Lures and Snares of Old New York*, Random House, NY, 1992

◆ SALWEIN (Peter): *Upper West Side Story*, Abbeville Press, NY 1989

◆ SHEPARD (Richard F.): *Broadway from Battery to the Bronx*, Harry Abrams, NY, 1987

◆ STARR (Roger): *The Rise and Fall of New York City*, Basic Books, NY, 1985

◆ TRACHTENBERG (Alan): *Brooklyn Bridge: Fact and Symbol*, Univ. of Chicago Press, Chicago, 1979

◆ TRAGER (James): *Park Avenue: Street of Dreams*, Atheneum, NY 1990

◆ WALLOCK (Leonard) ed.: *New York: Culture Capital of the World, 1940–1965*, Rizzoli, NY, 1988

## ◆ ARCHITECTURE ◆

◆ ALPERN (Andrew): *Luxury Apartment Houses of Manhattan*, Dover, NY, 1993

◆ BADGER (Daniel D.): *Badger's Illustrated Catalogue of Cast-Iron Architecture*, Dover, NY, 1982

◆ BOYER (M. Christine): *Manhattan Manners, Architecture and Style 1850–1900*, Rizzoli, NY, 1985

◆ BREEZE (Carla): *New York Deco*, Rizzoli, NY 1993

◆ CROMLEY (Elizabeth Collins): *Alone Together: A History of New York's Early Apartments*, Cornell Univ. Press, Ithaca, 1990

◆ DOLKART (Andrew S.): *A Guide to New York City Landmarks*, Preservation Press, NY, 1992

◆ DUNLAP (David W.): *On Broadway, A Journey Uptown over Time*, Rizzoli, NY, 1990

◆ FRIEDMAN (Joe) and BERENHOLTS (Richard): *Inside New York: Discovering New York's Classic Interiors*, Harper Collins, NY, 1992

◆ GILLON (Edmund V.), REED (Henry. H.): *Beaux-Arts Architecture in New York*, Dover, NY, 1988

◆ GOLDBERGER (Paul): *The Skyscraper*, Alfred A. Knopf, NY, 1983

◆ HAWES (Elizabeth) : *New York, New York*, Alfred A. Knopf, NY, 1993

◆ HOOD (Clifton): *722 Miles: The Building of the Subways and How They Transformed New York*, Simon & Schuster, NY, 1993

◆ IRACE (Fulvio): *Emerging Skylines: The New American Skyscrapers*, Whitney Library of Design, NY, 1990

◆ KLOTZ (Heinrich): *New York Architecture, 1970– 1990*, Rizzoli, NY, 1989

◆ MACKAY (Donald A.): *The Building of Manhattan*, Harper Collins, NY, 1989

◆ ROSEN (Laura): *Top of the City*, Thames and Hudson, London, 1983

◆ ROTHSCHILD (Nan): *New York City Neighborhoods: The 18th Century*, Academic Press, NY, 1990

◆ SHAPIRO (Mary J.): *A Picture History of the Brook-lyn Bridge*, Dover, NY, 1983

◆ SILVER (Nathan): *Lost New York*, Schocken Books, NY, 1967

◆ STERN (Robert. A.),

◆ GILMARTIN (G.), MELLINS (T.): *New York Nineteen Thirty*, Rizzoli, NY, 1987

◆ WHYTE (William H.): *City: Rediscovering the Center*, Doubleday, NY, 1989

◆ WOLFE (Gerard R.): *New York: A Guide to the Metropolis*, McGraw-Hill, NY, 1994

## ◆ ARTS ◆

◆ ABBOTT (Berenice): *New York in the Thirties*, Dover, NY, 1973

◆ AVEDON (Richard): *Autobiography*, Random House, NY, 1993

◆ CHWAST (Seymour) and HELLER (Steven) ed.: *The Art of New York*, Harry Abrams, NY, 1983

◆ COHEN (Barbara) CHWAST (Seymour) and HELLER (Steven) ed.: *New York Observed: Artists and Writers Look at the City*, Harry Abrams, NY, 1987

◆ FIELDS (Armond and Marc L.): *From the Bowery to Broadway: Lew Fields and the Roots of the American Popular Theatre*, Oxford University Press, NY, 1993

◆ HINE (Lewis): *Men at Work*, Dover, NY, 1977

◆ KIRSTEIN (Lincoln): *Mosaic*, Farrar, Straus & Giroux NY, 1994

◆ WILLIS-BRAITHWAITE (Deborah): *Van Der Zee, Photographer*, Harry Abrams, NY, 1993

## ◆ LITERATURE ◆

◆ AUSTER (Paul): *New York Trilogy: City of Glass, Ghosts, The Locked Room*, Viking Penguin, NY, 1990

◆ BELLOW (Saul): *Seize the Day*, Viking Penguin, NY, 1984

◆ CAPOTE (Truman): *Breakfast at Tiffany's*, Random House, NY, 1994

◆ CARR (Caleb): *The Alienist*, Random House, NY, 1994

◆ DOCTOROW (E. L.): *The Waterworks*, Random House, NY, 1994

◆ DONLEAVY (J. P.): *A Fairy Tale of New York*, Atlantic Monthly, NY, 1989

◆ DOS PASSOS (John): *Manhattan Transfer*, Houghton-Mifflin, NY, 1991

◆ EDMISTON (Susan) and CIRINO (Linda D.): *Literary New York*, Gibbs Smith Pubs., Indianapolis, 1991

◆ ELLISON (Ralph): *The Invisible Man*, Random House, NY, 1989

◆ FITZGERALD (F. Scott): *Tender is the Night*, Macmillan, NY, 1977

◆ GOOCH (Brad): *City Poet: The Life and Times of Frank O'Hara*, Alfred A. Knopf, NY, 1993

◆ HALEY (Alex): *The Autobiography of Malcolm X*, Ballantine, NY, 1992

◆ HIMES (Charles): *A Rage of Harlem*, Random House, NY, 1989

◆ JAMES (Henry): *The American Scene*, St. Martin's Press, NY, 1987

◆ LORCA (Federico Garcia): *Poet in New York*, W. W. Norton, NY, 1940

◆ MITCHELL (Joseph): *Up in the Old Hotel*, Pantheon, NY, 1992

◆ WAKEFIELD (Dan): *New York in the '50s*, Houghton-Mifflin, NY, 1992

◆ WHARTON (Edith): *Age of Innocence*, Alfred A. Knopf NY, 1993

◆ WHITMAN (Walt): *Leaves of Grass*, Random House, NY, 1993

◆ WOLFE (Thomas): *Bonfire of the Vanities*, Farrar, Straus & Giroux, NY 1987

## ◆ PAINTING ◆

◆ COOPER (Martha), CHALFANT (Henry): *Subway Art*, Henry Holt and Co., NY, 1988

◆ GLUECK (Grace): *New York: The Painted City*, Gibbs Smith Pubs., Indianapolis, 1992

◆ MAJOR (Mike): *Drawings & Paintings of New York*, Main Graphics, 1990

◆ WALDMAN (Diane): *Roy Lichtenstein*, Guggenheim Museum, NY, 1993

◆ WATSON (Steven): *Strange Bedfellows*, Abbeville Press, NY, 1991

## ◆ FILM ◆

◆ *Annie Hall*, Woody Allen, 1977

◆ *Breakfast at Tiffany's*, Blake Edwards, 1961

◆ *A Bronx Tale*, Robert DeNiro, 1993

◆ *Carlito's Way*, Brian de Palma, 1993

◆ *Do the Right Thing*, Spike Lee, 1989

◆ *The French Connection*, William Friedkin, 1971

◆ *Ghostbusters*, Ivan Reitman, 1984

◆ *The Godfather Parts I–III*, Francis Ford Coppola, 1972–90

◆ *Manhattan*, Woody Allen, 1979

◆ *The Man in the Grey Flannel Suit*, Nunnally Johnson, 1956

◆ *Miracle on 34th Street*, George Seaton, 1947

◆ *On the Waterfront*, Elia Kazan, 1954

◆ *Raging Bull*, Martin Scorsese, 1980

◆ *Rear WIndow*, Alfred A. Hitchcock, 1954

◆ *Seven Year Itch*, Billy Wilder, 1955

◆ *Six Degrees of Separation*, Fred Schepisi, 1993

◆ *Taxi driver*, Martin Scorsese, 1976

◆ *West Side Story*, Robert Wise, 1961

◆ *The World of Henry Orient*, George Roy Hill, 1964

◆ *Year of the Dragon*, Michael Cimono, 1985

# ◆ LIST OF ILLUSTRATIONS

436

# ◆ ACKNOWLEDGMENTS

**We would like to thank the following for their assistance:**

Seymour Durst, *Old New York Foundation*
Gordon MacCollum, *American Architecture Archives*
Luis Cancel, *former commissioner of the New York City Department of Cultural Affairs*
Deborah Bershad, Margaret Hammerle, *Art Commission of the City of New York*
Idilio Gracia-Peña, *commissioner of the New York City Department of Records and Information Services*
Kenneth Cobb, *NYC Municipal Archives*
Jane Harris, *Manhattan Sites*
Jane Hausen, *The NYC Landmarks Preservation Commission*, all rights reserved.
Sherrill Wilson, Tuesday Brooks, *The Office of Public Education and Interpretation*
Cathy del Priori, Betsy Becker, *Madison Square Garden*
Robert M. Browning, *National Baseball Hall of Fame and Museum*
Anne Marie Gilmartin, *N. Y. Rangers*
Paul Spinelli, Lisa Shulman, Frank Ramos, *Jets NFL Properties*
Ro Lohin, *The New York Studio School*
Nancy Cricco, *New York University*
Kathleen Goncharov, *The New School for Social Research*
Janet Parks, *Avery Library, Columbia University*
Robert MacDonald, Leslie Nolan, Marguerite Lavin, Tony Piasani, Terry, Ariano, Peter Simmons, Billie Heller, Marty Jacobs, *Museum of the City of New York*
Alison Whiting, Mary Beth Betts, *The New York Historical Society*
Diana Pardue, Jeffrey S. Dosik, Geraldine Santoro, Kevin Daley, *Ellis Island Immigration Museum*
Amy Hines, Neil Calvanese, Sarah Cedar Miller, *Central Park Conservancy*
Tom Ching, *Parks Horticulture*
Barbara Treitel, *The Jewish Museum*
*The Jewish Forward*
Lori Duggan Gold, *Brooklyn Botanic Garden*
Karen L. Saber, *New York Botanical Garden*
Linda Corcoran, *NYZS The Wildlife Conservation Society*
Harry Hunter, *National Museum of American History, Smithsonian Institution*
Mary Ison, *Prints and Photographs Division, Library of Congress*
Michelle Saffir, *Asia Society*
Susan George, *Fraunces Tavern*
Charles Juno, *Empire State Building*
Patty Schickram, *Macy's*
James Reed, Celeste Torello,

Rockefeller Group
Joe Grabowski, Ken Walmsley, *The Woolworth Corporation*
Geraldine Barnett, *US Post Office Bowling Green Station*
Lisa Berlin, *US Post Office*
Steve Gilkenson, *McAuley Mission*
Mons. Anthony Dalla Villa, Thomas Young, *Saint Patrick's Cathedral*
The Very Rev. James P. Morton, William Logan, *The Cathedral Church of Saint John the Divine*
Rebecca Carlisle Blind, *Saint James Episcopal Church*
Joan Baachus-Patterson, *Riverside Church*
Eric Hilton, *First Presbyterian Church*
Sister Rita King
Sister Margarita Smith
Anthony Bellov, *Abigail Adams Smith Museum*
Paul Glassman, *Morris-Jumel Mansion*
Kathy Stocking, *New York State Historical Association*
Aldon James, Carol Lowrey, *The National Arts Club*
Tom Gilbert, *AP/Wide World Photos-Inc.*
Helaine Pardo, *Commerce Graphics*
Dan May, Karl Nemchek, *Met Life*
Barbara Cohen, Judith Stonehill, Francis Morrone, *New York Bound Bookshop*
Mike Regan, *World Trade Center*
Leon Haft, *Marshall Chelsa Club*
Ian Ginsberg, *Bigelow Pharmacy*
Major Waddington, *Salvation Army*
Melissa L. Burian, *US Dept. of Commerce*
Lloyd Morgan, *Morgan Press*
Don Luck, Ester Smith, *Institute of Jazz Studies*
Donna Walker Collins, *Dance Theater of Harlem*
Nancy Lassale, Steve Miller, *New York City Ballet*
James Johnson, *Martha Graham*
Yee Chan, *Alvin Ailey*
Ellen Jacobs, *Merce Cunningham*
Nicole Vandestienne, *Paul Taylor Dance Company*
*RCA Archives*
Azita Corton, *CBS*
Scott Fain, Carol Brokaw, *ABC*
Betty Hudson, *NBC*
Lida Lauffer, *HBO*
Richard Betz, *La Verne*
J. Carter, Stacey Friedman, *MTV Networks*
Mark Magner, Kingson Chou, Richard Termini, *Children's Television Workshop*
William L. Noble
Walter Gasnick
Rev. Stephen S. Garney

**We would like to thank the following for permission to reproduce the extracts on pages 114 to 128**

◆ DONADIO & ASHWORTH, INC: Excerpt from *Good As Gold* by Joseph Heller, copyright © 1979 by Joseph Heller. Reprinted by permission of Donadio & Ashworth, Inc. (UK) Excerpt from *Good As Gold* by Joseph Heller, published by Jonathan Cape Ltd, reprinted by permission of Jonathan Cape Ltd, London.

◆ ELIZABETH H. DOS PASSOS: Excerpt from *Manhattan Transfer* by John Dos Passos (Harper and Brothers, 1925). Reprinted by permission of Elizabeth H. Dos Passos, Co-Executor, the Estate of John Dos Passos.

◆ THE DREISER TRUST: Excerpt from *The Color of a Great City* by Theodore Dreiser, copyright © 1923 by Boni & Liveright, Inc. copyright renewed 1951 by Mrs Theodore Dreiser, as widow of the author. Reprinted by permission of The Dreiser Trust, Harold J. Dies, Trustee.

◆ FABER AND FABER LIMITED: "Broadway" by Vladimir Mayakovsky, translated by Peter Jukes from *A Shout in the Street* by Peter Jukes (1990). Reprinted by permission of Faber and Faber Ltd. Also reprinted in the U.K. by permission of Faber and Faber Ltd.

◆ FARRAR, STRAUS & GIROUX, INC.: Excerpt from *I Thought of Daisy* by Edmund Wilson, copyright © 1953 by Edmund Wilson, copyright renewed 1981 by Helen Miranda Wilson. Reprinted by permission of Farrar, Straus & Giroux, Inc. Also reprinted in the U.K. by permission of Farrar, Straus & Giroux, Inc.
– Excerpt from "Harlem Literati" from *The Big Sea* by Langston Hughes. Copyright © 1940 by Langston Hughes. Copyright renewed 1968 by Arna Bontemps and George Houston Press. Reprinted by permission of Hill and Wang, a division of Farrar, Straus & Giroux, Inc.

◆ HARPERCOLLINS PUBLISHERS, INC.: Excerpt from 'Here is New York' from *Essays of E. B. White* by E. B. White, copyright © 1949 by E. B. White, copyright renewed 1977 by E. B. White. Reprinted by permission of HarperCollins Publishers, Inc.

◆ ALFRED A. KNOPF, INC: Excerpt from *Souvenir and Prophecies* by Holly Stevens, copyright © 1966, 1976 by Holly Stevens. Also reprinted in the U.K. by permission of Alfred A. Knopf, Inc.

– Excerpt from *Odd Jobs*, by John Updike, copyright © 1991 by John Updike. Reprinted by permission of Alfred A. Knopf, Inc.
(UK) Excerpt from *Odd Jobs*, by John Updike (Penguin Books 1992, first published in the U.K. by André Deutsch) copyright © 1991 by John Updike. Reprinted by permission of Hamish Hamilton Ltd.

◆ LITTLE, BROWN AND COMPANY: "A Brief Guide to New York" from *Verses from 1929 On*, by Ogden Nash, copyright © 1940 by Ogden Nash. Reprinted by permission of Little, Brown and Company.
(UK) "A Brief Guide to New York" poem published in *Many Long Years Ago*, Little, Brown 1945 © 1945 by Ogden Nash. Reprinted in the UK by permission of Curtis Brown Ltd.

◆ MACMILLAN PUBLISHING COMPANY: Excerpt from *The Diary of George Templeton Strong* by Allan Nevins and Milton Halsey Thomas, copyright © 1952 by Macmillan Publishing Company, copyright renewed 1980 by Milton Halsey Thomas. Reprinted by permission of Macmillan Publishing Company.

◆ NEW DIRECTIONS PUBLISHING CORP.: Excerpt from *The Crack-Up* by F. Scott Fitzgerald, copyright © 1945 by New Directions Publishing Corp. Reprinted by permission of New Directions Publishing Corp.
(UK) Excerpt from *The Crack-Up* by F. Scott Fitzgerald, published by the Bodley Head, reprinted by permission of the Fitzgerald Estate and the Bodley Head, London.

◆ PANTHEON BOOKS: Excerpt from *Up in the Old Hotel* by Joseph Mitchell, copyright © 1992 by Joseph Mitchell. Reprinted by permission of Pantheon Books, a division of Random House, Inc.

◆ THE WALLACE LITERARY AGENCY, INC : Excerpt from *Great Jones Street* by Don DeLillo, copyright © 1973 by Don DeLillo (Penguin Books). Reprinted by permission of The Wallace Literary Agency, Inc. Also reprinted in the U.K. (published there by Picador Books) by permission of The Wallace Literary Agency, Inc.

◆ A. P. WATT LTD: Excerpt from *What I Saw in America* by G. K. Chesterton (Hodder & Stoughton, London, 1922). Reprinted by permission of A. P. Watt Ltd on behalf of the Royal Literary Fund.

# INDEX